VILLAGE REVOLTS

VILLAGE REVOLTS

Social Protest and Popular Disturbances
in England, 1509–1640

Roger B. Manning

CLARENDON PRESS · OXFORD
1988

Oxford University Press, Walton Street, Oxford OX2 6DP
Oxford New York Toronto
Delhi Bombay Calcutta Madras Karachi
Petaling Jaya Singapore Hong Kong Tokyo
Nairobi Dar es Salaam Cape Town
Melbourne Auckland
and associated companies in
Beirut Berlin Ibadan Nicosia

Oxford is a trade mark of Oxford University Press

Published in the United States
by Oxford University Press, New York

British Library Cataloguing in Publication Data
Manning, Roger B.
Village revolts: social protest and
popular disturbances in England 1509–1640.
1. Peasant uprisings — England —
History. 2. Great Britain — Politics
and government — 1485–1603 3. Great Britain
— Politics and government — 1603–1649
I. Title
942'.009'734   DA315
ISBN 0-19-820116-8

Library of Congress Cataloging in Publication Data
Manning, Roger B. (Roger Burrow)
Village revolts.
Bibliography: p.
Includes index.
1. Great Britain — History — Tudors, 1485–1603.
2. Great Britain — History — Early Stuarts, 1603–1649.
3. Riots — England — History.   4. Social movements —
England — History.   5. Villages — England — History.
6. Peasantry — England — History.   I. Title.
DA315.M36   1988   942.05   87-22050
ISBN 0-19-820116-8

Phototypeset by Dobbie Typesetting Service,
Plymouth, Devon
Printed in Great Britain
at the University Printing House, Oxford
by David Stanford
Printer to the University

For my Mother
and in memory of
my Father

Acknowledgements

IN a commonwealth of knowledge many contribute to a scholarly enterprise, and it is my good fortune to be able to acknowledge numerous acts of kindness and assistance. The idea for this book originated in an undergraduate special topics course on 'Peasant Revolts and Peasant Movements', which I organized in 1973 and to which a number of my colleagues at Cleveland State University contributed lectures in their special fields. The National Endowment for the Humanities, the Penrose Fund of the American Philosophical Society, and the College of Graduate Studies of Cleveland State University provided financial assistance for travel to England. Research was carried on in the Public Record Office, the Corporation of London Record Office, the Guildhall Library, the British Library, the Institute of Historical Research, the Cleveland Public Library, and the Cleveland State University Library, and I have to thank the archivists and librarians of those institutions. I must also acknowledge the kindness of the editor of *Albion* for permission to reprint as chapter 2 (ii) a revised version of an article which first appeared in that journal.

Colleagues and friends have helped in countless ways. Clifford Davies, Anthony Fletcher, and Keith Lindley read various chapters in earlier drafts; Barrett Beer not only read the entire manuscript, but patiently endured many hours of discussion and argument. Andrew Charlesworth, James Cockburn, Louis Knafla, Peter Brandon, J. S. Taylor, Bertram Wyatt-Brown, Brian Kerr, William Robison, and Cornelia Wallisfürth have answered queries, called important sources to my attention, or otherwise rendered assistance. Anthony Fletcher, Clifford Davies, Clive Holmes, Keith Lindley, and the Reverend J. F. Larkin all graciously allowed me to see typescripts or proofs of essays or books in advance of publication. Anyone whose investigations carry him into the labyrinthian way of the agrarian, social, and legal history of Tudor and early-Stuart England must also be conscious of the great debt which he owes to pioneering scholars such as R. H. Tawney, W. G. Hoskins, Joan Thirsk, Christopher Hill, Eric Kerridge, M. E. James, and Thomas G. Barnes.

LueVenia Richardson and Diane Monreal typed and retyped various drafts of the manuscript and Ivon Asquith expertly guided it through the press. My greatest debt is to Anne, my wife, who never ceased to encourage me to persevere and who provided me with the leisure to write this book.

R.B.M.

Cleveland, Ohio
August 1986

Contents

x   *Contents*

List of Maps

Abbreviations

Place of publication is London unless otherwise indicated.

Acts PC	*Acts of the Privy Council of England*, ed. J. R. Dasent (32 vols.; 1890–1907).
Ag. HR	*Agricultural History Review*
AHR	*American Historical Review*
AHEW	*The Agrarian History of England and Wales*, iv. *1500–1640*, ed. Joan Thirsk (Cambridge, 1967).
BIHR	*Bulletin of the Institute of Historical Research*
BL	British Library
C.	Chancery
Cal. SP	*Calendar of State Papers*
CLRO	Corporation of London Record Office
DL	Duchy of Lancaster
DNB	*Dictionary of National Biography* (22 vols.; Oxford, 1917–).
Ec. HR	*Economic History Review*
EHR	*English Historical Review*
Hist. MSS Comm.	Historical Manuscripts Commission
HJ	*Historical Journal*
JBS	*Journal of British Studies*
L. & P., Hen. VIII	*Letters and Papers, Foreign and Domestic of the Reign of Henry VIII*, ed. J. S. Brewer *et al.* (23 vols. in 38 parts; 1862–1932).
MNH	*Manor Northern History*
OED	*Oxford English Dictionary*
P. & P.	*Past and Present*
PRO	Public Record Office
Rep.	CLRO, Repertories of the Court of Aldermen
REQ	Court of Requests
SP	State Papers
SR	*Statutes of the Realm* (9 vols.; 1810–22).

STAC	Court of Star Chamber
Staffs. QSR	*The Staffordshire Quarter Session Rolls*, ed. S. A. H. Burne (Wm. Salt Arch. Soc., 4 vols.; 1930–6).
TED	*Tudor Economic Documents*, ed. R. H. Tawney and E. Power (3 vols.; 1924).
Trans. R. Hist. Soc.	*Transactions of the Royal Historical Society*
TRP	*Tudor Royal Proclamations*, ed. P. L. Hughes and J. F. Larkin (3 vols.; New Haven, 1964–9).
VCH	*Victoria History of the Counties of England*, ed. William Page (1900–).

Introduction

BETWEEN the Great Revolt of 1381 and the Monmouth Rebellion of 1685 England saw 'three centuries of recurrent regional uprisings'.[1] Not including the English Civil Wars, which were fought on a wider scale, there were between 30 and 35 of these regional rebellions. This book seeks to study some of the hundreds of 'village revolts' which occurred between the accession of Henry VIII and the meeting of the Short Parliament in May 1640.[2] Although manifestations of social protest, usually defined in legal terms as riots, were more localized in extent and more limited in aims than the rebellions of the late-medieval and early-modern periods, they also proved to be a more persistent phenomenon. Village revolts against seigneurial exploitation began long before the Great Revolt of 1381, while other species of social protest, such as game poaching, food riots, machine smashing, and anti-turnpike riots continued into the eighteenth and nineteenth centuries.

Since riots were more numerous than rebellions and have left a larger body of evidence—especially in the records of the Tudor and early-Stuart Court of Star Chamber and other equity courts, their study is likely to yield much knowledge about the nature of popular protest. The forms of popular protest become more intelligible when studied with reference to legal norms and standards of justice. The outbreak of popular disturbances usually reflected a deterioration in the quality of justice dispensed. The rituals of protest employed by demonstrators frequently mimicked judicial ceremonies, while legal distinctions between categories of crimes (i.e. high treason, felony, and misdemeanour) imposed constraints upon how far collective protest might prudently be carried without endangering family, household, and property.

---

[1] E. B. Fryde, *The Great Revolt of 1381* (Historical Association, 1981), 7.
[2] Throughout this work, old-style dates are retained with regard to the day and the month; however, the new year is taken to begin with 1 January instead of 25 March.

Even where popular concepts of justice diverged from those of
the governing élite, the former were derived from the latter. Most
petitioners first carried their grievances to their lords or magistrates.
They resorted to violent demonstrations only when their governors
failed to heed warnings or to redress grievances, displayed partiality,
or did not discharge their traditional duties of rendering justice
and resolving disputes.[3] Since the grievances were usually quite
specific, the use of violence was both controlled and selective and
was usually aimed at the property rather than the person of the
victim. The employment of the customary symbols and rituals of
festive misrule or affirmations of loyalty served to reassure the
governors that the protestors were not challenging the social or
political order. These forms of social protest in local communities
could be expected to remain within these traditional limits unless
the system of justice broke down or some external influence, such
as rumours or political prophecies, supplied the basis for more
generalized protest and, perhaps, expanded the sphere of social
conflict. It was at this point that village revolts sometimes coalesced
into regional rebellions.[4]

Except where aristocratic manipulation or gentry factionalism
complicate the picture, the participants in village revolts usually lack
rights of political participation outside their local communities; their
motives are devoid of political consciousness and their writings or
utterances do not employ a political vocabulary. Precocious political
awareness is more characteristic of urban protests, especially those
of London, than rural protests. Political protest, as embodied, for
example, in regional rebellions, is generally supposed to be more
sustained and less spontaneous than social protest. But, in examining
the latter, one must avoid focusing only upon the riots, which by
themselves appear to be episodic, and look also at the litigation,
which frequently accompanied anti-enclosure riots and tenurial and
rent disputes and which was necessarily more sustained—sometimes
across generations. Although anti-enclosure riots may be regarded
as displaying primitive or pre-political behaviour because they failed
to develop into some more modern form of protest or participation

---

[3] J. Brewer and J. Styles (eds.), *An Ungovernable People: The English and their
Law in the Seventeenth and Eighteenth Centuries* (New Brunswick, NJ, 1980),
17–18.
[4] R. B. Manning, 'Violence and Social Conflict in Mid-Tudor Rebellions', *JBS*
16 (spring 1977), 18–40.

in the political nation, the participants often displayed a remarkable degree of legal sophistication.[5]

Between the great mid-Tudor rebellions of 1536 and 1549 and the English Civil Wars, there were only a few popular disturbances which could be dignified by the name of 'revolt': the Midland Revolt of 1607 did result in one battle; the Western Risings of 1626–31 were essentially large-scale anti-enclosure riots; while the Enslow Hill Rebellion of 1596 never got beyond the conspiratorial stage. In terms of the level of violence, the number of participants and geographical extent, none of these Elizabethan and early-Stuart insurrections quite compares with the pitched battles and 'camping days' of the Western Rebellion or Kett's Rebellion of 1549. These lesser risings more closely resemble the hundreds of riots protesting enclosures of commons and wastes, drainage of fens and disafforestation which reverberated across the century or so between 1530 and 1640. The term 'village revolt' seems appropriate because these riots were almost invariably contained within the confines of one or several local communities and, typically, were responses to alterations in land use.

The inclusion of a chapter on London apprentices' riots in a book which purports to deal with village revolts and social protest may strike the reader as odd. London was, after all, something more than a village. But popular disturbances in the metropolis, from early in the reign of Henry VIII to the end of the Jacobean period, no longer displayed that awareness of national and international issues which had characterized London's participation in the Great Revolt of 1381 or Jack Cade's Rebellion of 1450. Rather, London riots and insurrections during this period reveal the same pattern of localism and sub-political behaviour found in village protests, even if they did arise from problems which were uniquely urban and metropolitan. From the beginning of Charles I's reign, popular demonstrations in London began to take on a distinctive political flavour, and by 1640 the metropolis once again displayed something like the degree of political awareness which was evidenced by the late-medieval revolts. But the persistence of localism in popular protests in provincial England undoubtedly contributed to the widespread neutralism of the Civil Wars.[6]

---

[5] E. J. Hobsbawm, *Primitive Rebels: Studies in Archaic Forms of Social Movement in the 19th and 20th Centuries* (New York, 1965), 2–3.

[6] J. S. Morrill, *The Revolt of the Provinces: Conservatives and Radicals in the English Civil War, 1630–1650* (1976), 88–99.

Most of the agrarian protests of sixteenth- and early seventeenth-century England were directed against enclosures of commons and manorial wastes. Because sustained demographic growth, beginning *c.*1520, tended to increase grain prices, the earlier practice of converting arable land to pasture practically ceased, except in a few parts of the Midlands which were not well served by markets and transport. The reorientation of English agriculture from subsistence to commercial production disrupted rural communities by emphasizing the differences between large farmers and smallholders. Many of the latter failed to survive the prolonged late-Elizabethan and early-Stuart crises, and rural as well as urban communities faced worsening problems of providing for poor relief and regulating masterless men. In the countryside, vagrants and artificers frequently squatted upon wastes in woodland-pasture regions, while paupers were housed in poor-law cottages built upon the village common. Older tenants often had trouble distinguishing between the two practices and tore down such hovels.

Following the crises of the 1590s, the pace of agrarian change appears to have accelerated: convertible husbandry became more widely diffused in mixed-farming communities, while the movement of surplus population from fielden to pastoral and sylvan regions together with the development of rural industry becomes more discernible. Whichever pattern of development a particular community followed, change brought more intensive land use and greater demands upon resources of food, fuel, and water. Some far-sighted landlords certainly introduced improved agricultural technology, but more resorted to 'fiscal seigneurialism', i.e. reviving forgotten manorial obligations and exactions, extracting higher rents and entry fines, commercially exploiting fuel, mineral, timber and water resources, or settling new tenants upon the manorial waste.

All of these practices constituted an unprecedented assault upon the important resources of commons and wastes which traditionally had been shared by the village and manorial community and upon which the English husbandman was dependent if tillage was to be maintained. Popular determination to defend use-rights against the incursion of the modern doctrine of absolute and exclusive rights of private property can tell us much about the degree to which a sense of community survived in a particular manor or village. The evidence presented in this book suggests that the extent to which individualism had permeated late-medieval and early-modern English society may have been exaggerated.

Historians have generally assumed that the peasantry disappeared from England in the eighteenth century as the ownership of land, no longer held of the king by conditional tenures, came to be concentrated in the hands of the gentry. This is supposed to have followed upon the disappearance in the sixteenth and seventeenth centuries of small peasant proprietors who had been forced to sell their holdings. Although a few gentlemen managed their own estates, most of the land was leased to farmers and worked by labourers for wages.

Alan Macfarlane has raised the question of whether smallholders in Tudor and Stuart England were peasants, or, indeed, whether peasant society even existed in England in earlier periods. Dr Macfarlane argues that the 'central feature of "peasantry" is the absence of absolute ownership of land, vested in a specific individual'.[7] By concentrating on a detailed analysis of inheritance customs, Macfarlane easily demonstrates that English law (leaving aside a discussion of trusts and corporate bodies) vests property only in individuals, and that smallholders frequently alienated land without much regard for family interests. But Dr Macfarlane does not succeed in establishing the existence of an absolute and unqualified legal doctrine of private property, or what is usually called 'individualism' or 'possessive individualism'. Dr Macfarlane's argument for the existence of a doctrine of unqualified private property rights in the seventeenth century ignores several considerations. Nowhere does he mention the survival of use-rights, which the courts upheld and protected, when those rights could be documented, and which necessarily limited the 'landowner's' title. The continued exercise of seigneurial jurisdiction, the extraction of manorial dues and services, and the survival of servile tenures all modified the terms of land-holding. Although a 'tenurial revolution' may have been in progress, it certainly was not yet completed. Moreover, no clear and unqualified definition of 'property' can be found in any legal dictionary or the works of any legal writer before the eighteenth century. Seventeenth-century legal writers, including Sir Edward Coke, are vague on the question of 'property' except to say that, ultimately, all property is

---

[7] A. Macfarlane, *The Origins of English Individualism: The Family, Property and Social Transition* (New York, 1979), 78–80.

vested in the king.[8] The abolition of the Court of Wards and Liveries may be said to have ended feudal tenures, but that did not dispose of the question of common rights, which remained the subject of much litigation in late seventeenth-century Chancery cases.

A sense of community, whereby neighbours acted together to protect manorial custom, would seem to be a necessary characteristic of peasant society. Moreover, Henry Kamen has suggested that neighbourliness may have been a stronger social bond than kinship in many northern European village communities.[9] When a claim to common rights was articulated and stoutly defended, there must have remained something more than a vestigial sense of community. Even in communities where common rights had been extinguished, the memory of such rights still inspired collective social protest in the form of anti-enclosure riots, widespread hedge breaking, game poaching, and participation in Digger communal experiments. Although many landholders, both large and small, were attempting to stake out claims to private property unqualified by any rights of usufruct, there were those who viewed the enclosure of their commons as symbolic of the loss of a sense of community.[10]

[8] G. E. Aylmer, ' "Property" in Seventeenth-century England', *P. & P.*, no. 86 (Feb. 1980), 87–97. See also C. G. A. Clay, *Economic Expansion and Social Change: England, 1500–1700* (2 vols.; Cambridge, 1984), i. 64–5.

[9] H. Kamen, *European Society, 1500–1700* (1984), 17.

[10] J. Stow, *A Survey of London*, ed. C. L. Kingsford (2 vols.; repr. Oxford, 1971), ii. 77–8.

PART I
Agrarian Change and Social Protest

1

Agrarian Change and Common Rights

UNTIL well into the early-modern period many Englishmen assumed that the clearing of forests represented the triumph of civilization over savagery. When contemporary observers gazed upon the summer landscape of sixteenth-century England and saw a predominance of green, they were not struck by its beauty, as would be the case with a present-day traveller. The preponderance of woodland and pasture was especially offensive to the eye of the Tudor surveyor — that harbinger of agricultural improvement; it reminded him that the indolent denizen of sylvan and pastoral areas could get an easy living by stock-rearing and dairying. Gold was the colour that he longed to see in the rural landscape, because an increase in corn growing was taken to be the sign of agricultural progress. It was axiomatic that uncultivated heaths, moorlands, and forests were nurseries of beggars, thieves, and sectaries, but the husbandman who followed the plough had little time to get into trouble. It was not just a need to increase corn production to feed a growing population that prompted the efforts to extend the amount of land under cultivation; it was also a determination to bend the idle to labour.[1]

i. The Agricultural Revolution

Even more significant than the extension of tillage were the revolutionary new methods of utilizing land. Eric Kerridge has argued that the Agricultural Revolution occurred in England during the period between 1560 and 1760 and not between 1750 and 1850 as was generally supposed by earlier writers. Indeed, the most significant technological innovations were introduced in the first century of that two-hundred-year period. The period after 1750 saw economic growth in agriculture because yet more land was brought under

---

[1] K. Thomas, *Man and the Natural World* (New York, 1983), 194–5; *AHEW*, vol. iv, pp. xxix–xxxvii; C. Hill, *Society and Puritanism in Pre-revolutionary England* (1966), 278; John Aubrey, *The Natural History of Wiltshire*, ed. J. Britton (1847), 11.

cultivation, but the new methods and systems that constitute the technological revolution in agriculture for the most part had been worked out in the earlier period. The most striking evidence for this argument is to be seen in the increased yields, measured in seed-return ratios, which were becoming widespread after 1600.[2]

In addition to the pressure of demographic expansion, the rapidly rising agricultural prices and increases in land values also stimulated more intensive cultivation. But the impact of the Agricultural Revolution was selective both geographically and socially. The new agricultural techniques required considerable investments of capital and the conversion in land use had to be spread over many years; thus wealthy landowners were in a better position to take advantage of such innovations than smallholders. In the initial stages of agrarian change the geographical extent of a market economy and the avail-ability of reasonably fertile soils generally limited the benefits of the Agricultural Revolution to the fielden areas of the Midlands and southern England.

The essential ingredient of the Agricultural Revolution was the elimination of the distinction between permanent tillage, given over exclusively to the cultivation of foodstuffs, and grassland permanently used for grazing. This was replaced by land permanently cultivated, but alternating between the growing of corn and legumes and the planting of ley-grasses. Leys, such as perennial rye and the various varieties of clover — also known as 'artificial' grasses because they were sown from seed and were not necessarily indigenous, had the function of restoring nitrogen to the soil and increasing the supply of grass for grazing. The medieval husbandman had looked upon arable and pasture as being permanently separate categories. The object of this modern, 'up-and-down' or 'convertible' husbandry was to put every ounce of manure back into the soil and to exploit the natural fertilizing advantages of nitrogen-fixing leys. All up-and-down land was thus permanently cultivated and never fallow in the sense of being unpro-ductive or left to the slow natural recovery of indigenous grasses.[3] Of course, not all land was suitable for up-and-down husbandry. The temporary cultivation of marginal land on wastes yielded small returns and was, in any case, no innovation. Water-meadows that were too wet did not repay ploughing and were better left for growing hay.

[2] E. Kerridge, *The Agricultural Revolution* (New York, 1967), 24, 328.
[3] Ibid., pp. 181 ff.

The application of convertible husbandry to grain production resulted in a dramatic technological breakthrough. Moreover, the increase in yields measured in seed-return or seed- yield ratios, which were observable by 1600, remained for two centuries a uniquely English phenomenon. In Russia at the same time the seed-return ratio was somewhere between 3 : 1 and 5 : 1. The seed-return ratio in France at the beginning of the French Revolution did not much exceed 5 : 1.[4] Grain production increased in eighteenth-century France, but only by bringing more land under cultivation and requiring more hours of labour from those who tilled the soil. But in England in 1600 seed returns of 20 : 1 were not unusual. Water meadows in the Cheshire Cheese country could produce a yield as high as this with crops of oats, barley, and rye. In the south-west-Wales coastal region marled and composted land sown with barley displayed seed returns of between 10 : 1 and 14 : 1. The fertile common fields of the Midland Plain, which had produced returns of 10 : 1, could yield 20 : 1 when converted to up-and-down husbandry. On the average, the application of convertible farming to cereal production doubled previous yields. The precariousness of subsistence agriculture in the North of England stands in stark contrast. Unfertilized land in the lowlands of Northumberland and Durham, planted with oats and winter wheat, provided seed-yield ratios of only between 3 : 1 and 5 : 1.[5]

The breakthrough in the yields of grasses for fodder and grazing was just as important as the increase in the yields of grains. Grass yields could quadruple where the system of convertible husbandry was combined with the sowing of clovers, lucerne, sainfoin, and other artificial grasses. The 'floating' or artificial irrigation of water-meadows produced even higher yields. The subsequent addition of root crops such as turnips in the seventeenth century completed the regimen that allowed animals not only to be carried over the winter season, but actually to be fattened on winter stocks of fodder. This was the foundation for the great increase in the production of milk, meat, hides, and manure.[6] Each of these technological innovations

---

[4] R. Mousnier, *Peasant Uprisings in Seventeenth-century France, Russia and China*, trans. B. Pearce (New York, 1972), 162; E. LeRoy Ladurie, 'The Fantastical Accounts of Gregory King', in M. Ferro (ed.), *Social Historians in Contemporary France: Essays from 'Annales'* (New York, 1972), 141.

[5] Kerridge, *Agricultural Revolution*, pp. 130, 155, 159–60, 330–1.

[6] Ibid., p. 331.

was important, but the sum was greater than the parts, for the full benefits could be reaped only when combined into a carefully regulated system of farming.

In consequence of this remarkable productivity of English agriculture, widespread famine or crises of subsistence disappeared from southern England in the sixteenth century and from the poorest and most isolated parts of England by the second quarter of the seventeenth century. By contrast, regions in France such as the Beauvaisis were afflicted with crises of subsistence throughout the seventeenth century; such crises occurred, on average, every decade and could carry off 10 to 15 per cent of the population.[7] A crisis of subsistence was a famine marked by a 'mortality crisis' resulting in, at minimum, a doubling of the number of burials. Although southern England no longer suffered mortality crises from famine, the plague could still produce even sharper increases in mortality in urban areas, as in London in 1592 and 1603.[8] In contradistinction to crises of subsistence, Tudor-Stuart England still suffered periodically from dearth, a situation characterized more by high grain prices than by famine.[9] Dearth produced deep suffering, as in London and other parts of southern England in 1597 when burials increased by 50 per cent. Dearth was more likely to be experienced by the landless poor, by textile workers thrown out of work in times of high grain prices, in regions that were not self-sufficient in grain, and where transport was bad and the market economy underdeveloped. The fear of, or actual presence of dearth, marked by steep increases in the price of corn, could precipitate grain riots, in which mobs would attempt to block shipments of grain and perhaps compel the open sale of such grain stocks at what were deemed popularly to be fair prices — a species of social protest sometimes known as *taxation populaire*.[10]

Andrew Appleby's study of famine in Cumberland and Westmorland allows us to catch a horrifying glimpse of the last crises of subsistence in England and their impact on an underdeveloped region. Whereas

---

[7] P. Goubert, 'The French Peasantry of the Seventeenth Century: A Regional Example', in T. Aston (ed.), *Crisis in Europe, 1560–1660* (1965), 159.

[8] A. B. Appleby, *Famine in Tudor and Stuart England* (Stanford, Calif., 1978), 135, 138–9.

[9] J. Walter and K. Wrightson, 'Dearth and the Social Order in Early Modern England', *P. & P.*, no. 71 (May 1976), 23.

[10] E. P. Thompson, 'The Moral Economy of the Crowd', *P. & P.*, no. 50 (1971), 76–136.

the crisis of 1597 displayed an increase in the mortality rate of 50 per cent in southern England, in Cumberland and Westmorland it resulted in burial rates that were three or four times the usual rate.[11] The crisis of 1623 began like that of 1597 with a series of bad harvests brought on by wet weather during the grain-ripening season. Burials tripled in Lancashire, while in Cumberland and Westmorland there is again evidence of burials increasing fourfold with the number of baptisms also dropping very sharply.[12] These two north-western counties did not experience any comparable crises after 1623. The explanation is not to be found in new agricultural techniques but, rather, in a stabilization of population and grain prices and a return to those forms of pastoral agriculture most appropriate to the environment. As a market economy spread more widely through the North, the region could exchange the products of animal husbandry for grain grown elsewhere.

Not all of the forty or so farming 'countries' of England and Wales were suited to the convertible husbandry of the Agricultural Revolution. In the early sixteenth century this system of agriculture was confined mostly to the Cheshire Cheese and Lancashire Plain farming countries. After 1560 convertible husbandry spread rapidly to other areas, but Eric Kerridge admits that only half of the farmland of England had made the transition by 1660.[13] The Chalk and Cheese countries of Wiltshire illustrate the selective penetration of the new farming techniques. The chalky soils of the former required inordinate quantities of manure from sheep fed on extensive downs to maintain the fertility of smaller amounts of arable and thus were not easily adapted to up-and-down husbandry. The transition from the older sheep-and-corn husbandry with its separate arable and pastoral lands was still taking place in the eighteenth century when unenclosed commons and fields remained much in evidence. The Cheese and Butter countries, which had undergone enclosure at an early date, remained areas of small family farms and the characteristic economic development was the extension of rural industry rather than agrarian change.[14]

[11] Appleby, *Famine in Tudor and Stuart England*, pp. 145–7.

[12] Ibid., p. 168.

[13] Kerridge, *Agricultural Revolution*, pp. 39, 129, 144, 194.

[14] Ibid., 42, 123, 299; J. Thirsk, 'Industries in the Countryside', in F. J. Fisher (ed.), *Essays in the Economic and Social History of Tudor and Stuart England in Honour of R. H. Tawney* (Cambridge, 1961; repr. 1974), 74.

Within a particular village community acceptance of new farming methods was also selective. At Wigston Magna, Leicestershire, approximately 20 per cent of the open fields were subjected to convertible husbandry. Although Wigston was close to the county town of Leicester, the latter's six hundred families did not constitute much of a market in the mid-sixteenth century; most farming in Wigston was of a subsistence variety, and this had changed little by the end of the century. Only two or three of the largest farmers had significant surpluses to sell in Leicester. Although Wigston was perhaps more backward than other Leicestershire villages in this respect, Professor Hoskins concluded that Leicestershire small-holders were remarkably impervious to the commercialization of agriculture.[15]

While experiments with convertible husbandry can be found in Lincolnshire as early as the mid-sixteenth century, generally, the methods of the Agricultural Revolution penetrated Lincolnshire relatively late. Lincolnshire possessed a wide variety of farming regions and soil types, including the fens, the marshes, the chalk wolds, and the claylands. Although the fens saw an incomplete application of the new convertible husbandry after drainage in the seventeenth century, the Agricultural Revolution took place largely in the eighteenth century and did not begin to reach the claylands until the third quarter of the nineteenth century.[16]

The transition to convertible husbandry unquestionably produced hardship for many during the late sixteenth and early seventeenth centuries. In the initial stages, continuous tillage required heavy manuring by large flocks of animals. The extensive grazing require-ments of these animals appears to have been a more significant cause of overcharging commons than the demand for wool, which was weak during this period. The problem of feeding them was solved only gradually by the growing of fodder crops other than hay, and was made more economical by the increasing demand for animal

[15] W. G. Hoskins, *The Midland Peasant: The Economic and Social History of a Leicestershire Village* (1965), 164, 175, 178.

[16] R. W. Ambler and M. Watkinson, 'The Agrarian Problem in Sixteenth-century Lincolnshire: Two Cases from the Court of Star Chamber', *Lincolnshire History and Archaeology* 11 (1976), 13–19; J. Thirsk, *English Peasant Farming: The Agrarian History of Lincolnshire from Tudor to Recent Times* (1957), 222–3, 238, 245, 257, 283; G. A. J. Hodgett, *Tudor Lincolnshire* (History of Lincolnshire 6; Lincoln, 1975), 66–7.

products which came only in the seventeenth century. As long as grain prices remained high, people who could hardly afford bread-corn were in a poor position to purchase animal products.[17] The smallholder who lived in areas specializing in corn production or sheep-corn husbandry was especially vulnerable to price fluctuations in these commodities. Although corn could rise steeply in price during a year of dearth (such as 1596 when the general average price reached 50s. a quarter, or 83 per cent above the norm), the price could also drop very sharply, as in 1603 (when the general average price was 23s. per quarter or 24 per cent below the norm).[18] At the same time the general rise in wool prices which had persisted through the sixteenth century came to an end in 1603 and fell abruptly in the next decade. Generally speaking, the prices of meat and dairy products held up better in the seventeenth century than grain prices, which began to fall after 1660. Thus a smallholder or even a cottager in a region of traditional pasture-farming was better off than his equivalent in the fielden areas.[19]

Those who argued for the improvement of forests and fens in the seventeenth century claimed that their schemes would increase employment and feed more people. An increase in corn growing was still taken to be a sign of agricultural progress—despite signs of over-supply and sagging prices in the first half of the seventeenth century. This became a permanent phenomenon after 1660, and the government was then obliged to encourage the export of surpluses. But the improvers continued to be more worried about the numbers of masterless men in pastoral and sylvan regions and the hordes of squatters that their abundant wastes attracted. They wished to impose gentry control on the more egalitarian societies that these economies spawned. The costly improvements that were undertaken to increase corn production in pastoral areas met with violent popular resistance—especially in the fenlands. It was only towards the end of the seventeenth century that some reformers came to realize that dairying, or the growing of industrial crops such as flax and hemp, could support a much larger population than corn-growing.[20]

---

[17] A. R. Bridbury, 'Sixteenth-century Farming', *Ec. HR* 2nd ser. 27 (1974), 545.

[18] W. G. Hoskins, 'Harvest Fluctuation and English Economic History, 1480–1619', *Ag. HR* 12 (1964), 28–46.

[19] J. Thirsk, 'Seventeenth-century Agriculture and Social Change', *Ag. HR* 18 (1970), 149–50, 157.

[20] Ibid., pp. 169, 175.

The process of agrarian change can be traced to the late fourteenth and early fifteenth centuries when the demographic disasters following the Black Death caused labour shortages, rising wages, and a shrinking market for agricultural produce. The lords of large estates abandoned the system of overall estate management and direct exploitation of demesnes and began leasing their demesnes at fixed annual rents, thus shifting the economic risks to the farmers of their demesnes. Marginal land ceased to be cropped and a greater emphasis was placed upon sheep-farming, which was more profitable during that period. This, in turn, dictated a reduction in the labour services owed by tenants, which were commuted to rents. To replace the labour services of tenants, wage labour was hired as needed. Successive archbishops of Canterbury and bishops of Worcester practised these estate-management policies from the late fourteenth century in order to produce a predictable income in uncertain times.[21]

The phenomenon of demesne-leasing stimulated both social mobility and agrarian change. At first demesnes were leased in small parcels to a number of tenants within the manor in accordance with each tenant's social standing, but later the practice was to lease the demesne in one parcel to a large-scale farmer. The earlier leasing practices buttressed the existing social structures and probably reflected a desire to preserve manorial custom in so far as possible; the later leasing practices not only altered the social structures, but also introduced technological innovations, profoundly altered land use, and began orienting farming practices towards commercial production. The larger farmers of demesnes were frequently gentlemen, but where good transportation provided access to the London market, merchants sometimes invested in demesne farms and then sublet them to smaller men.[22] The influx of these new men into manorial communities was destructive of traditional practices: customary tenures were converted into leases, smallholders speculated in the more fluid land market, and enclosure proceeded apace. These trends form the social and economic background to the Great Revolt of 1381 and Jack Cade's Rebellion of 1450.

---

[21] C. Dyer, *Lords and Peasants in a Changing Society: The Estates of the Bishopric of Worcester, 680–1540* (Cambridge, 1980), 113, 141–9, 209; F. R. H. DuBoulay, *The Lordship of Canterbury: An Essay on Medieval Society* (New York, 1966), 218–19.

[22] Dyer, *Lords and Peasants*, pp. 213–14; R. H. Hilton, *Bond Men Made Free: Medieval Peasant Movements and the English Rising of 1381* (1973), 169–70.

Enclosure of the demesne was usually the next step in agricultural improvement after demesne-leasing. Open-field farming was still widespread in the Midlands in the sixteenth and seventeenth centuries, and we can observe in detail how enclosure of demesnes could disrupt and diminish the tenants' exercise of their common rights. Enclosure necessitated consolidation of demesne lands scattered among the tenants' lands, which meant exchanges of land with the tenants. From the landlord's point of view, this had the advantage of producing one large consolidated farm, which could be used as a pasture or for convertible husbandry, and which would be a more attractive commercial proposition to a competent farmer seeking a lease. However, there were disadvantages for the tenants, especially the poorer tenants. Although their arable holdings would not be diminished, their common rights certainly would be. While the lord had most likely abandoned his common rights on unenclosed pasture, the tenants no longer had access to the demesne lands for gleaning, which was important to the poorer sort. Moreover, the lord's hedges would most likely make it difficult and time-consuming for tenants to drive their beasts to commonable pastures. Enclosure of the demesne would have the effect of disrupting customary arrangements and causing the manorial system to break down. The net result was that it became easier to persuade the tenants to accept what the lord wanted in the first place—namely, total enclosure of the whole manor. Since considerable opposition could be expected at every stage, and a substantial capital investment would be required for making fences, planting hedges, and digging ditches and mounds, it was unusual for total enclosure to be effected in a single stage.[23]

The ability of the tenants to withstand such pressure from manorial lords or their farmers very much depended upon the viability of their agrarian customs. Such resistance was more effective where a fully developed common-field system existed than where the arable fields were merely open. The distinction, which Joan Thirsk insists upon, between 'common fields' and 'open fields' helps to provide a measure of the survival of a sense of community and the degree to which it regulated farming practices within a particular manor or village.[24]

[23] M. E. Finch, *The Wealth of Five Northamptonshire Families, 1540–1640* (Northants. Rec. Soc. 19; 1956), 154–60; R. H. Tawney, *The Agrarian Problem in the Sixteenth Century* (repr. New York, 1967), 232–3.

[24] J. Thirsk, 'The Common Fields', in R. H. Hilton (ed.), *Peasants, Knights and Heretics: Studies in Medieval English Social History* (Cambridge, 1976), 10–11; and

In an open-field village, the arable strips of tenants and, perhaps, the lord would be found interspersed and lying together but not subject to common rights of pasture; individual parcels might be temporarily enclosed to secure fallow grazing for the animals of the person holding that parcel of land. In a fully-developed common-field system the strips of each tenant would be scattered throughout the arable fields and meadows and would be subjected to common of pasture after the harvest and while lying fallow; the time of ploughing, sowing, and harvesting, as well as the crops to be planted, would be subject to community decisions and husbandry by-laws made in the manorial court or village assembly. In addition, all tenants, as commoners, would enjoy use-rights over the uncultivated waste, which included the right to pasture animals needed to work their holdings or supply their households. Commoners also possessed the right to gather fuel for household consumption, and stone and timber in order to make repairs to their dwellings and barns, but not for sale outside the manor. Dr Thirsk's 'common fields' and 'open fields' represent conceptual models, and most fielden communities in the sixteenth century fell somewhere between the two because of the widespread erosion of use-rights. As the case of Wigston Magna indicates, open fields did not necessarily present an obstacle to agricultural improvement or temporary enclosures, and might even allow the exercise of somewhat attenuated common rights.[25] But in a common-field system viable common rules of husbandry and the exercise of customary use-rights did impede individual efforts at agricultural experimentation and improvement.[26] Conversely, the absence of communal control by a village assembly and the erosion or extinction of use-rights facilitated the enclosure of open fields and resulted in the land being held in severalty by individuals—all of which were prerequisites for agricultural improvement.

ii. *Common Rights*

Commons, or 'manorial waste', as they were known to lawyers, are peculiar to England and Wales. Manorial wastes are not to be found

the same author's introduction to the Third Edition of C. S. and C. S. Orwin, *The Open Fields* (Oxford, 1968), pp. ix–x.

[25] Hoskins, *Midland Peasant*, p. 164.

[26] J. Thirsk, 'The Local History of Enclosing and Engrossing', *AHEW* iv. 200–5; W. E. Tate, *The Enclosure Movement* (New York, 1967), 43–4.

in Scotland and Ireland because they are necessary adjuncts of the manorial system to which the latter two countries were never subjected—passing as they did from tribal or clan ownership to the modern system of absolute proprietorship. Although the soil of the waste was vested in the manorial lord, his possession was qualified by the recognition in English common law of use-rights attaching to copyholds and freeholds within the manor. In the twentieth century a million and a half acres of commons still survive unenclosed. They are to be found not only in rural areas, but also within Greater London, where all can still take delight in the open expanses of Hampstead Heath or Clapham Common. The modern use of commons is primarily recreational and local societies have sprung up to preserve the public's access to them, just as smallholders in earlier times fought to defend them against enclosure and encroachment.[27]

Wastes consisted of land on the periphery of manors beyond the normal extent of cultivation, and extended to the wastes of adjoining villages or manors. Most of them provided the very roughest sort of grazing. More desirable pasturage would be found on meadows after hay-harvest ('Lammas lands'), drier grasslands classified as pasture, and on fallow arable land or arable land following harvest.[28] The primary consideration in the exercise of common rights of pasture was to feed the plough beasts. After that necessity was assured, the keeping of a few dairy cows was desirable. Another part of the waste might be set aside for horses. Generally, only cattle, oxen, sheep, and horses were considered commonable beasts. Where the waste was abundant, voracious feeders such as geese and swine might be tolerated; the latter were more generally turned loose to browse for nuts, roots, and herbaceous plants in wooded areas.[29]

After common of pasture the next most important of the use-rights attaching to wastes was common of estovers, which permitted the

[27] G. J. Shaw-Lefevre, Lord Eversley, *Commons, Forests and Footpaths* (1910), 1–5; I. Whyte, *Agriculture and Society in Seventeenth-century Scotland* (Edinburgh, 1979), 31, 83; J. W. Jeudwine, *The Foundations of Society and the Land* (1918; repr. New York, 1975), 177; F. G. Emmison, *Elizabethan Life: Home, Work, and Land: From Essex Wills and Sessions and Manorial Records* (Chelmsford, 1976), 243–4; W. G. Hoskins and L. D. Stamp, *The Common Lands of England and Wales* (1963), 102–3.

[28] C. Lane, 'The Development of Pastures and Meadows during the Sixteenth and Seventeenth Centuries', *Ag. HR* 28 (1980), 18.

[29] Tate, *The Enclosure Movement*, pp. 38–9; A. W. B. Simpson, *An Introduction to the History of the Land Law* (Oxford, 1961), 104–7.

gathering of wood for fuel and for repairing dwelling houses and barns. Large timbers and crucks of trees were needed for the frames of houses; bracken, heather, and rushes furnished thatching for roofs; dead wood and the new sprouts of pollarded willows, together with clay, provided the materials for wattle and daub walls. Stone and slate were also quarried from wastes where available. The fuel available to commoners varied from region to region. Heaths and moors provided furze and gorse, and wooded areas dead wood which were bound into faggots. In fens and mosses peat was dug for use as domestic fuel (common of turbary). In other areas coal was mined from outcroppings and shallow veins.[30]

The question of who was legally entitled to rights of common and precisely what those rights comprehended varied according to manorial custom. Freehold tenants of manors with arable holdings had only to establish their claim to that tenure in order to secure their rights to common of pasture; customary tenants were obliged to show a grant or demonstrate long usage. In pastoral and sylvan areas where wastes were ample common of pasture was generally allowed to all inhabitants and the commons were said to be unstinted. In most fielden communities commoning was restricted to tenants in the sixteenth century and pasturage was beginning to be stinted or rationed.[31] Because of the fear of masterless persons squatting on wastes the royal courts began limiting common rights to tenants in the early seventeenth century.[32]

Access to adequate grazing was absolutely necesssary for the maintenance of tillage by smallholders.[33] In 1533 two husbandmen of Bransby, Yorkshire complained to the Court of Star Chamber that whereas formerly they had pastured their animals on the town commons and on the common fields after harvest, the manorial lord, 'of his extort and myghty powre', lately had enclosed arable fields and commons to the total of 400 acres so that the tenants no longer could feed their draft animals. The consequence was that where there had formerly been 15 or 16 ploughs there remained only six.[34] At

[30] Hoskins and Stamp, *The Common Lands*, pp. 47–9.

[31] Simpson, *History of the Land Law*, pp. 104–7; Hoskins and Stamp, *The Common Lands*, p. 50; Tate, *The Enclosure Movement*, pp. 38–9.

[32] Below, ch. 4.

[33] Tawney, *The Agrarian Problem in the Sixteenth Century*, pp. 239–41.

[34] *Yorkshire Star Chamber Proceedings* iii, ed. W. Brown (Yorks. Arch. Soc., Rec. Ser. 41, 1913), 45–7.

Burnham, Somerset the copyholders complained that their absentee lord, by making intakes and enclosures of the common, had rendered it impossible for several tenements to maintain tillage.[35] Within the lordship of Thomley, Oxfordshire enclosure of the waste was causing the abandonment of tenancies. Tenants attempting to claim common of pasture found that Sir John Brome impounded their beasts and levied fines of 5*d*. per day on each animal in a locality where the average daily wage for labourers was 1/2*d*.[36] The royal manor of Orwell, Cambridgeshire suffered from a severe shortage of both common pasture and fuel. Located on clay soils at the edge of the Midland Plain, it produced mainly corn under a two-course system of rotation and depended upon a fold-course for fertilization. Yet there existed in the early seventeenth century only 200 acres of meadow and pasture classified as Lammas lands to service 1450 acres of arable. These meagre common lands disappeared during the course of the century. The years between 1607 and 1627 saw a decrease in the number of smallholders with between 15 and 50 acres and a sharp increase in the number of cottagers holding two acres or less. The villagers' custom of making provision in their wills for all offspring and widows undoubtedly contributed to the fragmentation of smallholdings.[37]

Disputes concerning the exercise of common rights were frequently intertwined with the other conflicts. On the royal manor of Tewkesbury, Gloucestershire the customary tenants of three hamlets in the tithing of Northey were obliged to rent a common close from the steward of Northey, Ralph Asheley, gent., in order to graze their plough oxen. Asheley also brought in a surveyor and began converting copyholds to leaseholds. Although the tenants complained to Sir Anthony Kingston, high steward of the manor, who ordered Asheley to cease troubling the tenants, they remained afraid of Asheley because he was known to be a favourite of Anne Boleyn. Instead of going to law they made peace with Asheley by offering him 40*s*. But the Edwardian steward of Northey, Sir John Ribalde, was even more extortionate. He employed another surveyor, who discovered that the tenants' holdings were not by copy of the court roll, but were part of the demesne and the tenants would have to

[35] PRO, REQ 2/8/135.   [36] Ibid., STAC 2/31/149.
[37] M. Spufford, *Contrasting Communities: English Villagers in the Sixteenth and Seventeenth Centuries* (Cambridge, 1974), 94–6, 100–1, 118.

pay re-entry fines in order to renew their leases. Moreover, the surveyor told the tenants that continued use of the common close would cost them 13s. 4d. per acre for a lease that would expire upon the death of Ribalde. Some tenants compounded to secure new leases, but the remainder brought a complaint against Ribalde in the Court of Requests.[38]

Although the yearly cycle of activities for townsmen was in many ways quite different from the rhythm of the husbandman's year in rural communities, urban life was not wholly divorced from agricultural activities. Townsmen still depended upon the use-rights that they claimed on nearby commons in order to feed their horses and obtain fresh milk. At Coventry access to the city's Lammas lands helped to shape the civic calendar. The reversion of Lammas pastures to private hands on 2 February coincided with the beginning of the civic year when the mayor was inaugurated. The reopening of the Lammas lands to communal access on 1 August signalled the beginning of autumn.[39] By the early sixteenth century few Londoners could afford to keep a cow on the commons skirting the city's suburbs, but they continued to look to such open spaces for exercise and recreation. Sometime in 1513 or 1514 the inhabitants of Islington, Shoreditch, and Hoxton enclosed their commons. Apprentices and citizens who continued to use those commons to practise archery or simply to walk upon were prosecuted and told to confine themselves to the highways.

This sayeng sore greved the Londoners, and sodainly . . . a great number of the citee assembled them selfes in a mornynge, and a turnar in a fooles cotte came cryenge through the cytee, 'shouels and spades!'; and so many people folowed that it was a wonder and within a short space all the hedges about the townes were cast downe, and the diches filled, and euery thing made plain the woorkemen were so diligent.[40]

The fields remained open for many years thereafter, but by the reign of Elizabeth London's growth encroached upon the surrounding commons. John Stow viewed the failure to preserve such open spaces as symbolic of the loss of a sense of community:

---

[38] PRO, REQ 2/18/125.
[39] C. Phythian-Adams, 'Ceremony and the Citizen: The Communal Year at Coventry', in P. Clark and P. Slack (eds.), *Crisis and Order in English Towns, 1500–1700: Essays in Urban History* (Toronto, 1972), 70.
[40] Edward Hall, *Hall's Chronicle* (1809; repr. New York, 1965), 568.

Wee now see the thing in worse case than ever, by meanes of inclosure for Gardens, wherein are builded many fayre summer houses, and as in other places of the Suburbes, some of them like Midsommer Pageantes, with Towers, Turrets, and Chimney tops, not so much for vse or profite, as for shewe and pleasure, bewraying the vanity of mens mindes, much vnlike to the disposition of the ancient Cittizens, who delighted in the building of Hospitals, and Almes houses for the poore, and therein both imployed their wits, and spent their wealths in preferment of the common commodities of this our Citie.[41]

iii. *Enclosure*

Possessed as we are of the advantage of hindsight, we can identify the pressure of an expanding population and rapid technological change in agricultural practice as principal causes of economic and social dislocation in Tudor-Stuart England. Enclosure was merely a stage in the alteration of land use, but it was upon that symbolic act that contemporary debate focused and it was upon the enclosing hedge that villagers with a sense of wrong vented their rage. Because arable land being converted to up-and-down husbandry was first laid down to pasture for several years to recover its fertility after being enclosed, the popular perception was that such land was withdrawn from tillage. This, in turn, was perceived as causing the decay of houses of husbandry and the depopulation of villages. Enclosure also was widely blamed for causing dearth. That is why anti-enclosure riots were a much more widespread form of protest in the sixteenth and early seventeenth centuries than grain riots.[42]

Both contemporary and modern writers have attempted to distinguish between the different types of enclosure. John Hales, whose supposedly inflammatory rhetoric in the charges to the commission for redress of enclosures was widely blamed for the extensive rioting of 1548–51, admitted that enclosure could benefit the commonwealth; an example he gave was where no one's common rights were violated and the object was to increase the supply of timber. It was the kind of enclosure that led to depopulation or loss of use-rights that he condemned.[43] Depopulation could follow

---

[41] Stow, *Survey of London*, ii. 77–8.

[42] Walter and Wrightson, 'Dearth and the Social Order in Early Modern England', p. 30.

[43] Hales's charge, which he insisted upon reading at every meeting of the commissioners, is printed in John Strype, *Ecclesiastical Memorials* (3 vols.; Oxford, 1816),

from enclosures that either resulted in the conversion of arable to pasture or extinguished use-rights on the commons, and the introduction of up-and-down husbandry certainly resulted in some depopulation. The crucial questions were, first, whether other land was available to compensate those who suffered loss and, second, whether enclosure was carried out in a fair or a high-handed manner. If the former, it was possible to secure the tenants' agreement, and enclosure could proceed amicably.[44] But depopulation might still follow if an enclosure agreement excluded inhabitants who were not tenants from the waste. Enclosures of arable for permanent sheep pasture were more prevalent in the earlier Tudor period while wool prices remained high;[45] in the reign of Elizabeth and thereafter the kinds of enclosure that provoked the most popular resistance were enclosures for convertible husbandry or intakes of waste. Intakes and enclosure of manorial waste were usually a prelude to cultivation of the waste and could lead to the phenomenon of impopulation, or an increase of population in a particular community.[46] The practice of enclosing and improving wastes was an especially controversial issue in the seventeenth century. Those who advocated the practice pointed out that it increased food production, furnished a means of absorbing the surplus population of other communities, and turned such persons into proper husbandmen to the exclusion of squatters and masterless men. It was assumed that such persons would be subjected to gentry control and that manorial lords would increase their income from rent. But the older copyholders and freeholders usually objected because their use-rights on the waste were thereby diminished, and their rents and entry fines were frequently increased as part of a general scheme of improvement. Moreover, the older tenants usually considered the new tenants to be undesirable as neighbours and little better than vagrants.[47]

Another type of enclosure that was especially resented was empark-ment. The sport of the chase was an integral part of aristocratic

ii/2. 145. See also F. W. Russell, *Kett's Rebellion in Norfolk* (1859), 11; *DNB*, s.v. John Hales.

[44] Tate, *Enclosure Movement*, pp. 61–2; Kerridge, *Agrarian Problems*, pp. 119–21.

[45] Finch, *Five Northamptonshire Families*, pp. 114–16.

[46] E. Kerridge, *Agrarian Problems in the Sixteenth Century and After* (1969), ch. 6.   [47] Cf. below, ch. 7 (ii).

culture, and many a country gentleman coveted his own deer park. Scores of new deer-parks were enclosed during the Tudor-Stuart period, and were especially numerous in the Weald of Sussex. Usually emparkments were intakes from the waste or enclosures of wooded areas which extinguished the common rights of pasture and estovers, but emparkment of arable land was not unknown.[48] As symbols of aristocratic arrogance, emparkments invited both anti-enclosure riots and widespread poaching. Where previously there had been a tangible expression of a sense of community in the collective exercise of use-rights, the appearance of the enclosing hedge in the landscape served notice that henceforth the commodity of one individual was to be preferred.

Enclosures of common fields and wastes were procured in several ways. The simplest method was where one person acquired by purchase all tenements and their appurtenant common rights. A few privileged courtiers in the Tudor period enclosed by special licence of the monarch. When Henry VIII created the honour of Hampton Court, he secured enclosures on Hounslow Heath by Act of Parliament. In the seventeenth century various individuals obtained enclosures by private Act of Parliament, and this method was employed frequently after 1727. The usual method of securing general enclosure in the late sixteenth and early seventeenth centuries was by means of an agreement between the landlord and tenants, which was embodied in a Chancery decree. Early seventeenth-century Chancery decrees specified that enclosure agreements were subsequently to be 'made perfect' by an Act of Parliament. Manorial lords also continued to make partial enclosures of waste under the provisions of the Statutes of Merton (1235) and Westminster (1285). All of these were legal methods of securing enclosure, but they frequently concealed the use of force, fraud, and intimidation against the tenants.[49]

The materials used for constructing enclosing hedges depended upon what was available locally. Each type possessed its own peculiar symbolism. In Cornwall, stone walls were considered 'hedges' and afforded protection against Atlantic gales. Enclosures were more

---

[48] J. E. Jackson, *Wiltshire: The Topographical Collections of John Aubrey* (Devizes, Wilts., 1862), 130-1.

[49] G. Slater, *The English Peasantry and the Enclosure of Common Fields* (repr. New York, 1968), 6-7; Finch, *Five Northamptonshire Families*, pp. 14-16; 37 Hen. VIII, c. 2, *SR* iii. 986-7; cf. ch. 5 below.

acceptable in a pastoral society and many such enclosures in the West Country were already ancient by the sixteenth century. Mounds and ditches were much employed in the Cambridgeshire fens, but became associated with unpopular drainage schemes in the seventeenth century. A 'dead hedge' was a kind of temporary fence, widely used in the medieval period, which was constructed 'of dead wood, well staked and thick plashed'. Dead hedges were distinguished from 'quick hedges' or living hedges, which were planted as 'quick-sets', or nursery transplants. The plashed or wattle types of dead hedges were always temporary enclosures. But the increasing use of quick hedges implied a permanent division of land henceforth to be held in severalty. Of all the several hundred species of flora found in English hedgerows today, the whitethorn or hedging hawthorn (*Crataegus Monogyna*) was the most widely employed and was meant to afford an impenetrable barrier to man and beast. Eventually, birds would disperse other species of plants, shrubs and trees into the hedgerows. The defenders of enclosure liked to point out that hedging and ditching provided employment for the poor, and subsequently furnished them with nuts, berries, and fuel.[50]

A piece of land need not be surrounded by a physical obstacle in order to be enclosed. Thus, a 'close' may be said to represent in law a man's rights over his own property. A trespass can be perpetrated simply by farm animals straying across an imaginary boundary line and transgressing upon a 'close'.[51] Hedge-breaking and depasturing of cattle in a close were the symbolic ways of reclaiming lost rights of common of pasture. Under manorial custom hedge-breakers were liable to have their animals distrained in the manorial pinfold or pound. In a manorial community undergoing enclosure, pound-breach and rescue of distrained cattle also became expressions of popular resistance to enclosure.[52]

The physical presence of the enclosing hedge emphasized that trespass was an unlawful act. F. W. Maitland points out that trespass had always been regarded as a crime in common law during the Middle Ages.[53] Even when a close was surrounded by an imaginary

---

[50] E. Pollard *et. al.*, *Hedges* (New York, 1975), *passim*, esp. 38, 79–85. An ancient hedgerow may be dated by the number of species of flora which it contains.

[51] H. A. Lloyd, *The Gentry of South-West Wales, 1540–1640* (Cardiff, 1968), 72–3.

[52] Tate, *Enclosure Movement*, pp. 29–30; PRO, STAC 2/34/50.

[53] *Select Essays in Anglo-American Legal History*, ed. Association of American Law Schools (3 vols.; Boston, 1908), ii. 589.

boundary, English law assumed that breaking that close implied violence; but when an actual hedge was broken, the law assumed that force was required, and the act was said to be done *vi et armis* — with force and arms. If three or more people, having made menacing gestures or speeches, destroyed an enclosure, the trespass was considered a riot.[54] By emphasizing the seriousness of the crimes of riot and trespass, the law was tending to come down on the side of theories of possessive individualism. By destroying an enclosing hedge, the dispossessed restored, if only momentarily, a sense of community and dramatized their own concept of justice. Thus, their action carried a symbolism of its own and almost invariably proceeded according to prescribed rituals.

Because population had continued to decline in the arable areas of southern and midland England until the 1520s, the historian encounters comparatively few instances of enclosure disputes before 1530. While the records of quarter sessions are scanty in the early sixteenth century, early-Tudor Star Chamber cases are numerous enough to make it clear that enclosure riots became commonplace only after 1530.[55] The enclosure riot remained the pre-eminent form of social protest during the period from 1530 to 1640. Enclosure riots may not have been quite as numerous as poaching offences, but it can be argued that the former displayed a higher degree of political awareness because enclosure riots frequently combined controlled levels of violence with sophisticated legal manoeuvres on the part of tenants in the common-law and equity courts. It is difficult to avoid the conclusion that enclosure disputes were primarily a response to the pressure of expanding population upon available land resources after 1530.

The bitterness of enclosure disputes first manifests itself in the Midlands, while areas with abundant wastes, such as Lancashire and Yorkshire, remained for some time relatively free of such conflict and were more tolerant of squatters upon the waste.[56] Protests against enclosure of manorial waste became especially numerous in the mid-Tudor period and during the late-Elizabethan crises. The Statute of Merton of 1235, re-enacted in 1549, allowed lords to

---

[54] Michael Dalton, *The Countrey Ivstice* (1622; repr. New York, 1972), 177.
[55] I. Blanchard, 'Population Change, Enclosure, and the Early Tudor Economy', *Ec. HR*, 2nd ser. 23/3 (1970), 440–2; below, ch. 2 (ii).
[56] Thirsk, 'The Local History of Enclosing and Engrossing', *AHEW* iv. 202–203.

enclose and improve manorial waste provided they left sufficient commons for their tenants, and that legal principle was still accepted by the courts in the sixteenth century.[57] Thus, when tenants of Winterton, Norfolk complained that they were denied common of pasture and turbary by an enclosure that Sir William Paston had made on a waste lying between Winterton and Somerton, he pleaded that he had only severed some six or seven acres out of 100 acres. Paston was considered a harsh landlord, and the complainants pointed out that, by contrast, Sir John Clere, lord of the manor of Winterton, had always punished 'overcharging' of comons in his manorial court.[58] On the manor of Ilam, Staffordshire the demesne farmer and tenants had for some time been in the habit of cultivating part of a waste consisting of 1000 acres, but beginning in the reign of Edward VI they found themselves challenged by others who intercommoned on the same waste.[59] Large wastes that had supported intercommoning by several communities 'since time immemorial' became scenes of riotous disputes as inhabitants of one community sought to deny use-rights to rival communities. Sometimes the injured parties were driven to erect enclosures to prevent their cattle straying and being impounded by officers of rival villages.[60]

There were areas of England, such as the highland zone of Devonshire west of the River Exe, where the arable land had long been enclosed. Lower-lying wastes and forests had been cleared between 1150 and 1350 by colonists who had obtained freeholds by socage tenure, which entailed very few obligations beyond the payment of rent and rendering suit to the manorial court. In contrast to the nucleated villages and common fields of the Midlands, Devon farmers had held their land in severalty from the beginning and lived in isolated farmsteads and hamlets. Because vast amounts of waste, to be found on Dartmoor, Exmoor, and the Culm Measures, were readily accessible, common rights on fallow fields did not obstruct

[57] *VCH Stafford* vi. 51–2.   [58] PRO, REQ 2/14/171.
[59] Ibid., REQ 2/19/29.
[60] Ibid., STAC 2/16, fos. 50–3, printed in *Lancashire and Cheshire Cases in the Court of Star Chamber*, ed. R. Stewart-Brown (Lancs. and Ches. Rec. Soc. 71; 1916), 99–100 (Sutton and Macclesfield, Ches.); PRO, REQ 2/12/137 (Horley and Hensington, Oxon.); PRO, STAC 2/20/254, printed in 'Star Chamber Proceedings, Hen. VIII and Edw. VI [Staffs.]', ed. W. K. Boyd, *William Salt Archaeological Society* (1912), 111–12 (Wolverhampton, Staffs.).

agrarian change in Devonshire. The very rapid increase in population in sixteenth-century Devon, the growth of the clothing industry, and the victualling needs of the ships of Plymouth led to new colonization of wastes on higher ground, but the cultivation of this additional land resulted in very few enclosure disputes.[61]

The ramifications of enclosure and the extinction of common rights reached beyond the issues of land use, concepts of property rights, and agricultural improvement. Mervyn James, for example, has concluded that the abundant wastes and moors of the highland areas of County Durham, by providing a livelihood for younger sons, preserved strong kinship groups and partible inheritance long after the nuclear family and its weakened bonds of kinship and a high rate of emigration prevailed in lowland Durham.[62] Certainly, contemporaries appreciated the far-reaching effects of enclosure. In a debate in the House of Lords on the problem of depopulating enclosures shortly after the suppression of the Midland Revolt of 1607, one speaker warned against any hasty legislation regulating enclosures with the assertion that the activities of the Edwardian commissioners for redress of enclosures had provoked anti-enclosure riots, and 'may move the people to seek redress by the like outrage'. Repeating the commonplace about unenclosed wastes being 'nurseries of beggars', he added that enclosed counties such as Essex, Somerset, and Devonshire not only produced more prosperous inhabitants but also supplied high proportions of able-bodied men for the county musters and paid higher returns on parliamentary subsidies than unenclosed counties such as Northamptonshire. The speaker was more concerned about overpopulation than depopulation and suggested that population surpluses might be sent 'to the wars' or transported to the colonies. Hedgerows, he added, would also obstruct the movements of any foreign invaders.[63]

So frequently was the issue of enclosure discussed that the enclosing hedge came to symbolize, depending on the writer's point of view, the imposition of order upon disorderly and seditious persons, or the abridgement of freedom and economic independence. Thus, the

---

[61] Hoskins, *Devon*, pp. 14–19, 62–3, 70–2.

[62] M. E. James, *Family, Lineage and Civil Society: A Study of Society, Politics and Mentality in the Durham Region, 1500–1640* (Oxford, 1974), 22–5.

[63] BL, Cotton MSS, Titus F. iv, fos. 322–3, printed in *Seventeenth-century Economic Documents*, ed. J. Thirsk and J. P. Cooper (Oxford, 1972), 107–9, and in Kerridge, *Agrarian Problems*, pp. 200–3.

metaphor of the enclosing hedge was frequently applied to contemporary debates on church government and religious toleration. Philip Henry, although later a Nonconformist himself, did not like Independents because 'they pluck up the hedge of parish order'.[64] Gerrard Winstanley came to equate all churches and sects with theories of possessive individualism: 'for all your particular churches are like the inclosures of Land which hedges in some to be heires of Life, and hedges out others'.[65] After the suppression of the Midland Revolt of 1607 it became axiomatic that those who levelled hedges were bent also upon levelling social distinctions — and it was from this time onwards that the term 'leveller' began to acquire the connotation of political radicalism. Some of those who found themselves dispossessed by enclosure and agricultural improvement looked to the communal cultivation of wastes and commons as the only means to free themselves from what Gerrard Winstanley called 'all Norman enslaving lords of manors'.[66]

The same Cromwellian and Restoration Parliaments which strengthened the property rights of the gentry by abolishing military tenures failed to grant security of tenure to copyholders or to regulate enclosure. Unfortunately, the policy of maintaining houses of husbandry against depopulating enclosures, which Privy Council and Star Chamber attempted to enforce sporadically until the breakdown of the Laudian regime, came to be viewed as subordinate to the problem of enclosing and improving wastes and regulating the mobility of masterless men. Proponents of enclosure still justified their schemes in terms of agricultural improvement, but increasingly the real issue became one of restoring and maintaining social control.[67]

---

[64] Quoted in C. Hill, *The World Turned Upside Down: Radical Ideas during the English Revolution* (New York, 1972), 81.

[65] *Fire in the Bush* (1649?), in *The Works of Gerrard Winstanley*, ed. G. H. Sabine (repr. New York, 1965), 445-6.

[66] Quoted in C. Hill, *The Century of Revolution, 1603-1714* (New York, 1961), 148-9.

[67] Ibid.; Hill, *The World Turned Upside Down*, ch. 17.

2

Enclosure Riots, 1509–1548

ANTI-ENCLOSURE riots were the most typical and widespread manifestations of agrarian protest in early-modern England and Wales. Although such disturbances had occurred during the medieval period, the riotous levelling of hedges became especially prevalent during the 1530s and 1540s. Before 1548 such protests were not sharply focused and were more usually directed against outsiders of any rank who introduced innovations in agrarian practice into local communities—especially those in which a tradition of self-government survived. The earlier localized protests need to be distinguished from the widespread destruction of enclosures during the years 1548–52, which were more specifically anti-aristocratic and which were, in many instances, sympathetic responses to the regional rebellions of the period. These latter more generalized disturbances were touched off by the spread of seditious rumours.

Enclosures of land for both pasturage and tillage had been undertaken since the beginning of English agriculture and did not usually cause conflict. Indeed, considerable amounts of enclosed land had long existed in counties such as Devon and Kent. But the rapid increase in population in the early sixteenth century pressed hard upon the available supply of land. The necessity of increasing the food supply speeded up the process of enclosure and the introduction of new methods in agriculture and thus altered the familiar patterns of land use in many local communities. Production of corn and meat could not be increased significantly without the year-round use of enclosed and consolidated plots of land, which was inconsistent with communal access to common pastures and waste and the stubble remaining after harvest on arable lands.[1]

Other causes of friction in mid-Tudor agrarian society included the greater fluidity of the land market and the litigation that accompanied

---

[1] J. Thirsk, *Tudor Enclosures* (repr. Historical Association, gen. ser. 41, 1970), 4–10; ead., 'The Local History of Enclosing and Engrossing', *AHEW* iv. 200–5; Tawney, *The Agrarian Problem*, pp. 177 ff.; Kerridge, *The Agricultural Revolution*, pp. 15, 39–40.

the conveyance of tenancies and estates to outsiders as distinct from the more traditional pattern of inheritance. The development of a market in copyhold land and freehold farms was already evident by 1520. The dissolution of the monasteries and the subsequent sale by the Crown of expropriated church lands resulted in a market in manorial-sized properties, with the consequence that more medium-sized estates were built up at the expense of large estates.[2]

The many changes taking place in rural English society are reflected in the increased number of enclosure disputes between *c*.1530 and 1549. Considering the tensions bred thereby, the social relationships between landlords, farmers, smallhold tenants, landless labourers, and rural artisans could hardly remain unaffected.

i. *The 'Agrarian Problem' and Demographic Pressure*

The 'agrarian problem', as R. H. Tawney saw it, consisted of the impact of rising prices upon the relations between landlord and tenant. The former were supposed to have reacted by squeezing and evicting the latter. We now know that rising prices became a problem only in the second half of the sixteenth century, and that therefore the adaptations that Tawney attributes to landlords in the earlier part of the century would have been inappropriate to the actual economic circumstances. Tawney lacked the quantitative data that allow us to see that the real agrarian problem arose from the pressure of population growth upon the land beginning in the second quarter of the sixteenth century.[3]

Although early-Tudor social critics continued to decry depopulating enclosures, that phenomenon had largely ceased, and 'sustained population growth' had begun by about 1520. Their passionate denunciations of 'sheep eating men' are more comprehensible when one remembers that the sites of deserted medieval villages were still discernible and that the grazier had become a convenient scapegoat for the lack of available arable land. Although the population of mid-Tudor England was not as great as it had been in the mid-fourteenth century, it was difficult to absorb the population increase in the

---

[2] J. Youings, *Sixteenth-century England* (Harmondsworth, Middx., 1984), ch. 7.
[3] W. G. Hoskins, *The Age of Plunder: King Henry's England, 1500–1547* (1976), 63–4.

sixteenth century because, as a consequence of the engrossing of farms, there were fewer tenancies to be had than formerly. In earlier times, the surplus population had been accommodated by colonizing the waste, but much less waste was available for enclosure and the creation of new tenancies in the sixteenth century. Moreover, smallhold tenants were often reluctant to allow further encroachments because of the worsening shortage of pasture. This was especially true in lowland or fielden England, but shortages of pasture attributable to impopulation were also developing in certain areas of the highland zone in the northern counties. Since few among the surplus population could find tenancies, 'it would have been the landless wage-earners whose numbers were swelled'. These artisans and labourers—rather than smallholders—constituted the bulk of the crowd during the riots and rebellions of 1549.[4]

It is paradoxical that although the incidence of anti-enclosure protests increased between *c*.1530 and 1549, probably no more than 2 per cent of the land was enclosed during the sixteenth century. By contrast, perhaps a quarter of the arable and common waste was hedged in during the seventeenth century. The apparent problem arises from the fact that contemporaries used the term 'enclosure' as shorthand for a variety of agricultural practices that resulted in depopulation, the decay of tillage, engrossing, encroachment upon wastes or overcharging common pastures, or the assertion of absolute rights of private property that led to the extinction of common use-rights—whether or not the land was actually hedged and ditched. The usual way to express community displeasure about any of these agrarian innovations was to employ the traditional and symbolic form of agrarian protest of levelling hedges. That is why hedges, which had stood unchallenged for years or generations, were sometimes suddenly destroyed. Thus an increase in enclosure protests does not necessarily argue an increase in actual enclosing. But under sixteenth-century conditions it is symptomatic of sustained demographic pressure and rapid agrarian change. Nor need population pressure be found within a particular local community in order to produce rapid change; rather, agrarian

---

[4] Blanchard, 'Population Change, Enclosure, and the Early Tudor Economy', pp. 428, 434, 440; *TED* iii. 12–62 *passim*; Hoskins, *Age of Plunder*, pp. 63–4; Dyer, *Lords and Peasants*, p. 243; B. L. Beer, *Rebellion and Riot: Popular Disorder in England during the Reign of Edward VI* (Kent, Ohio, 1982), 189–93.

innovations could come about in response to regional or national market developments resulting from population increase.[5]

Demographic pressure upon land resources after c.1530 is especially noticeable in the midland counties. This was the region where most of the late-medieval and Tudor depopulating enclosures and conversions of arable to pastoral land had occurred and, in a few instances, continued to occur as late as the early seventeenth century. Althouth the practice was not very common after c.1520, popular memory of it endured and the reaction to these few instances of depopulating enclosures in the Midlands was especially bitter during the early-Jacobean period.[6]

On the Duchy of Lancaster lands in the uplands of north-west Derbyshire, the response to this demographic pressure took the form of an increase in stock grazing on the part of smallhold tenants as well as crown farmers. This called forth complaints about rising pasture rents and the overstocking of commons. Sheep were kept for commercial wool production and served the West Riding clothing industry. Cattle were bred as well, and then fattened on pastures in Leicestershire and Cambridgeshire. On the bishop of Worcester's estates in Worcestershire, the manorial courts, which had opposed enclosure in the fifteenth century, came to favour it in the late 1530s as a means of bringing more land into cultivation.[7]

There were also problems of severe overpopulation in certain parts of the North. Although pasturage continued to be plentiful in the upland areas of Durham, little unused waste remained in the lowland townships. In the lowland areas of Cumberland demographic pressure was especially severe, so it made little sense to convert such land to pasture. Enclosure in Cumberland and Westmorland usually took the form of encroachment upon wastes in the foothills of the Cumbrians and Pennines and in the royal forests of Inglewood and Westward. Although overpopulation resulted in such areas, conflict

---

[5] J. R. Wordie, 'The Chronology of English Enclosure, 1500–1914', *Ec. HR* 2nd ser. 36/4 (Nov. 1983), 484, 489–93; M. L. Bush, *The Government Policy of Protector Somerset* (Montreal, 1975), 44; D. M. Palliser, *The Age of Elizabeth: England under the Later Tudors, 1547–1603* (1983), 179.

[6] Blanchard, 'Population Change, Enclosure and the Early Tudor Economy', pp. 428, 440; Palliser, *The Age of Elizabeth,*, pp. 165, 181; *A New Historical Geography of England*, ed. H. C. Darby (Cambridge, 1973), p. 256; see also below chs. 4 and 9.

[7] *The Duchy of Lancaster's Estates in Derbyshire, 1485–1540*, ed. I. Blanchard (Derbys. Arch. Soc., Rec. Ser. 3; 1967), 6–7, 15; Dyer, *Lords and Peasants*, pp. 335–6.

between lords and old tenants was minimal since they often shared the profits of settling cottagers upon the wastes as under-tenants. Those who suffered were the landless poor who did not participate in such enclosures of waste or forest. Not only were they deprived of grazing rights, they were also rendered more vulnerable to crises of subsistence since the north-west was not self-sufficient in grain. It appears that only the poorest were involved in enclosure riots in Cumberland and Westmorland, except where the lord attempted to settle cottagers upon the waste without consulting the ancient tenants.[8]

In Devonshire and Cornwall arable land was almost wholly enclosed by the latter part of the sixteenth century and farmers turned to unimproved heath and moorland to reclaim more land. Enclosures of waste in the West Country were carried out in order to increase the supplies of wool, meat, cheese, and grain for the burgeoning populations of wool towns.[9]

In descriptive terms, these examples represent some of the actual responses of agrarian communities to the problem of sustained population growth. For analytical purposes, historians continue to disagree upon whether the thrust of these changes is best characterized as the development of an agrarian capitalism which destroyed the old social relationships, a technological revolution carried out through the co-operation of lord and tenant, or a seigneurial reaction in which lords, sometimes in partnership with their ancient tenants, merely exploited the opportunities with a view to quick profit. The last category of change does not imply innovation.

One of the features of the 'agrarian problem' that most writers posit is the development of capitalism in agrarian society as a result of the increasing shift from subsistence to commercial agriculture. As a consequence, an agrarian society consisting of feudal lords and customary tenants is supposed to have given way to one divided into three main categories: landlords more interested in profits than the

---

[8] R. I. Hodgson, 'The Progress of Enclosure in County Durham, 1550–1870', in H. S. A. Fox and R. A. Butlin (eds.), *Change in the Countryside: Essays on Rural England, 1500–1900* (1979), 85; A. B. Appleby, 'Agrarian Capitalism or Seigneurial Reaction? The Northwest of England, 1500–1700', *AHR* 80/3 (1975), 575–80; id., 'Common Land and Peasant Unrest in Sixteenth-century England: A Comparative Note', *Peasant Studies Newsletter* (1975), 20–3.

[9] W. G. Hoskins, 'The Reclamation of the Waste in Devon, 1550–1800', *Ec. HR* 13 (1943), 80–92.

loyalty of their tenants, farmers holding consolidated farms by leasehold rather than customary tenures, and landless labourers who worked for wages. Tawney argued that landlords, faced with the inflationary spiral of prices in the sixteenth century, tried to maintain their income by evicting smallholders and enclosing arable common fields, thus causing rural depopulation and setting adrift a horde of landless, masterless men. Other landlords, unable to raise annual rents fixed by custom, attempted to extract a higher return by raising the entry fines. In an attack upon Tawney, Eric Kerridge argues that the application of capitalist principles of estate management produced a technological revolution in agriculture that was able to feed England's expanding population. This could only be carried through by lords and tenants working in partnership, and such co-operation was possible only if tenants possessed security of tenure and were protected against unreasonable rents. Tawney believed that the commercialization of agriculture in the sixteenth century was accompanied by much clamour and protest (although he never studied that topic systematically), while Kerridge failed to notice any agrarian disturbances other than the Caroline forest riots in the west.[10]

Both explanations of agrarian change possess a degree of validity but cannot be applied to all parts of England without qualification. Certainly, after the 1520s it was encroachment upon commons and wastes and the extinction of tenants' common rights rather than the enclosure of common arable fields that caused most of the conflict. Tawney undoubtedly exaggerated evictions of tenants, who were more usually driven off the land by a combination of harvest failures and indebtedness. Kerridge, on the other hand, overstated the extent of capitalist agriculture and technological innovation.[11]

The argument for a seigneurial reaction rests upon the assumption that most country gentry lacked the capital, and probably the technical knowledge, to invest in capital-intensive agricultural innovations which, in any case, might not yield a profit for many years. Andrew Charlesworth also maintains that landlords had fewer alternatives than Tawney and Kerridge imagined. Manorial lords had lost much ground to tenants in the fifteenth century, which they sought to regain in the more favourable land market of the early

---

[10] A. Charlesworth, *An Atlas of Rural Protest in Britain, 1548–1900* (Philadelphia, 1983), 8–10; Appleby, 'Agrarian Capitalism or Seigneurial Reaction?', pp. 574–5, 592.
[11] Ibid., Charlesworth, *An Atlas of Rural Protest*, pp. 10–11.

sixteenth century. Because most of these tenants were now free rather than servile, seigneurial options were limited and rarely aimed at eviction. Rather, they consisted of direct exploitation of the demesne (instead of leasing to tenants and farmers) and increasing the size of seigneurial flocks and herds on the common pastures. An extreme example of this kind of seigneurial reaction in preference to new agricultural technology is found in the persistence of the fold-course system in the sheep-corn country of Norfolk. The seigneurial defence of the fold-course method of fertilizing not only was detrimental to tenants' rights but also impeded the introduction of convertible husbandry. In addition to attempting to raise rents or, more usually, entry fines, some lords revived half-forgotten manorial dues and taxes or carved new tenancies out of the manorial waste to let at improved rents. The latter set of strategies is referred to in this book as 'fiscal seigneurialism'. In short, many landlords preferred to squeeze money out of their tenants in the old-fashioned manner because it was quicker; technological innovations required too much time and investment before profits could be realized.[12]

Not all Henrician landlords milked their tenants; some still showed a paternal regard for their neighbours. Sir John Gostwick might fairly be regarded as an upstart, since his ancestors were yeomen and his fortunes, through the patronage of Wolsey and Cromwell, were founded upon royal office-holding and shrewd purchases of monastic land. After acquiring the manor of Willington, Bedfordshire from the Duke of Norfolk in 1529, Gostwick applied rational and capitalistic principles to the management of his estate in so far as he gave his tenants 21-year leases, which could be called in earlier for renewal. But his conscience and his desire for social prestige would not allow him to rack-rent his tenants unless they did the same to their subtenants. Gostwick specifically warned his heir against raising rents or enhancing entry fines.[13]

---

[12] Ibid.: K. J. Allison, 'The Sheep-Corn Husbandry of Norfolk in the Sixteenth and Seventeenth Centuries', *Ag. HR* 5 (1957), 22–30; N. W. Alcock, *Warwickshire Grazier and London Skinner, 1523–1555: The Account Book of Peter Temple and Thomas Heritage* (British Academy Records of Social and Economic History, new ser. 4; 1981), 38; id., 'Enclosure and Depopulation in Burton Dasset: A 16th Century View', *Warwickshire History* 3 (1977), 180–4.

[13] A. G. Dickens, 'Estate and Household Management in Bedfordshire, *c.*1540', *Bedfordshire Historical Record Society*, 36 (1956), 38–45; H. P. R. Finberg, 'The Gostwicks of Willington', ibid., pp. 72–3.

Demographic pressure seems to be the most satisfactory explanation for the more rapid rate of agrarian change after about 1520, but the responses of lords and tenants in diverse local communities cannot be comprehended within a single model of change. This diversity and complexity should also warn us to beware of stereotypes of agrarian protest which assume that the typical anti-enclosure riot was perpetuated by an exasperated peasantry venting their rage upon the hedges and ditches of a commercially-minded, grasping gentry.

ii. *Patterns of Violence and Protest*

The impact of sustained demographic pressure on agrarian society is reflected in the more than fourfold increase in enclosure riots after *c.*1530. Of my sample of 75 enclosure-riot cases prosecuted before the Court of Star Chamber between 1509 and 1553, 13 (or 17 per cent) of these cases were heard between 1509 and 1529, and 56 (or 75 per cent) came before the court between 1530 and 1553. Six cases (or 8 per cent) are without date. Based upon Dr John Guy's statement that the Court of Star Chamber under Cardinal Wolsey dealt with 35 cases of riot, rout, and unlawful assembly, we may conclude that enclosure disputes constituted roughly one-third of the breaches of public order examined by Star Chamber.[14]

Except for those riots that accompanied the Pilgrimage of Grace and the Rebellions of 1549, the early- and mid-Tudor enclosure riots remained primitive or pre-political forms of social protest.[15] The largest body of evidence pertaining to these disturbances is found among the richly-documented proceedings of the Court of Star Chamber. The records of the Duchy Court of Lancaster also contain similar evidence. An analysis of the 75 Star Chamber cases dealing with enclosure riots during the reigns of Henry VIII and Edward VI demonstrates that the peerage and gentry played a more significant part in initiating the forcible destruction of enclosures than did smallholders or artisans. To put it more concretely, of the 75 cases involving enclosure riots, in 29 instances the casting down of hedges was procured by peers or gentlemen, in four cases by order of a

---

[14] J. A. Guy, *The Cardinal's Court: The Impact of Thomas Wolsey in Star Chamber* (Hassocks, Suss., 1977), 52; Beer, *Rebellion and Riot*, p. 9; cf. R. J. Hammond, 'The Social and Economic Circumstances of Ket's Rebellion', Ph.D. thesis (London, 1934), 89–92.

[15] I employ here the categories discussed in Hobsbawm, *Primitive Rebels*, pp. 2 ff.

manorial court or municipal officials, and in three cases riots were the indirect result of failure to comply with a crown order commanding the removal of enclosures. In four cases the destruction of enclosures can be assigned to townsmen, and in three cases to clerics; in another four cases we find clergy or lesser gentry leading tenants and small-holders; but in only 12 instances can we confidently state that the levelling of hedges was initiated by yeomen, husbandmen, labourers, or craftsmen. Even if we add in the 14 cases where the social status of the anti-enclosure rioters cannot be determined accurately, only about one-third of these riots are attributable to the initiative of smallholders or persons of lesser rank.[16]

Enclosure riots were merely one species of violence employed by the gentry in pursuing quarrels with rival gentry or enforcing uniformity of agricultural usage upon their tenants. Enclosure riots against rival gentry were frequently accompanied by organized poaching affrays in the warrens and parks of their enemies and sometimes by violence or the threat of violence upon their persons. The gentry combined this calculated use of violence against rivals or tenants with harassment in courts of law. Apparently, it did not occur to the early-Tudor aristocracy that they might be setting a bad example for their social inferiors.[17]

Even where smallholders appear to be the principals in violent enclosure disputes, gentry rivalries can sometimes be discerned in the background. In the case of *John Grevys, husbandman* v. *Sir William Cavendish*, the larger issue was the wardship of Francis Leche, which was disputed between Cavendish and Lord Vaux. Grevys had leased from the ward's father a parcel of enclosed pasture which Cavendish maintained was part of his manor of Chatsworth, Derbyshire. When Cavendish depastured several horses in the

[16] Cf. Table 2.1.

[17] George Rudé argues that in so far as the pre-industrial crowd employed violence against persons, it was due to the corrupt example of the governing classes: *Paris and London in the Eighteenth Century: Studies in Popular Protest* (repr. New York, 1971), 26–8. For a discussion of other aspects of the use of violence by Tudor peers and gentry, cf. R. B. Smith, *Land and Politics in the England of Henry VIII: The West Riding of Yorkshire, 1539–1546* (Oxford, 1970), 144–51; L. Stone, *The Crisis of the Aristocracy, 1558–1641* (New York, 1967), 107–13; M. E. James, *A Tudor Magnate and the Tudor State: Henry, Fifth Earl of Northumberland* (York, Borthwick Papers 30, 1966), 10–11; *Proceedings of the Court of Star Chamber in the Reigns of Henry VII and Henry VIII*, ed. G. Bradford (Somerset Rec. Soc. 27; 1911), 21–2; S. E. Lehmberg, 'Star Chamber, 1485–1509', *The Huntington Library Quarterly* 24 (1961), 189–214.

disputed close, the complainant drove them out in so forcible a manner that one of the horses died. Later Cavendish put some oxen in the close, but these were driven off a hill into a pond and drowned. Thereupon, Cavendish assembled several servants, who plucked open the complainant's enclosure, beat him, and turned dogs loose upon him. One is tempted to believe that Grevys would not have been so bold unless he was encouraged by others.[18]

There were situations where the appearance of a hedge on the horizon could represent a threat to lord and smallholder alike. In farming countries where pasture was scarce, enclosures interfered with the traditional right of shack or shackage, that is, the right of lord and tenant to graze their cattle and sheep on arable lands between harvest time and spring-planting. In those parts of Norfolk and Suffolk where sheep-corn husbandry was practised, heavy dunging and treading of the open fields by sheep was necessary to maintain the fertility of the light, sandy soils before the introduction of the modern system of convertible husbandry. Here, enclosures obstructed the East-Anglian manorial lord's fold-course, which the seigneurial flocks pursued across the tenants' land. When manorial lords behaved with restraint, tenants as well as lords benefited from this system; but where lords abused their privileges by ignoring planted fields or overcharging the grazing resources of arable and waste, then it was in the interests of the tenant to enclose his land. Landlords usually permitted enclosures only after easements were guaranteed for the seigneurial sheep.[19]

Where rights of shack were violated it was not difficult to incite villagers to violence against the offending tenant. When John Rogers, husbandman of Brumstead, Norfolk, attempted to mark off the northern boundary of his holding with quickset hedges, the squire assembled together the parish priest, five husbandmen, and 20 other persons who came by night and removed his enclosures and assaulted him. Rogers was afraid to return to his holding and complained that the squire 'beyng a man of ffeire lands & well alied [allied]' intended to drive Rogers off his 'lyvyng & Inheritance'. Denial of the right of shack was also the issue that provoked Sir Thomas Cuppeldike

---

[18] PRO, STAC 3/5/60.
[19] Hammond, 'The Social and Economic Circumstances of Ket's Rebellion', pp. 73–74; Allison, 'The Sheep-Corn Husbandry of Norfolk in the Sixteenth and Seventeenth Centuries', pp. 12–30 *passim*; A. Simpson, *The Wealth of the Gentry, 1540–1660* (Chicago, 1961), 83.

to assert his authority as lord of Great Carbrooke manor in Norfolk against John Payne. The latter, a relative newcomer, had hedged and ditched part of his three-acre copyhold tenement, which precipitated 'certeyn varyance, debate and stryve' between himself and the other villagers. Fearful of his safety, Payne obtained a warrant of the peace, which he gave to the town constable to enforce. The constable then turned the warrant over to Cuppeldike, who reportedly exclaimed: 'By goddes soule ther[e] shalbe no warrants servyd withyn my Town for I am lord and kynge ther my selfe!' Taking offence because Payne had ignored the authority of the manorial court, and had refused to attend its sessions and obey an order to remove his enclosure, Cuppeldike assembled seven or eight servants to remove the offending hedges. While they were at work, they sang the following rhyme:

> Syr Sowter [cobbler] loke owght
> thy dyke goo downe
> and yf thowe come owght
> to prate or speake
> thowe shall have a broken crowne
> and be of good chere
> ffor thy Lawer [quickset] shall no longer grow here![20]

The authority of a manorial court was also employed to remove several enclosures on the royal manor of Bakewell and it produced a complicated series of disputes. John Sharp of Derby, gentleman, who apparently was trying to expand his leaseholdings in the area, was presented by a jury of 13 elected tenants of the manor and borough of Bakewell at the court leet and baron held at Michaelmas in 1542 for wrongfully enclosing two common fields plus other lands and tenements of the manor as well as certain lands belonging to George Vernon, esquire, the chief tenant of the manor. Sharp was accused of keeping the common fields to 'hym[self] in seueraltie contrary to all lawes and customs used in the said manor', and was further accused of enclosing part of the king's highway that ran from the Castle of the Peak to Derby. When Sharp refused to obey the order of the manorial court to remove the enclosures and restore the rights of shack and common pasture to the tenants of Bakewell Manor, George Vernon, as the presiding judge of the court, ordered

---

[20] *John Rogers, husbandman v. Henry Dengayn, gentleman* (1545), PRO, STAC 2/29/100; *John Payne v. Sir Thomas Cuppyldyke* (1544), ibid., STAC 2/29/13 and 29/65.

the jurors themselves to level the enclosures and open the king's highway. When Sharp caused the jurors to be subpoenaed before the Court of Star Chamber at Westminster, Vernon helped them pay their legal expenses.[21]

George Vernon may also have had a hand in the riot that occurred two months later which levelled the hedges environing two closes which Sharp had leased from a chantry priest in Bakewell. Some of the jurors were among the 26 persons whom Sharp, in another Star Chamber action, accused of destroying his enclosures and then depasturing their cattle within them. Although the defendants admitted that some of the closes were held in severalty, they maintained that the hedges, in effect, denied them the right of shack which they had previously exercised there. However, John Sharp was not to be deterred. In 1545 he was accused of enclosing by 'force of arms' 30 acres of waste and denying the right of common pasture to the other tenants of Bakewell Manor.[22]

The pattern of anti-enclosure protests was very similar on the manors of Enfield and Edmonton, Middlesex, which were also parcel of the Duchy of Lancaster. During the late fifteenth and early sixteenth centuries there were frequent attempts by the demesne farmers to enclose the commons. Several noteworthy features of these early cases of resistance to the extinction of common rights stand out: the tenants from the four manors of Edmonton, Enfield, South Mimms, and Monken Hadley acted in concert in protesting such enclosures to the duchy officials; the leadership was provided by the gentry tenants of the manors, who also suffered losses of common rights; and the duchy officials condoned or encouraged the tenants to remove the enclosures themselves—even though this resulted, as in 1528, in somewhat unruly assemblies of 200 or 300 persons. This suggests that there may have been a long tradition of such community action enjoying official sanction. Despite this popular resistance, the enclosure of both pasture and arable proceeded apace, and over 300 acres were taken in during the late fifteenth and early sixteenth centuries. Another 100 acres were enclosed between 1515 and 1530. In 1531 a duchy commission ordered the restoration of common

---

[21] *John Sharp, gentleman* v. *George Vernon, esquire* (1542), ibid., STAC 2/34/33.

[22] *John Sharp* v. *William Bone, yeoman* (1542), ibid., STAC 2/29/18; *Robert Wolsencrafte, yeoman* v. *John Sharp* (1545), ibid., STAC 2/31/65.

rights, and enclosures ceased for a time on Enfield manor, but continued on the other three manors.[23]

The inhabitants of Tudor towns kept horses and cattle and thus were also drawn into enclosure disputes. In a case involving lands outside Chepping Wycombe, Buckinghamshire, John Raunce, yeoman of Chepping Wycombe, accused the mayor and burgesses of inciting a midnight riot that resulted in the cutting down and burning of Raunce's hedges and the depasturing of his lands. The land in question was leased by Raunce from the Dean of Windsor and contained 20 acres of arable, which the defendants maintained lay within a common field, where the townsmen claimed right of shack after the corn was cut. Raunce had hedged and ditched the land, intending to convert it to pasture held in severalty. When the mayor and burgesses complained about Raunce's enclosures to the Dean of Windsor and to Edward, Lord Windsor, the steward of the Dean's estates, Lord Windsor, came and viewed the common field and ordered Raunce to remove his enclosures. Although Raunce agreed to this decision at the time, he later refused to comply with Lord Windsor's order and continued to deny the townsmen of their right of shack, assaulting and driving out the common herdsman and impounding beasts caught upon the enclosed land. The mayor and burgesses denied the allegation of forcible destruction of enclosures, but it is difficult to believe that they would have hesitated very long after their betters had pronounced such enclosures illegal.[24]

The lesser folk among townsmen were subjected to various kinds of pressures and inducements to take part in enclosure riots. One such riot at Lichfield on 6 May 1549 began when the bellman rang the bell to summon people together in Boore Street and read to them a proclamation which said 'that every man that had any cattle within the said town should bring them forth and claim their common'. Apparently, some of the citizens had enclosed the common recently, and a bailiff of the city had instigated a riot to harass some of his rivals among the citizens. Approximately 100 people, armed with spades and hedging bills, proceeded to the common and cast down the hedges and ditches. Some were persuaded to take part

---

[23] D. O. Pam, *The Fight for Common Rights in Enfield and Edmonton, 1400–1600* (Edmonton Hundred Hist. Soc., occasional papers, new ser. 27; 1974), 4–5, 9.

[24] *John Raunce, yeoman* v. *George Petyfere, Mayor of Chepping Wycombe* (1542–3), PRO, STAC 2/32/119.

by the threat that their cattle would be maimed if they did not participate.[25]

Enclosure disputes were merely one of several issues that led to conflict between landlord and tenant. Manorial courts were less and less able to resolve such disputes, and royal authority, exercised through courts such as Star Chamber or special local commissions, was not always able to fill the void left by the decay of manorial courts. This is well illustrated by a feud that raged between the inhabitants of Finedon, Northamptonshire and two generations of manorial lords over a period of thirty years. In 1509 the freeholders and tenants complained that the lord of the manor, John Mulsho, esquire, had enclosed their commons and a balk (a raised path between two ploughed fields) which they had used for village processions, and had bred a great number of rabbits which were destroying their corn. Mulsho refused to remove the enclosures although ordered to do so by the King's Council. Quite the contrary, Mulsho was making more enclosures with a view to converting arable lands to pasture. Whereas it was the custom of the manor for an heir to a copyhold to pay a fine of a year's rent upon taking up the copyhold, Mulsho was demanding an entry fine of nearly two years' rent, contrary to a royal letter commanding him not to charge more than the customary entry fines. Moreover, Mulsho was accused of despoiling the village woods by cutting excessive amounts of timber and making a forcible entry with eight armed men into a wood belonging to Henry Selby, husbandman. A local commission appointed by the Court of Star Chamber imposed a compromise whereby Mulsho was to keep certain of the closes open for part of the year, but the compromise only served to generate more litigation. In 1529, the enclosures were removed by order of the sheriff. Following that, several husbandmen riotously assembled themselves to chop up gates and gateposts. Later, 60 villagers gathered together to dig up the roots so that the hedges would not grow back again. They continued at this task for eight days with 'knelling of bells, hooting and shouting in most Riotous manner'. Mulsho replied to this by impounding the villagers' cattle, but they broke into the common pound to retrieve their beasts and led them into one of Mulsho's pastures, where his grass was quickly consumed. When Mulsho attempted to carry their

[25] 'Suits in the Court of Star Chamber. Temp. Henry VII and Henry VIII', ed. Boyd, pp. 115–19.

animals to the pound at Northampton — 13 miles distant — the villagers seized the distraint order and again rescued their animals. Moreover, the inhabitants of Finedon had put together a common purse of £20 to spend on lawsuits against Mulsho. Subsequently, the villagers were ordered to replant those hedges that were illegally removed, but that being done, another riot occurred in which they were cast down again.[26]

Intervention by the Court of Star Chamber, local commissioners, and the Court of Chancery failed to put an end to the feuding between Mulsho and the villagers of Finedon. By 1538 Mulsho's part in the dispute had been inherited by his son, John, who in that year put in a bill of complaint in Star Chamber about a copyholder, Henry Selby, who had disputed the elder Mulsho's high entry fines. Sustained by a common purse, Selby had fought the matter in Star Chamber and Chancery for twelve years without paying an entry fine. A Chancery decree finally ordered Selby to make a submission to Mulsho the younger at a session of the manorial court. When the manorial court was convened, Selby appeared, but, encouraged by his neighbours, he refused to make a submission. The other business of the manorial court was also obstructed because the jurors refused to make presentments, thus denying the manorial lord his revenue from amercements.[27]

Abbots and priors of monasteries frequently behaved no differently from their gentry neighbours in pursuing violent feuds. The prior of Malton set his brother, also a canon regular, upon a neighbour, William Percehay, esquire, who was seriously wounded in the ambush. The abbot of Fountains procured six large anti-enclosure riots between 1497 and 1499 against a neighbouring gentleman for imparking a portion of a disputed waste. Intercommoning disputes were often the basis of such conflict, as in the case of the abbot of Leicester and the tenants of Over Haddon, Derbyshire, who appear to have been encroaching upon and overcharging each other's portion of an adjoining common waste. Each accused the other of suborning witnesses in trials before the Duchy Court of Lancaster. When the Over Haddon tenants levelled the abbot's hedges and poached fish from his millpond, his servants fired volleys of arrows at them. The

---

[26] *Selected Cases before the King's Council in Star Chamber* (1477-1544), ed. I. S. Leadam (2 vols.; Selden Soc. 16, 25; 1903, 1911), ii, 6 ff., 40-7.

[27] Ibid., ii, 63-6.

tenants of Over Haddon retaliated by drowning a number of the abbot's cattle. In 1532, an intercommoning dispute between the prior of Lytham, Lancashire and Dame Margaret Butler and her son, Thomas, gave rise to three large enclosure riots stirred up by the Butlers. The monks of Lytham prevented an attack upon the monastery by a crowd of 300 persons only by taking advantage of the Lancashire countryman's reverence for the sacrament and holding up the Eucharist before the menacing crowd.[28]

Except during the mid-Tudor rebellions, these agrarian disorders were nearly always contained within a single local community except where several villages commoned upon the same disputed waste. The small scale and isolated character of most of these riots can be better understood when one considers that in the 43 Star Chamber enclosure-riot cases (out of the sample of 75 cases), where precise information on the number of rioters is given, in 32 instances the number of persons participating was 30 or fewer. In only 6 of these 43 cases were more than 100 rioters involved. These larger-scale enclosure riots were the work of peers, gentry, and townsmen. For example, Edward Stanley, Lord Mounteagle, procured 400 persons to destroy the pales with which Edmund Talbot, esquire, had emparked land in Bashall, Yorkshire, while William Holcroft, esquire, was twice able to send crowds of 300 and 400 persons to destroy enclosures made by city aldermen on lands leased from Chester Abbey and lying outside the walls of Chester.[29]

Moreover, outside the years of rebellion, there are only two or three instances where one can argue that a connection existed between agrarian protests, involving anti-enclosure riots, in several different local communities. The most interesting example occurs in the East Sussex Weald, within the area bounded by Laughton, Mayfield, and Chiddingly. The disturbances, which began in 1520 and continued into the 1530s, are attributable to a gang of poachers, whose activities ranged more freely than the usual smallholder

---

[28] *Yorkshire Star Chamber Proceedings*, i. 180–1, ii. 137–9; Lehmberg, 'Star Chamber, 1485–1509', pp. 197–8; *The Duchy of Lancaster's Estates in Derbyshire, 1485–1540*, ed. Blanchard, pp. 18–19, 29–30, 38–42, 57–60; *Pleadings and Depositions in the Duchy Court of Lancaster*, ed. H. Fishwick (3 vols.; Rec. Soc. Lancs. and Ches., 1896–9), ii. 9–18.

[29] PRO, STAC 2/15, fos. 37–8; *Yorkshire Star Chamber Proceedings*, iii. 161; *Lancashire and Cheshire Cases in the Court of Star Chamber*, ed. Stewart-Brown, pp. 102–4.

protests, and subsequently developed into a more general conspiracy to destroy noblemen's parks.

The chain of events began in 1520 when Ellis Midmore, a mercer by trade, and a dozen hooded men broke into John Brooke's dovehouse, stole a number of pigeons and escaped on horseback. They must have been suspected of more than small-time game poaching, because several of the defendants were lodged in the Tower of London and at least one of them, Robert Sage, was racked. The latter confessed, but later retracted his confession. A Sussex grand jury was sceptical when presented with conflicting evidence, and so dismayed by their discovery that one of the defendants had been tortured that they complained to the King's Council. The Council, presided over by Cardinal Wolsey, found Midmore, who had steadfastly refused to confess, guilty of riotous poaching and perjury and convicted Robert Sage of slandering a peer for accusing Thomas Fiennes, Lord Dacre, of causing his torture in the Tower. Later, Midmore and several other of the defendants also accused Lord Dacre of maliciously promoting the prosecutions and extracting the confessions by intimidation. Dacre then prosecuted Midmore and his companions in the Court of Common Pleas on a charge of *scandalum magnatum*. Wolsey ordered Midmore to be pilloried.[30]

In 1524 a disputed debt led Midmore to hire a couple of labourers 'with hoodes and their heddes and fayces discolored' to assault John Praty of Chiddingly. While under indictment for that offence, Midmore hired more men — some from Kent — to set fire to Praty's house and hedges and steal his cattle, and then obtained Praty's imprisonment for debt. Between 1530 and 1532 Midmore and a fellow conspirator, Richard Frankwell, at the head of a gang of a dozen men, terrorized the neighbourhood in numerous attacks upon enclosed woods, parks, dovecots, fishponds, and breeding places for waterfowl, as well as acts of arson. The principal victim of these protests was Sir William Pelham, whose enclosure of 1200 acres of

[30] *Abstracts of Star Chamber Proceedings relating to the County of Sussex: Henry VII to Philip and Mary*, ed. P. D. Mundy (Suss. Rec. Soc. 16; 1913), 46–7; Guy, *The Cardinal's Court*, pp. 61–3; BL, Lansdowne MSS, 639, fo. 56; G. R. Elton, *Policy and Police: the Enforcement of the Reformation in the Age of Thomas Cromwell* (Cambridge, 1972), 313–14. This Lord Dacre was the grandfather of the ninth Lord Dacre, who was hanged in 1541 for killing a man during a poaching affray: M. A. Lower, 'The Trial and Execution of Thomas, Lord Dacre', *Sussex Archaeological Collections* 19 (1867), 170–2.

commonable waste for deer-parks and coppices to provide fuel for his ironworks, was the occasion for the outbreak of rioting. Vengeance was also visited upon John Brooke, John Praty, and several other middling landowners. Midmore and Frankwell were imprisoned in the Tower of London for several months, but upon their discharge they returned to Sussex and their old habits of inciting enclosure riots. This is the last that we hear of Midmore and Frankwell, but attacks upon aristocratic parks in the Weald of Sussex and Surrey were frequent in the mid-Tudor period. No evidence exists that would connect these disturbances with Midmore and Frankwell, but a conspiracy to attack the Archbishop of Canterbury's park and murder his gamekeeper, which was uncovered during the period when they were active, probably was, at the least, a sympathetic protest. The leader of the conspiracy, William Nusell of Mayfield, was described as 'a person of noo good name and fame' who 'intendeth to destroy other noblemen's parks in those parts'.[31]

Two other waves of anti-enclosure rioting broke out in Yorkshire in the years preceding the Pilgrimage of Grace. The riots against Henry Clifford, Earl of Cumberland, on his Craven and Westmorland estates have often been cited as examples of protests by smallhold tenants caused by the fiscal seigneurialism of a harsh landlord. Lord Darcy called Cumberland 'the worst beloved that I ever heard of, and specially with his tenants'. Although Cumberland was much hated, the discontent among his smallhold tenants was exploited by his own mesne tenants and rival magnates and it is difficult to separate the aristocratic feuds from the popular protests.[32]

The bad feeling between Cumberland and his tenants and neighbours reached back to the beginning of the sixteenth century. In about 1531 trouble broke out in the lordship of Kirkby Malzeard in Craven, the jurisdiction of which was disputed between Cumberland and

---

[31] *Star Chamber Proceedings . . . Sussex*, pp. 44–5, 58, 64–5, 70, 72–3, 76–7, 148; J. S. Moore, *Laughton: A Study in the Evolution of the Wealden Landscape* (Leicester Univ., Dept. of English Local Hist., occasional papers 19; 1965), 44–5; PRO, STAC 2/29/151, 3/3/49; *VCH Surrey*, iv. 430–1.

[32] M. H. and R. Dodds, *The Pilgrimage of Grace, 1536–37 and the Exeter Conspiracy, 1538* (2 vols.; Cambridge, 1915), i. 73–4; R. Reid, *The King's Council in the North* (1921; repr. Wakefield, W. Yorks., 1975), 124–5; S. M. Harrison, *The Pilgrimage of Grace in the Lake Counties, 1536–7* (R. Hist. Soc., Studies in History 27; 1981), 60–6; M. E. James, 'The First Earl of Cumberland (1493–1542) and the Decline of Northern Feudalism', *NH* 1 (1966), 60–1; *Clifford Letters of the Sixteenth Century*, ed. A. G. Dickens (Surtees Soc. 172; 1957), 25.

Anne, Countess of Derby, who leased the farm of the lordship to John Norton of Norton Conyers, a well-known Percy client who was later to command the siege of Skipton Castle during the Pilgrimage of Grace. When Norton tried to hold court in Kirkby Malzeard, Cumberland sent in Christopher Aske and other clients with 60 men, who broke up the sessions and carried away the court rolls. Norton also alleged that Cumberland's men terrorized the former's tenants, poached his deer, and killed 40 of the Countess of Derby's deer in Netherdale Chase. Norton counterattacked in what Cumberland called 'the greattest insurrection . . . that hath bene of late tyme in that county'; for this riot Norton and 91 others were indicted at Leeds. When Cumberland sent his son and heir to preside over the disputed court, Norton and other members of the gentry gathered 200 persons (including sanctuary men from Ripon) to demonstrate against Lord Clifford's proceedings.[33]

In June 1535, 400 persons assembled in a series of three riots to remove the enclosures which the Earl of Cumberland had recently erected at Giggleswick in Craven. Eighty-two persons were indicted— half of them tenants of the Earl of Cumberland and his steward, John Lambert, and the remainder tenants of the Earl of Northumberland. Mervyn James thinks there is good reason for believing that it was Northumberland who fomented the disturbances. Sir Richard Tempest, the magistrate who restored order, disingenuously told Thomas Cromwell that no person of substance was involved and that most of the rioters were women and children whose names he could not discover. By July the anti-enclosure rioting had spread into Lancashire, Cumberland, Westmorland, and Northumberland. Several northern peers and gentry were ordered to muster their followers to suppress the disorders, but this led to several armed confrontations when rival bands of aristocratic retainers sought to settle old scores instead of restoring order.[34]

There were other outbreaks of rioting among the royal tenants of Galtres Forest in East Yorkshire in December 1535 and April 1536. The trouble seems to have started with encroachments upon commonable waste made by Sir Thomas Curwen. Although an

[33] R. B. Smith, *Land and Politics in the England of Henry VIII: The West Riding of Yorkshire, 1539–1546* (Oxford, 1970), 197–201; *Yorkshire Star Chamber Proceedings*, ii. 48–50, iii. pp. 200–1.

[34] *L. & P., Hen. VIII*, viii. 863, 970, 984, 991–2, 1008, 1030, 1046, ix. 150, 196, 427; James, 'The First Earl of Cumberland', pp. 60–2.

indictment for treason was secured against one 'simple person', the gentry sitting on the jury at Topcliffe sessions prevented indictments for rioting being returned against the other participants 'in spite of the evidence'. The second Galtres Forest riot of April 1536 provides clear evidence of aristocratic manipulation. The actual rioting was precipitated when Lord Darcy, as justice of Galtres Forest, ordered the tenants to make perambulations—presumably to remove the enclosures from the encroachments made by Curwen and Wharton. The latter two attempted to have 80 of the royal tenants summoned to Westminster at 'barley seed-time', but Cromwell interceded to prevent the tenants from having to undergo this hardship.[35]

Excluding those riots which accompanied the mid-Tudor rebellions, these are some of the largest manifestations of agrarian protest in early sixteenth-century England. The Craven riots spread beyond particular local communities because of aristocratic manipulation and magnate feuds and because the Earl of Cumberland was an especially nasty landlord with extensive estates. The more widely-dispersed agrarian riots of July 1535 in the far north and north-west are unique and appear to be sympathetic responses to the Craven riots of the previous month; they more closely resemble the enclosure riots which accompanied the rebellions of 1536 and 1549. Only the East Sussex disorders reveal non-gentry leadership and appear to have been the work of artisans and labourers. Parks were notoriously thick on the ground in the forest areas of Sussex, and the Wealden iron industry was also beginning to encroach upon woodland pastures in an area already suffering from demographic pressure. Except for the Craven riots, none of these agrarian disorders spread outside a locale more than 15 miles in extent. There would appear to be no justification for calling any of these protests a 'peasant movement'.

Another way of examining the complexity of motivation involved in enclosure riots is to analyse the victims of such violence. The most typical victim of an enclosure riot was the outsider. Merchants attempting to buy their way into the landed gentry were particularly vulnerable to enclosure riots, as were farmers of leases. New owners and farmers were the victims of enclosure riots in 24 of the 75 Star Chamber cases. A closely-related category consists of six absentee gentlemen. Only 20 resident gentry were victims, while 14 smallhold tenants had their enclosures forcibly removed. In three cases the

---

[35] *L. & P., Hen. VIII*, x. 77, 733; Dodds, *Pilgrimage of Grace*, i. 73–4.

victims were townsmen; in one instance, a clergyman. In four cases the social status of the victims is unknown.[36]

Merchants and farmers who were outsiders were prone to enclosure riots because they did not understand or care to understand local agricultural customs, and were less likely to be respected by their tenants or by neighbouring members of the gentry than longer-established landholders. John Grymes, citizen and 'clothworker' of London, had been granted the manors of Wetton and Butterton, Staffordshire by letters patent in 1546. Four years after an agreement to enclose, a dispute as to whether a wood and pasture were held in common or in severalty resulted in 18 husbandmen from Wetton pulling down the stone walls and hedges with which Grymes had recently enclosed the disputed land. Although Grymes had complained to Lord Ferrers, the lord lieutenant, and brought charges against the rioters, he had been unable to secure indictments for rioting. Lawerence Malham, who called himself a 'gentleman' but who began his career as a 'pewterer', rising to become in turn chamberlain and sheriff of York, was in similar circumstances. Shortly after purchasing the manor of Kirkby Misperton (also known as Kirkby Overcarr), situated near Pickering, Malham enclosed three pastures. Approximately 20 husbandmen broke open his closes and depastured their horses and cattle. Although Malham obtained indictments against them, that did not deter the defendants from returning to destroy the hedges.[37]

Farmers of leases were even more vulnerable to enclosure riots because their interest was often more speculative and their commitment to the local community more tenuous than that of the parvenu lord of the manor. John Gryndall leased the farm of a tenement and pasture in Cumberland formerly belonging to St Bees' Priory, which was let to him by the executors of Sir Thomas Challenor, the principal lessee. A number of persons, by the procurement of John Skelton, esquire, spent several days in October and November 1549 destroying his hedges and also made an affray upon his son. When Thomas Strete, esquire, came into possession of a lease of lands formerly belonging to the Priory of Ruislip, Middlesex and subsequently passing through the hands of a number of speculators, he began to enclose several pastures. In April 1549, upwards of 16

---

[36] Cf. Table 2.1.
[37] 'Suits in the Court of Star Chamber. Temp. Henry VIII and Edward VI [Staffs.]', ed. Boyd., pp. 197–201; *Yorkshire Star Chamber Proceedings*, iv. 47–58.

persons cast down his enclosures. Five days later, they returned and chopped up the gate and gateposts. The next day they brought their cattle to feed upon Strete's grass, and resisted attempts by his servants to carry the villagers' cattle to the pound. Later, the rioters repeated the whole ritual on another close and assaulted one of Strete's servants.[38]

Farmers leasing ecclesiastical lands also suffered much at the hands of enclosure rioters. Tristram Teshe, gentleman of the city of York, notary and principal registrar to the Archbishop of York, had obtained from the Archbishop a 40-year lease of barns, eight enclosed pastures, three crofts, and three orchards lying just outside the city. On the last day of September 1534 ten inhabitants of York, led by a merchant, a draper, and a tanner entered the closes, destroyed the enclosures, and depastured their own beasts to the number of 500, and caused them to be kept in the pastures by the common herdsman for 30 days. On 2 October, the rioters returned with 300 persons to finish casting down the hedges and poles, and on this occasion depastured 1000 horses, cows, and sheep. Three different juries empanelled to investigate Teshe's complaints refused to find a riot: 'And som[e] of the saide ryoutouse parsons were suffered to geve evidence to all three inquestes . . . by whose bragges and crackes the said thre[e] inquestes were put in feare that they neither wolde nor ded fynde the trewght of the saide riottes. . . .' The poorer citizens of the city of York had traditionally depended on the right of shack on arable lands during the winter months to keep a few cattle, and they steadfastly resisted all attempts at enclosure outside the city walls.[39]

The early-Tudor enclosure riot was in several respects a rather primitive form of social protest. Except during the years of rebellion, its objectives were to defend traditional use-rights against extinction and to prevent commons from being held in severalty. Not particularly directed against the rich, the enclosure riot was most frequently employed against those who introduced innovations. In its most primitive form it was merely a means of pursuing a feud. The

[38] *John Gryndall* v. *John Skelton, esquire*, PRO, STAC 3/5/51; *Thomas Strete, esquire* v. *John Ferne et al.*, ibid., STAC 3/3/48.
[39] *Yorkshire Star Chamber Proceedings*, iv. 103–5; D. M. Palliser, *Tudor York* (Oxford, 1979), 29, 49, 84.

early-Tudor enclosure riot was also small in scale: it was precipitated by very specific agrarian conditions associated with a limited geographical area. Some catalyst other than a local enclosure dispute was required to produce riots on a larger scale. One such precipitating influence was supplied by the propaganda of John Hale and the commonwealthmen, who exaggerated the extent of enclosures and depopulation; the inflammatory proceedings of Protector Somerset's enclosure commissioners in 1548–9 provided another. The outbreak of popular rebellion produces what Pitirim Sorokin calls 'the transformation of speech-reactions'. During the rebellions of 1536–7 and 1548–9 there are countless examples of deferential speech patterns among commoners giving way to demands for ridding England of all gentlemen. Yet such bloodthirsty talk produced very little personal violence against gentlemen outside the field of battle. The commoners may have transferred their dislike of agrarian innovation and altered land-use to the gentry in 1549, but it was upon the symbolic enclosing hedge that they vented their hatred. Similarly, the agricultural labourers who rioted during the Captain Swing risings of 1830 sent threatening letters to gentlemen, farmers, and parsons, but did them no harm and smashed threshing machines and burned ricks instead.[40]

Even where it was a manifestation of a larger-scale popular rebellion, the enclosure riot was restrained and followed traditional rituals. In contrast to the bloody religious riots of sixteenth-century France, violence in the enclosure riot was directed at property and rarely touched persons. The number of instances where crown or manorial officials ordered or condoned the removal of enclosures prior to the riots and rebellions of 1548–9 also reveals both an official disapproval of enclosures and a tolerance for enclosure riots as a form of popular justice. Moreover, the leaders of the larger-scale enclosure riots frequently exhibit a desire to legitimate their actions

---

[40] Strype, *Ecclesiastical Memorials*, ii/2. 348; Hammond, 'The Social and Economic Circumstances of Ket's Rebellion', pp. 106–8; Hist. MSS Comm., *Thirteenth Report* (1907): Hereford Corp. MSS, xiii/4. 317; PRO, SP 10/8/11; *AHEW* iv. 222–4; P. Sorokin, *The Sociology of Revolution* (repr. New York, 1967), pp. 41 ff.; Raphael Holinshed, *Holinshed's Chronicles*, iii. 965–9, 973–4, 979; *L. & P. Hen. VIII*, xii/1. 200, 336; F. Rose-Troup, *The Western Rebellion of 1549* (1913), 124–9; Tawney, *The Agrarian Problem*, p. 324; E. J. Hobsbawm and G. Rudé, *Captain Swing* (New York, 1968), 197–220; Manning, 'Violence and Social Conflict in Mid-Tudor Rebellions', pp. 18–40.

by causing church bells to be rung and having the town bailiff or village constable read proclamations in the king's name ordering enclosures to be cast down.[41]

In many of the enclosure riot cases, the use of violence is obviously calculated, controlled and combined with sophisticated legal manoeuvres. Smallholders as well as gentry learned that enclosure disputes might be taken out of the hands of local juries, which were easily influenced or intimidated, and transferred to Star Chamber or other prerogative courts by allegations of riot. Frequently, villagers put together a common purse for legal expenses and agreed not to make separate settlements. Unfortunately, we rarely know the outcome of Star Chamber cases because the decrees have long since vanished. But what is known about the work of contemporary royal commissions and inquests looking into enclosures suggests that until the big landowners succeeded in overthrowing Protector Somerset, the smallholder could hope for some measure of justice from the prerogative courts.

[41] John Stow, *Annales, or a Generall Chronicle of England* (1631), 890; N. Z. Davis, 'The Rites of Violence: Religious Riot in Sixteenth-century France', *P. & P.*, no. 59 (May 1973), 51–91; *TRP i, no. 342*.

3
Elizabethan Enclosure Riots

ENCLOSURE riots during the reign of Elizabeth were, for the most part, small in scale, although numerous and widely dispersed throughout the realm. In contrast to the widespread anti-enclosure rioting that accompanied the rebellions of 1548–9 and continued until 1552, Elizabethan enclosure riots continued to resemble those of the 1530–48 period until about 1590. Of the 105 cases of enclosure riots analysed in this chapter, in 55 instances the number of those participating in the riots is specified. Twenty-seven riots were perpetrated by ten or fewer persons; 13 riots involved between 11 and 20 persons; eight included as many as 21 to 30 persons. Only seven instances reveal involvement of more than 30 persons. Thus, within a few years of the 1548–9 rebellions, the enclosure riot had reverted to its more traditional pattern of an agrarian dispute arising from localized grievances, usually confined to one or two village communities. Under these more normal circumstances that characterize the early and mid-Elizabethan periods, the enclosure riot employed low-level violence, rarely revealed social conflict, and, indeed, frequently involved feuding among the gentry. But the crises of the late-Elizabethan period present a more sinister face. The repeated harvest failures of the 1590s and the growing tensions between landlord and tenant, resulting from the introduction of more rationalized systems of estate management, rack-renting, and tenurial disputes, not only precipitated the rebellions of 1596 and 1607, but also contributed to a proliferation of enclosure disputes after 1590 in which social conflict once again becomes more explicit.

The small scale of Elizabethan enclosure riots is not without legal significance. The penalties prescribed for or inflicted upon rioters depended upon the number of persons involved, their intent, and the threat to public order as perceived by Parliament, the Privy Council, or the judges at any particular moment. In the wake of the 1548–9 rebellions, Parliament had made it treason for 40 or more persons to assemble together for two hours or more for the purpose of destroying by force enclosures, parks, fishponds, or killing game, burning hayricks, and the like, having been ordered by proclamation to disperse.[1] Marian and Elizabethan statutes reduced the same offences to capital felony, but required only 12 or more persons to be assembled for the space of one hour after a magistrate had read the proclamation to disperse. A riot committed by three to eleven persons was a misdemeanour punishable by one year's imprisonment.[2] The important distinction was between a forcible destruction of hedges growing out of an enclosure dispute within one or two villages, which was considered a private dispute, and a situation where rioters went from village to village advocating the general destruction of enclosures, which was considered a public matter.[3] In the troubled times of the 1590s the attorney-general, Edward Coke, and the judges construed the latter as levying war against the Queen and therefore treason. In such a situation the intention of the rioters was more significant than the number of rioters (provided there were at least three).[4]

In actuality, there is no evidence that the statutory penalties against 12 or more enclosure rioters were ever applied at the quarter sessions or assizes during the reign of Elizabeth. Complainants to the Court of Star Chamber alleging riotous destruction of enclosures continued to initiate suits as private parties until the 1590s when the attorney-general became more active in prosecuting such cases *pro rege*. The penalties of high treason were, however, applied to the leaders of the London Apprentices' Insurrection of 1595, the Enslow Hill Rebellion of 1596, and the Midland Revolt of 1607, but in each instance the judges resorted to a constructive extension of the basic Treason Statute of 1352 or the Elizabethan Statute of 1571.

The Court of Star Chamber deemed the basic elements of a riot to be present when three or more persons assembled together and both attempted and intended to perform an unlawful act by force. If three persons conspired to perform an unlawful act by force but only two persons actually perpetrated the act, the court could still find a riot because procurers of riots were considered to be at least

---

[1] 3 & 4 Edw. VI, c. 5, *SR* iv. 104–8.
[2] 1 Mary, St. 2, c. 12, *SR* iv. 211–12; 1 Eliz. I, c. 16, *SR* iv. 377.
[3] Sir William Holdsworth, *A History of English Law* (13 vols.; 1922–52), viii. 327–38.
[4] Sir Edward Coke, *The Third Part of the Institutes of the Laws of England* (4th edn.; 1669), 9–10; Sir Matthew Hale, *The History of the Pleas of the Crown* (2 vols.; 1800), i. 145.

as guilty as actual rioters. Although the colourful language in which complainants allege a riot in order to secure a hearing before Star Chamber must sometimes be taken with a grain of salt, most riot cases did involve some degree of violence. In any case, it was not necessary to prove the actual use of force and violence in order to obtain a conviction for riot in Star Chamber. It sufficed to prove that provocative or intimidating words were accompanied by the bearing of weapons. Thus, a situation that might lead to a breach of the peace could be construed as a riot.[5] In an enclosure dispute of 1594 in Llandilo, Radnorshire, the complainant specified the weapons carried by those who destroyed his hedges and also charged that the defendants had published scandalous letters and verses libelling him.[6] In another dispute apparently involving intercommoning on a meadow in Trewyn, Denbighshire in 1595, the principal complainant said that the defendants, who came from Bryn Kymry, were armed with 'gonnes, pistolls, huge calliuers, privy coats, longe pikes, staves, halberds, pitchfortes, fforeste Bills, welshe hooks, swords and Bucklers and daggers' and had threatened 'to spoile, kill, hurte and wounde' the inhabitants of Trewyn 'whensoever they shoulde see them'.[7] It goes without saying that an enclosure riot involved, at the very least, the destruction of hedges or other kinds of enclosures, and this necessitated the use of hedging bills, forest bills, and spades, which were considered to be weapons.

An analysis of the types of enclosure destroyed during the Elizabethan period is very revealing about the sources of agrarian protest. In 89 per cent of all enclosure-riot cases studied, the participants were attempting to assert a claim to the exercise of use-rights on wastes, commons and woodland. Only one case arose out of the enclosure of arable land previously lying in open or common fields. The largest category (36 per cent) of such disputes about use-rights involved intakes and enclosures of wastes and commons; 26 per cent concerned the enclosure and subsequent holding in severalty of pasture and meadow, which had mostly been regarded as Lammas lands open part of the year for common of pasture. Wooded pasture was also being enclosed for coppicing on a significant scale in order to produce more timber (19 per cent of the sample), while

[5] Guy, *The Cardinal's Court*, pp. 18, 58–9, 149.
[6] *Edward Daunce, gent.* v. *Hugh Lloyd, clerk*, PRO, STAC 5/D25/20.
[7] *Hugh Griffith* v. *Rees ap John Llewelyn*, PRO, STAC 5/G3/5.

the love of the aristocracy for the pleasures of the hunt resulted in protests against the emparking of wooded pasture in 8 per cent of the cases. In 7 per cent of the cases there is a clear and unmistakable indication that the wastes and commons were being improved and utilized for convertible husbandry, and the actual proportion is almost certainly higher.[8] The clearest economic trends revealed are increasing demographic pressure upon arable and pastoral resources and a rising demand for timber, peat, and coal for building materials and fuel.[9]

The reasons for the increased demand for arable, pasture, timber, and fuel become more apparent when the distribution of enclosure-riot cases is broken down by geographical region. In the early- and mid-Tudor periods there is an unusual concentration of enclosure riots in Staffordshire (11 cases) and Derbyshire (9 cases), which represents more than one-quarter of the sample of 75 cases (Table 2.2). Generally, the east and west Midlands account for nearly half of all enclosure-riot cases in the Court of Star Chamber in the first half of the sixteenth century. The cause was most likely demographic expansion, which, in turn, led to increased pressure on commons from sheep- and cattle-rearing. During the reign of Elizabeth, enclosure disputes dwindle to practically nothing in the east Midlands (Table 3.2), but the proportion of enclosure riots occurring in the west Midlands rises to 34 per cent of the sample. If one adds in the Welsh-Border counties (which are not counted for the earlier period because of the paucity of Welsh enclosure disputes among the mid-Tudor Star Chamber records), then it becomes evident that something like 50 per cent of all enclosure-riot cases for Elizabethan England and Wales occurred in the west Midlands and on the Welsh Border.[10] This is surely symptomatic of the remarkable development of rural industry in the Severn, Avon, and upper Trent valleys and their hinterlands during the late-Elizabethan and early-Stuart periods.[11]

---

[8] See Table 3.1.   [9] See ch. 10 (iii).

[10] I have relied upon R. H. Hilton, *A Medieval Society: The West Midlands at the End of the Thirteenth Century* (repr. Cambridge, 1983), 8–15, in defining the west Midlands. Cf. *The Duchy of Lancaster's Estates in Derbyshire, 1485–1540*, ed. Blanchard, pp. 6–7, 15.

[11] B. Trinder, *The Industrial Revolution in Shropshire* (1973), ch. 2; W. H. B. Court, *The Rise of the Midland Industries, 1600–1838* (repr. Oxford, 1953), 5–17; C. Wilson, *England's Apprenticeship, 1603–1763* (New York, 1965), 82. The Severn, notable for its freedom from tolls, was Europe's busiest navigable river after the Meuse in the seventeenth century. For a discussion of the connection between the rapid

The influx of artisans and labourers into the west Midlands and Welsh Borderland to dig coal, fashion iron products, and weave cloth made new demands upon the agricultural and fuel resources of this region. The concentration of one-half of the enclosure riots in a region of predominantly pastoral, sylvan, and proto-industrial economies also supports the view that demonstrations of popular protest occurred more freely in the looser social structures of these economies than in fielden England. Thus, the development of rural industry may be nearly as significant a cause of social protest as agrarian change.

Where the needs of a growing population pressed upon land resources, stinting, or the regulation and limitation of grazing rights, was frequently a prelude to general enclosure. In Tring, Hertfordshire the overcharging of meadows after Lammas day was so destructive to the grass that the manorial lord sought to limit common of pasture to cattle only. He prosecuted his tenants in Star Chamber for testifying in the Court of Common Pleas that manorial custom allowed common of pasture for sheep as well as cattle.[12] There was also a growing tendency to limit pasture rights to those freeholders and copyholders who could prove a strong claim to such use-rights. John Smyth of Nibley, the antiquarian and steward of the hundred and liberty of Berkeley in Gloucestershire, noted with distaste how at Matford Mead in Alkington, 'The inhabitants . . . pretend their ill custome, vizt. hand over head, pell-mell, on Lammas day, to thrust in all manner of their cattell, whether they have any ground therein or not; whereby the herbage to the small benefit of anyone is in one weeke or sooner eaten vp and consumed.'[13]

On the large Duchy of Lancaster manor of Wakefield, before the expansion of its clothing industry brought an influx of population, in general anyone could graze an animal or two on the commons. When the cottage industry began to grow, Halifax sub-manors began requiring a prohibitively expensive grazing licence from non-tenants. The custom of the manor reserved half of the common pasture for tenants, while the Crown, as lord of the manor, was free to enclose and rent out parcels of the other half. In 1583, John Savile, a gentleman-freeholder within the manor, and other tenants contested a recent

---

expansion of coal-mining in late sixteenth-century County Durham and 'the first wave of enclosures', cf. Hodgson, 'The Progress of Enclosure in County Durham, 1500–1870', p. 90.

[12] *Robert Hyde, esq. v. John Jennynges*, PRO, STAC 7/12/43.
[13] J. Smyth, *The Berkeley Manuscripts*, iii. 51.

crown enclosure. Subsequently, the manorial tenants determined to exclude recent immigrants from the commons. However, the influx of population demanded a solution, and the JPs not only permitted more enclosures, but also allowed cottages to be erected on the waste.[14] Further evidence of a severe shortage of pasture is found in a number of intercommoning disputes both among the tenants of the sub-manors of Wakefield and with neighbouring manors. In 1597 a quarrel developed between the town of Horbury and the adjacent honour and manor of Pontefract after a series of storms had altered the bed of the River Calder, which marked the manorial boundaries, and shifted part of Horbury Common to the Pontefract side. The matter was litigated before the Council of the North and arbitrated by a duchy commission. The Court of Duchy Chamber ordered the tenants of Horbury to depasture their cattle on the far side of the river and the Pontefract tenants to distrain them in order to bring the matter to trial at the York Assizes. The suit was settled in favour of the Horbury tenants, who were ordered to restore the ancient watercourse.[15] In 1615 the tenants of another Wakefield township attempted to gain more meadow by altering a watercourse to their advantage, but the Duchy Court ordered them to restore the stream to its former course.[16] At Woodeaton, Staffordshire a greedy farmer new to the neighbourhood tried to increase his hay crop by cultivating the common way which provided access to his neighbours' meadows; they had their revenge by riding their hay-wains four abreast through his grass before he could cut it.[17]

The many cases of pound-breach are also symptomatic of a shortage of pasture and attempts to defend use-rights. In Norfolk, the efforts of the bailiff of the town of Carleton Rode, which was part of the honour of Richmond, to draw a precise boundary on the waste shared by that community and New Buckenham was disputed by the latter village. When he impounded the sheep and cattle from New Buckenham as waifs and strays their owners marched to Carleton Rode 'in most terrefying, fearefull and insulting manner', and demanded the return of their beasts. This being refused, the New Buckenham men forcibly rescued their animals. After

---

[14] M. J. Ellis, 'A Study in the Manorial History of Halifax Parish in the Sixteenth and Early Seventeenth Centuries, Part II', *Yorks. Arch. Journal* 61 (1961), 420–5.
[15] PRO, DL 5/19, fos. 215–16.   [16] Ibid., DL 5/27, fo. 332.
[17] *Thomas Astley, yeoman v. John Walter, gent.*, PRO, STAC 5/A22/3.

threatening to shoot and set their dogs upon the tenants of Carleton Rode, a riot ensued. The case was prosecuted by the attorney-general, who accused one defendant of perjuring himself with false testimony concerning past usages of common rights.[18] In Dorset, a widow's attempt to preserve an enclosed pasture on the manor of Over Compton provoked repeated resistance in the form of hedge-breaking and pound-breach to rescue distrained cattle.[19]

As good agricultural land grew more scarce, it was only natural that manorial lords and prospective tenants would be tempted to encroach upon wastes to meet the growing demand for corn, fodder, and pasturage. Such intakes from the waste had occurred before when population increases outstripped agricultural resources, and involved merely a temporary use of marginal land, which was soon exhausted and returned to its primary use as rough grazing. In the sixteenth century one can distinguish between several categories of intake from wastes. In large, sylvan parishes such as Condover, Shropshire, wooded land was still being assarted, or cleared for cultivation, in the sixteenth century.[20] Such communities were havens for squatters, who might by long, undisturbed occupation secure a claim, if not a title, to their little hovels and gardens and were frequently allowed common rights on the remaining waste. Alternatively they were settled on wastes in cottages erected at parish expense as a cheap form of poor relief. The term 'improvement of wastes', however, usually meant that intakes were made by authority of the lord of the manor, who enclosed the intakes in severalty, created new messuages, and conveyed them to old or new tenants as copyholds or leaseholds. Because of the heavy capital investment in new agricultural techniques, the erection of farm houses, and the altered legal status of the new messuages, such land was permanently alienated from the waste. Frequently, the response of the older tenants was to reclaim their lost use-rights by the destruction of hedges, the intimidation of the new tenants, the spoliation of herbage and crops, and, sometimes, the destruction of offending houses of new tenants and cottagers.[21] Such improvements of wastes only intensified already existing intercommoning disputes between two

[18] *Edward Coke, esq., Attorney General* v. *John Cower*, PRO, STAC 5/A33/28.
[19] *Mary Abington, widow* v. *Richard Pike*, PRO, STAC 5/A22/39.
[20] *VCH Shropshire*, viii. 28–33.
[21] PRO, STAC 5/A29/33, A3/32, 7/15/8, 5/V6/9.

or more neighbouring communities. When Thomas Leveson, farmer of the ecclesiastical manor of Hilton, Staffordshire, enclosed a coppice and erected a cottage in 1591 upon a wooded waste shared with the manor of Essington, he provoked a revival of enclosure rioting that had broken out 41 years earlier as a result of an attempt to demarcate a boundary dividing the waste between the two manorial communities.[22] After Sir John Savage discovered that his improvements on a waste brought endless lawsuits and repeated enclosure rioting by the burgesses of Frodsham, Cheshire, he ordered a tenant to level his own hedges in order to avoid further complaint. The unhappy tenant obeyed his lord and then found himself bound over to appear at the next court leet for the offence of hedge-breaking.[23] But many landlords thought that the profits to be made from the exploitation of wastes were worth pursuing. Three different Pelham heirs to the manor of Laughton, Sussex fought the Duchy of Lancaster's efforts to deny them use of 450 acres of Dicker Waste; suits and cross-suits were filed in the Courts of Duchy Chamber, Wards and Liveries, Star Chamber, and King's Bench before the Duchy recognized the Pelham claim. By that time the duchy officials reasoned that there was little of value remaining, since the duchy farmer had stripped the waste of timber.[24]

In its exploitation of wastes the Crown acted as an exemplar to other enclosing landlords, as the improvement of Hounslow Heath demonstrates. Hounslow Heath was parcel of the new honour of Hampton Court, which was created by Act of Parliament in 1539.[25] This statute annexed to the manor of Hampton Court numerous manors in Middlesex and Surrey recently acquired by expropriation from dissolved religious corporations, transfer from the Duchy of Lancaster, and purchase from private owners. The act gave copyholds of inheritance to all current tenants of the newly acquired manors, established a royal chase, and authorized commissioners to survey, divide up, and allot the soil of Hounslow Heath among inhabitants of the towns lying at the edge of that huge waste. The terms were that the prospective tenants should receive their allotments as leaseholds for 21 years, during which time they were to hold such parcels in

[22] *Henry Vernon, esq.* v. *Thomas Leveson, esq.*, ibid., STAC 5/V8/6.
[23] *Richard Trewman* v. *William Modesley*, ibid., STAC 7/15/28.
[24] *R.* v. *Thomas Pelham, esq.*, ibid., DL 5/19, fos. 16ᵛ–17ᵛ, 37ᵛ–39ᵛ.
[25] 37 Hen. VIII, c. 2, *SR* iii. 986–7.

severalty and convert them to tillage and high-quality pasture and meadow. Tenants who successfully improved their allotments would, at the end of their leases, have their tenancies confirmed as copyholds of inheritance. Tenants who could raise the capital needed for improvements stood to benefit; those who could not apparently received no recompense for lost use-rights. However, Hounslow Heath was a vast tract of 4,293 acres and the process of improvement proceeded slowly; by 1602 only 800 acres had actually been surveyed and partitioned. Two hundred and twenty-one acres were granted to certain inhabitants of the parish of Bedfont, but a group of dissidents, led by Ambrose Coppinger, a Middlesex JP, and two other gentlemen, hatched a conspiracy to keep the 221 acres in common and to levy a common purse to maintain lawsuits against enclosure. Coppinger also took more direct action when, on the evening of May Day 1602, he led 100 men and women in the levelling of 1,000 rods of quickset hedges environing the Bedfont allotment.[26]

Landlords also exploited the fuel and mineral resources of wastes. The tenants of Petworth, Sussex had possessed ample common pasture before the manor was bequeathed to the Crown by Henry, sixth Earl of Northumberland. Although Petworth had already contained two enclosed parks, Henry VIII emparked additional common pasture. Most of the hedges and pales surrounding these parks were cast down during the riots of 1548–51. Queen Mary restored Petworth to the seventh Earl of Northumberland, and he and the eighth Earl began making enclosures of more commons. Neither would tolerate any opposition from tenants, but both attempted to deal with their tenants personally and to compensate them for the loss of use-rights. The ninth Earl, when he looked about for ways of raising money from his Petworth estates, first considered evicting his tenants, but rejected the idea because he was advised that some tenants were freeholders and the remainder possessed copyholds that were quite secure in law. Instead, he turned to iron-founding and made extensive intakes from the Petworth wastes and commons in order to cut timber for charcoal and dig iron ore. The once-prosperous Petworth tenants, increasingly deprived of pasture

---

[26] *Edward Coke, esq., Attorney General* v. *Ambrose Coppinger, esq.*, PRO, STAC 5/A29/22. The Bedfont Heath Enclosure Allotment of *c.*1546, which divided 220 acres into 140 individual holdings, is printed in Kerridge, *Agrarian Problems*, pp. 166–73.

and pannage rights, kept fewer cattle and pigs than 50 years earlier, and had fewer animal products to sell. The evidence clearly indicates that their standard of living declined.[27]

While enclosure riots most frequently demonstrated popular opposition to alterations in land-use, they sometimes protested various forms of seigneurial oppression such as rack-renting. In Warwickshire, John Alderford incurred heavy debts during the 1590s through the extensive rebuilding of the manor house of Abbots Salford, formerly a residence of the abbots of Evesham. He may only have been following the example of the Crown when he resorted to raising money by extorting 'vnreasonable and vnconstionable . . . compositions' from his tenants to confirm their copyholds.[28] The tenantry—women as well as men—retaliated by levelling hedges enclosing 100 acres of pasture which Alderford held in severalty. When the task at first proved to be too great, the tenants recruited their neighbours and came back and finished the job two months later.[29]

Further light is shed upon the motivation behind enclosure riots during the Elizabethan period when the 105 cases in this sample are analysed to determine the social status of those who led or procured such disturbances and those who were the victims. As in the period before 1548–9, the gentry were more frequently the procurers of such riots. But in the Elizabethan period, they were responsible for only 33 per cent of the riots, as compared to 41 per cent in the earlier period, while the proportion instigated by smallholders, cottagers, artisans, and squatters increased from 16 per cent to 31 per cent. In the earlier period the gentry were the victims of hedge-breaking in 35 per cent of the cases, but in the Elizabethan period that proportion rose to 49 per cent.[30] While a number of these enclosure disputes reveal long-standing feuds among the gentry, one must remember that gentlemen also suffered economic loss through abridgement of their use-rights. Moreover, the lesser gentry, when they possessed tenancies within a manor, were inclined to side with their husbandmen-neighbours against the greater gentry who possessed seigneurial

[27] P. Jerrome, *Cloakbag and Common Purse: Enclosure and Copyhold in 16th Century Petworth* (Petworth, Suss., 1979), 16–18, 32–4. I owe this reference to Cornelia Wallisfürth.

[28] Cf. ch. 6.

[29] *VCH Warwickshire*, iii. 156–60; *John Alderford, esq.* v. *William Turke*, PRO, STAC 5/A3/37.   [30] See Tables 2.1 and 3.1.

jurisdictions. Even where one landlord incited a rival's tenants for purely selfish reasons, his rival's tenants might still possess legitimate grievances. In the light of abundant evidence of seigneurial encroachment upon wastes, it seems reasonable to detect a renewal of popular resentment of the gentry during the late Elizabethan period. Increased social conflict is implicit in the significant increase in the number of enclosure riots during the 1590s and becomes quite explicit in the rebellions of 1596 and 1607.

However, in some instances where gentlemen were accused of instigating enclosure riots, it is evident that this was merely one manifestation of violent feuding between two rival factions. Complaints that use-rights were denied by illegal enclosures was merely a pretended or, at best, a peripheral issue. In the parish and township of Northerden, Cheshire in 1596, both Edward Vawdrey and William Tatton claimed a part of the lordship of the township. In actuality, each farmed a portion of the manor of Northerden for the Dean and Chapter of Chester Abbey. Both had made intakes and enclosures of the common waste upon which each had erected cottages and installed tenants. Each disputed the other's enclosures: Tatton had destroyed some of Vawdrey's hedges; Vawdrey had obtained a judgment from the Court of Exchequer confirming his rights of common. When Vawdrey sought to remove his rival's hedges, he was prevented from doing so by 20 armed persons procured by Tatton. Tatton also denied Vawdrey's tenants access to the highway, dammed the River Marcy for a millpond which flooded a ford, and prevented them from watering their cattle. Tatton's followers also assaulted several of Vawdrey's tenants, but perhaps the worst blow to Vawdrey's pride was that Tatton, who occupied first place in the parish church, ripped out Vawdrey's pew, which he and his ancestors, being accounted third in rank in the parish, had customarily occupied.[31] At Newport Pagnell, Buckinghamshire, George Annesley and Robert Johnson each alleged a title to common of pasture, but were merely pursuing an old feud between their two families when they levelled hedges and destroyed one another's copses.[32]

---

[31] *Edward Vawdrey, gent.* v. *William Tatton, esq.*, PRO, STAC 5/V7/21, 23.
[32] *George Annesley the younger, gent.* v. *Robert Johnson, gent.*, ibid., STAC 5/A29/38.

A notorious gentry feud disturbed late-Elizabethan Wiltshire. The hostility probably originated in the adherence of Sir Walter Long and his followers to the Puritan faction, against whom Sir John Danvers displayed a strong dislike. Numerous insults were exchanged, and in one encounter a servant of Danvers was killed. Long obstructed a coroner's inquest that may have been investigating the same murder. Two of Danvers' sons confronted Long and his followers while the latter were at dinner, and in the scuffle that followed, shot and killed Long's brother. Danvers died of grief, according to his widow, after the fugitive Danvers brothers fled overseas. Two of their servants were caught and hanged for murder. Long then attempted to stir up Lady Danvers' tenants against her by encouraging them to revive a claim to common rights on a waste that had been enclosed and improved 17 years earlier. Lady Danvers, an Italian by birth, asserted that the waste had been enclosed with the tenants' consent and that they had received other commons as compensation. The tenants got together a common purse for legal expenses and Long consulted a barrister of the Inner Temple who told them that they might evade a charge of riot by avoiding all weapons except shovels and spades and by working only two at a time in removing the hedges. The Court of Star Chamber, however, was not deceived and reckoned that a total of 28 persons participated and punished Long and the lawyer for procuring a 'palliated' or cloaked riot. Long's son, granted immunity from prosecution for testifying against his father, deposed that his father had been but a short distance from the scene of the riot urging on the tenants with cries of: 'Well done, Masters! This is the waye. If you do not preuayle, I will gyue you as muche lande oute of my parke', and 'Holde together, for there was never multitude helde together & failed of there purpose.' Sir Edward Coke prosecuted the case, charging the defendants additionally with libel, perjury, and subornation of perjury. Long was fined £200, four leading tenants £100 each, and the remaining tenants 100 marks each. All were sentenced to imprisonment, although Long may not have served that part of his sentence. He was retained on the commission of the peace even though he had been removed from the bench on two previous occasions.[33]

[33] John Hawarde, *Les Reportes del Cases in Camera Stellata, 1593–1609*, ed. W. P. Baildon (1894), 49–52; BL, Harley MSS, 2143, fo. 66'; A. Wall, 'Faction in Local Politics, 1580–1620: Struggles for Supremacy in Wiltshire', *Wilts. Arch. Magazine* 72–3 (1977–8), 123–4; John Aubrey, *Aubrey's Brief Lives*, ed. O. L. Dick (1950), 77.

It was not unusual for justices of the peace to abuse their power in pursuing such feuds. Robert Peyton of Isleham, Cambridgeshire used his authority as a magistrate to prevent the servants of Henry Veysey from hedging and ditching an intake from the waste, secured an indictment against him for illegal fishing, unfairly assessed him for a parliamentary subsidy, and harassed him with suits and warrants for his arrest. Yet Peyton himself was encroaching upon the same waste.[34] A Welsh copyholder in Berewe, Montgomeryshire sought justice from the Court of Star Chamber after Arthur Price, JP, led some 20 persons in destroying his hedges because he perceived that all of the Montgomeryshire justices were allied with Price.[35] When Thomas Harriets gathered together his neighbours in Arrow, Warwickshire in order to level Sir John Conway's newly-erected enclosure of a waste, they raised 40s. among themselves with which to bribe Sir John Throckmorton, chief justice of Chester and vice-president of the Council in the Marches of Wales. Throckmorton agreed to ignore the matter provided the hedge-breakers undertook to work two at a time in order to avoid allegations of riot.[36]

The judges of the Court of Star Chamber were not unmindful of the corrupt example that aristocrats displayed when they summoned their tenants to pursue feuds. When questioning defendants and witnesses, the interrogatories drawn up by the court frequently reveal the suspicion that a gentleman was the procurer of the disturbances.[37] There were still landlords who could muster large numbers of tenants to do their bidding. Lord Dudley of Dudley Castle, Staffordshire became embroiled in a dispute about grazing rights with a member of the Littleton family in the 1590s. He assembled 600 tenants on one occasion and nearly as many on another occasion; armed with pikes and bows, they seized several hundred head of Littleton's cattle and drove them into Worcestershire. Just before sentence was to be passed against Dudley in Star Chamber, the chief baron of the Exchequer said that 'the riot was such as has not been heard of in the Queen's time'; he believed that 'The greater the man, the greater the punishment [ought to be] as an example to others.' What

---

[34] *Henry Veyse, gent. v. Robert Peyton, esq.*, PRO, STAC 5/V6/34, V8/20.
[35] *Evan Vaughan v. Arthur Price, JP*, ibid., STAC 5/V6/29.
[36] *Sir John Conway v. Henry Lawgher*, ibid., STAC 7/11/15, 5/C10/3, C11/16.
[37] For example, cf. *John Graunger, husbandman v. Thomas Stafford, husbandman*, ibid., STAC 7/2/49, 15/15.

especially alarmed the chief baron was that Dudley's tenants were
not just simple husbandmen but were, for the most part, nailers and
coal-miners 'who live all their days in drink'. Clearly, the prospect
of mobs of artisans committing crimes against property alarmed
him.[38] The expansion of the nail-making and coal-mining trades in
Staffordshire had been accompanied in the 1590s by a marked
increase in presentments at the quarter sessions for hedge-breaking,
illegal timber-cutting, poaching, and related crimes committed by
artisans and labourers.[39] At the Michaelmas 1599 sessions the
inhabitants of Tutbury presented a petition complaining that William
Bateman had hired a number of roughnecks to intimidate them and
prevent them from exercising their pasture-rights on the town
commons.[40] The chief baron warned the defendants in the case of
Littleton v. Lord Dudley: 'let the servant beware how he perform[s]
his master's wish in unlawful acts, for the servant himself shall be
punished.' The Star Chamber sentenced Lord Dudley to pay 500
marks for the first riot and £500 for the second; the lesser defendants
were fined £20 apiece for each riot.[41] Retaining continued to be a
problem in the west Midlands and the Borderland—a legacy of the
earlier bastard feudalism of the Marcher lordships, and may help
to explain the numerous enclosure riots and gentry faction-fighting
in that area.

Enfield, Middlesex was another community where some of the
local gentry presented a corrupt example by hiring artificers to
commit crimes against other people's property as well as by their
own acts of oppression. The population of Elizabethan Enfield grew
very rapidly: Enfield Chase attracted squatters while the influence
of the London market economy brought about enclosures for new
orchards and the building of cottages for artisans and the poor. In
1581 Sir Thomas Wroth, a Middlesex magistrate who owned mills
in the Lea Valley, apparently quarrelled with the persons who
shipped his flour and malt to London, and hired, with the help of his
henchman, the constable of Edmonton Hundred, a number of
artificers from Enfield and adjacent towns to destroy the banks of
the River Lea 'to th'entent not only to hynder, but even to overthrowe
the passage between Ware and London'. William Fleetwood, recorder

---

[38] *Littleton v. Lord Dudley*, in Hawarde, *Reportes*, pp. 34–6.
[39] *Staffs. QSR*, vols. ii, iii, iv, *passim*.
[40] Ibid., iv. 118–20.   [41] Hawarde, *Reportes*, pp. 34–6.

of London, who was sent down to take evidence in the case, thought Wroth 'over muche puffed in pride, with over much lyvyng and wealthe.'[42] Sir Thomas's son Robert was also a JP and a principal tenant of the manor of Enfield which belonged to the Duchy of Lancaster. He and Henry Middlemore, who farmed the manor for the duchy, enclosed 100 acres of common pasture, of which Wroth took half while Middlemore and the other larger tenants received smaller parcels. On 7 July 1589 forty women, for the most part wives of artisans and labourers, destroyed the offending enclosures. Twenty-nine of the women were arraigned at a petty sessions before Robert Wroth and Middlemore, and 24 of them sent to Newgate Gaol to await trial at the Middlesex Sessions. A number of them were pregnant and seven actually gave birth while in Newgate. They were still imprisoned on August 20 when they wrote to Lord Burghley seeking relief.[43]

An earlier outbreak of enclosure rioting had occurred in 1584. The previous farmer of Enfield manor, John Taylor, who was also a duchy receiver, had enclosed 52 acres of demesne subject to common-rights. The lesser tenants had presented Taylor in the manorial court, which threatened him with a fine if the enclosures were not removed. Taylor counter-sued the tenants in the Court of Duchy Chamber, which upheld him. Taylor argued that previous farmers of the manorial demesne had neglected to maintain earlier enclosures. Since Enfield Chase had become so overcharged with population, he was obliged to restore the enclosures and maintain the demesne in severalty in order to graze his draft animals. The tenants were not prepared to accept defeat, and in 1584 they breached Taylor's hedges and depastured over one hundred head of cattle.[44]

In cases where litigants alleged an illegal enclosure and were able to establish a prior claim to common-rights over the enclosed parcel of land, a court order could be obtained to remove the offending enclosure. But such orders often met with resistance. When Ralph Leake of East Leake, Nottinghamshire was compelled to answer a

---

[42] T. Wright, *Queen Elizabeth and Her Times* (2 vols.; 1838), ii. 159–61; K. Fairclough, 'A Tudor Canal Scheme for the River Lea', *London Journal* 52 (Nov. 1979), 223.
[43] Pam, *Common Rights in Enfield*, pp. 9–10; BL, Lansdowne MSS, 59, fos. 31, 59–60ᵛ.
[44] Pam, *Common Rights in Enfield*, pp. 9–10.

complaint in Star Chamber in 1570 that he had breached a close, he explained that he had demonstrated a claim to common-rights on the disputed parcel between May Day and Lammas Day on behalf of his tenants at the Nottingham Assizes, and the lord chief justice, Sir James Dyer, had ordered the hedges and fences removed before 1 May of that year. When the enclosures, made by two brothers who may have been piqued by an inability to raise a crop of hay on the land, remained standing, Leake ordered two of his tenants to make a gap in the hedge in peaceful fashion. The following day the gap was again closed, and Leake had one of his tenants reopen it.[45] On the crown manor of Llanstephan in Carmarthenshire, the farmer of the demesne was presented at the court baron for encroaching on the waste. Members of the homage jury, described as poor men who spoke only Welsh, then took it upon themselves to level the farmer's hedges and ditches. The farmer subsequently complained to the court of Star Chamber and accused the jurors of perjured testimony concerning the customs of the manor and his alleged encroachment as well as unlawful assembly and forcible entry.[46]

The inability of manorial courts to reconcile such disputes increasingly caused litigants to resort to royal courts. On the manor of St Cullombe in Cornwall, a number of copyholders were gentlemen who leased to under-tenants. A group of opposing tenants prevented the under-tenants from digging peat on the manorial waste by building a stone wall blocking the common way. The obstruction was twice presented at the court baron. When the manorial lord, Sir John Arundell, ordered the bailiff to remove the wall, the latter was riotously resisted by 30 armed tenants who discharged firearms in an effort to frighten him. The defendants were subsequently indicted at the general sessions, but Sir John ultimately had to complain to the Court of Star Chamber.[47]

Outsiders—whether farmers of tenements or demesne, new tenants, absentee landlords, London merchants acquiring rural estates for investment, or even families which after a generation still had not been accepted by their neighbours—were the most vulnerable victims of enclosure riots. Such persons were more disposed to the

---

[45] *Gabriel Stapleton v. Ralph Leake, gent.*, PRO, STAC 7/15/7.
[46] *Griffith Morgan of Llangain, gent. v. Thomas Nichols of Llangunog*, ibid., STAC 5/M19/31; *Griffith Morgan v. Griffith Nicholas*, ibid., STAC 5/M29/2.
[47] *Sir John Arundell v. Richard Carter*, ibid., STAC 5/A3/5.

introduction of agrarian novelties and might be ignorant of local customs, but part of the resentment can only be explained by the traditional English hostility to strangers. When Benjamin Beconsawe purchased a grange and a farm from Sir Philip Constable in 1602 and took up residence in Middle Rasen, Lincolnshire, he complained that his neighbours, knowing him

not to haue any ffrynds, kindred, or allies in the said countie of Lyncolne, and therefore trusting to there might power and ffriends, they . . . did complott confedeorat and conspire to gether howe and in what manner to driue your subject being a meare straynger in the saide countye of Lincolne out of the saied countye; and to make him forsake his saied ffarme Graunge & premisses; and to inforce him to retorne to the . . . county of South [ampton] as if your saied subject were not a naturall Englishman and your maiesties subiect.[48]

In order to persuade him to repatriate himself, five of Beconsawe's neighbours destroyed the enclosures surrounding two pastures planted with leys, drove out his cattle, depastured their own cattle, and beat his servants when they tried to reclaim his cattle from the pound.

John Vicary, the farmer of the manorial demesne of Southquarne, Somerset, was more resourceful. Vicary had enclosed a valuable wood, in which the tenants claimed the right to cut timber. The tenants, led by a gentleman-copyholder, successfully brought an action of trespass against Vicary in King's Bench for illegal timber-cutting, and proceeded to cut nine loads of wood. The tenants attempted to prevent Vicary from interfering by barricading the access road and arming themselves with swords and pistols. Vicary and his servants attacked and drove the tenants off by firing arrows at them. Vicary subsequently hired some ruffians from Wales to ambush the tenants. While the Welshmen were in the neighbourhood, it was alleged that they committed several robberies.[49]

Crown farmers especially appear to have been resented because they were frequently the instruments of large-scale or total enclosure. On the Duchy of Lancaster manor of Southcrop, Gloucestershire, the principal farmer, Thomas Conway, who was an officer of the royal household, and the other farmers of the demesne agreed among

[48] *Benjamin Beconsawe, gent.* v. *Robert Boxholme, yeoman,* ibid., STAC 8/61/63.
[49] *John Vicary, husbandman* v. *Roger Sydenham, gent.,* ibid., STAC 5/V8/8.

themselves to enclose and hold in severalty both the open-field arable and the common pasture. They encountered strong opposition from a group of tenants led by Henry Keeble, who also farmed the neighbouring manor of East Leach-Martin for the Dean and Chapter of Gloucester. The dissident tenants were forcibly excluded from the commons and their cattle distrained. As the leader of the resistance, Keeble was singled out for retaliation: Conway and the other farmers caused Keeble's sons and servants to be assaulted and beaten, infringed upon his hunting and fishing rights on the manor of East Leach-Martin, and had him summoned before the Privy Council.[50] In Brecknockshire, the crown farmers of the Forest of Ffynant or Gwernffynant, in the lordship of Dinas adjacent to Dinas Castle, undertook an extensive scheme of enclosure and improvement, and brought in tenants to occupy the cottages which they erected. John Vaughan of Clement's Inn, London, continuing the work begun by his brother several years earlier, argued that the new leaseholds in severalty provided subsistence for many poor people, while the work of hedging and ditching provided them with labour. Yet the inhabitants excluded from their former commons were poor also, and were easily incited to resist. Armed assemblies of up to 200 persons repeatedly levelled the hedges, assaulted those erecting the enclosures, and threatened to tie them to horses' tails. Vaughan charged that the riots were procured by persons of such power that the defendants dared not name them. Vaughan also owned land in the parish of Llanyrvill, Montgomeryshire which formerly belonged to Strata Marcella Abbey, where his tenants were harassed by enclosure riots.[51]

On the royal manor of Bristlington, Somerset, most of the common-field arable had been enclosed many years before, and tenants were encroaching upon the commons for growing oats, but common of pasture was not completely extinguished until the farmer, John Lacy, citizen of London, subleased the remainder of the common pasture to another tenant c.1579. When a substantial coyholder, possessed of 120 acres, attempted to claim common of pasture in the midst of the subtenant's 30 acres of corn, his cattle were maimed and killed, and he was sued for trespass at the Taunton Assizes.[52]

[50] Henry Keeble, yeoman v. Thomas Conway, ibid., STAC 7/3/31.

[51] John Vaughan, gent. v. Roger Vaughan; John Vaughan v. John Cadwalader; John Vaughan v. Hugh ap John, yeoman, ibid., STAC 5/V7/29, 7/16/3, V9/14.

[52] Richard Vaughan, gent. v. John Lacy, citizen of London, ibid., STAC 5/V7/18, V9/14.

Absentee landlords found it difficult to protect their enclosures from hedge-breakers. William Albany, a merchant tailor who lived mostly in London, complained that his enclosure of a wooded common on the manor of Whittington, Shropshire was repeatedly breached over a period of two or three years. At first he could not identify the culprits because he was a stranger in the county and they worked at night, but eventually the hedge-breakers grew bolder and did their work by daylight. Albany finally identified the ringleader as a tenant who worked six messuages comprising 200 acres.[53] That Albany was a cloth-merchant and a number of the rioters were weavers suggests another source of conflict besides the loss of use-rights. A comparable situation also existed on the manor of Condover, Shropshire where the antipathy between clothiers and weavers was more explicit.[54] The once-mighty earls of Northumberland, formerly able to raise private armies among their tenants, had to appeal to the Privy Council for help in quelling anti-enclosure rioting among their northern tenants during their enforced residence in the South.[55]

New landlords were frequently greeted by hostility even when they were resident. Richard Andrewes was the eighth owner of Haresfield Park, near Gloucester, in less than 50 years; he may have inherited ill will from an earlier owner, Sir Anthony Kingston, the provost-marshal who, with a jest ever upon his lips, had hanged rebels in 1549. Certainly, Andrewes's extensive mills, dovehouses, fishponds, orchards, gardens, coppices, meadows, pastures, and deer-parks excited envy and provoked hedge-levelling and timber-cutting by 30 neighbours in 1595.[56] Gentlemen who acquired freeholds and copyholds within manors were notorious for encroaching upon common land and were sometimes denied rights of common by other tenants on the merest suspicion of acquisitiveness. Lord Sandys, a ward of the crown in 1561, was told that he could exercise the rights of common of pasture pertaining to his holdings within the manors of King's Enham and Knight's Enham, Hampshire, but his farmer could not.[57]

[53] *William Albany, citizen and merchant tailor of London* v. *Randall Hamner*, ibid., STAC 5/A22/32.
[54] *Henry Vynar, gent.* v. *Richard Harris*, ibid., STAC 5/V8/12, V6/17.
[55] *Acts PC* xvi. 116; xxii. 527–8.
[56] *Richard Andrewes, gent.* v. *William Harris, yeoman*, PRO, 5/A29/10.
[57] *Francis Vaughan, esq.* v. *Richard Spicer, gent.*, ibid., STAC 5/V9/21; *John Blake* v. *Edward Richards, husbandman*, ibid., STAC 7/10/47.

In Staffordshire, the piecemeal sale by George Touchet, Lord Audley, of his holdings and two-thirds interest in the large manor of Tunstall caused a bitter feud lasting nearly 20 years between Ralph Sneyde and William Unwin as each vied for the lordship of the manor. Religious differences only intensified the rivalry: Sneyde was a recusant sheltering a cousin who was a Marian priest and former chaplain to Bishop Bonner of London; Unwin alleged that Sneyde had dissuaded the churchwardens and parishioners of Wolstanton from selling the Catholic vestments and sacred vessels because they might be put to a lot of expense 'to buye such newe ornaments yf there came a chaunge or alteration of the Relygyon'. Unwin, for his part, was a Puritan who took offence at Sneyde for prophaning the sabbath, but Sneyde prevailed among the 60 or so tenants of the manor by depicting Unwin as a greedy upstart, who engrossed holdings, drove up the price of land, enclosed commons, and extorted high fees for grinding corn on the manorial mills.

When Lord Audley began selling off his properties in 1576, Unwin possessed a capital messuage of 200 acres by copyhold of inheritance, and Sneyde was well established on the commission of the peace. Lacking sufficient capital himself to buy out Lord Audley, Sneyde was unable to prevent Unwin from acquiring several freehold properties, including the manorial mills. Unwin began consolidating his holdings by making exchanges with the other tenants—sometimes persuading them to agree by making gifts of small parcels of land. Although Sneyde could not keep up with Unwin's land-purchases, he did acquire the seigneurial jurisdiction, which included the right to hold a court leet. He used his seigneurial authority repeatedly to incite the tenants to destroy Unwin's enclosures and cut his timber.

Unwin also charged that Sneyde had been appointed a captain by the Earl of Essex and commissioned to raise a company of soldiers from among his tenants to help suppress the Northern Rebellion of 1569. Having raised money to arm and furnish his soldiers, Sneyde got himself discharged of his obligation to assist in suppressing the rebellion, but kept the money and maintained the recruits as liveried retainers without licence to do so. Sneyde employed his retainers to ambush Unwin, level Unwin's hedges, and to serve as leet jurors and present Unwin for various offences. When Sneyde was appointed sheriff in about 1579 he used his authority to get Unwin impanelled on numerous juries, arrested and denied bail, indicted at the Assizes, and tried by a jury made up of Sneyde's relatives and retainers. When

Sneyde's term as sheriff was completed he continued to prosecute Unwin in the court leet for illegal enclosures and erecting cottages that encroached upon the waste. In 1587 the steward of the manorial court persuaded the leet jury to declare that all of Unwin's land acquisitions violated the customs of the manor and were therefore forfeited to the lord of the manor.[58] By this time, a number of Tunstall tenants, maintained by Sneyde, had commenced several suits against Unwin in Chancery and other courts. In 1594 Unwin, still harassed by lawsuits, was obliged to flee; he was arrested in Lincoln's Inn Fields and committed to Newgate Prison. He secured his release, only to be arrested a month later in Newcastle-under-Lyme.[59] Between 1576 and 1594 Unwin began at least five separate suits in Star Chamber against Sneyde and his retainers, charging them with fraud, perjury, subornation of perjury, maintenance, champerty, assault, forcible entry, and riotous destruction of hedges, yet there is no evidence that Sneyde was ever punished. Although Unwin was not without friends in the parish, none dared come forward to testify against Sneyde. The Tunstall tenants were ranged solidly behind Sneyde, which made prosecution very difficult.

Sixteenth-century tenants possessed other forms of social protest, such as rent-strikes and the raising of common purses to pay the costs of litigation, but these were usually used in conjunction with anti-enclosure riots. Rent-strikes had been widely employed in the fifteenth century to resist payment of individual rents and a variety of seigneurial exactions. Refusal to pay rents remained effective only as long as labour was relatively scarce and tenants were prepared to abandon their holdings, or where strong gentry leadership was forthcoming from among or in support of the tenants.[60] Only a few instances of rent-strikes have been uncovered in the sixteenth century and most occurred in Wales and the Borderland. In the first quarter of the century Edward Stafford, third Duke of Buckingham, practised fiscal seigneurialism on a large scale in his marcher lordships. When he attempted to extract higher entry fines from his customary tenants,

---

[58] Either the steward made no distinction between the court leet and the court baron, or Unwin could not perceive any difference.

[59] *William Unwin, gent. v. Ralph Sneyde, esq.*, PRO, STAC 5/U1/33, U1/9, U2/1; *William Unwin v. Hugh Smith*, ibid., STAC 5/U1/12, U1/37; *William Unwin v. John Lovatt, gent.*, ibid., STAC 5/U1/14; *William Unwin v. Lawrence Loggin*, ibid., STAC 5/U1/20.

[60] Dyer, *Lords and Peasants*, pp. 275–7.

many expressed a determination to surrender their tenancies rather than submit to the Duke's demands. Judging from the amount of unoccupied land inventoried at the time of the Duke's attainder and execution in 1521, many had carried out that threat. The amount of resistance offered by Buckingham's tenants to his demands for manorial dues and services and amercements for failure to attend the Grand Sessions of his marcher lordships had already necessitated intervention by the Privy Council in 1518.[61] Two other cases of large-scale rent-strikes occurred on the Denbighshire and Caernarvonshire lands of John, Lord St John of Bletsho, in the 1590s, and were led by high-ranking Welsh gentry who had long displayed an aversion to the acquisitiveness of English courtiers. Both estates had been granted to the Earl of Leicester and had passed through the hands of his brother, the Earl of Warwick, and Warwick's widow to Lord St John. The leader of the resistance in the lordship of Chirk, Denbighshire was John Edwards, who had represented the county in the Parliament of 1588.[62] Edwards had been a protégé of Lord Chancellor Hatton, who had secured him a place in the commission of the peace despite Edwards's recusancy. St John charged that during 1593–4 Edwards had used his position as magistrate to encourage recusancy in Chirkland, to organize resistance to paying rents, and to destroy enclosures of wastes and commons at Glyn Fechan, Llanarmon, and Llangollen Fechan recently erected by St John. It is uncertain how many of the Chirkland tenants actually participated, but they were organized into companies in at least six of the townships and sent 40 of their leaders to Edwards's house, where they planned strategy, agreed to raise a common purse to keep the enclosures open, and discussed how they might alter the customs of the manor.[63] St John's position in Caernarvonshire was that of royal patentee to search out encroached lands in the Forest of Snowdon and crown tenant of those lands, and, like his predecessor, the Earl of Leicester, was attempting to force those occupying such lands to compound

---

[61] B. J. Harris, 'Landlords and Tenants in England in the Later Middle Ages: the Buckingham Estates', in R. H. Hilton (ed.), *Peasants, Knights and Heretics: Studies in Medieval Social History* (Cambridge, 1976), 216–20.

[62] A. H. Dodd, 'North Wales in the Essex Revolt of 1601', *EHR* 59 (1944), 355.

[63] *John, Lord St John of Bletsho v. John Edwards of Chirke, esq.*, PRO, STAC 5/S62/33; P. Williams, 'The Welsh Borderland under Queen Elizabeth', *Welsh Historical Review* 1 (1960), 29; id., *The Council in the Marches of Wales under Elizabeth I* (Cardiff, 1958), 93, 237.

with him and the Queen in order to secure confirmation of their titles without incurring the legal status of bondmen.[64] During 1594–5 fifteen gentlemen (four of them were esquires) and six yeomen organized resistance to the payment of the composition and the rents; they had also canvassed the entire county to raise a common fund for the purpose of maintaining counter-suits against St John. A commission to inquire into the encroachments was entrusted to Sir Robert Salusbury and Sir Robert Bulkeley, an old rival of the Earl of Leicester; the sheriff summoned a jury composed of the leaders of the rent-strike, who were unable to discover any encroachments in the face of the evidence. The leaders of the resistance had also entered into bonds with one another to hold together until their purpose was secured—namely, to raise the common purse and deny the rents. In his complaint to the Court of Star Chamber St John alleged that the act of gathering a common purse was 'seditious' because it was a conspiracy to alter the Queen's laws.[65]

An early-Tudor statute enabled poor persons, needing to bring a suit in any court of record in the kingdom, to obtain free legal counsel and remission of court fees if they declared themselves paupers.[66] Tenants involved in suits before the Court of Star Chamber showed a preference for sharing the costs of litigation among the whole community by raising a common purse—although this made them vulnerable to allegations of maintenance. Contemptuous of other people who begged, copyholders were probably reluctant to plead as paupers and unwilling to accept the passive role that court-appointed legal assistance would have assigned them. Moreover, many tenants possessed enough knowledge of the law to know that the choice of a lawyer was important, and they understood that in litigation, as in war, a good defensive strategy was to attack by bringing counter-suits. When William Veysey, lord of the manor of Abbots Wyck, Essex, began requiring his tenants to purchase licences for timber-cutting, his tenants defied him and forcibly resisted confiscation of the timber that they continued to cut. The copyholders seized the initiative by entering into bonds with one another to get

[64] ibid., p. 239.

[65] *Lord St John* v. *William William, esq.*, PRO, STAC 5/S29/36.

[66] 11 Hen. VII, c. 12, *SR* ii. 578; Kerridge, *Agrarian Problems*, p. 81; W. J. Jones, *The Elizabethan Court of Chancery* (Oxford, 1967), 323.

together a common purse of 18s. and brought a suit against Veysey in Star Chamber. Veysey then countered with a suit against them for maintenance.[67] In Wimbledon, Surrey, Henry Vyne attempted to encroach upon an enclosed wooded pasture belonging to a recusant. When Vyne began cutting timber and preparing to erect a cottage, John Harding, who claimed to have the farm of the pasture, breached the hedges with a hired mob of 40 persons and chopped the timber into small pieces. Harding assured his men that he would defend them against prosecution even if it cost him £200. When one of Harding's followers gave testimony that led to Hardings's indictment at the Croydon Sessions, Harding both verbally and physically abused the informer. Harding defended himself by saying that his attorney advised him that he might seize the timber if he did so in a quiet manner; he had hired only as many workmen as were necessary to load and move the cut timber.[68]

When the eighth Earl of Northumberland made extensive enclosures of commons on his Petworth estates, he could count on support from among tenants who were employed as manorial officials or labourers on demesne land. Those who expressed reservations about yielding up their use-rights were intimidated by threats of vengeance out of the Earl's own mouth. The opposing faction among the tenants raised a common purse and brought a series of Chancery suits against the ninth Earl in the 1590s, and won a few minor concessions, but the Earl refused to abide by the Chancery decree embodying the settlement, while the Earl's lawyers wearied the tenants with legal proceedings. The ninth Earl resorted to a number of other shabby tricks: sometime in the 1590s William James, the principal leader of the opposing tenants, was 'pressed for a soldier' and sent overseas; after James returned home, the Earl's servants bribed James to consent, in 1607, to a new Chancery decree, which was much less advantageous to the tenants than the first decree. Subsequently, James changed sides and once again took up the cause of the tenants. The Earl, now imprisoned in the Tower of London for supposed complicity in the Gunpowder Plot, accused James of putting together a common purse and duping some illiterate tenants into entering into covenants and bonds to continue the litigation against Northumberland. Northumberland also accused James of attempting to persuade the

[67] *William Veysey, gent.* v. *Michael Rolfe*, PRO, STAC 5/V8/7.
[68] *Henry Vyne* v. *John Harding, yeoman*, ibid., STAC 5/V6/9.

Petworth tenants to emulate the participants in the Midland Revolt of 1607 by generally destroying all enclosures in Petworth. The Earl's resources for 'waging law' were much greater than those of the tenantry, and ultimately they had no alternative but to make peace with him.[69]

The act of raising a common purse enforced unity among tenants and required a more sustained opposition to alterations in land-use than enclosure riots—especially when reinforced by covenants and bonds requiring tenants to hold together, but it could also be construed as the crime of maintenance under certain circumstances. The courts generally ruled that tenants could levy a common purse only where they had 'a joint and equal interest' and all participated in the suit. This interpretation meant that customary tenants whose interest or reversion was determinable by the will of the lord could maintain, but freeholders and copyholders by inheritance could not.[70] To raise a common purse where no suit actually followed was considered to be the worst form of maintenance, 'for that it putteth ffuel to all suites'.[71]

In the last decade of the sixteenth century there was a marked increase in the number of enclosure-riot cases. Based upon the sample of 105 cases in England and Wales during the reign of Elizabeth, the number of enclosure riots in the 1590s increased 76 per cent over the average number of cases per decade for the previous twenty years. The types of enclosure destroyed suggest that severe shortages of pasture, timber, and fuel were the immediate cause of the protests. That the increase in such disorder occurred in the 1590s was most likely a consequence of the demographic expansion of the previous two decades which crested after 1590.[72] The influence of the harvest failures of the middle years of the decade is more difficult to discern, although shortages of bread-corn almost

---

[69] Jerrome, *Cloakbag and Common Purse*, pp. 78–97.

[70] William Noy, *Reports and Cases Taken in the Time of Queen Elizabeth, King James and King Charles* (1656), 99; Richard Crompton, *Star-Chamber Cases* (1630; repr. Amsterdam, 1975), 47.

[71] BL, Lansdowne MSS, 639, fo. 99.

[72] Peter Clark, *English Provincial Society from the Reformation to the Revolution: Religion, Politics and Society in Kent, 1500–1640* (Hassocks, Suss., 1977), 235, 244; Stone, *Crisis of the Aristocracy*, p. 329; W. G. Hoskins, *Provincial England: Essays in Social and Economic History* (repr. 1965), 187–94; E. A. Wrigley and R. S. Schofield, *The Population History of England, 1541–1871* (Cambridge, Mass., 1981), 208.

certainly made the inhabitants of sylvan and pastoral areas more dependent upon dairy products. That social conflict played a more significant role in the enclosure disputes of the 1590s may be inferred from the increasingly higher proportion of enclosure riots directed against the greater gentry and peerage. But it must be remembered that even during the 1590s the gentry sometimes still organized protests against absentee landlords such as Lord St John, as the Chirkland and Snowdonia disorders reveal, and that faction-fighting among the gentry, if anything, intensified during the decade.

Because enclosure disputes frequently involved issues other than alterations in land-use, such as tenurial disputes and rack-renting, the increased incidence of enclosure disputes in the 1590s is compatible with the emphasis that some historians have put upon this period as a time when both great landowners and smallholders, carrying an increasing burden of indebtedness, were faced with financial insolvency after a sequence of harvest failures. Landlords resorted to more rational and less paternalistic forms of estate management by attempting to convert customary tenures to leaseholds of fixed duration and to extract higher entry fines and rents.[73] Smallholders, for their part, became more determined to defend ancient use-rights and to resist the encroachments upon commons and wastes of manorial lords and farmers.

A simple enclosure riot, perpetrated once by poor husbandmen, cottagers, or artisans, is hardly more than a skimmington, and thus a fairly primitive form of social protest. But one or more enclosure riots, led by substantial yeomen or gentlemen tenants or freeholders, when combined with rent-strikes or complex legal manoeuvres, must be viewed as a more highly-developed and sustained form of social protest. While some enclosure riots merely protested alterations in land-use, the more complicated disputes were also directed at various forms of fiscal seigneurialism. The most politically-sophisticated forms of agrarian protest were those which raised common purses to pay for legal counsel and commence counter-suits, and enforced community solidarity by exchanging bonds and signing covenants to hold together until litigation was finished. This probably represented the safe limits of social protest, because those who sought to broaden

[73] Stone, *Crisis of the Aristocracy*, pp. 324–34; *AHEW* iv. 690–1; E. Kerridge, 'The Movement of Rent, 1540–1640', *Ec. HR*, 2nd ser. 6 (1953), 16–34.

resistance by persuading other village communities to join them in a more general protest against enclosures might be charged with treason, which put their lives and estates and the welfare of their families and households at risk. Thus, protestors almost always confined their resistance within the local community, because the most that they could be accused of was riot and maintenance, which were misdemeanours normally punished only by fines. Since wider demonstrations of protest were too dangerous, their resistance to the erosion of use-rights and their determination to preserve customary tenures could only become more effective through the more skilful use of royal courts of law. However, the ability to pay increased legal costs would differentiate the more substantial copyholders from their poor neighbours; and the increasing use of royal courts undermined the usefulness of manorial courts in resolving conflict. Either way, the cohesiveness of the local community was weakened.

4

Early-Stuart Enclosure Riots

THE late Elizabethan crises resulted in three popular insurrections, a general increase in individual crimes against property, and a greater frequency of violent social protests. The incidence of enclosure riots in the 1590s was nearly double the average number for the previous two decades. Although the samples of enclosure riots for the reigns of Elizabeth I and James I are not perfectly comparable, violent enclosure disputes appear to have continued at an unusually high rate through the first decade of the seventeenth century. Of the 125 enclosure-riot cases which constitute the sample for the Jacobean period, 75 occurred between 1603 and 1609, 32 during the years 1610–19, 12 between 1620 and 1625, and six are undated. Violent enclosure disputes were endemic to many parts of rural England during the Tudor and early-Stuart periods, but the late-Elizabethan crises, which appear to have persisted between approximately 1590 and 1610, seem to have resulted in a doubling of the usual frequency of agrarian protests.[1]

Jacobean enclosure riots were also larger in scale than those occurring in the previous reign. Whereas only 24 per cent of all Elizabethan enclosure riots included more than 20 participants, 32 per cent of the Jacobean cases (where the number of participants is specified) fall into this category. The largest anti-enclosure riots of the reign of James I were, of course, those usually associated with the Midland Revolt of 1607, where the number of participants was said in every case to have exceeded one thousand. But even after excluding these cases, 5 per cent of all remaining Jacobean enclosure riots still included more than 150 persons. The largest of these occurred at Ladbroke, Warwickshire in 1607 and numbered over 400 participants.[2]

The rituals of enclosure riots appear to have grown more elaborate in the early seventeenth century as the rioters imitated the military ceremony of militia musters or affected the carnivalesque behaviour

---

[1] See Table 4.1. [2] PRO, STAC 8/61/35.

of May Day processions. In the larger enclosure riots, the participants are described as marching in companies led by captains, as at Stixwold, Lincolnshire in 1607. The Ladbroke rioters of the same year were led by a captain on horseback and a man playing a pipe and a tabor. The Great Wishford men in 1621 wore red badges and stuck red feathers in their caps. The Norfolk rioters who assembled on Westland Heath in 1632 to level enclosures were led by a captain, a lieutenant, and a drummer. Ceremony and dignity were important to Englishmen even when they were tearing up hedges by the roots. But the rioters of Blunham, Bedfordshire trooped behind a drunken peddlar on horseback while the real leader marched in their midst.[3]

The influence of the Midland Revolt upon early-Stuart enclosure disputes reveals itself in several ways. Just as rumours about the riots and rebellions of 1548–9 emboldened tenants and smallholders in other parts of England to destroy hedges — even those that had stood for years — so also the example of the Midland Rebels reverberated across the countryside, and encouraged their descendants to protest the new agricultural methods and the enclosure in severalty of common pasture and waste. Again, even long-standing enclosures were levelled, extorted enclosure agreements were repudiated, and alterations in the tenure of land detrimental to tenants were stoutly resisted. Sympathetic demonstrations emulating the Midland Rebels of 1607 undoubtedly explain the high incidence of enclosure riots during the period from 1607 to 1609.

The records of the Jacobean Court of Star Chamber contain numerous allusions to the Midland Revolt. Complainants sometimes sought to discredit enclosure rioters by attempting to associate their protests with the Midland Revolt and thus depict them as rebels and 'levellers' — men who would level not only hedges but social distinctions as well. When, in 1607, William Brereton of Hanford, Cheshire prosecuted his tenants for destroying hedges, he mentioned the practices of 'the late Levellers', and charged that they had threatened to destroy the enclosures again if they were repaired.[4] In Shropshire in 1608 a crafty lawyer, representing Humphrey Briggs of Haughton, attempted to disguise a case of forcible entry as an enclosure riot by exploiting the reaction to the

[3] Ibid., STAC 8/15/13, 68/3, 153/6, 156/32; *Historical Collections*, ed. John Rushworth (2nd edn., 8 vols.; 1721–2), ii/2, app., pp. 53–4.
[4] *William Brereton, esq. v. Reginald Finlowe, yeoman*, PRO, STAC 8/60/7.

Midland Revolt.[5] In Morton Pinkney, Northamptonshire the failure of a manorial lord to honour an enclosure agreement provoked his tenants, in 1609, to destroy twenty-year-old hedges. The complainant, his farmer, described this as an attempt 'to raise and stirr a newe rebellion . . . not much vnlyke the Late rebellious tumoult for inclosures'.[6] In another case, where 50 rioters in Escott, Warwickshire in 1615 destroyed a close upon which corn was growing, the complainant accused the defendants of 'makeing greate braggs and vsinge most vile and lewde speeches sayeinge that they woulde overthrowe all inclosures in the countrye and that Captain Pouche and his fellowes should not excell theire doinges. . . . '[7] The memory of the Midland Revolt endured, and even as late as 1624 a gentleman of Cricklade, Wiltshire referred to Lammas Day rioters as 'levellers'.[8]

Early-Stuart enclosure protestors were probably more sophisticated than their Elizabethan predecessors. One-fifth of the enclosure rioters in the Jacobean sample were accused of raising common purses to pay for the costs of litigation, as contrasted with 7 per cent of the Elizabethan sample. Many of them also entered into bonds and covenants with one another to hold together until their purpose was accomplished.[9]

As in the Tudor period, most enclosure disputes arose from enclosures of waste, commons, pasture, meadow, and woodland pasture. During the reign of Elizabeth 89 per cent of the cases fall into this category, and the proportion for the Jacobean period is 76 per cent. Within this broad category two significant trends emerge. The proportion of disputes arising from the enclosure of wastes and commons has increased from 36 per cent for the reign of Elizabeth to 49 per cent for the reign of James I. During the same period, the proportion of enclosure-riot cases caused by the enclosure of high-quality pasture, meadow, and woodland pasture has declined from 53 per cent to 27 per cent.[10] The significance of these two developments seems to be that the amount of unenclosed high-quality grazing land and woodland pasture had declined dramatically, and the assault upon unenclosed waste and common was increasing. The

---

[5] *Humphrey Briggs, esq.* v. *Thomas Morton, gent.*, ibid., STAC 8/47/9.
[6] *Thomas Fossan, yeoman* v. *Thomas Bryars*, ibid., STAC 8/148/7.
[7] *Richard Duncombe, esq.* v. *William Gardiner*, ibid., STAC 8/122/17.
[8] *Daniel Browne, gent.* v. *Edmund Cusse*, ibid., STAC 8/63/10.
[9] See Table 4.1.   [10] Cf. Tables 3.1 and 4.1.

movement to improve wastes is especially evident in Lancashire in the early seventeenth century.[11] Another trend is that the proportion of violent protests arising from the enclosure of arable land doubled from 8 per cent to 16 per cent. Most of the Jacobean cases occurred in the Midlands—especially in Warwickshire and Northamptonshire—and involve depopulating enclosures where arable land was converted to sheep pasture.

An analysis of the geographical distribution of enclosure riots during the reign of James I shows that the west Midlands continued to generate the largest number of violent enclosure disputes. The proportion of the total (30 per cent) had not altered significantly since the reign of Elizabeth (34 per cent).[12] Within the west Midlands the largest concentrations of riots occurred in Warwickshire, Shropshire, and Staffordshire. The proportion of enclosure riots occurring in the North of England rose from 9 per cent to 17 per cent and all of these cases come from Yorkshire, Lancashire, and Cheshire. The high incidence of enclosure disputes in these counties is probably attributable to the influx of population and the expansion of rural industry as well as the settlement of moors and mosses. The proportion of enclosure riots in the east Midlands increased from 3 per cent to 18 per cent between the late-sixteenth and early-seventeenth centuries. Most of the enclosure riots here were concentrated in Lincolnshire and Northamptonshire. The east Midlands were troubled by population pressure and a shortage of pasture. The heavy-clay areas were better suited to permanent pasture and the regions of lighter soils benefited from convertible husbandry employing temporary leys and heavy manuring by sheep. Already, the Midlands were becoming the main area in England for grazing.[13]

In those areas where pasture became increasingly scarce, copyholders turned to the courts to exclude cottagers, artisans, and labourers. The conflict seems to have been especially sharp where more than one village shared a common and overgrazing resulted. The judicial decision in *Gateward's Case* in 1607 is generally regarded as a significant legal development in defining rights of common pasture more strictly.[14] The defendant, Stephen Gateward, had

---

[11] Cf. ch. 5. [12] Cf. Tables 3.2 and 4.2.
[13] Thirsk, 'The Local History of Enclosing and Engrossing', *AHEW* iv. 247–50.
[14] *Robert Smith* v. *Stephen Gateward, gent.*, Court of Common Pleas, Coke, 6 *Reports*, fo. 59ᵛ.

championed the cause of the poorer villagers in the vicinity of Stixwold, Lincolnshire and defended the customary use-rights of all inhabitants. The custom, the judges ruled, was against the law because it was too vague and had no reference to whether or not an inhabitant possessed an interest in a dwelling house. In effect, the right of common might be claimed only by copyholders or leaseholders. No one could claim right of common who had no estate or interest in his house, but possessed only a mere habitation. The legal consequence was to exclude cottagers because the right of common pasture attached to houses of husbandry and not to persons. E. P. Thompson cites *Gateward's Case* as an example of the tendency of judges to reify or materialize intangible use-rights and thus limit them.[15] Although, in practice, cottagers continued to be afforded use-rights where wastes were abundant, the movement to exclude them was spreading widely in the seventeenth century.[16]

The judicial decision in *Gateward's Case* continued to be opposed in Stixwold and other villages surrounding the disputed waste which included Calscott, Edington, and Stixwold or Stipwood Moors. The protagonist of the copyhold and freehold tenants of the Duchy of Lancaster lands in the area was Richard Evington, the 60-year-old constable of Stixwold.[17] He was prosecuted by the attorney-general for procuring a riot that occurred soon after the Midland Revolt. At first the attorney-general had thought that this was an anti-enclosure riot, but subsequently he discovered that Evington and the constables from Horsington had led 60 persons from those villages in riotously erecting an enclosure on Calscott Moor. They had intended to divide the enclosed parcel of waste among themselves and hold it in severalty. Evington's supporters organized themselves into companies and posted watches to defend their enclosures against rival villagers. The attorney-general added that Evington's supporters had destroyed enclosures which they found offensive on another part of the waste.

Stephen Gateward, a tenant of the Earl of Lincoln, determined to launch a counter-attack on Evington's enclosures. By forging

[15] E. P. Thompson, 'The Grid of Inheritance: A Comment', in J. Goody, J. Thirsk, and E. P. Thompson (eds.), *Family and Inheritance: Rural Society in Western Europe, 1200–1800* (Cambridge, 1976), 339. Lord Eversley, *Commons, Forests and Footpaths*, pp. 10–11.

[16] Ibid., pp. 10–14.

[17] *Sir Henry Hobart, Attorney-General* v. *Richard Evington, gent.*, PRO, STAC 8/15/13.

a warrant purporting to be from Henry, Earl of Lincoln, and threatening people with the Earl's displeasure, Gateward gathered together 60 persons from six other villages surrounding the waste and kept them busy for over a week in the spring of 1608 filling in more than 1,000 rods of Evington's ditches. Evington accused Gateward of attempting 'to rayse newe Tumults and insurreccons' like the recent Midland Revolt. Gateward replied that his followers had understood that enclosures were condemned by the king's recent proclamations and that Evington's enclosure was illegal because the Duchy of Lancaster had not authorized an enclosure agreement.[18]

Robert Freeston complained that his manor of Thimbleby, Lincolnshire consisted entirely of champion, or unenclosed land, and possessed 'small store of pasture'. His family was large and grazing was insufficient for the cattle, horses, and 'draught cattle' necessary to maintain his household, so he enclosed six acres of meadow in severalty. The enclosed land was part of a field upon which the inhabitants of Horncastle claimed common of pasture. Freeston charged that Richard Enderby, a lawyer and high steward of Horncastle, had procured poor persons from Horncastle and other nearby towns, and, threatening to 'revive the late quieted vprores', they had destroyed Freeston's close and depastured 500 head of cattle there. Enderby was accused of unlawful maintenance and champerty.[19] The lesser defendants were accused of raising a common purse and binding themselves together by covenants to maintain suits.[20]

Both pasture and water-rights were at issue in a series of riots in Radnorshire between 1617 and 1623. Edmund Sawyers of London and his farmer had made improvements on the manor of Elwell, which were opposed by the smallholders who claimed Lammas-Day rights by tenant-right on the manorial demesne and common rights in Colwyn Forest, which was part of the manor. The manorial tenants swore 'deep oathes' to maintain anyone who might be sued, and then proceeded to destroy enclosures and weirs, pull down barns encroaching upon the waste, rescue distrained cattle, and then depasture them on Sawyers' enclosed pastures and arable lands.

---

[18] *Richard Evington, v. Steven Gateward*, ibid., STAC 8/129/13.
[19] The crime of illegally supporting a suit in which a person had no natural interest in order to make a profit.
[20] *Robert Freeston, gent. v. Edward Lamm*, PRO, STAC 8/145/20.

Crowds of up to 100 persons frequently gathered at night to burn hayricks.[21]

When Thomas Box, who held the manor of Nettlebed, Oxfordshire, made an intake of four acres from the waste for a new orchard to replace the one cut down when he rebuilt and extended his house, he claimed that he had the consent of most of the commoners. Although the waste consisted of 400–500 acres the loss was resented by the poorer commoners who received no recompense. Box also enclosed a pond, to which every commoner required access, in order to obtain water for household use as well as watering his cattle because the area was dry and poorly supplied with water. To make matters worse Box overcharged the common with cattle, sheep, and swine, the last of which were not usually commonable beasts. The poorer inhabitants complained to members of the local gentry, who mediated the dispute and attempted to work out a compromise in the form of a written agreement, but Box refused to sign. That course of action having failed, Richard Butler, husbandman, and several artisans and labourers decided 'to try by the course of common law there right to the saide common of pasture' by making a breach in Box's hedges. Part of the disputed waste belonged to Sir Francis Stonor of Stonor, and it is likely that the defendants enjoyed his support.[22]

In earlier times it was not unusual to allow temporary intakes from the waste for growing corn. It was understood that after two or three years the land would revert to commonable waste. But such intakes came to be viewed with suspicion because of the fear that they would be permanent. Temporary intakes had been allowed in Holme Walfield, Cheshire in Elizabethan times, but when Ralph Davy, who farmed William Brereton's lands while the latter was a ward of the crown, enclosed part of the waste for cultivation, his intakes encountered resistance because Davy was an outsider and claimed to hold the intakes in severalty. Henry Haworth, a gentleman-tenant, led the other tenants in destroying Davy's hedges and said that they would be levelled again if any attempt were made to replant them.[23] On the manor of Arcott, Shropshire Roger Cardiffe's under-tenants

---

[21] *Sir Thomas Coventry, Attorney-General* v. *Peter David* alias *Powell*, ibid., STAC 8/29/4.

[22] *Thomas Box, gent.* v. *Richard Butler, husbandman*, ibid., STAC 8/64/21.

[23] *William Brereton of Hanford, esq.* v. *Reginald Finlowe, yeoman*, ibid., STAC 8/60/7.

enclosed intakes from the waste and planted corn without seigneurial permission. Anne Corbett, a widow who held the manor by dower right, allowed the under-tenants to maintain the enclosure until the corn was harvested because they had pleaded poverty. But when they subsequently refused to honour their promise to abandon the illegal intakes and planted another crop, she ordered her other tenants to remove the hedges. It appears that Cardiffe was trying to settle under-tenants permanently on the waste and that they did not farm any part of his two messuages.[24] In Litton, Derbyshire Thomas Bagshaw, the manorial lord, enclosed large portions of the waste which he converted to arable use. He was opposed by his tenants who repeatedly tore down stone walls and depastured their animals. The tenants referred to him as an 'improving landlord', and used the term in a pejorative sense.[25]

The most disruptive enclosures of the Jacobean period were those that occurred in the Midlands and involved large-scale conversions of arable land to sheep pasture. These enclosures are supposed to have caused extensive depopulation and to have led to the Midland Revolt. Ladbroke, Warwickshire was the scene of a larger anti-enclosure riot in June 1607 which a complainant in Star Chamber attempted to link with the Midland Revolt (without, however, providing any evidence to prove that allegation). The attorney-general, Sir Henry Hobart, stated that enclosures for sheep runs in Ladbroke had caused the decay of 18 houses of husbandry.[26] The Ladbroke enclosure dispute is unusually well documented, and it appears that the attorney-general may have oversimplified a very complicated situation. Although there can be no doubt that depopulation occurred, it is not solely attributable to enclosure, because the enclosure agreement of 1597 had been preceded by considerable engrossing of tenements. Moreover, the evidence concerning one parcel of land, a freehold of 200 acres within Ladbroke manor leased to William Burton, suggests that some of the land was converted to up-and-down husbandry rather than permanent sheep pasture.[27]

---

[24] *Roger Cardiffe of Great Bolas, gent.* v. *Anne Corbett*, ibid., STAC 8/87/20.

[25] *Thomas Bagshaw* v. *Ralph Oldfield*, ibid., STAC 8/64/4.

[26] *Sir Henry Hobart, Attorney-General* v. *William Burton the elder, yeoman*, ibid., STAC 8/10/18; *VCH Warwickshire*, vi. 143.

[27] *William Burton the elder, yeoman* v. *Edward Clarke*, PRO, STAC 8/68/3; *William Burton* v. *Francis Harrolde, gent.*, STAC 8/61/35.

Whatever the causes of depopulation were, most of the surviving tenants were unhappy about the way in which the enclosure agreement was carried out and some continued to dispute the agreement and to claim use-rights extinguished by the agreement 40 years after the event.[28]

One cause of the strife was a lack of seigneurial continuity and firm direction in carrying out the enclosure agreement. Ladbroke Manor had been inherited by Robert Catesby, later one of the Gunpowder-Plot conspirators, who sold it in 1597 to Sir Robert Dudley, illegitimate son of the Earl of Leicester. Dudley also purchased another large estate in Ladbroke from Sir John Spencer of Althorp, and immediately began a scheme for total enclosure in an area of open-field agriculture. The land was carelessly surveyed and little heed paid to the quality or value of the several parcels when they were portioned out among the tenants. While some tenants benefited, most were worse off than before enclosure and there was much resentment concerning the inequitable manner in which the redistribution of land was handled. Meanwhile, Dudley's failure to establish his claim to his father's title led him to abandon his family and his lands, and he went into exile in Italy in 1605. His estates were subsequently administered by the crown on behalf of his wife and children.[29]

When the great Ladbroke enclosure riot occurred on 1–3 June 1607, the work of apportionment and enclosing was uncompleted. William Burton, who held 60 acres of his own land in addition to the 200 acres leased from Thomas Thornton, a freehold tenant of the manor, stated that his leasehold land was dispersed in scattered parcels, which he had enclosed himself about eight years earlier. According to Burton, the participants in the riot came from 15 villages in Warwickshire and one in Northamptonshire, and a representative of the rebels at Cottesbach, Leicestershire had promised help from that village. Burton tried to depict the Ladbroke riot as part of a general rising against enclosures, but he let the cat out of the bag when he admitted in another bill of complaint that the hedge-levelling was directed only against him, despite the existence of other enclosures in the neighbourhood. Morever, the rioters were procured and led by several members of the neighbouring

[28] *John Thorneton, esq.* v. *John Radford*, ibid., C. 78/396/13.
[29] Ibid.; *VCH Warwickshire*, vi. 143.

gentry, who paid many of the participants, furnished them with food and drink, and provided music for their amusement.[30]

It is curious that popular resentment was directed against Burton rather than Dudley. Burton's neighbours presented him to the royal commissioners inquiring into depopulating enclosures for having caused the suppression of two houses of husbandry and having been an accessory in the depopulation of 15 or 16 more; they secured his indictment for enclosing the highway between Ladbroke and Hardwick; and they accused him of swallowing up and enclosing part of a common pasture claimed by the adjacent village of Napton.[31]

A year later, Burton sought his revenge against those who had incited the rioters by writing a libellous ballad attacking them and distributing 40 copies of it around the country. In order to deflect suspicion elsewhere, Burton and his son included themselves among the people whom they slandered in the eclogue and affixed the name 'Thomas Vnhedgall' to it. Their ruse was discovered and the attorney-general prosecuted them for seditious libel.[32]

The enclosure dispute at Great Wolford, Warwickshire arose from circumstances similar to those at Ladbroke. The conspirator Robert Catesby also held the manors of both Great and Little Wolford between 1600 and 1605. When Catesby was forced to sell, the purchaser was James Bishop, from whose father Catesby had originally purchased Great Wolford. Great Wolford had earlier consisted of open-field arable, and when Bishop acquired the manor he enclosed seven messuages, which had previously been engrossed and depopulated. Bishop attempted to compel the twelve remaining freehold and copyhold tenants to abandon their rights to common of pasture on the newly-enclosed land, but, under the leadership of Edward Ockley, a gentleman-tenant, they resisted by bringing suit in Chancery and seeking the mediation of a justice of the peace. The tenants continued to claim their use-rights, and destroyed Bishop's hedges on three different occasions in 1606. When Bishop's servants offered resistance, the tenants swore out warrants of the peace against them and obtained the assistance of the tithing-man in enforcing the warrants. Bishop prosecuted the tenants for trespass in the Court

---

[30] PRO, STAC 8/68/3, 61/35. John E. Martin's discussion of the Ladbroke enclosure riot of June 1607 fails to establish a connection between that protest and the Midland Revolt of 1607: *Feudalism to Capitalism: Peasant and Landlord in English Agrarian Development* (Atlantic Highlands, NJ, 1983), 168–70.

[31] PRO, STAC 8/68/3, 10/18.   [32] Ibid., STAC 8/10/18, 59/6.

of Common Pleas and for riot and maintenance in Star Chamber. The tenants raised a common purse by assessing each tenant 5s. per yardland per term to pay for legal expenses, and the assessment continued to be collected for two years.[33]

Because of the perception that depopulating enclosures had caused the Midland Revolt, several landowners and clergymen of the region had spoken out against this species of enclosure. The issue was quite divisive in Warwickshire, as the enclosure dispute at Welcombe, near Stratford-upon-Avon, reveals. This contoversy is also notable because it involved William Shakespeare, who had purchased a half-share in a lease of tithes at Welcombe. When, in 1614, William Combe proposed to enclose the open fields at Welcombe and convert from arable farming to sheep pasture, Shakespeare offered no objection, despite the depopulating nature of the enclosure, because he had been assured that his own share of the tithes would remain undiminished. The corporation of Stratford declared their opposition to the Welcombe enclosure and a couple of members of the corporation acquired leases in Welcombe which gave them a claim to use-rights on the land to be enclosed. On that pretext they began filling in the ditches newly dug for hedges. Combe, mounted on horseback, appeared with his men to oppose the two 'diggers', and called them 'puritan knaves & underlings in their colour'. Thomas Greene, the leader of the diggers and a friend of Shakespeare, returned the next day with a group of women and children to continue levelling the enclosures. Combe proceeded nonetheless and depopulated the whole village except for his own house. By this time Shakespeare had had second thoughts and declared that 'he was not able to beare the enclosinge of Welcombe'. Greene continued to oppose Combe, and after petitioning the lord chief justice and the Privy Council, he obtained a warrant ordering Combe to remove the enclosures.[34]

In the lordship of Elton, Herefordshire the enclosures of open-field arable made between 1611 and 1622 by John Bridgwater, a freehold tenant, encountered opposition because he swallowed up

---

[33] *VCH Warwickshire*, v. 216; *James Bishop, esq.* v. *Edward Williams*, PRO, STAC 8/15/13; *James Bishop* v. *Robert Workman, husbandman*, ibid., STAC 8/78/13.

[34] M. Eccles, *Shakespeare in Warwickshire* (Madison, Wisc., 1961), 104, 136–8; E. K. Chambers, *William Shakespeare: A Study of Facts and Problems* (2 vols.; repr. Oxford, 1963), ii. 144–52; Dyer, *Lords and Peasants*, pp. 254–5.

other people's land and had repeatedly refused to make compensation. Bridgwater also caused offence because he overcharged the common with cattle. The other tenants finally banded together and levelled his hedges and impounded his cattle every time they appeared on the common. Bridgwater prosecuted them for riot in Star Chamber, but the principal defendant persuaded Bridgwater to accept the arbitration of the vicar of Wigmore. The award was accepted by both complainant and defendant and the case was settled out of court. Bridgwater agreed to pay compensation.[35]

As in the Tudor period, gentlemen continued to play a significant role in procuring or leading anti-enclosure riots. Indeed, the proportion of violent enclosure disputes attributable to gentry leadership increased slightly between the Elizabethan and Jacobean periods (from 33 per cent to 39 per cent).[36] The gentry may have abandoned some of the more extreme forms of violence in the century preceding the Civil Wars, but they remained attached to lesser species of violence such as levelling their neighbours' hedges in pursuit of feuds.[37] As in the reign of Elizabeth, half of all victims of enclosure riots were gentlemen; some of these cases involve gentry feuds, but most arise from conflict between manorial lords or large landowners and smallholders.

A significant trend during the transition from the late sixteenth to the early seventeenth century is that the proportion of anti-enclosure protests organized and led by smallholders nearly doubled (from 23 per cent to 43 per cent).[38] Smallholders invariably participated to some degree in enclosure disputes, but it appears that in the early seventeenth century they became more inclined to initiate violent enclosure riots themselves. The distinction that I have made between gentlemen and smallholders when analysing the procurers and victims of enclosure riots is somewhat misleading, because gentlemen were found among tenants—especially on large manors. In some of these cases it would be better to distinguish between gentry-tenants and gentlemen who possessed seigneurial jurisdiction. If this were done,

---

[35] *John Bridgwater, gent.* v. *John Bridgwater, yeoman*, PRO, STAC 8/67/1. The vicar of Wigmore also bore the name of John Bridgwater and all three may have been related.

[36] Cf. Tables 3.1 and 4.1.

[37] Cf. M. E. James, *English Politics and the Concept of Honour, 1485–1642* (*P. & P.* supplement 3, 1978), 13, 17.

[38] Tables 3.1 and 4.1.

then the proportion of enclosure riots procured or led by tenants would be much greater. This would strengthen the argument that social conflict in agrarian disputes was increasing in the early seventeenth century.

Jacobean tenants were better organized to resist enclosures than their mid-Tudor predecessors and were better prepared to defend themselves in court—even though they did not always achieve success when opposing well-connected landowners. When George Gunter, who claimed to be the lord of the adjoining manors of Racton and Woodmancot in West Sussex, enclosed 60 acres of a waste shared by those two manors and the manor of Aylsworth, he was surprised by the opposition he encountered. The customary tenants of Aylsworth, led by Edward Maunde, bound themselves together 'with many Solempne [solemn] vowes' and, early in January 1604, 30 of them destroyed most of Gunter's hedges and fences. When Gunter prosecuted Maunde in Star Chamber, the latter presented a carefully-argued defence, which is worth considering in some detail. Maunde said that Gunter had no authority to make intakes from the waste because he possessed no seigneurial jurisdiction over the waste. No court baron had been held on the manors of Racton and Woodmancot for at least 50 years. Most of Gunter's lands, said Maunde, were held of Lord Lumley as part of the manor of Stanstead, and the rest were held as customary tenancies within the manor of Aylsworth, to which the enclosed portion of the waste belonged. Each tenant of Aylsworth was allowed by custom to graze 60 sheep for each yardland he possessed. Since the waste had a total area of 300 acres and 1900 sheep, there was not sufficient pasturage to permit intakes from the waste. The answer of the second defendant, George Blythe, was constructed with equal care.[39] That they had retained competent legal counsel is evident, but one suspects that the defendants were well informed themselves concerning the legal aspects of enclosure.

Several other Sussex gentry were also aggressively improving wastes during this period. Sir Henry Compton, for example, was not over-careful about securing title to the lands that he enclosed on Chailey Common in East Sussex. On one parcel, the inhabitants of Chailey parish destroyed his enclosures and burnt the houses which he had erected because they maintained that the land belonged to

---

[39] *George Gunter, esq.* v. *Edward Maunde, husbandman*, PRO, STAC 8/153/22.

Lord Howard of Effingham and was commonable after Michaelmas. When the inhabitants of Fletching, a neighbouring village, destroyed Compton's fences on another part of Chailey Common, they were attacked by his servants and dogs, and serious gunshot wounds were inflicted on one villager.[40] Another improvement scheme on Chailey Common was begun by the third Earl of Dorset, Lord Abergavenny, Sir George Goring, and Sir Edward Bellingham, who were joint lords of the manor of Howndeane. An agreement had been drawn up to enclose 511 acres of the waste in severalty and to practise convertible husbandry. One hundred and sixty acres were to be retained as manorial demesne and the remaining 351 acres apportioned among eight copyholders and one freeholder at an annual rent of ½ d. per acre and 6d. herriot. After the Earl of Dorset died in 1624 and his interest passed to his widow, the copyholders rebelled and cast down the dowager countess's fences. The Court of Chancery ordered the tenants to perform the agreement.[41] In 1600 Nicholas Challoner allowed a tenant to enclose ten acres of waste from Chiltington Common in East Sussex, but his son discovered that the land had valuable timber growing on it and attempted to renegue on the enclosure agreement.[42]

Orwell, Cambridgeshire was a royal manor where no lord had resided since the reign of Richard II and the tenants had grown used to managing their own affairs. For a long time they had leased the manorial demesne directly from the crown, and met in the parish church to take community action. When Queen Elizabeth granted a lease of the demesne arable to Mrs Jean Audley, the tenants approached her in order to strike a bargain. There was a severe shortage of pasture land in proportion to the amount of arable, and when Mrs Audley demanded what they considered to be exorbitant entry fines and rents for the pasture, the tenants complained in 1605 to the Court of Exchequer. The son of one of the more substantial tenants, Thomas Butler, a student at Gray's Inn, offered to try to obtain a lease of meadow and pasture from the crown. The tenants agreed to pay him an annual retainer fee and also to allow him to enclose and hold in severalty a small piece of the village common.

---

[40] *Sir Henry Compton v. Robert Martin, husbandman*, ibid., STAC 8/104/9; Anthony Fletcher, *A County Community in Peace and War: Sussex, 1600–1660* (1975), 56.

[41] *Anne, dowager countess of Dorset v. John Godley*, PRO, C. 78/279/9.

[42] *Edward Howell, yeoman v. Richard Challoner, gent.*, ibid., C. 78/180/13.

When Butler failed to prevent Mrs Audley from forcing the tenants to lease directly from her, they destroyed the hedges surrounding his close and depastured their cattle. However, by 1627 Thomas Butler's widow and members of his family had obtained possession of two-thirds of the available pasture in Orwell.[43]

Access to scarce pasture land was an issue that pitted copyholders against cottagers and artisans on the manor of Wimbledon, Surrey. William Child, a customary tenant who also worked as a notary public in London, enclosed two parcels of meadow from the common pasture. He maintained that manorial custom permitted this and that other tenants were doing the same. Bartholomew Carter, a blacksmith, claimed that manorial custom had allowed common of pasture to cottagers on the same footing as tenants; in 1614 he led 20 other persons, including carpenters and joiners, in destroying 40 perches of Child's hedges.[44]

Women played a significant role in Tudor and Stuart social protest. Their participation in food riots is especially notable,[45] and they were involved in at least 13 anti-enclosure riots (11 per cent of the sample) during the reign of James I. Indeed, several enclosure riots were entirely feminine protests. The legal accountability of women involved in protests confined within a village community was unclear. William Lambarde held that

if a number of women (or children under the age of discretion) do flocke together for their own cause, this is none assembly punishable by these statutes, unless a man of discretion moved them to assemble for the doing of some unlawfull act. . . .

Lambarde then qualified this statement by noting that

sundry women were punished in the Star Chamber, and that worthily: because putting off that fastnesse which beseemeth their sexe they arrayed themselves in the attire of men, and (assembling in a great number) they most riotously pulled down a lawfull enclosure.[46]

---

[43] Spufford, *Contrasting Communities*, pp. 97–8.
[44] *William Child, Notary Public* v. *Bartholomew Carter, blacksmith*, PRO, STAC 8/93/18.
[45] J. Walter, 'Grain Riots and Popular Attitudes to the Law: Maldon and the Crisis of 1629', in J. Brewer and J. Styles (eds.), *An Ungovernable People*, 62–3.
[46] William Lambarde, *Eirenarcha, or of the Office of Iustice of Peace* (1602), 169–70. Cf. Michael Dalton, *The Countrey Iustice* pp. 146–7, 205, 245.

Just as there existed a popular legal myth that no riot could be committed when protesters against enclosures worked only two at a time to level hedges, so also there was another popular belief that married women, as *femmes covert*, were 'lawless' and could level hedges with impunity. The judges of the Court of Star Chamber, in their efforts to curb disorder, assailed this popular legal mythology and consistently maintained that women, and their husbands or masters as procurers, could be punished for riots.[47]

In 1608 a group of husbandmen in Waddingham, Lincolnshire considered how they might reclaim their Lammas-Day rights in a couple of enclosed pastures.

But they the said persons, thinkeing as yt should seeme That the castinge downe of the ffences and hedgs of the said closes would be a gretter offence and more greevously punished in them, then if yt should be done by weomen, ... did ... move, persuade and procure diverse weomen to the number of fortie or thereabouts to go to cast downe the said hedge and ffences.[48]

The women were mostly the wives of husbandmen, and their husbands waited together within a couple of hundred yards should they be needed. Both husbands and wives were prosecuted by Star Chamber for riot and the women were charged additionally with assault.

Another all-female riot occurred on the manor of Dunchurch, Warwickshire in 1609. The tenants were upset because the manorial lord, Sir Francis Leighe, had enclosed eight acres of pasture, which obstructed their access to a common pasture. Fifteen women, including wives, widows, spinsters, unmarried daughters, and servants, took it upon themselves to assemble at night to dig up the hedges and level the ditches. All were named as defendants along with husbands, fathers, and masters. The women denied that the men had procured their actions and asserted that the wife of Leighe's bailiff had told them that they might pull down a stile that was dangerous to climb over and make a small gap in the hedge.[49] The female defendants' attempt to argue that their husbands had no knowledge of their actions was undoubtedly rejected because, in a similar case in 1605, the Court of Star Chamber had ruled 'that if

[47] Cf. ch. 3.
[48] *Philip Adams, gent.* v. *William Burrell, husbandman*, PRO, STAC 8/42/11.
[49] *Sir Henry Hobart, Attorney-General* v. *John Chaundeler*, ibid., STAC 8/16/14.

women offend in trespass, riot or otherwise, and an action is brought against them and their husbands, they [the husbands] shall pay the fines and damages, notwithstanding the trespass or the offence is committed without the privity of the husbands.'[50]

Protagonists in enclosure disputes resorted to a variety of dodges to avoid implicating themselves. When a farmer on the royal manor of Ravensworth, Yorkshire enclosed several parcels of woodland pasture that he had recently leased, the other tenants immediately began to conspire to remove the enclosures and reclaim their common of pasture. But being

men of wealth [who] might be questioned and trubled for the same, they therefore to avoyde there owne danger . . . did cunningly and privately moue, stirr & persuade divers poore menn dwelling neare abouts to Ioyne & assemble togeather & to pull downe the said hedges & fences in the night tyme, promising to beare them out therein, & encouridging them with diverse disgraceful & threatning speeches . . . That never a fellow in England shoulde keepe vpp the said hedges.[51]

In Great Wishford, Wiltshire, on the edge of Groveley Forest, the title to a meadow was disputed between Sir Richard Grobham and Sir Robert Bassett. Grobham, the complainant, charged that Bassett had hired about 60 vagrants to take possession of the meadow and hold it. Grobham attempted to depict the incident as a case of forcible entry. But the defendants actually included a clergyman, gentlemen, yeomen, husbandmen, shepherds, and warreners, plus wives and children. They wore red badges and feathers in their caps, marched in companies, levelled hedges, and kept up their protests over a period of at least five years; in short, they behaved more like a village community than a rabble of vagrants. On one occasion they marched past Grobham's house in Great Wishford uttering 'hideous cries' and shouting that he was 'an vnworthie knight, a base knight, a bald knight & an irreligious knight!'[52]

Many protests against the extinction of use-rights were intended to secure the sympathetic intervention of magistrates to whom the protesters looked for justice. The case of Sir Henry Barker, a Middlesex JP, reveals how vulnerable such persons were when they encountered hostility in a magistrate. Barker farmed the tithes of the

---

[50] Hawarde, *Reportes*, p. 247.
[51] *John Felton, gent.* v. *James Ponsonby*, PRO, STAC 8/142/8.
[52] *Sir Richard Grobham* v. *Sir Robert Bassett*, ibid., STAC 8/153/6.

rectory of Fulham. The poorer people of the parish claimed the right to glean the fields after the corn harvest. One of Barker's servants brutally beat several women whom he discovered gleaning a field after the tithe-corn had been harvested in August 1605. When one of the women, Joanne Belgrave, complained to Barker about his servant's assault, Barker had her and another woman placed in the stocks and shut up within a cage in Hammersmith for a day and a half. Joanne Belgrave's husband, Thomas, complained to other members of the Middlesex Bench, but when Barker got wind of the complaint he committed Thomas Belgrave to Newgate Prison on perjured evidence that Belgrave had conspired to ambush and maim Barker's servant. The plague was raging in Newgate at that time, but Barker remained incarcerated for five days until lord chancellor Ellesmere ordered everyone charged with a bailable offence to be released. Barker further revenged himself upon Belgrave by ordering his servants to destroy the hedges and fruit trees in Belgrave's orchard. Still bound over to appear before the Middlesex Sessions, Belgrave appealed to Sir Edward Coke, the attorney-general, who prosecuted Barker in the Court of Star Chamber.[53]

During the reign of Elizabeth only one peer, Lord St John, was the victim of enclosure rioting, but enclosure protests were directed against several peers in the Jacobean period. As might be expected, the riots were organized and led by gentlemen rather than smallholders, but the amount of violence occasioned by these riots is unusual. Two enclosure riots protested the sharp practices of Thomas Howard, Earl of Suffolk. Suffolk had acquired the manor of Hoddenham, near Ely, from the crown, which included two recently enclosed meadows. Suffolk leased parts of the manor to a series of farmers who came and went in rapid succession, but retained an interest in the two meadows, upon which several neighbours, including John Jowles, claimed common of pasture. In 1604 Jowles procured a crowd of 200 persons—many of them women—to destroy Suffolk's fences, ditches, and bridges by promising to share his rights of common pasture with them. The rioters gathered up all of the cattle in the neighbourhood (500 head in all) to consume the hay crop. They also attacked and beat the Earl's officers and servants, and assaulted the two justices of the peace who read the proclamation

[53] *Sir Edward Coke, Attorney-General v. Sir Henry Barker*, ibid., STAC 8/8/4.

ordering them to disperse. When a JP ordered the arrest of one of Jowles's servants the next day, the rioters rescued him.[54] A few years later, Suffolk enclosed 40 acres of common pasture on his manor of Newport in Essex against the will of his freehold tenants. When the freeholders filed several suits against him, the Earl sought to stay the suits by arranging a conference between his lawyers and the freeholders. He offered them Lammas-Day rights by way of a compromise and agreed to pay £20 annually to the overseers of the poor. Suffolk claimed that his tenants agreed to those conditions and the enclosure agreement was subsequently ratified by a Chancery decree. When Suffolk was fined and imprisoned for embezzlement in 1619, the Crown sequestered the manor in order to secure payment of his debts.[55] Subsequently, in May 1620, a series of riots broke out and the enclosures surrounding the meadow were destroyed, a house was pulled down, and one of Suffolk's servants was wounded. Thomas Nightingale was prosecuted for leading the riot and in his defence said that the disputed pasture had been shared by the inhabitants of the parish of Widdington, who were not party to the Earl's enclosure agreement. Nightingale and the other defendants swore that there was no Chancery decree confirming the enclosure, but rather that the Earl had filed a bill of complaint in Chancery in which he made reference to a fictitious decree.[56]

When the Earl of Clanricard married the Earl of Essex's widow, who was also Suffolk's niece, he acquired the use of a woodland pasture in Walford, Herefordshire which he promptly enclosed. Resistance was organized by several of the gentry of the parish who led crowds of up to 60 persons in a series of riots in March 1604 that destroyed nearly 1,000 rods of hedges.[57] The Earl of Kent's attempt to sever and enclose nine acres from the waste of his manor of Blunham, Bedfordshire also met with well-organized resistance from his tenants. Their leader, Robert Ball, was the village constable,

---

[54] *Sir Edward Coke, Attorney-General* v. *John Jowles, esq.*, ibid., STAC 8/5/21.

[55] Suffolk was Lord Treasurer from 1614 until removed from office in 1618 for embezzlement, bribery, and extortion (*DNB*, s.v. Thomas Howard, 1st Earl of Suffolk).

[56] *Sir Thoms Coventry, Solicitor-General* v. *Thomas Nightingale, esq.*, PRO, STAC 8/34/5.

[57] *Richard de Burgh, Earl of Clanricard* v. *Anthony Stratford, gent.*, ibid., STAC 8/84/19.

who gathered them together in the parish church and collected 40s. from each tenant for a common purse. Ball made the plans for the removal of the fences surrounding the enclosed parcel, which the Earl used as a horse pasture, and then absented himself during the two days of rioting that followed. The tenants were divided into companies and Ball left a deputy constable in command. Sixty persons participated, including wives and female servants, and Ball's deputy also recruited outsiders, including:

one Thomas Reyner, a dissolute fellowe, a rogue and one who wandered aboute the country selling of acquavite, whome they vsed as captayne of their riotous and rebellious assembly, [while] they, all weaponed, . . . came marching in warlike and rebellious manner to the saide close. . . . And the saide Thomas Reyner . . . in most riotous and rebellious manner, flourishing his staffe which he then had above his head, cryed out with a lowed [loud] voice: . . . 'Now for King James and for the commons of Blunham!'[58]

On the manor of Charlton Horethorne, Somerset, misunderstandings concerning the details of an enclosure scheme initiated by the Earl of Pembroke in the 1560s led to a violent clash 50 years later between the Jacobean manoral lord, James Gilbert, and his tenants. Both Gilbert, whose father had purchased the manor from Pembroke, and his tenants admitted that the agreement had resulted in the enclosure, exchange, and consolidation of scattered parcels of arable, high-quality pasture, and meadow. Gilbert maintained that after his father's death his mother had granted parcels of the waste in severalty to tenants who complained about the lack of adequate pasture. When he came into his inheritance he found himself short of pasture and enclosed a further portion of the waste for his own use. His tenants maintained that the original agreement specified that common rights on the waste were to remain unabridged. They were willing to agree to total enclosure of the waste provided the apportionment was carried out in an equitable manner, but Gilbert had already grabbed 60 acres, which was more than his fair share. The tenants destroyed Gilbert's enclosures and depastured their cattle on two separate occasions in 1611 and 1612, and allegedly made threatening speeches against Gilbert. On the last occasion, the tenants met forcible resistance from Gilbert and his servants. One tenant, Roger Downe,

---

[58] *Henry Grey, Earl of Kent v. Robert Ball, constable of Blunham*, ibid., STAC 8/156/32.

said that Gilbert, mounted on horseback, had charged at him with a lance and threatened to kill him. Downe replied that 'althoughe he were but a poore man yet the lawe woulde punishe the complainant [Gilbert] for the doinge thereof', and proceeded to defend himself with his own staff.[59]

Religious conflict aggravated a number of Jacobean enclosure disputes. During the time of the Midland Revolt, William Burrows, constable of Belton, Leicestershire, incited the inhabitants of the village to destroy hedges belonging to John Beaumont, lord of the manor of Grace Dieu, and to reclaim common rights taken from them 40 years earlier. When Beaumont's servants attempted to dissuade the hedge-breakers, Burrows arrested them as rogues and vagabonds who were known to frequent alehouses. Burrows and the villagers defended themselves before the Court of Star Chamber by arguing that as an indicted recusant Beaumont was presumed to be excommunicated and outlawed and thus disabled from bringing suits at law.[60] Sir William Acklam's attempts to improve the waste on his manor of Moreby were frustrated when Sir Ralph Ellerker commanded his tenants on the neighbouring manor of Stillingfleet to destroy Acklam's enclosures or face eviction. Acklam sought to demonstrate Ellerker's factiousness by accusing him of being a church-papist and his wife of being 'an obstinate popish recusant'. Moreover, Ellerker's tenants frequented alehouses and drank 'healthes' in the intervals between digging up Aklam's hedges.[61]

In the Vale of Evesham, Thomas Allen used his power as foreman of the Worcestershire grand jury and assessor for the parliamentary subsidy of 1602 to make life difficult for recusants. Allen suspected that the Copley family sheltered seminary priests and recusants who had been outlawed. When Allen ordered several visitors to the Copley house in Bredon pilloried as vagrants, the Copleys and their friends retaliated by destroying hedges and trees in a close belonging to Allen. Members of the Copley circle of recusants also ambushed and assaulted Allen on several occasions, wounded him twice, and nearly killed him on one occasion.[62]

---

[59] *James Gilbert, esq.* v. *Roger Downe, husbandman*, ibid., STAC 8/155/10.
[60] *John Beaumont, esq.* v. *William Burrows, yeoman*, ibid., STAC 8/71/6.
[61] *Sir William Acklam* v. *Sir Ralph Ellerker*, ibid., STAC 8/40/9; *VCH Yorkshire, East Riding*, iii. 104–7.
[62] *Thomas Allen, gent.* v. *John Copley, gent.*, PRO, STAC 8/46/5.

Enclosure disputes in urban communities tended to be more bitter and social conflict more explicit than in rural areas. Whereas manorial lords and gentlemen-tenants sometimes championed the use-rights of their tenants or neighbours, poorer townsmen could perceive a direct connection between the growth of oligarchy in municipal government and the extinction of their rights of common pasture. Frequently, town lands were enclosed and leased to farmers or graziers in order to increase municipal revenues. Usually, rights of common pasture were thereafter restricted to burgesses, or other privileged members of the corporation, who were selected by co-option.[63]

At Coventry, the importance of sheep to the city's cloth trade in the early sixteenth century was used to justify the alienation, enclosure, or overcharging of the common lands. At the end of that century the town lands were leased for growing grain to be stored against emergencies. Popular sentiment was against the abridgement of common rights for whatever reason, and anti-enclosure riots protesting such policies occurred in 1525, 1548, 1603, and 1638. The conflict was only intensified by intrusive lawyers and gentry who meddled in Coventry's affairs: during the Midland Revolt rioting broke out quite close to Coventry and two rival factions accused one another of attempting to incite anti-enclosure riots among the inhabitants of the city.[64]

The burgesses of Daventry, Northamptonshire granted a 99-year lease of a town meadow to a farmer in order to pay off old debts. In 1604, a crowd of 40 persons, including artisans who claimed that rights of common pasture after Michaelmas attached to the cottages which they rented from the Duchy of Lancaster, challenged the lease by destroying the farmer's hedges and depasturing 200 head of cattle. Many of the protesters were said to be infected with the plague, and only two could sign their names.[65]

---

[63] Kerridge, *Agrarian Problems*, pp. 98–9; J. Waylen, *A History Military and Municipal of the town of Marlborough* (1854), 103, 110, 118, 123, 131; *The Third Book of Remembrance of Southampton, 1514–1602*, ed. A. L. Merson (2 vols.; Southampton, 1952, 1955), ii. 20–1; Sir Francis Hill, *Medieval Lincoln* (Cambridge, 1965), 302, 331.

[64] *VCH Warwickshire*, viii. 202–4; *John Ferrour, esq. v. William Hallett*, PRO, STAC 8/144/24.

[65] *Richard Farmer, gent. v. William Wildye, chandler*, PRO, STAC 8/145/7. For an account of earlier enclosures on the manor of Daventry, see E. M. Leonard, 'The Inclosure of Common Fields in the Seventeenth Century', *Trans. R. Hist. Soc.*, 2nd ser. 18 (1905), 104–6.

In Stratford-upon-Avon, the enclosure of the town commons by Sir Edward Greville, the lord of the borough, provoked the burgesses to elect Richard Quiney as bailiff without seeking Greville's approval. Quiney and several townsmen then levelled the hedges and were prosecuted by Greville for riot. Greville also charged Quiney with levying tolls upon grain sold in the market without any authority for doing so. Their quarrels generated numerous cross-suits: the bailiff attempted to retain the attorney-general, Sir Edward Coke, as his counsel; Greville's wife bragged that she possessed more than enough influence with various judges to prevail. Greville's methods were more violent than those of his wife, and his servants menaced the bailiff who had to take sureties of them to keep the peace. Quiney, a friend of Shakespeare, subsequently died of head wounds inflicted upon him by one of Greville's servants while attempting to stop a brawl.[66]

When Robert Barnard, a barrister, purchased an estate near Huntingdon and became the borough's recorder, he persuaded the common council, which consisted of 24 inhabitants elected annually, to alter the town's government by vesting it in a closed corporation consisting of 13 aldermen elected for life, a mayor, and himself. The burgesses evidently consented to the abolition of democratic government because many found the expense incurred by municipal office-holding burdensome, but were outraged to discover that the revised charter granted by Charles I in 1630 permitted the new oligarchy to restrict rights of common pasture. Oliver Cromwell, a member of the borough commission of the peace, took up the cause of the popular party with such vehemence that he was reprimanded by the Privy Council. The Earl of Manchester was called upon to arbitrate the dispute and recommended restoration of the commoners' pasture rights.[67]

The borough of Malmesbury was disturbed by a series of especially violent enclosure riots between *c.*1590 and 1610. The corporation, consisting of an alderman discharging the functions of a mayor and 12 burgesses, secured the enclosure of the town's commons in order to discourage the influx of unemployed clothing workers. The corporation's first attempt at enclosure in about 1590 was halted

[66] Eccles, *Shakespeare in Warwickshire*, pp. 76–7, 97–9.
[67] Sir Charles Firth, *Oliver Cromwell and the Rule of the Puritans in England* (1900; repr. 1953), 30–2.

by the destruction of the enclosures; renewed efforts to enclose at the beginning of the next reign precipitated riots in 1603, 1606, 1607, 1609, and 1610. The conflict was undoubtedly connected with problems of underemployment and over-production in the Wiltshire woollen industry, and the prosecution of certain clothiers for employing unapprenticed textile workers.[68] The members of the corporation included clothiers, drapers, and glovers, who were described as 'the Richer sort' and 'men that sway the whole towne'. The popular party, made up of fullers and other artisans, refused to recognize the authority of the corporation and claimed that all householders were burgesses, and thus all were seised of the common, known as King's Heath, which had been granted by King Aethelstan in return for their help in repelling the Danish invaders. The leaders of the popular party testified that they had retained Robert Berry, a solicitor, to advise them in opposing the corporation's attempt to enclose King's Heath. Instead, he betrayed his trust and helped the alderman and burgesses to draw up by-laws vesting 300 acres of common land in the hands of the corporation. Mediation by the Bishop of Salisbury supported the new by-laws, and they were confirmed by a Chancery decree obtained from lord chancellor Ellesmere in about 1609 and upheld in another ruling by the Court of Chancery in 1612. Of the 300 acres enclosed, 100 acres were assigned to the exclusive use of the 13 members of the corporation, and the remainder divided among the other three 'companies': the 'four and twenty', the 'landholders', and the 'commoners'. The leaders of the popular party complained that this caused the 'vtter impoverishing of . . . aboue twoe thowsand persons & more, all inhabitants'; the commoners' company henceforth were limited to grazing eight beasts in summer and 50 in winter.[69] At the beginning of this period of strife, the young Thomas Hobbes lived in the borough; he may have acquired his dislike for democracy

---

[68] B. E. Supple, *Commercial Crisis and Change in England, 1600–1642* (Cambridge, 1964), 26–7, 43–5; M. G. Davies, *The Enforcement of English Apprenticeship: A Study in Applied Mercantilism, 1563–1642* (Cambridge, Mass., 1956), 139–40.

[69] *John Cowy, baker* v. *Humphrey Elkington, alderman of Malmesbury*, PRO, STAC 8/93/2; *Robert Evans, glover* v. *Humphrey Elkington*, ibid., STAC 8/138/8; *William Webb, alderman of Malmesbury* v. *Robert Terry the elder*, ibid., STAC 8/290/22; *Humphrey Elkington* v. *Henry Palmer, tiler*, ibid., STAC 8/130/3; *John Cooper, baker* v. *William Hobbes, burgess*, ibid., C. 78/174/5.

from the tumultuous affairs of Malmesbury before he ever read Thucydides.[70]

The shortage of pasture continued to be the single most important cause of anti-enclosure riots during the early seventeenth century. Violent protests against the enclosure of open-field arable, whether for permanent pasture or conversion to up-and-down husbandry, were confined almost entirely to Warwickshire and Northamptonshire. The most significant agrarian trend revealed by this analysis of Jacobean enclosure riots is the encroachment upon commons and wastes by improving landlords, who enclosed this marginal land in order to develop more arable and high-quality pasture. The demand for more pastoral land arose from the grazing requirements of draft animals, the need for manure to maintain or increase corn production, and the need on the part of artisans and cottagers to produce butter and cheese to sustain themselves through the economic crises of this period. There is no evidence of any extension of sheep-grazing to produce more wool. The geographical distribution of enclosure protests produced by shortages of pasture bears a close correlation to those areas, such as the west Midlands, where the expansion of rural industries encouraged the influx of population.

The apparent doubling of the frequency of enclosure riots between 1590 and 1610 emphasizes how serious the late-Elizabethan crises were and suggests that the nature and structure of these crises deserve more investigation. Moreover, the frequent references to the Midland Revolt in the proceedings of the Court of Star Chamber and the wave of sympathetic riots that followed in its wake serve to remind us how divisive the issue of agrarian change and the extinction of use-rights by enclosure in severalty could become.

Tenants increasingly took the initiative in going to law to defend their common rights in the early seventeenth century. In 20 per cent of the enclosure-riot cases in the Jacobean sample, tenants were accused of raising common purses for legal expenses and an even higher proportion retained legal counsel. The arguments that tenants were able to present in defence of their common rights reveal a growing legal sophistication among copyholders despite the evidence that literacy rates remained low among husbandmen. But literacy was almost universal among gentlemen at this time and stood at

[70] Cf. John Aubrey, *Aubrey's Brief Lives*, pp. 147–8.

a high rate among yeomen.[71] Probably two-thirds of gentry households and one-third of yeomanry households possessed books.[72] Thus, effective copyholder resistance still depended upon leadership from gentlemen and yeomen. Both smallholders and townsmen who sought to prevent the enclosure of their commons complained about avaricious lawyers who took on such cases in order to acquire land by fraudulent means. Clients and lawyers both exploited uncertain points in the law of riot, and this produced a reaction among judges who maintained that in riots as in treason 'there be noe Accessories but all [are] principalls.'[73]

The survival of only one bundle of Star Chamber proceedings from the reign of Charles I makes it impossible to undertake a thorough investigation of enclosure riots during that period. There is reason to believe that the Court of Star Chamber continued, at least sporadically, to discourage violence in enclosure disputes, but, at the same time, refused to countenance illegal enclosures. In the Westland Heath enclosure-riot case of 1632, the judges heavily fined the leaders of the riot, but refused to award damages to the plaintiff because 'some of the Defendants had had two Verdicts for Common in the said Ground'.[74] But the most telling evidence about crown policies towards enclosure and the extinction of ancient use-rights comes from a study of royal manors within the Duchy of Lancaster. While the early-Stuart Court of Star Chamber attempted to deal with enclosure disputes in an even-handed manner, the administration of crown estates by the Duchy of Lancaster displayed an official policy of imposing enclosure agreements and improving rents in the face of opposition from the tenants of Duchy lands.

---

[71] D. Cressy, *Literacy and the Social Order: Reading and Writing in Tudor and Stuart England* (Cambridge, 1980), 119, 152–3, 159–62.

[72] P. Clark, 'The Ownership of Books in England, 1560–1640: The Example of Some Kentish Townsfolk', in L. Stone (ed.), *Schooling and Society: Studies in the History of Education* (Baltimore, 1976), 101; see also H. S. Bennett, *English Books and Readers, 1558–1603* (Cambridge, 1965), 159–62, for a discussion of law books written for laymen.

[73] BL, Lansdowne MSS, 639, fo. 39.

[74] *Historical Collections*, ed. Rushworth, ii/2, app., pp. 53–4.

5

Resistance to 'Enclosure by Agreement'

THE method of enclosure favoured by advocates of agricultural improvement was the multilateral enclosure agreement—also known as 'enclosure by commission'. Enclosure by agreement was supposed to incorporate the assent of the lord and freeholders within the manorial or village community. Sometimes the consent of copyholders also was solicited and they were made parties to the agreement, but more frequently they were ignored.[1] The more complicated agreements were drafted by lawyers; surveyors might be brought in to measure and assess the quality of the allotments where the division of open fields necessitated exchanges of land in order to consolidate holdings. In order to guarantee a clear title and to enforce enclosure agreements, a decree in Chancery was increasingly sought; where crown lands were involved, the enclosure agreements were confirmed by decrees from the Court of Exchequer or the Court of Duchy Chamber of the Duchy of Lancaster. Another legal advantage of a decree from the Court of Chancery or other equity court was that it enabled trustees or guardians to consent to enclosure on behalf of their wards and it also bound dissentients to the agreement.[2]

The advantages of enclosure by multilateral agreement were several: without a secure title and exclusive possession lords, farmers, and tenants were unlikely to undertake capital-intensive agricultural improvements. Agricultural land that was enclosed by multilateral agreement was more attractive to prospective buyers or farmers than land still subject to use-rights. Enclosure agreements were also useful in ending intercommoning disputes where more than one manorial or village community shared the waste.

---

[1] Kerridge, *Agrarian Problems*, pp. 103–6, 112–14; *Reports of Cases Decided by Francis Bacon . . . Lord Chancellor in the High Court of Chancery*, ed. J. Ritchie (1932), 184, 187. The exclusion of copyholders from enclosure agreements, in practice, was not as restrictive as it might appear, because the distinction between freeholds and copyholds of inheritance was unclear (the royal courts afforded them the same protection), and because many tenants possessed both freehold and copyhold land and would have been consulted in the former capacity.

[2] Leonard, 'The Inclosure of Common Fields in the Seventeenth Century', p. 109.

But it must not be supposed that the assent of all manorial freeholders and copyholders was easily obtained, despite the assertion by Professor Maurice Beresford that the opposition mentioned in suits, in most instances, was pretended, in order to get the case heard in the Court of Chancery and to secure a decree confirming the enclosure agreement.[3] It has already been noticed in preceding chapters that tenants who agreed in principle to enclosure were dismayed by inequitable apportionment arising from careless surveying, and that resistance to enclosure agreements frequently continued many years after the event.[4] Nor can one assume that all of the land specified in enclosure agreements was, in fact, enclosed. Lack of capital, continuing litigation and anti-enclosure rioting caused many delays. The more participants there were who had to be appeased in the negotiations, the more difficult it was to secure agreement and then compliance. For this reason, compliance with enclosure agreements seems to have been more difficult to secure on larger manors—especially crown manors where the presence of gentlemen-tenants stiffened resistance.

Moreover, the difficulty in securing agreement to enclosure and compliance from customary tenants was sometimes complicated by accompanying tenurial and rent disputes. After the union of the two crowns of England and Scotland in 1603 ended warfare on the Scottish border, manorial lords in northern England began to undermine tenant right, the tenure peculiar to that region which had required the tenant to render military service in the border wars. Lords in other parts of England attempted to compel tenants possessing copyholds of inheritance to exchange them for more economic leaseholds of shorter duration. Also, Eric Kerridge has demonstrated a general upward movement of rents, especially in the late sixteenth and early seventeenth centuries, as landlords demanded higher entry fines for both copyholds and leaseholds. Market conditions were such that outsiders could always be found who were willing to pay the higher rents. Rent increases and modifications of tenure on crown lands had lagged behind practices in estate

---

[3] M. Beresford, 'Habitation Versus Improvement: The Debate on Enclosure by Agreement', in F. J. Fisher (ed.), *Essays in the Economic and Social History of Tudor and Stuart England in Honour of R. H. Tawney* (repr. Cambridge, 1974), 57; id., 'The Decree Rolls of Chancery as a Source for Economic History, 1547–*c*.1700', *Ec. HR*, 2nd ser. 32 (1979), 2–3.

[4] See ch. 3 and ch. 4.

management on non-royal manors during the reign of Elizabeth, and the imposition of economic rents on crown tenants and the rationalization of tenures early in the reign of James I were therefore more abrupt and encountered greater resistance.[5]

Although enclosure by agreement often concealed both coercion by the lord and resistance on the part of the tenants, yet this method of enclosure became more common in the late sixteenth century and had become the usual method in the seventeenth century. Multilateral enclosure agreements confirmed by court decree withstood the scrutiny of the Privy Council, which still employed the Court of Star Chamber sporadically to prosecute illegal enclosures in the late-Elizabethan and early-Stuart periods. Towards the end of the reign of James I government policy began to allow enclosures that could not be proved to be depopulating, and the general increase in corn production removed fears of dearth.[6]

Enclosure by agreement during this period was made possible by the increasing social diversification among copyholders. Landlords in the seventeenth century found that in the long run enclosure schemes encountered less opposition if they sought support from among their more substantial tenants and made them parties to the agreement.[7] This was sometimes done by leasing parcels of newly enclosed waste to these tenants on favourable terms. The fear of poor persons squatting or being settled upon the waste was often as strong a motive for the more prosperous tenants to acquiesce in enclosure as the financial inducements. The poorer tenants, and cottagers who were commoners by custom, were frequently not adequately compensated for their lost use-rights, and they suffered the most from shortages of pasture, fuel, and building materials.

Enclosure agreements were generally harmful to the Church. Glebe lands were swallowed up in exchanges; tithes were commuted to fixed payments in an age of rising prices; common lands set aside for the repair of church fabric might also be lost. So great was the scandal that Archbishop Laud took it to be axiomatic that enclosure agreements were not good for the Church, and began compiling glebe

---

[5] Kerridge, 'The Movement of Rent, 1540–1640', pp. 29–33; F. C. Dietz, *English Public Finance, 1485–1641* (2 vols.; 1964), ii. 298; G. Batho, 'Landlords in England', *AHEW* iv. 269–71.

[6] J. Thirsk, 'Agrarian History, 1540–1640', *VCH Leicester*, ii. 202–3; ead., *AHEW* iv. 237–8, 254–5; *Seventeenth-Century Economic Documents*, ed. Thirsk and Cooper, 121–2.   [7] Ibid.

terriers as a prelude to recovering glebe lands and tithes lost through enclosure. Agricultural improvement produced higher yields, but alterations in land use might increase the great tithes to the benefit of a lay impropriator and reduce the small tithes, to the impoverishment of a vicar.[8] When, in 1620, the rector of Charwelton, Northamptonshire sued to recover tithes and 24 acres of glebe land plus pasture, he complained that the Elizabethan enclosure agreement gave a 70-year lease of those properties to Sir Ewesby Andrew, the manorial lord and patron of the benefice, because Andrew's ancestors had been in the habit of presenting younger sons to the benefice, keeping the tithes and profits from the glebe, and paying the incumbent a small stipend.[9]

Although many suits in the Court of Chancery which sought decrees confirming enclosure agreements were collusive and evidence of opposition fictitious—especially on smaller manors where fewer freeholders had to be persuaded and appeased—Professor Beresford has overstated his case.[10] It is not difficult to discover many cases in the Chancery Decree Rolls where resistance to enclosure was both vehement and protracted. Enclosure agreements confirmed by decrees in Chancery or other equity courts continued to generate so much litigation and hedge-breaking that their legality was questioned, and a bill was introduced in Parliament in 1666 to legalize all enclosure agreements made in the previous 60 years. Thereafter the practice of ratifying enclosure agreements with Chancery decrees declined, and private Acts of Parliament became the preferred means.[11] Moreover, opposition to enclosure was especially widespread and bitter on crown manors, where the situation was exacerbated by tenurial and rent disputes, as the Entry Books of Decrees of the Duchy Court of Lancaster demonstrate. Evidence of widespread anti-enclosure rioting on Duchy of Lancaster manors undergoing enclosure may also be found in the Star Chamber Proceedings. Used together these various kinds of evidence provide several detailed case-studies of both royal and non-royal manors where complex agrarian disputes continued over considerable periods of time.

---

[8] C. Hill, *Economic Problems of the Church from Archbishop Whitgift to the Long Parliament* (Oxford, 1956), 100–5; *Reports of Cases Decided by Francis Bacon*, ed. Ritchie, pp. 183–6.   [9] PRO, C. 78/252/3.
[10] Beresford, 'Habitation Versus Improvement', p. 57; id., 'The Decree Rolls of Chancery', pp. 2–3.
[11] Leonard, 'The Inclosure of Common Fields', pp. 109–110 and n.

Bills of complaint in Star Chamber were frequently filed to initiate cross-suits, and the disputes were often resolved in other courts. The Entry Books of Decrees of the Court of Star Chamber were destroyed after the abolition of that court, but determination of enclosure and tenurial disputes referred to in Star Chamber Proceedings may sometimes be recovered from the Chancery Decree Rolls (PRO, C. 78) and the Entry Books of Decrees of the Court of Duchy Chamber (PRO, DL 5), as well as from draft decrees (PRO, DL 6). The number of cases initiated in Star Chamber had increased from 732 in 44 Elizabeth to over 1000 cases in 2 Charles I, but the court probably never heard more than 50 cases a year. The attorney-generals' prosecutions were usually given precedence, and probably most were heard and determined.[12]

It is likely that the Court of Star Chamber heard fewer cases dealing with violent enclosure disputes in the reign of Charles I, because the Court was devoting more time to cases of seditious libel. Moreover, there are strong indications that official opposition to illegal and depopulating enclosures was weakened by the desire of the Stuart monarchs to raise more revenue. Under James I the officials of the Duchy of Lancaster favoured enclosure and improvement of wastes on duchy manors, no matter how much opposition had to be overcome. In the reign of Charles I the policy of prosecuting perpetrators of depopulating enclosures began to yield to one of allowing the culprits to compound for their offences with fines or even to buy licences to enclose.[13]

Four large manors in Lancashire belonging to the Duchy of Lancaster provide the first group of case-studies. All four involved enclosure of the manorial waste only, and it is worth considering the uses to which the enclosed waste was put. There was some extension of cultivation, and a smaller part of the new arable land appears to have been subjected to convertible husbandry. Agricultural improvement in Lancashire consisted largely of the reclamation of moors, wastes, marshes, and mosses. Reclamation of mosses such as Chat Moss yielded reasonably fertile land that would later prove suitable for potato culture. The draining of mosses was very

---

[12] H. E. I. Phillips, 'The Last Years of the Court of Star Chamber', *Trans. R. Hist. Soc.*, 4th ser. 21 (1938), 113.
[13] M. Beresford, 'The Deserted Villages of Warwickshire', *Trans. Birmingham Arch. Soc.* 66 (1945–6), 60.

expensive and did not prevent periodic flooding. Also, the practice of burning the covering of mosses, together with draining, lowered the level of neighbouring lands. Altogether, the reclamation of wastes in Lancashire proved to be an expensive and sometimes wasteful undertaking, and not infrequently land prepared for tillage had to be returned to permanent pasture.[14]

Much of the waste enclosed and improved for cultivation was divided into tenancies created primarily to produce rents. These were usually sublet to under-tenants in such small parcels that the consequences were more likely to be overpopulation and inefficiency than agricultural innovation.[15] The remaining encroachments on the wastes of these manors resulted in the commercial exploitation of peat and coal. Quite simply, the enclosures in this sample of Lancashire manors reveal some evidence of agricultural innovation, and abundant evidence of a seigneurial assault upon the resources of commons and wastes, rent exploitation, and a movement to abolish perpetual tenures. These last three tendencies were characteristic of a 'seigneurial reaction', or fiscal seigneurialism, which was taking place all over Europe in the sixteenth and seventeenth centuries.[16] The ninth Earl of Northumberland, when presented with the choice of converting to up-and-down husbandry or raising rents, chose the latter because it was easier. When he discovered that his tenants on the manor of Petworth could not be evicted because they possessed copyholds of inheritance, he instead ruthlessly exploited the resources of the wastes and commons. He cut timber worth £20,000 within the space of a few years, and scarred the commons with pits where he had dug iron-stone.[17] The officials of the Duchy of Lancaster made the same choices and preferred immediate increases in revenue to long-term agricultural improvement.

[14] T. W. Fletcher, 'The Agrarian Revolution in Arable Lancashire', *Trans. Lancs. Ches. Antiquarian Soc.* 72 (1962), 94-7.

[15] J. Thirsk, 'The Farming Regions of England', *AHEW* iv. 85-6; G. E. Tupling, *The Economic History of Rossendale* (Chetham Soc. 86; 1927), 70-97.

[16] M. Bloch, *French Rural History: An Essay on its Basic Characteristics*, trans. J. Sondheimer (Berkeley, Calif., 1966), 102-27, 182-5; Appleby, 'Agrarian Capitalism or Seigneurial Reaction?', p. 592; id., 'Common Land and Peasant Unrest in Sixteenth-century England', pp. 20-3. Dr Appleby noted the same tendency in Cumberland and Westmorland towards impopulation as a consequence of tenancies on enclosed parcels of the waste being sublet to under-tenants.

[17] G. R. Batho, 'The Finances of an Elizabethan Nobleman: Henry Percy, Ninth Earl of Northumberland (1564-1632)', *Ec. HR*, 2nd ser. 9 (Apr. 1957), 436, 441; Jerrome, *Cloakbag and Common Purse*, pp. 32-4.

The agrarian conflict on the manor of Nether Wyresdale, Lancashire began with an attack on tenant-right tenure and the imposition of very high entry fines; this was followed by nearly total enclosure of a large waste. All of these seigneurial oppressions encountered stubborn resistance from the tenants, but ultimately prevailed. The crown moiety of Nether Wyresdale, in Amounderness Hundred, had been acquired by Sir Gilbert Gerard, Master of the Rolls, in 1574, and was inherited by his son and heir, Sir Thomas Gerard, Baron Gerard of Gerard's Bromley, Staffordshire, who purchased the other moiety in 1602. The disputes with the tenants of Wyresdale began immediately following the death of Lord Gerard's father in February 1593 and spread to the neighbouring manors of Carneforth and Scotforth, which he had also inherited. Lord Gerard denied the existence of tenant-right tenure, which meant that tenants could sell, bequeath, or lease their lands without permission of the lord, and asserted that the tenures were merely tenancies at will. Lord Gerard sued seven of the leading tenants of the three manors in the Court of Duchy Chamber in November 1593. The seven tenants held capital messuages totalling 800 acres between them, and Gerard alleged that they had obtained possession of the manorial court rolls and, together with 100 other tenants, conspired to enter forged conveyances by tenant right in the court rolls. When Gerard offered them leases for 21 years or three lives, they refused and bound themselves together by secret oaths to raise a common purse and defend their tenant-right tenure, which they claimed was the custom not only of the three manors but of adjoining manors as well. The trial lasted through 1593 and 1594 with many hearings; the officers of the Duchy Court made it clear that they inclined towards Lord Gerard's position that the tenant-right tenures were void. The tenants' plea of tenant-right tenure appears to have been referred to a common-law court for trial, but in the end the Court of Duchy Chamber disallowed it and ordered them to compound with Lord Gerard and accept leases for years or lives.[18]

Once Lord Gerard had consolidated seigneurial jurisdiction over the entire manor of Nether Wyresdale in 1602, he proceeded to enclose the waste (evidently under the provisions of the Statutes of

---

[18] *VCH Lancaster*, vii. 303; *Sir Thomas Gerard* v. *William Baines*, PRO, DL 1/163/G3, DL 5/21, pp. 5, 19; *Thomas, Lord Gerard* v. *Tenants of Nether Wyresdale*, ibid., DL 5/23, pp. 851–3.

Merton and Westminster of 1235 and 1285, which required that
the lord leave sufficient waste to allow the tenants to exercise their
common rights unabridged).[19] The land enclosed was leased to
substantial tenants at 12*d*. an acre for 21 years with entry fines of
40*s*. per acre or 40 years' improved rent. Enclosed and improved
waste in Lancashire was generally considered to be worth 4*d*. to 6*d*.
an acre in large parcels;[20] the courts considered entry fines of two
years' improved rent to be reasonable for copyholders of inheritance,
but two and a half years' rent was thought to be excessive.[21] The
entry fines and rents for leaseholds of enclosed parcels of waste that
Gerard offered to old tenants might seem extortionate, yet they were
apparently attractive and were meant to buy support among the
substantial tenants. This apparent paradox is explained by the fact
that the substantial tenants could sublease their leaseholds in small
parcels of an acre or so to under-tenants at many times the value
of the rents they paid to Gerard. Lord Gerard defended his enclosure
project before the Court of Star Chamber as a scheme for promoting
improved husbandry and setting idle people to work, but he makes
it clear that he leased only to old tenants. Had he rented directly
to new tenants, he said, he could have obtained entry fines of double
the amount of 40 years' improved rent. Instead, he allowed the
substantial old tenants to share the profits of exploiting the poor.
Having bought the support of some of the substantial tenants with
'easye and moderat ffynes', Gerard concluded an enclosure agreement
by indenture with them on 20 February 1603. It is clear that most
of the tenants were not parties to the agreement.[22]

The tenants who had been excluded from the negotiations for
enclosure protested violently. Two riots, on Shrove Tuesday, 21
February, and 17 April 1604 destroyed a total of 400 rods of
enclosures. Sixteen women, alleged to have been procured by their
husbands, perpetrated the first riot; the second riot included at least

---

[19] Kerridge, *Agrarian Problems*, p. 94.

[20] Tupling, *The Economic History of Rossendale*, p. 63.

[21] Prof. Kerridge says that the courts did not rule on the reasonableness of entry
fines for leaseholds or copyholds for life; these were entirely at the will of the lord
and reflected market conditions: *Agrarian Problems*, p. 39. Cf. also the dispute about
manorial customs and entry fines on the manor at Audley, Staffordshire, in which
Lord Gerard was admonished by Lord Chancellor Ellesmere not to demand unreasonable entry fines (ch. 6).

[22] *Thomas, Lord Gerard v. William Sykes the elder*, PRO, STAC 8/153/3.

25 participants.[23] The resistance was led by a gentleman, Robert Plessington, who told the protesters 'that woemen were lawles and . . . might boldly without anie ffear of punishment pull downe the hedges and ditches'; others spread rumours that Lord Gerard had been killed and 'that yt was a tyme wherein there was no lawe by reason of her Maiesties death'.[24]

The interrogatories administered by the Court of Star Chamber reveal the motives for opposition to the enclosure agreement. Some tenants were resentful because they had not been consulted; others complained that the enclosures hindered access to the remaining waste. One tenant said that the enclosure scheme might have been a good idea if the enclosed waste had been let to the poorer inhabitants at reasonable entry fines. Plessington said the real issue was not whether the waste should be enclosed, but rather it concerned the equitable division of the waste. There was also disagreement concerning how much waste was actually enclosed, since Lord Gerard undertook his scheme under the provisions of the Statutes of Merton and Westminster, which allowed the lord, as owner of the soil of the waste, to make intakes or approvements provided adequate waste was left to the tenants. Lord Gerard had told the Court of Star Chamber that he was enclosing 1,000 out of 8,000 acres. Plessington thought that the total area of the waste amounted to only 3,000 acres and that the better part of it had been enclosed. A Duchy of Lancaster survey of 1605 revealed that only 21 acres of commons remained unenclosed, and the whole manor consisted of only 4,215 statute acres in the nineteenth century.[25] It seems fairly clear that Lord Gerard had lied both to the Court of Star Chamber and to the Duchy Chamber when he said that he had enclosed only one-eighth of a waste consisting of 8,000 acres.

[23] Star Chamber was still interrogating defendants in Jan. 1605. John Carlons, husbandman, was questioned because his wife Janet was named a defendant. He had ignored previous subpoenas to appear before the court and had gone into hiding. He was arrested by Lord Gerard's officers on a warrant from Star Chamber and imprisoned. He claimed that his lawyer had told him that he need not answer because he was not himself named a defendant in the bill of complaint. When interrogated about his complicity in the first enclosure riot, he said that the Court would have to prove that Janet Carlons was his wife. Carlons also complained about being made to walk 12 miles to Preston, having to pay for a copy of the bill of complaint, which was 'exceedingly Tedious and longe', and being required to post £100 surety guaranteeing his appearance in London: PRO, STAC 8/153/2.   [24] Ibid.
[25] Ibid., STAC 8/153/3, DL 5/23, pp. 851–3; Edward Baines, *The History of the County Palatine and Duchy of Lancaster*, ed. J. Croston (5 vols.; 1893), v. 428.

Eighty-six tenants had originally sealed the enclosure agreement by indenture, and five more subsequently assented. On 16 November 1604 the Duchy Court indicated that it favoured the enclosure agreement:

> this courte dothe think it very hard and not agreeable to equitie that a matter so beneficiall to the said Lord and tenauntes brought to soe new a poynt of perfection tendinge soe apparantly to publique good and agreed and consented vnto by soe greate a number vnder theire hands and seales should be diverted and frustrated by a few humorouse and contentiouse persons.[26]

The court therefore issued an injunction compelling assent to the agreement by the remainder of the tenants and established a commission consisting of three local gentry to see that the agreement was carried out. However, in May 1605 the Court noted that there were still numerous incidents of hedge-breaking and illegal digging of peat on the enclosed waste; three tenants were imprisoned in the Fleet Prison in London for continuing to oppose the enclosure agreement.[27]

On the manor of Penwortham, in the hundred of Leyland, intakes and enclosures on the waste had been made in piecemeal fashion since the time of Henry VIII and Edward VI. Sir Henry Farrington, who was the steward of the manor in those days of more lax administration of the Duchy of Lancaster, had been permitted to enclose portions of Penwortham Moss and create demesne copyholds, which the tenants regarded as inheritable estates. In 1567, the stewardship, along with the seigneurial jurisdiction, came into the hands of William Fleetwood, who recently had purchased the former priory of Penwortham. Sir Henry Farrington's son and heir, William, was the farmer of the manor of Penwortham, but continued to lay claim to the seigneurial jurisdiction that his father had exercised. Perceiving the increasing value of peat as a fuel, he began treating the demesne copyholds as tenancies at will and attempting to expel the tenants and seize the profits of the demesne tenancies, as well as exploiting the unenclosed parts of the waste.[28] The first William

---

[26] PRO, DL 5/23, pp. 851–3.   [27] Ibid., pp. 879–80.
[28] Sir Robert Somerville, *History of the Duchy of Lancaster* (2 vols.; 1953), i. 505; Baines, *County Palatine and Duchy of Lancaster*, iv. 206; *Robert Charnock v. William Farrington*, PRO, DL 6/33, unsorted draft decrees, 27 Eliz. For a discussion of demesne copyholds, which were, strictly speaking, tenancies at will, see Kerridge, *Agrarian Problems*, pp. 86–90. For a discussion of commercial peat digging, in

Farrington's son, William II, became the farmer of Penwortham in about 1602, and enclosed another 40 acres of Penwortham Moss, which was leased to a tenant for coppicing and commercial peat-digging. William Farrington II's peat-digging operations left many 'mosspits', which filled with water, and created hazards for the cattle and sheep belonging to the other tenants. These other tenants also complained about the abridgement of their common rights of pasture and turbary, and eight of them sought revenge in February 1604 by destroying Farrington's new enclosures.[29] Richard Fleetwood also claimed the seigneurial jurisdiction, and it is quite probable that he encouraged the rioters, because Farrington had sought to expel Fleetwood and his tenants from enclosures that Fleetwood's father had made on Penwortham Moss. Farrington persisted in regarding Fleetwood and his tenants as tenants at will; Fleetwood, for his part, boasted to the Duchy Court that Farringtons had always been tenants of Fleetwoods. The decree handed down by the Court of Duchy Chamber in 1608 recognized Fleetwood's jurisdiction in the manorial court of Penwortham and confirmed the enclosures made by Fleetwood's father, as well as Fleetwood's title to them.[30]

In addition to the lordship of Penwortham, Richard Fleetwood also possessed the seigneurial jurisdiction of the neighbouring duchy manor of Farrington, which he exploited for all it was worth. Emulating his rival, William Farrington, he dug large amounts of peat on Penwortham Moss. This provoked violent protest from those who viewed with alarm the rapidly dwindling fuel resources of the waste. Several gentlemen-tenants led their subtenants in riots in 1610 and 1612, which destroyed 200 wagon-loads of turves stacked for drying. In a third riot, the same persons also destroyed hedges environing approvements upon which Fleetwood had settled tenants in order to grow corn. The attacks upon Fleetwood's intakes from the waste continued as late as 1614, when he found it necessary to seek a decree in the Court of Duchy Chamber in order to confirm the enclosures, which had been made in the 1590s. Fleetwood's

competition with coal-mining, see J. Langton, *Geographical Change and Industrial Revolution: Coalmining in South West Lancashire* (Cambridge, 1979), 56–7, 101–2.

[29] *William Farrington of Worden, esq.* v. *William Hollinhurst*, PRO, STAC 8/144/12.

[30] *Richard Fleetwood, esq.* v. *William Farrington, esq.*, ibid., DL 5/24, pp. 657–9.

amercement of his tenants for failure to give suit to the manorial court also contributed to the conflict.[31]

The duchy manor of Sutton, located in the parish of Prescott and the hundred of West Derby, provides another instance of two rival families disputing possession of the seigneurial jurisdiction and bequeathing that feud to the next generation. The conflict was also fed by the protests of the freehold tenants against the settlement of new tenants on the waste and the commercial exploitation of Sutton Heath for coal and peat. Ultimately, the duchy imposed an enclosure agreement upon the manorial lord, Richard Bold, and the tenants in an attempt to restore peace.

Richard Bold's seat was at Old Bold Hall, which he rebuilt in 1616. The Bolds were a predatory family who gathered into their hands numerous manors formerly belonging to their neighbours. Richard Eltonhead and William Holland questioned Bold's title to the seigneurial jurisdiction of Sutton and attempted to establish their own claim to the lordship by accusing Bold of concealing crown lands. Both Eltonhead and Holland were freeholders on the manor and their families had long resided in the parish of Prescott. Holland's family lived in the manor house of Sutton in the reign of Elizabeth, and Eltonhead's great uncle had disputed possession of the seigneurial jurisdiction with Bold's uncle. The elder Bold's title to the lordship had been upheld in 26 Elizabeth by the Court of Duchy Chamber and that court and the common-law courts had ruled in the younger Bold's favour more recently. The Duchy Court dismissed Eltonhead's case in 1619.[32]

Eltonhead and Holland were discouraged from bringing any more suits in the Court of Duchy Chamber, but they found it easy to stir up the smaller freehold tenants. The Duchy Court noted that 16 anti-enclosure riots were directed against Bold between August 1619 and June 1620. Bold, in a Star Chamber suit, alleged that there were actually 18, and they were all procured by Eltonhead and Thomas Worsley, whom he described as 'ringleaders'.[33] The

---

[31] *Richard Fleetwood, esq. v. Joseph Huddleston, esq.*, ibid., STAC 8/139/28; BL, Lansdowne MSS, 639, fo. 39; *Richard Fleetwood v. Francis Orrell, gent.*, PRO, DL 5/27, fos. 61, 67, 89.

[32] Baines, *County Palatine and Duchy of Lancaster*, v. 21–3; *Rex, ex relation. Richard Eltonhead, gent. v. Richard Bold, esq.*, PRO, DL 5/28, fos. 198ᵛ–199, 201ᵛ.

[33] Since it is difficult to determine where one enclosure riot ends and another begins in a sequence of riots, I have made it a practice, for statistical purposes, to

defendants regarded Bold's enclosures on the waste as illegal—even though some of them had stood for 40 or 60 years. They said that they had initiated numerous suits in the Duchy Chamber and common-law courts in order to recover their commons. They felt that the various lawsuits had failed to obtain justice, and they could not afford to continue paying legal costs. After consulting with 'counsell learned in the lawes',

they were advysed and directed by there said counsell that they might in peacible and quiet manner, beinge not aboue the number of towe at a tyme, not weaponed, nor with anye other to aide and assiste them, pull downe in peacible manner the said Inclosures.

This advice they followed. Although they claimed to have worked in peaceful fashion, they asserted that they were assaulted several times by Richard Bold and his servants. Richard Eltonhead, in his answer, still maintained that the freeholders did not recognize Bold as the manorial lord and denied that Bold had any title to the waste. Eltonhead claimed that by right of his holdings he was entitled to one-quarter of the waste and that some of his claims to common of pasture and turbary had been let to his under-tenants along with their messuages.[34]

The 1620 suit in the Court of Duchy Chamber was filed by eight tenants, who were recognized as freeholders and 'charterers'.[35] They alleged that Bold had settled 25 new tenants on the waste and had also dug extensive coalpits and mosspits on the waste, which endangered their cattle and greatly diminished their access to common of pasture. The court's decree upheld Bold's right to mine coal, 'which is an vsuall thing for the Lords of waste to doe in that cuntrey', but also ruled that Bold was obliged to fence off the coalpits to prevent harm to cattle and to fill in the pits when he was finished. The court issued several injunctions ordering Bold to fill in the abandoned pits, to no avail.[36] It was probably for this offence that Bold was fined £20 by the Court of Star Chamber in Easter term 1632.[37]

count only one riot per month. Thus Table 4.1 includes only six of these riots. It was the practice of Star Chamber to count one riot per day for each specified location.

[34] *Richard Bold* v. *Richard Eltonhead*, PRO, STAC 8/70/12; *Richard Roughey* v. *Richard Bold*, ibid., DL 5/28, fos. 310ᵛ–311, 313.

[35] Cheshire and Lancashire dialect for freeholder.

[36] PRO, DL 5/28, fo. 345.

[37] T. G. Barnes, 'Fines in the High Court of Star Chamber, 1596–1641' (typescript list in PRO Round Room), 150.

Here was a dispute that was likely to continue generating both violence and litigation. The duchy officials decided that an enclosure agreement was the best way to impose peace, and a local commission was established in 1622 to survey the manor and draw up articles of agreement. It is significant that it took 12 years to hammer out that agreement. Total enclosure of the waste probably appealed to the freeholders because it would impose some limitations upon Bold's depredations. As finally decreed by the Court of Duchy Chamber in June 1634, the enclosure agreement gave 24 acres of the waste to Bold and the remainder was to be divided up among Eltonhead and the freeholders in proportion to the sizes of their messuages. Several mosses were reserved as a source of peat for the freeholders as well as a bowling green. Bold was to have no access to the approvements allotted to the freeholders except for digging coal, which he could do almost anywhere because he was still lord of the soil of the manor. The only restriction placed upon his mining activities was that he could not dig in or under any of the common ways or lanes of the manor.[38]

On the duchy manor of Raunds, Northamptonshire, an officer of the crown used his influence to secure permission of the Duchy of Lancaster to enclose intakes from the waste and hold them in severalty. Two decades later the tenants of the manor destroyed those enclosures. Subsequently, the duchy officials discovered several defects in the tenants' tenures and threatened to void their estates. The tenants were compelled to offer a composition to the crown in order to obtain copyholds of inheritance and to submit to an agreement for total enclosure.

Robert Gage, an attorney of the Court of Common Pleas and the clerk of the peace for Northamptonshire who held the neighbouring 'Gage's Manor', had enclosed 17 acres from the waste of the manor of Raunds in about 1582. Gage testified that an enclosure agreement in which he made compensation to the tenants of Raunds for lost common rights had been confirmed by the Court of Duchy Chamber. Gage was also appointed a local commissioner to divide up the land specified in the enclosure agreement between himself and two other persons. The tenants emphatically denied that any of them had ever been a party to such an agreement or had received compensation.

[38] *Richard Eltonhead v. Richard Bold*, PRO, DL 5/31, fos. 600ʳ&ᵛ; J. U. Nef, *The Rise of the British Coal Industry* (2 vols.; repr. 1966), i. 305–9.

Moreover, Gage had also obtained indictments against the tenants of Raunds for attempting to exercise their right of shack on the unenclosed common fields of the manor after harvest. The tenants were too poor to go to law to recover their lost use-rights. But when Gage denied them access to a common pathway across the waste to the village church, they were moved to violent protest. Led by Michael Pickering, a gentleman-copyholder, and by the village constable, the 'greatest parte of the nowe inhabitaunts of Raunds' destroyed Gage's enclosures in November 1603 and depastured their cattle in Gage's closes. They were resisted by Gage and his family and servants, who impounded some of the cattle, and these were then forcibly rescued by Pickering's son. The encounter was especially bloody and several of the combatants sustained serious wounds. The defendants' answers emphasized that Gage was a covetous man. Gage himself noted that while three persons had benefited from the 1582 enclosure agreement, his were the only enclosures destroyed.[39]

When Gage prosecuted Pickering and the other tenants in the Court of Star Chamber for riot, Pickering countered with a suit complaining of illegal enclosures of royal demesne land. The Star-Chamber judges appear to have considered recommending that the defendants be prosecuted for treason, probably because of allegations made by Gage that the rioters included persons from 'other neighbouring Townshipps'. This motion was rejected, and the judges, in answer to Gage's accusation of maintenance, allowed that 'In a common cause it is lawfull to make a common purse'.[40] The controversy left a legacy of bitterness in the community: ten years later a relative of one of the tenants was part of a conspiracy to accuse Robert Gage's younger son, Thomas, of burglary.[41]

There was a danger in making themselves conspicuous as the tenants of Raunds and other crown tenants soon realized. The officials of the Duchy of Lancaster discovered that the manorial steward, Robert Castle, esq., and his predecessors had been careless about protecting the interests of the crown. The manorial stewards and under-stewards had accepted the tenants' assertion that their estates were copyholds of inheritance demisable at the will of the

---

[39] *Robert Gage, gent.* v. *Michael Pickering, gent.*, PRO, STAC 8/159/16; *Michael Pickering* v. *Robert Gage*, STAC 8/241/21.

[40] BL, Stowe MSS, 397, fo. 9.

[41] *Thomas Gage, gent.* v. *John Saunderson, yeoman*, PRO, STAC 8/160/30.

tenant, that the entry fines were certain and fixed by custom at one year's rent, and that the sum was also fixed by custom. The stewards had granted a large part of the demesne and waste as copyholds of inheritance, which was illegal. Furthermore, copyholds were not surrendered in the manorial court upon alienation but could be surrendered to any two copyholders who straightened it out with the steward subsequently—sometimes as much as a year after the lands had, in fact, changed hands. The customary tenants not only conveyed their holdings as they pleased, but entailed them and made and broke uses at will. Small wonder that Castle was dismissed.[42]

Perhaps no body of tenants in England had rendered themselves so vulnerable to the crown's policy of fiscal seigneurialism as those of the manor of Raunds. A survey of the manor was probably under way when, in June 1618, the leading tenants offered to the duchy a composition of 40 years' ancient rent to compensate for past entry fines declared to be due to the crown and to make entry fines certain and fixed in future.[43] The composition was accepted and the entry fines established at one year's rent for copyholds alienated. Tenants who had not originally petitioned to be allowed to compound could not be compelled to pay the composition; if they did not subscribe their entry fines were to be set at two and a half years' rent. The old tenants were to pay one half of the composition after obtaining a decree from the Court of Duchy Chamber and 'the other half vpon an act of Parliament for establishing the said composition'. In future, new tenants were to pay the composition in instalments.[44]

It was probably after the manorial survey had been completed that Sir Edward Moseley, attorney-general of the Duchy of Lancaster, prosecuted all of the customary tenants of Raunds for fraud and declared that 'theire severall estates were voyde in lawe'. Moseley specifically charged that the tenants' claim to hold demesne copyholds was fraudulent, that they did not possess copyholds of inheritance because most of their land was held by 'bondhold' tenure, which was devisable only for life or lives with no right of inheritance, and that they had trespassed upon the King's demesne by falsely claiming

---

[42] *R. v. Customary Tenants of Raunds*, PRO, DL 5/27, fo. 1285ʳ&ᵛ; *R. v. William Catelyn, esq., and Customary Tenants of Raunds*, ibid., DL 5/28, fos. 73–78ᵛ.

[43] These tenants included Robert Gage's heir, John Gage, esq., and William Catelyn, esq., lord of the manor of Furnells in Raunds: *VCH Northampton*, iv. 32.

[44] PRO, DL 5/27, fo. 1285ʳ&ᵛ.

common of pasture.[45] They had also committed perjury by making false presentments regarding manorial custom to the court baron.[46]

Moseley's prosecution was a naked ploy to compel all tenants to agree to pay the composition of 40 years' ancient rent, which, it was calculated, would yield £1,640 to the Crown. The whole body of tenants had no choice but to compound. In return the Court of Duchy Chamber would confirm all copyhold, customary, and bondhold lands, as well as demesne tenancies, as ancient copyholds.[47] It would also recognize the tenants' title to common rights on the remainder of the waste. In order to avoid a multiplicity of lawsuits the duchy also required the tenants to agree to total enclosure of the common fields and to make such exchanges of land (including freehold land) as the enclosure commissioners might appoint. The tenants of the adjacent manors of Chelston and Colcott were also ordered to adhere to the composition and enclosure agreement. Tenants who did not join the composition and enclosure agreement or who defaulted in payment of the composition would forfeit their lands.[48] The Act of Parliament confirming the decree of the Court of Duchy Chamber was passed in the Parliament of 1624.[49]

On the manor of Ingleton in the West Riding of Yorkshire, a seigneurial attack upon the tenants' claim to hold their estates by tenant right was unsuccessful, but the legal costs to which the tenants were put in defending their tenures so exhausted their financial resources that they could not offer effective resistance to seigneurial encroachments on the waste. They were forced to submit to an enclosure agreement which they did not desire in order to secure peace. But the enclosure agreement was so complicated and imperfectly devised that it disrupted the exercise of common rights by the tenants of other manors throughout the honour of Skipton.

---

[45] Alexander Savine considered bondhold land to be a survival of base tenure, and stated that it usually carried with it higher entry fines than customary tenure: 'English Customary Tenure in the Tudor Period', *Quarterly Journal of Economics* 19 (1905), 48–9. The defendants pleaded that the diversity of tenures and tenurial customs was confusing; they admitted that freehold, copyhold, and bondhold land lay 'promiscuously intermingled' in the common arable fields: PRO, DL 5/28, fos. 73–78ᵛ.   [46] Ibid.

[47] The reason why the tenants offered a composition of 40 years' rent is that possession for 40 years was required in order to make an 'ancient' copyhold (information courtesy of Dr Stuart Jenks).

[48] PRO, DL 5/28, fos. 73–78ᵛ.

[49] 21 Jac. I, c. 2, *SR* iv. 1210–11.

The tenants of Ingleton claimed to possess tenant-right estates, for which they paid fixed and certain fines and rents, as well as the right to exercise common of pasture and turbary on Ingleton Moor. The lord of the manor, Richard Cholmondeley, maintained that their claims 'were not sufficient in lawe' and proceeded to institute suits at common law against them. The tenants sought relief in the Court of Chancery and obtained a decree in 1592 confirming their tenant-right tenures and their common rights. The Chancery decree also fixed the fine upon alienation at 15 years' rent, seven years' rent for an inheritance, and one year's rent when a new lord of the manor succeeded, together with 'a runninge girsome [gressum]' of two years' rent payable every seven years. In addition, the decree ordered the tenants to pay Cholmondeley £600 'in consideration of the perpetuall establishinge and confirmation of the said customes'. When Richard Cholmondeley II succeeded his father he immediately began to challenge their tenures with lawsuits and 'to take vpp, ymprove and enclose the greatest parte of the saide moores and common'; the tenants countered with another complaint in Chancery against Richard Cholmondeley II and against Gerard Lowther, lord of the manor of Calcoates or Cold Cotes, who was also encroaching upon Ingleton Moor. The Court of Chancery in 1608 once again upheld their tenures and claims to common rights.[50]

Gerard Lowther continued to encroach upon Ingleton Moor in defiance of the Chancery decree of 1608 and vexed the tenants with many lawsuits. Moreover, sometime between 1608 and 1611 he purchased the manor of Ingleton from Richard Cholmondeley II. The tenants of Ingleton and Calcoates,

beinge wearyred and ympoverished with longe suites and verie desirous to live in peace and to give theire landlords anye satisfaction, did conclude and agree with the said Gerrarde Lowther for the ymproveinge and takinge vpp of parte of the saide common and wastes by the saide Gerarde Lowther to holde to his own vse and profitts, and that the complaynauntes might have some other parte of the saide common and moores to be inclosed and laide

---

[50] *Thomas Holmes and tenants of Ingleton and Calcoates v. Gerard Lowther, esq.*, PRO, C. 78/192/14. R. W. Hoyle's excellent essay, containing an independent study of the manor of Ingleton, came to my attention after I had completed this chapter: 'Lords, Tenants, and Tenant Right in the Sixteenth Century: Four Studies', *NH* 20 (1984), 48–52.

to theire tenementes . . . to hold in customarie estate in suche sorte as they
holde theire tenements. . . .[51]

Because the articles of agreement required negotiations and adjust-
ments of common rights with the lords and tenants of several
neighbouring manors, the final agreement was not drawn up until
January 1611. The arbitrator, Serjeant Richard Hutton, proposed
that Lowther and the tenants of Ingleton and Calcoates enclose and
divide between them 215 acres. The tenants of the two manors would
give up all common rights on Ingleton Moor except the right of
turbary in one small mosspit; in future they were to confine their
rough grazing to more distant and less desirable fells or outmoors.
Fifty acres would be yielded to the lords and tenants of the manors
of Twistleton and Scales in exchange for the latter giving up their
right to intercommon on the portion of Ingleton Moor that was
to be enclosed. The lord of Twistleton was to make additional
satisfaction to the tenants of Scales for lost use-rights. The tenants
of Ingleton would also agree to cede their use-rights on other moors
to the tenants of three other manors in the parish of Bentham. When
the final covenants were ready for signing, Lowther changed his mind
and refused to affix his signature. He ignored two Chancery decrees
ordering his adherence before he finally submitted in November
1612. The tenants told Lord Chancellor Ellesmere that the enclosure
agreement was meant to protect them from Lowther's encroachments
on the waste.[52]

Through a misunderstanding, a parcel of land belonging to the
tenants of Calcoates, known as the Two Penny Lands, had been
included in the 215 acres enclosed on Ingleton Moor. Therefore the
enclosure agreement of 1612 had to be amended once again in 1616.
The Two Penny Lands had been enclosed 80 years earlier by the
tenants of Calcoates in order to exclude other villagers, but were
held as common pasture rather than being divided into severalty.
The Two Penny Lands were now to be held in severalty and the
Calcoates tenants were compensated with other enclosed land. The
new parcel of enclosed waste allotted to the tenants of Calcoates was
to be held in severalty by tenant-right tenure, but was not to be
subject to entry fines. This was because Lowther, who had been made

[51] Ibid. The tenants of Calcoates also held their estates by tenant right.
[52] Ibid.; *AHEW* iv. 30.

a justice of the Irish Court of Common Pleas in 1610, had sold a half interest in the seigneurial rights to Sir Ralph Bosville, who, in turn, had leased them to the tenants of Calcoates.[53]

In the Vale of Berkeley in Gloucestershire, the paternalistic Lords Berkeley and their freehold tenants co-operated in various enclosure schemes to protect their interests against the influx of large numbers of poor people, but resistance to enclosure on the part of the poorer inhabitants continued for at least sixty years. The Berkeley estates lay in a pastoral-sylvan region and consisted, for the most part, of abundant wastes with lush grazing and woodland pasture well supplied with oaks. The extravagance of Henry, thirteenth Lord Berkeley (1534–1613), had forced him to sell off lands worth £41,000 over a period of 60 years. Much of these lands, and the leases of the remaining Berkeley estates, came into the hands of the Countess of Warwick and Sir Robert Sidney, Viscount Lisle and later Earl of Leicester; their hostile presence and indiscriminate leasing policies contributed to many intercommoning disputes. Lord Lisle's sale of timber from Micklewood Chase led to the erection there of a furnace and a forge that drew poor charcoal burners and iron workers from the Forest of Dean. The wastes and parks attracted squatters and bands of deer-stealers, while riverine poachers impinged upon Lord Berkeley's valuable fishing rights in the Severn River, which extended to mid-channel. Tenants and farmers subdivided and subleased approved parcels of waste and woodland to large numbers of under-tenants. The Civil Wars brought marauding soldiers and other landless persons into the Vale of Berkeley and resulted in further depredations.[54]

In the parish of Slimbridge there was a large waste, consisting of the Old Warth and the New Warth, or the 'newly gained groundes', which had been deposited by the flow of the Severn. This waste was shared by the freeholders, copyholders, and leaseholders of four manors including Frampton and Slimbridge. Intercommoning disputes were frequent and there was an enclosure riot in May 1598. The New Warth came to be held by Lord Lisle, who leased it to farmers; their attempt to enclose the New Warth and tax the inhabitants for

[53] *Sir Ralph Bosville of Bradbourne, Kent and tenants of Calcoates v. Gerard Lowther, esq., Justice of the Common Pleas in Ireland*, PRO, C. 78/249/6; *DNB*, s.v. Sir Gerard Lowther (d. 1624).
[54] Smyth, *The Berkeley Manuscripts*, ii. 265, iii. 296–300, 328, 354–5; PRO, C. 78/142/7, C. 78/517/2, 3.

rights of pasture provoked another riot in 1610. In 1631 the government uncovered a conspiracy, led by a soldier from Frampton, to destroy the enclosures again; the Gloucestershire justices investigated a rumour that the leading culprits were lieutenants of John Williams, the leader of the 'Lady Skimington' Riots in the Forest of Dean.[55] The many 'beggarly cottages, inmates, and alehouses and idle people' that crowded the waste alarmed Lord Berkeley's steward, the antiquarian John Smyth of Nibley; he wrote in 1639 that the parish was ripe for total enclosure and division of the Warth in severalty as King Charles was doing in the Forest of Dean. In 1646, 'diverse disorderly persons, taking advantage of the late warres' destroyed the enclosures surrounding 300 acres of the New Warth, which had been made in 1610, and burnt numerous cottages. The rioters appear to have come mostly from the Manor of Frampton. In an attempt to restore peace, George Berkeley volunteered to open up 80 acres of his own lands on the New Warth in order to satisfy the claims of the men of Frampton to exercise common of pasture there. He obtained the assent of 178 tenants of the four manors and secured confirmation of the agreement with a decree in Chancery in 1652.[56]

The benevolent George Berkeley maintained a flexible attitude in attempting to settle enclosure disputes among his tenants. Micklewood Chase, a forest of 500 acres which was parcel of the demesne of the manor of Alkington, had been largely denuded of its valuable oaks while it was in the hands of Lady Warwick and Lord Lisle, and Henry, Lord Berkeley, had cut more timber to help pay his debts. In order to protect the remaining oaks and their valuable mast and to exclude outsiders, the freehold and copyhold tenants petitioned Lord Berkeley in 1611 for an enclosure agreement. The chase also included a deer-park of 100 acres, but the pales were in disrepair and permitted the deer to stray into the common pasture. Lord Berkeley disparked the deer-park and removed the deer and fences to other parks. A new, enclosed common pasture of 100 acres was marked off for the tenants; the remaining 400 acres were enclosed in severalty and leased to 'divers tenants'. During the Civil Wars the oak trees in the common pasture were much wasted—apparently by soldiers

---

[55] *John Clifford, esq.* v. *Martin Flower*, PRO, STAC 7/11/2; *Cal. SP, Dom., 1631–1632*, 87–8; B. Sharp, *In Contempt of All Authority: Rural Artisans and Riot in the West of England, 1586–1660* (Berkeley, Calif., 1980), 105–7.

[56] Smyth, *The Berkeley Manuscripts*, iii. 328; Sharp, *In Contempt of All Authority*, p. 243 and n.; *George Berkeley, esq.* v. *Nathaniel Stephens, esq.*, PRO, C. 78/517/2.

and squatters—and the tenants approached George Berkeley to amend the enclosure agreement of 1612 with a view to preserving the remaining oaks. The second enclosure agreement of 1652 is a remarkable document. Provision was made for cutting timber in the common pasture above the number of 40 oaks, which were to be retained to produce mast for cattle; the tenants' share of the profits from the sale of surplus timber was to 'bee ymployed for releife of the poore Inhabitants of the Tything of Alkington and for binding out theire poore children [as] Apprentices'.[57] Thus the tenants of Alkington, in the midst of civil war, devised among themselves an imaginative solution to the related problems of wood-stealing and poor relief. The leading tenant, 'John Smith, Esquire', was quite probably the son of John Smyth of Nibley.

Henry, thirteenth Lord Berkeley, was reputed to be 'the best landlord that England had', and certainly through successive generations the Berkeleys displayed paternalistic consideration for their tenants.[58] Yet it must be remembered that the indebtedness arising from Berkeley extravagance necessitated extensive sales and leases that exposed their tenants to predatory courtiers and farmers and disrupted local agricultural customs. Nor were the Berkeley estates free from acrimonious tenurial and rent disputes.[59] Rising prices as well as heavily mortgaged lands drove the Berkeleys to exploit the wastes and woodlands for fuel and rents from approvements. These policies differed little from those pursued by manorial lords in Lancashire, Shropshire, or Staffordshire. The only difference is that the Berkeleys showed some restraint in exploiting their seigneurial rights. The Chancery suits which led to confirmation of enclosure agreements clearly resulted from collusion between the Berkeleys and their tenants, but there is abundant evidence that resistance was offered by the poorer inhabitants, who had been attracted to the Vale of Berkeley by the hope of a livelihood in a region of extensive wastes and woodlands. Thus the social cleavage was not between lord and tenants but rather between lord and tenants on the one hand, and cottagers and landless persons on the other.

[57] Smyth, *The Berkeley Manuscripts*, iii. 298–300; *Henry, Lord Berkeley v. Thomas Purnell*, PRO, C. 78/206/7; *George Berkley, esq. v. John Smith, esq.*, ibid., C. 78/517/3.   [58] Stone, *Crisis of the Aristocracy*, p. 306.
[59] For a discussion of the dispute between Henry, Lord Berkeley and the copyholders of Bosham concerning manorial customs governing entry fines, see Kerridge, *Agrarian Problems*, p. 57.

In conclusion, there is abundant evidence that the term 'enclosure by agreement' is deceptive. Historians must be wary of assuming that there was little or no resistance to enclosure agreements even where the evidence suggests that decrees of Chancery or other equity courts embodying such treaties resulted from collusive suits. The issues involved in enclosure—especially of wastes and commons—were complex and enclosure agreements frequently represented attempts to impose peace in a very troubled situation. In the early seventeenth century enclosure controversies were often complicated by tenurial and rent disputes. On larger manors there were more tenants to be reconciled, and the presence of gentlemen tenants provided effective leadership in resisting fiscal seigneurialism—or at least demanding a share in the profits. We are reminded of how numerous were the smaller gentry who held freehold or customary lands within the manor.[60] Undoubtedly only a small portion of these parochial gentry aspired to possess and exercise a seigneurial jurisdiction. They shared with humbler tenants a claim to common rights on the waste and could not be indifferent to seigneurial exploitation of the waste. Moreover, gentry feuds were unlikely to be ended by an enclosure agreement. On the manor of Sutton, Lancashire, the Bold–Holland struggle for seigneurial jurisdiction and the profits of the waste continued throughout the seventeenth century. The Bolds, who were the wealthiest parliamentarian family in Lancashire during the Civil War, lost the manor to the Hollands, who were royalists, and were not able to repurchase the manor until 1700.[61]

Nor should one assume that enclosure treaties were carried out in respect of every article of the agreements. In the first place, the actual undertaking of enclosure and agricultural improvement was expensive and was often delayed because of lack of capital. Legal challenges to the agreements frequently continued for a generation or more. Even when confirmed by a decree in Chancery or some other equity court, lawyers still could cast doubts upon their legality. It is true that enclosure agreements often went unchallenged for one or two generations, only to be challenged by enclosure rioting during times of crisis—a time-honoured ritual of protest even where no good

[60] *A Survey of the Duchy of Lancaster Lordships in Wales, 1609–1613*, ed. W. Rees (Cardiff, 1953), p. xxxi.
[61] B. G. Blackwood, *The Lancashire Gentry and the Great Rebellion, 1640–1660* (Chetham Soc., 3rd ser. 25; 1978), 58, 97.

reason existed. Copyhold tenants complained about lack of consultation in drawing up agreements, and those who did agree in principle could, with justice, complain about careless surveys and inequitable allotments. Enclosures surrounding approvements of wastes leased to cottagers and artisans were destroyed by old tenants who did not like their new neighbours; or cottagers and landless persons might destroy closes belonging to lords and tenants in order to gain access to scarce pasture and fuel resources. The root of the problem was usually excess population pressing upon dwindling resources of land.

6

Tenurial and Rent Disputes

COPYHOLD tenants in late-Elizabethan and early-Stuart England protested not only the erosion of their common rights and the imposition of enclosure agreements; on both royal and non-royal manors many tenants found that their tenures, which rightly or wrongly they regarded as customary estates of inheritance, were challenged by manorial lords, who argued that they were merely tenants at will, or who sought to compel tenants to exchange customary tenures for leaseholds for lives or years. Landlords, reacting to inflation, also tried to increase annual rents; however, since there were usually fixed by custom, they instead attempted to increase entry fines due upon the inheritance, conveyance, or leasing of tenancies. The royal courts afforded protection to copyholders where they could prove that manorial custom or previous agreements had afforded them lifehold or heritable estates. The royal judges also protected copyholders for lives or inheritance against unreasonably high entry fines, but not tenants at will or leaseholders. However, the protection of their economic rights was a constant struggle for even the most fortunate of copyhold tenants and required them to be perpetually vigilant and possessed of sufficient funds and legal knowledge to engage in long and expensive lawsuits.

Tenants of royal as well as non-royal manors were increasingly subjected to fiscal seigneurialism in the earliy seventeenth century. If the copyholders were found to be tenants at will and their entry fines uncertain and arbitrary, then the most satisfactory way to protect the interests of their families was to purchase, or compound for, estates of inheritance and certain entry fines. Quite commonly, the price for confirmation of estates of inheritance or ascertainment of entry fines, or both, was the equivalent of from 20 to 40 years' rent. For that price the tenant could secure an agreement that would be ratified by a decree of one of the equity courts. Early in the reign of James I the crown began a policy of enhancing rents on royal estates. Surveys revealed invalid grants of copyholds and lax administrative procedures in the previous century and assessed the current value of holdings with a view to improving rents. Royal tenants possessing invalid copyholds were allowed to compound in order to secure confirmation of estates of inheritance and ascertainment of entry fines. Some of them discovered that perfect security of tenure could be procured only by a second composition to obtain an Act of Parliament that would put the matter beyond dispute. Such agreements were common on large Duchy of Lancaster manors during this period. Substantial gentry tenants generally accepted these agreements, but poorer tenants regarded these species of fiscal feudalism as nakedly extortionate. There is evidence that the bitterness engendered by these tenurial and rent disputes sometimes determined patterns of allegiance during the Civil Wars.

Originally, all customary tenures were base in nature and held at the will of the lord according to the custom of the manor. This usually meant that the tenure was for one life or several lives, and the terms of service or rent were periodically renegotiated. If the tenancies of a manor became descendible by long usage, then a manorial custom was established which overrode the will of the lord. The terms of such tenure were frequently specified in a copy of the manorial court roll given to the tenant and in this way the customary tenant also became a copyholder. When a tenancy came to be descendible to heirs, the tenant acquired an interest in his holding that constituted an estate, in contradistinction to a mere chattel tenure. As long as he honoured the conditions of his tenure, a copyholder could not be ejected by his lord. If the lord attempted to do so, the copyholder might seek a remedy at common law by bringing an action of trespass against his lord.[1] Indeed, Sir Edward Coke states that the Court of Common Pleas ruled that a person possessing a copyhold for life or better was afforded the same protection against eviction by the common law as a freeholder.[2]

At one time the distinction between freehold and copyhold tenures was fairly clear: the first was limited to those of honourable status and the second to those of villein status. Subsequently, this distinction of status had become blurred as a fluid land market effected a redistribution of freehold and copyhold lands without regard to

---

[1] But this was a personal rather than a real action.
[2] Kerridge, *Agrarian Problems*, pp. 32–41; Sir Thomas E. Tomlins, *The Law Dictionary* (2 vols.; 1820), i, s.v. 'Copyhold'; *Brown's Case*, Michaelmas, 23 & 24 Eliz., Coke, 4 *Reports*, fo. 21.

personal status. Thus gentlemen came into possession of copyhold land to which base services had once attached, while husbandmen had purchased freehold lands. It was quite common for gentlemen of the highest rank to possess both copyhold and freehold land as well as seigneurial jurisdictions. Such was the case with Sir Arthur Pilkington, bart., a tenant of the manor of Wakefield, who confessed to an inability to sort out his freehold from his copyhold lands.[3] Although Coke stated that copyholders for life or better enjoyed the same security of tenure as freeholders, the distinction that he tried to maintain between the two types of tenure was too finely drawn. It confused contemporaries just as it has baffled modern historians such as Tawney.[4] Worse yet, it probably contributed to the increase in litigation in the early seventeenth century arising from tenurial disputes. Although copyhold tenure was base and servile in origin, in those instances where copyholders acquired an estate for life or of inheritance, they also gained status. In the seventeenth century such persons were deemed to be freeholders and were allowed to vote in county parliamentary elections, until an early eighteenth-century antiquarian rediscovered the distinction between the two kinds of tenure and copyholders of inheritance were disenfranchised.[5]

There are several reasons why tenurial and rent disputes occurred more frequently in the early seventeenth century. Prices of agricultural commodities had trebled in the second half of the sixteenth century, and the decade of the 1590s saw the sharpest increases since the 1550s.[6] Those agricultural producers who could survive the bad harvests of the 1590s and sell surpluses of corn could make substantial profits. Quite understandably, manorial lords whose income depended mostly on rentals were anxious to share in these profits. Generally, rents increased fourfold between the middle of the sixteenth and the middle of the seventeenth centuries, but most of the increase seems to have occurred in the second half of the sixteenth century.

[3] Sir Edward Coke, *The Compleate Copyholder* (1641), 4–7, 12–14, printed in Kerridge, *Agrarian Problems*, pp. 161–4; PRO, DL 5/33, fos. 298ᵛ–302.
[4] Tawney, *The Agrarian Problem*, pp. 289–90.
[5] Tomlins, *The Law Dictionary*, s.v. 'Copyhold'; D. Hirst, *The Representative of the People? Voters and Voting in England under the Early Stuarts* (Cambridge, 1975), 34–8.
[6] P. Bowden, 'Agricultural Prices, Farm Profits, and Rents', *AHEW* iv. 605.

Under-tenants and farmers with short leases could be charged rack-rents. The term 'rack-rent' properly meant rents that were adjusted annually to reflect current market conditions and harvest fluctuations. On leaseholds and tenancies where the fines were uncertain and arbitrary, the lord and the prospective tenant negotiated the amount to be paid. Given the rise in agricultural prices and the demographic pressure upon land resources, the demand for new holdings was such that farmers and prospective tenants were bidding rents up and old tenants for lives or years were buying the reversions of their own holdings in order to protect themselves.[7]

Extacting higher entry fines from copyholders of inheritance was more difficult. One way of doing this was by questioning the heritability of copyhold tenures, which, if successful, meant that the terms of the copyhold would eventually have to be renegotiated. The other method was for the manorial lord to argue that fines were uncertain. In this situation copyholders found that evidence from manorial court rolls showing that fines had become certain and fixed by long usage in the recent past was not accepted by the royal courts if the lord could prove that anciently the fines had been arbitrary and uncertain.[8] Only evidence of a formal agreement to ascertain fines was sufficient. Yet the royal courts did place limits on entry fines that were found to be uncertain and arbitrary, and the Court of King's Bench ruled in 1600 that they were not to be 'excessive and unreasonable'. The judges stated that copyholders might withhold fines which they believed to be excessive without fear of forfeiting their holdings until the royal courts decided whether or not the fines were reasonable. Coke says that it was a policy of the courts to protect the estates of copyholders.[9]

Consequently, it was advantageous for manorial lords to allow copyholders of inheritance to compound for ascertainment of fines. Generally, it was also beneficial for those tenants who could raise the necessary funds to pay the equivalent of 20 to 40 years' rent. Many of those who were able to do so could expect to recover their investments by screwing up the rents of their under-tenants. But it

---

[7] Kerridge, 'The Movement of Rent, 1540–1640', pp. 16–34; id., *Agrarian Problems*, pp. 46, 52; *VCH Stafford*, vi. 80.

[8] Kerridge, *Agrarian Problems*, p. 55.

[9] *Hobart v. Hammond*, Michaelmas, 42 & 43 Eliz., Coke, 4 *Reports*, fo. 27ᵛ; cf. also *Thomas, Lord Gerard v. William Abnett*, Trinity, 1615, PRO, C. 78/175/4.

does not follow that the suits in the equity courts which resulted in formal agreements confirming estates and ascertaining fines were collusive and the conflict fictional. Often there were other difficult issues to be resolved that touched upon manorial customs, such as the confirmation or abridgement of use-rights, enclosure agreements, mineral-rights, heriots, wardships, giving suit to the manorial court, and the like. Court cases reveal petty tyrants among the manorial lords and artful dodgers among the tenants. Both parties frequently resorted to force, fraud, and perjury to win their arguments. There is very little evidence that landlords wished to evict their tenants, but most landlords were determined to secure economic rents, which generally meant raising entry fines. Undoubtedly, many smallholders were forced to abandon their holdings because of mounting indebtedness and the inability to raise the funds needed for increased entry fines or for compounding for estates of inheritance and ascertainment of fines. Those copyholders who survived such crises were usually substantial men.

Tenurial and rent disputes were especially common on royal manors in the early seventeenth century. The income from the crown estates in the sixteenth century had not kept pace with either inflation or the general movement of rents on non-royal lands. The problem began with Henry VIII's alienation of well over half of the royal lands. Mary's practice of granting long-term leases was ended by Elizabeth, but crown farmers stripped the royal wastes and forests of timber, peat, and coal, while corrupt stewards of royal manors frequently granted invalid copyholds and pocketed entry fines. There was need for a thorough survey and evaluation of the crown estates, but under Elizabeth any attempt to charge economic rents was obstructed by the practice of granting royal servants leases and reversions of leases in lieu of salary increases. James I further diminished the income from the crown estates by granting and selling lands on a reckless scale. When Robert Cecil, Earl of Salisbury, became lord treasurer in 1609, he attempted to halt the alienations of crown lands and raise rents to market levels. Many of the agreements for confirmation of crown copyholders' estates and ascertainment of fines date from this period. It has been argued that the low rents on crown lands during the reign of Elizabeth reflected a desire to ensure the loyalty and support of crown tenants. But it seems that actually the reversions granted to courtiers not only impeded efforts at fiscal reform but also bred hostility among the tenants, who were much troubled by courtiers attempting to sell them reversions to the lands that they were already occupying.

Professor Kerridge concludes that the Jacobean reforms in the administration of crown lands never really displaced the system of rewarding officials and courtiers in favour of enhancing revenues for the royal treasury, but merely limited those profits to 'a small body of favourites'. When Salisbury's death ended his bold attempt to rationalize the administration of the crown estates, short-term expedients once again prevailed and the sale of crown lands was resumed.[10] Purchasers of royal lands were anxious to extract the maximum income from their new estates. Their attempts to do so also precipitated enclosure and tenurial and rent disputes.

The determination of the heritability of tenures and the certainty of fines started with manorial custom, which was first arbitrated in the court baron. When manorial custom was disrupted, the testimony of the oldest inhabitants or evidence of the customs of neighbouring manors might be accepted by the royal courts, but the most precise guide to custom was provided by the manorial court rolls. The bitter conflict concerning tenures, rents, and other sources of seigneurial income led both lords and tenants to manipulate or subvert manorial customs to their own ends.

In the middle of the sixteenth century, when the court rolls of Petworth Manor could still be consulted, no disagreement arose between the Earls of Northumberland and their tenants about customs, but sometime prior to 1592 the court rolls disappeared into the hands of the steward for recopying and were never seen again by the tenants. Henceforth, there was a steady erosion of manorial custom. Henry, ninth Earl of Northumberland had briefly considered evicting his numerous copyholders, but rejected that idea when his lawyers advised him that they possessed secure estates of inheritance. Instead, he devised various schemes to exploit the wastes and to overthrow those manorial customs that stood in the way of improving his income.[11] In 1591, 49 of the Petworth tenants complained to the Privy Council and the Court of Chancery that the Earl charged

---

[10] G. Batho, 'Landlords in England', *AHEW* iv. 265–70; R. B. Pugh, *The Crown Estate: An Historical Survey* (1960), 9–13; D. Thomas, 'Leases in Reversion on the Crown's Lands', *Ec. HR*, 2nd ser. 30/1 (Feb. 1977), 67–72; Kerridge, 'The Movement of Rent, 1540–1640', p. 33.

[11] For a discussion of enclosures and exploitation of the wastes of Petworth Manor, see ch. 3.

exorbitant entry fines, that the heriots demanded exceeded their customary value and were being levied upon widows' dower rights for the first time, and that amercements for failure to provide labour at harvest time were being revived. Although a Chancery decree in 1594 confirmed an agreement to ascertain entry fines at two years' rent, the Earl ignored the agreement and continued to treat entry fines as arbitrary and uncertain and negotiated the highest amount he could squeeze out of his tenants. The wardships of minor heirs of copyholders were a particularly sore grievance. Previously, custody of the heir and the tenancy had been granted only in open court after consultation with the homage jury, and the guardians appointed were usually relatives or neighbours. The ninth Earl began the practice of selling wardships to outsiders in order to bid up the price. In 1639 the wardship and marriage of an heir to a 40-acre messuage fetched £150.[12] Altogether, the evidence suggests that the royal courts were not very effective in restraining the Earl's exploitation of his tenants.

The copyholders of the mid-Tudor manor of Elmeley Lovett, Worcestershire were especially aggressive in pursuing a dispute about tenurial customs. Their copies of the court roll contained the words *sibi et suis*, which they interpreted as granting estates of inheritance, but the manorial lord, Sir Robert Acton, insisted that they held lifehold tenures only. The matter was pursued through the Courts of Chancery and Requests and the Council of Wales and the Marches, and the lord's interpretation was upheld in every instance. Early in the reign of Elizabeth, after Charles Acton had succeeded his father, the question of heritability was revived again when several copyholders pretended to hold some water-mills by estate of inheritance. Charles Acton accused his tenants of joining together with the tenants of neighbouring manors to give false testimony concerning their manorial customs at the assizes in Worcester Castle. The defendants contrived to keep a hungry jury locked up for 24 hours until the Judge declared a hung jury. Next, Acton's tenants attempted to have him indicted for burglary and, that failing, conspired to hire persons to ambush and murder him.[13]

---

[12] Jerrome, *Cloakbag and Common Purse*, pp. 12–13, 37, 41–9, 65, 75; Hugh Archibald Wyndham, Lord Leconfield, *Petworth Manor in the Seventeenth Century* (Oxford, 1954), 21–4.

[13] *Charles Acton, esq.* v. *Alice Harper*, PRO, STAC 5/A1/38. For a discussion of the confusion over the distinction between the terms *sibi et suis* and *sibi et heredibus*, see Kerridge, *Agrarian Problems*, p. 36.

The tenants of the Buckinghamshire manors annexed to the manor of Windsor were also alleged to have given perjured testimony in the court baron concerning certain manorial customs. One issue was whether a copyholder holding several messuages paid one or several heriots when he leased his lands or died. Another matter was concerned with the practice of coppicing in a woodland pasture where the tenants claimed common of pasture. The tenants maintained that custom allowed the temporary enclosure of a portion of the woodland while plantations of young trees matured. The Duchy of Lancaster, they complained, had recently enclosed and coppiced the whole woodland and permanently excluded tenants. In 1606 the tenants riotously destroyed the enclosure on two occasions. Sir John Fortescue, Chancellor of the Duchy of Lancaster, attempted to have the copyholds of several tenants declared forfeit because they had violated manorial custom by cutting timber on their copyholds without the licence of the manorial lord.[14]

A number of manorial customs and economic rights were disputed in the Court of Chancery in 1615 between Thomas, Lord Gerard and the customary tenants of Audley Manor in North Staffordshire. The tenants claimed that they possessed estates of inheritance, which they could lease at their pleasure, and that the entry fines were certain and fixed. Lord Gerard argued that the fines were uncertain and arbitrary and that tenancies were granted only by the lord or his steward in fee tail for terms of one, two, or three lives, or for 21 years or less. Moreover, any tenant attempting to sell or lease his copyhold without the licence of the lord forfeited the same. The tenants also claimed the right to dig coal and iron ore and cut timber on their copyholds without licence. Gerard said that, according to manorial custom, this constituted commission of an act of waste, which also brought forfeiture. Every single tenant, he said, had offended in this regard. Copyhold estates were, by this time, sufficiently secure that the threat of forfeiture was little more than a ploy. Nor did the Court of Chancery take seriously the claim of the Audley tenants to possess estates of inheritance. Instead the court turned to trial of the question of the certainty or uncertainty of fines and the matter of heriots. The tenants asserted that a tenant who held several copyholds was liable to only one heriot. Moreover, they conspired to sell their cattle and goods to one another in order to

---

[14] *Sir John Fortescue* v. *Robert Williott*, PRO, STAC 8/146/19.

defeat the collection of heriots. The court ruled that both common law and reason upheld the principle that several heriots should be paid where the tenant held several copyholds. The court dealt sympathetically with the tenants' assertion that entry fines were certain despite the fact that they had spirited away manorial court rolls, rent rolls, and customaries. The court also ignored their declaration that 'the customes of the said manor doe lye and rest in the breaste of the coppiehoulders', and instead used the written evidence of the court rolls to trace the history of entry fines on the manor back to the reign of Henry III. They discovered that entry fines had originally been uncertain, but began to grow more certain between the time of Henry VI and the reign of Elizabeth when the exceptions to the rule of certain fines became more common. Therefore it could not be proved that the custom of certain entry fines existed 'tyme out of mynde'. The court found for the complainant, Lord Gerard, but lord chancellor Ellesmere admonished him:

to take and accepte such reasonable and moderate fynes as the tennants might haue noe iuste occasion to complayne. And furthermore declared that if anye tennant whoe hereafter shall stand in case to paye a fyne shall finde himselfe grieved with a demand for an excessive fyne and withall shall offer a reasonable fyne that then euerie suche tennant preferring his Bill in this Courte for moderaccon shalbe heard and releived according to equitie.[15]

Cannock Chase, in Staffordshire, a large waste shared by several manors, was the scene of remarkable industrial development during the second half of the sixteenth century. The growth of iron-founding had placed a severe strain upon the fuel resources of Cannock Chase, while the expansion of the allied trades of charcoal burning and metal-working swelled the population and taxed grazing lands on the waste to the limit. Cottages were erected on approvements enclosed and severed from the waste and messuages were subdivided and leased to under-tenants. The limited supplies of water in the millponds which provided power for the hydraulic blast furnaces and forges precluded year-round employment of the artisans, who had to fall back upon the pastoral and fuel resources and game of Cannock Chase in order to eke out a living in off-seasons. Hence, there were numerous incidents of poaching and wood-stealing.

---

[15] *Thomas, Lord Gerard* v. *William Abnett, esq.*, PRO, C. 78/175/4.

Thomas, third Lord Paget was the leading landlord and owned most of the furnaces and forges in the neighbourhood as well as working several coal mines. The rapid alterations in land use caused by Paget's enterprises naturally led to many conflicts with tenants and neighbours, culminating in a series of anti-enclosure riots in 1581.[16] In the early seventeenth century, the Pagets no longer managed their iron-works and coal-pits on Cannock Chase, but instead limited their entrepreneurial activities to exploiting the coal-mines in Beaudesert Park on the edge of the chase. In 1606, William, fourth Lord Paget, and 139 of his tenants attempted to compose past differences by rationalizing tenures and agreeing upon a wide and comprehensive body of manorial customs involving the economic rights of lord and tenant. The Chancery suit that they filed was clearly collusive and reflected the significant social changes that rural industry and the influx of artisans had brought to Cannock Chase. Whatever differences had divided the Pagets and their tenants in the past, the cleavage was now between those who possessed land and the virtually landless craftsmen. By settling their differences concerning tenures, rents, and manorial customs, both Lord Paget and his copyhold tenants could get on with the business of leasing cottages and small plots of land to the artisans. From what we know of subleasing to under-tenants elsewhere, all stood to make substantial profits.

The 139 tenants, led by Sir Walter Aston and Sir Walter Leveson, were all copyholders on Lord Paget's manors of Cannock, Rugeley, Longdon, and Haywood. Within each manor the conditions of tenure varied considerably: some copyholds were held in fee simple and others in fee tail; some were granted for life or lives and some for years. In order to put an end to the many lawsuits that the confusion over tenures had occasioned in the past, and in return for a composition of £1,500, Lord Paget agreed to confirm their copyholds as estates of inheritance with the right to entail and make uses at the will of the tenant. Lord Paget retained the right to escheat the holdings of copyholders who died without issue, but daughters were to have the right of inheritance, widows were guaranteed dower rights, and the wardships of minor heirs and the custody of their lands were to be granted only to the next of kin. When the grant of a copy was for lives or years or to the use of an heir, the fine

---

[16] PRO, STAC 5/P12/25, P60/40, P63/16, A13/1; BL, Harley MSS, 2143, fo. 11. Fuller discussion and citations of sources appear in chs. 10 and 11.

due upon surrender and entry was limited to one year's rent; if demised to the use of another, two years' rent was allowed. Copyholders might lease their lands for up to 20 years without the lord's licence, but leases were to be recorded in the manorial court rolls so that the lord might know his tenants.[17]

The incidence of heriots and other seigneurial prerogatives was also carefully regulated. Heriots were to be limited to the best beast or, that lacking, to the best goods under the value of 4 marks. No heriot was to be collected when widows or female heirs succeeded, but only upon the death or surrender of heirs female. Heriots for cottages were not to exceed 6*d.* and no heriot was to be levied on any cottages erected upon ancient messuages. The Chancery decree that embodied this agreement also confirmed the copyholders' common rights on Cannock Heath and within Cannock Wood, which included the right to peat, ferns to burn for potash, marl, sand, and gravel. They, in turn, guaranteed the manorial lord the right to enclose and coppice woodland, provided the same was thrown open for common of pasture after nine years.

Finally, the treaty between Lord Paget and his tenants specified that although disputes about titles could be litigated in the royal courts, the interpretation of manorial customs was to be referred to a jury of 14 or 16 homagers drawn from that particular manor, one-half of whom were to be named by the lord's bailiff and the other half by 'twoe indifferente coppyholders'. No cottagers or servants were to serve on the homage juries, which were to be limited to sufficient freeholders and copyholders. The two copyholders, as well as the bailiff, would be provided with keys to the chest in which the court rolls were locked up in order to provide access to all tenants.[18]

Perhaps the most notorious tenurial dispute of the early-Stuart period was that involving the tenants of Clitheroe, which began in 1607 and was not finally settled until 1662. The honour of Clitheroe was a large royal estate comprising several manors that spread across the hundreds of Blackburn and Salford in south-eastern Lancashire. Within its boundaries lay the ancient forests of Pendle, Trawden,

---

[17] *Sir Walter Aston* v. *William, Lord Paget*, PRO, C. 78/165/8. For a discussion of entails and uses as applied to copyholds, see Simpson, *An Introduction to the History of the Land Law*, pp. 159–61. Entails and uses were employed to defeat the meaning of copyhold tenure.   [18] PRO, C. 78/165/8.

Tottington, and Rossendale, which had originated as chases and became part of the crown lands when the Duchy of Lancaster was annexed to the crown in 1399. Little woodland remained and disafforestation and enclosure were well under way at the beginning of the sixteenth century. After 1507 duchy officials granted many illegal copyholds of forest land and demesne, which the tenants of these copyholds regarded as estates held in fee simple. Although occasional questions were raised about the validity of their titles, the Clitheroe tenants subleased, alienated, and bequeathed their lands frequently in two or more portions to heirs both male and female, without hindrance from the duchy officials for a century. Consequently, the number of smallholdings multiplied. In Pendle, for example, the number of copyholders increased from 98 in 1527 to 230 in 1662, and one must remember that these statistics take no account of under-tenants or squatters. Despite great efforts to improve marginal land and bring it into cultivation, the economy of Clitheroe, especially in the Pendle and Rossendale districts, was essentially pastoral and sylvan. Cheese and butter were produced and nearly every household was involved in the weaving of wool and linen.[19]

In 1607, the officials of the Duchy of Lancaster prosecuted Sir Richard Towneley, Richard Shuttleworth, and other tenants of Clitheroe for unlawful entry and intrusion into the king's forests. In effect, their copyholds were declared void. The legal basis for this astounding action was Coke's dictum that 'custom never extendeth to a thing newly created'. In other words, the tenurial customs of the manor did not extend to grants of land from the lord's demesne and waste. No one, not even the manorial lord, had the power to create new copyholds, because copyhold tenure must exist by prescription, that is, it must have existed since time immemorial. Even though the lands assarted from the forests or approved from the wastes were conveyed by copy of the court roll 'according to the custom of the manor', the recipients possessed mere tenancies at will and the King could evict the Clitheroe tenants at

---

[19] Tupling, *The Economic History of Rossendale*, pp. 70–6, 95–7; id., 'The Causes of the Civil War in Lancashire', *Trans. Lancs. Ches. Antiquarian Soc.* 65 (1956), 17–18; M. Brigg, 'The Forest of Pendle in the Seventeenth Century', *Trans. Hist. Soc. Lancs. Ches.* 113 (1961), 65–96; 115 (1962), 65–90; W. S. Weeks, 'Clitheroe in the Seventeenth Century', *Trans. Lancs. Ches. Antiquarian Soc.* 43, 75.

his pleasure.[20] The tenants' position was, from a legal point of view, hopeless and they could not look to the gentlemen tenants to lead them in resistance. Even Sir Richard Molyneux, the Receiver-General of the Duchy of Lancaster, who had filed the information against the tenants in the Court of Duchy Chamber, was himself a Clitheroe tenant and had been prosecuted in a separate action.[21]

Thus, the Clitheroe tenants had no choice but to accept the King's offer to allow them to compound in exchange for perfecting their titles. In order to obtain copyholds of inheritance, the tenants of the manors of Accrington, Colne and Ightenhill offered a composition of 12 years' rent, but the Crown demanded and got 20 years' rent, which amounted to £3,954. A decree ratifying the agreement was handed down by the Court of Duchy Chamber and an Act of Parliament perfecting it was passed in 1609 (7 Jac. I, c. 21). The Clitheroe agreement of 1609 applied only to the lands assarted from the forests. Coke's pronouncement that new copyholds could not be created was also employed to void the copyholds carved out of the manorial wastes and demesnes, and in 1618, after more protracted resistance, the tenants of the manors of Derby, Accrington, Colne, and Ightenhill were milked for another composition in order to perfect their titles to these lands and also to obtain certain entry fines. This composition came to £5,574, the equivalent of 40 years' rent, of which Sir Richard Molyneux was to pay £1,812.[22] The composition of 1618 was to be paid in two instalments—with the second moiety due after another Act of Parliament was passed to confirm the agreement. A bill introduced in the Long Parliament in 1640 failed to pass, but another bill was enacted by the Rump Parliament in 1650, and the commonwealth's creditors, to whom the debt was turned over, began to collect from the Clitheroe tenants and to assess penalties for late payment. Finally, in 1662, the Cavalier Parliament relieved them of further obligations and confirmed their titles. G. E. Tupling estimated that by 1662 the Clitheroe tenants had paid the equivalent of 52 years' rent to obtain clear titles.[23]

---

[20] Tupling, *Economic History of Rossendale*, pp. 148–9; id., 'Causes of the Civil War in Lancashire', pp. 17–18; Prof. Kerridge's account of the Clitheroe tenurial dispute (*Agrarian Problems*, pp. 86, 88–9) fails to make a number of important distinctions.

[21] Tupling, *Economic History of Rossendale*, p. 150 n.

[22] Ibid., pp. 149–50; BL, Add. MSS, 12,496, fos. 373–374ᵛ.

[23] Tupling, *Economic History of Rossendale*, pp. 158–59.

Probably, no body of crown tenants suffered as much from the fiscal exactions of the early-Stuart kings as the men of Clitheroe. In 1642 they had their revenge when they defeated a detachment of royalist troops in a running battle between Chowbent and Lowton Common. Religious differences were probably also significant, since Blackburn and Salford hundreds were areas of notable Puritan influence. James, seventh Earl of Derby was generally considered a benevolent landlord, but after he purchased the manors of West Derby and Wavertree from the Crown in 1639, he oppressed the tenants by attempting to undermine their tenurial customs and raise their entry fines. The tenants of West Derby and Wavertree also supported the parliamentarian cause. Other tenurial and rent disputes between Cavalier landlords and their tenants weakened the royalist position in Lancashire and contributed to the spread of sectarianism. Yet, despite the extortionate sums that the tenants of Clitheroe and other Lancashire estates had to pay for confirmation of titles and ascertainment of fines, smallholders in many parts of Lancashire had become more numerous and more secure in their copyholds by the middle of the seventeenth century. The experience of litigation also seems to have instilled in them greater awareness of political issues. Perhaps the seventh Earl of Derby understood this when he advised his son to undertake 'no suit against a poor man . . . for then you make him your equal.'[24]

The tenants of Glatton and Holme, having already concluded an agreement with the Duchy of Lancaster to secure heritable estates and certain fines, discovered that the new owner challenged the validity of that agreement in an attempt to collect a second composition from them. Sir Robert Cotton, bart., purchased the manor in 1611 because it was close to his principal seat at Connington, Huntingdonshire, which he rebuilt in 1602. Possessed of considerable legal expertise and one of the most notable antiquarians of his age, Cotton used his great learning to oppress his new tenants in the most odious way.[25]

---

[24] Tupling, 'The Causes of the Civil War in Lancashire', p. 20; B. G. Blackwood, 'The Lancashire Cavaliers and their Tenants', *Trans. Hist. Soc. Lancs. Ches.* 117 (1965), 17–32; id., 'Agrarian Unrest and the Early Lancashire Quakers', *Journal of the Friends' Historical Society* 51, 72–6.

[25] Cf. K. Sharpe, *Sir Robert Cotton, 1586–1631: History and Politics in Early Modern England* (Oxford, 1979), 147–50, 152; *DNB*, s.v. Sir Robert Cotton. I hope to discuss the Glatton and Holme tenure dispute at greater length elsewhere.

The manor of Glatton and Holme was 10,000 acres in extent, but probably contained no more than about 2,000 acres of arable. There were, however, extensive pastures and meadows on the demesne, which were leased to farmers and had formerly carried great flocks of sheep. In addition, there were fens, which Cotton began to drain, as well as the fishing profits from Whittlesey Mere, reputed to be one of the greatest bodies of fresh water in the kingdom. Sir Robert Cotton purchased the manor for £2,800—a very low price; at the time of purchase the income from rents was £82 p.a. His son and heir, Thomas, in 1626 estimated the potential improved income from rents at £101 p.a., but complained that neither he nor his father had ever collected above £10 p.a. in rents because of a continuing rent strike on the part of the tenants.[26]

In 1590, the tenants of Glatton and Holme, who had been paying entry fines of one year's rent, offered the Queen fines of four years' rent in exchange for confirmation of their copyholds as estates of inheritance. When it became known in 1611 that commissioners of the Duchy of Lancaster had been empowered to sell the manor, Robert Castle, esq., a lawyer and tenant of the manor, who also claimed to be the bailiff, suggested that the tenants themselves purchase the manor. Cotton feared that he would lose out to the tenants, so he met with them and persuaded them to withdraw in his favour by promising, so they alleged, to honour the agreement establishing heritable estates and certain fines. Additionally, Cotton offered them the option of converting their copyholds to freeholds within two years. The grant of the manor was made to Sir Robert Cotton, his uncle John Cotton, and his son Thomas. Cotton and his son refused to honour the agreement establishing the heritability of the tenants' estates and proceeded to build a case for the fines being uncertain and arbitrary. Several heirs of the copyholders were denied entry into their copyholds because they refused to admit that their tenures were not heritable and would not pay the enhanced entry fines and annual rents that were demanded, and also because they were accused of employing uses in order to defeat the seigneurial prerogative of wardship. Cotton and his son researched manorial customs and rents back to before the time of Edward I: they claimed to have discovered evidence justifying the revival of annual payments for aids and in lieu of labour services, as well as for increasing the

[26] *Marsilian Sampson* v. *Sir Robert Cotton, bart.*, PRO, C. 78/300/1.

rate of heriots; they also proposed restoring rents and entry fines to the higher level that had been collected before the time of Henry IV, when they had been lowered because of 'a great murraine of cattle and decay of the tenants'. The Cottons also claimed to have discovered that a corrupt steward in the reign of Henry VIII had let some tenancies at half the reduced rent, and said that Robert Castle had detained court rolls and surveys to hide the evidence until the manorial documents were recovered by lawsuit. Thomas Cotton denied that his father had ever promised to accept and respect the copyhold tenures as estates of inheritance, but rather had promised to allow the tenants to purchase such estates. Thus Sir Robert Cotton had intended to compel his tenants to pay a second composition for confirming their estates.[27]

The Court of Chancery attempted to settle this dispute by arbitration, but neither party would compromise. The tenants petitioned for a judgment by the lord chancellor, who declared that they possessed estates of inheritance and certain entry fines. The lord chancellor's decree was to be confirmed by Act of Parliament. However, the decree did allow the Cottons to raise the annual rents by 20 per cent, thus restoring them to the amount collected before the time of Henry IV. The Cottons were able to prove that the demesne lands were enclosed and had been encroached upon by the tenants. These lands were to be returned into severalty. Tenant lands lying interspersed with demesne lands were to be exchanged for more outlying lands so that the demesne might be consolidated. The manorial lords' common rights were deemed to be extinguished on all commonable waste except fenland, and they were not to plough any part of the waste that had not been cultivated during the previous 30 years. Thus, Sir Robert Cotton and his son Thomas, for all their misguided antiquarian research, gained nothing more than a rent increase, which was probably below the prevailing market value of the land, and confirmation of enclosure of the demesne.[28]

The large crown manor of Wakefield affords another example of the impact of fiscal seigneurialism on a developing proto-industrial community in the early seventeenth century. Like other parts of the West Riding of Yorkshire and south-eastern Lancashire, limited agricultural land and impopulation had forced the inhabitants into by-occupations, and an extensive system of cottage manufacturing

[27] Ibid.   [28] Ibid.

of woollen textiles, specializing in the coarse cloths known as kerseys, had grown up by the end of the sixteenth century. The reputed prosperity of the West Riding clothiers had already been noticed by the government, and heavy assessments for ship money were laid on that region in the period from the 1590s to the 1630s. Because Wakefield and its sub-manors did not possess arable demesne, seigneurial income could only be improved by the rigorous exploitation of profits from rents, enforcing the monopoly of manorial corn and fulling mills, the amercement of tenants for failure to give suit to the manorial courts, and exploitation of wastes. As in the cases of Clitheroe and Cannock Chase, demographic expansion, whether by natural increase or immigration, resulted in extensive subleasing to under-tenants, which drove up the price of land. The Duchy of Lancaster and the lords of the sub-manors of Wakefield profited from these trends by taking compositions for the ascertainment of fines, confirming copyholds as estates, enfranchising copyholders,[29] and approving and subdividing the manorial wastes. Coal, ironstone, and lead mining and stone quarrying further diminished the pastoral and fuel resources of the wastes and compelled county magistrates to take positive steps towards the relief of poverty.[30]

Sir John Savile of Howley, who was steward of the manor of Wakefield as well as lord of several of the sub-manors, was commissioned by the duchy in 1603 'to persuade & drawe' the tenants to compound for copyholds of inheritance or enfranchisement. Many tenants seem to have been agreeable, but one copyholder was prosecuted for slander of justice in Star Chamber for saying that Savile had dealt with the tenants harshly and unjustly. Subsequently, Savile began treating with the tenants of the honour of Pontefract. Both Wakefield and Pontefract were surveyed in 1606 in connection with the composition scheme. The entry fines of the Wakefield and

---

[29] Enfranchisement meant the conversion of copyholds into freeholds held in fee-farm and subject to perpetual rents. Cf. Kerridge, *Agrarian Problems*, p. 53. Simpson is wrong when he says that fee-farm became an almost extinct tenure after the enactment of the Statute of *Quia Emptores* in 1290: *An Introduction to the History of the Land Law*, pp. 73-4.

[30] H. Heaton, *The Yorkshire Woollen and Worsted Industries* (2nd edn., Oxford, 1965), 68 ff., esp. 81-3; M. J. Ellis [François], 'Manorial History of Halifax', Part I, pp. 251-5, 259; ead., 'The Social and Economic Development of Halifax, 1558-1640', *Proc. Leeds Philos. and Lit. Soc.*, Literary and Historical Section, 11/8 (1966), 215-80; A. F. Upton, *Sir Arthur Ingram, c.1565-1642: A Study of the Origins of an English Landed Family* (Oxford, 1961), 48-9.

Pontefract tenants were uncertain and arbitrary, and Savile and the other sub-manorial lords (most of whom belonged to various branches of the Savile family) evidently exerted pressure by raising entry fines. The tenants of several sub-manors collected common purses to retain lawyers, of whom one drew up a document entitled 'The Breviate of Sowerby', which argued that the tenants of Sowerby had enjoyed certain fines and free status in the reign of Edward II. In 1609 the Crown fixed the composition for confirming copyholders' estates and ascertaining fines at 35 years' rent, but some copyholders preferred enfranchisement and were willing to pay up to 80 years' rent for it. As in the case of the Clitheroe copyholders, tenants of Wakefield who held lands enclosed from the waste were mulcted for another composition in 1618 to convert their 'encroachments' upon the wastes into heritable copyholds with fixed fines. Again, like the Clitheroe tenants, the copyholders of Wakefield were hounded by the Crown's creditors. Sir Thomas Monson, to whom Lionel Cranfield had promised the right to sell six baronetcies, was instead given the right to compound with Wakefield copyholders. Sir Arthur Ingram, another business associate of Cranfield, purchased the rectory manor of Halifax in 1609 and squeezed compositions for enfranchisement out of his new tenants.[31]

Encroachment on the waste inflicted hardship on the poor inhabitants of Wakefield as early as the 1580s. In 1583 the Court of Duchy Chamber decreed that Sir John Savile of Howley, George Savile, and Roger Pollard, who had enclosed and severed 90 acres of waste, were to pay 6*d.* per acre in perpetuity to the poor as compensation for loss of their commons. In 1600 the poor inhabitants complained to the Duchy Court that the Saviles and Pollard had never paid that assessment. The complaint was tried before Sir John Savile of Bradley, Baron of the Exchequer and a cousin of two of the defendants, who ordered the Yorkshire commissioners for trusts and charitable uses to see that the court's original decree was performed.[32]

---

[31] *Sir John Savile of Howley* v. *Robert Spaight, yeoman*, PRO, STAC 8/258/5; Ellis, 'Manorial History of Halifax', part I, pp. 254–5, 259–63; R. v. *John Thornehill, esq.*, PRO, DL 5/25, pp. 46–7; BL, Add. MSS, 12,496, fos. 373–374ᵛ; Upton, *Sir Arthur Ingram*, pp. 48, 100–1; R. H. Tawney, *Business and Politics under James I: Lionel Cranfield as Merchant and Minister* (Cambridge, 1958), 90 n. The price of the second Wakefield composition of 1618 was £5,410.

[32] *Inhabitants of Wakefield* v. *George Savile*, PRO, DL 5/22, p. 951.

In 1629, the manor of Wakefield was granted to Henry Rich, Earl of Holland and chief justice of the forests, who conveyed it to Sir Gervase Clifton, bart., as part of the marriage settlement when Clifton married his daughter.[33] The new manorial lord began negotiating with his tenants to enclose 590 acres from a large waste known as the Outwood and exploited their ambivalent feelings about enclosures of waste. Although the agreement of 1609 had assured the royal copyholders and freeholders of the townships of Wakefield and Stanley common of pasture and turbary in perpetuity, and commonable pasture had grown increasingly scarce, there were other considerations that made them amenable to persuasion. The many lawsuits arising from intercommoning disputes had wearied the tenants, and they feared that cottagers would continue to multiply, encroach upon their commonable lands, and drive up the poor rates. They also wished to have Clifton's large rabbit warren suppressed and were dismayed to discover the extent of Clifton's hunting and pasture rights in the Outwood. In 1634 Clifton obtained the assent of Sir William Savile, bart., Sir John Savile, and Francis Neville, esq., and 55 other tenants to an enclosure agreement. The agreement was not submitted to the Duchy Court until 1638 because a number of tenants, led by Sir Arthur Pilkington, bart., were opposed to the scheme, and others, who had already assented, discovered that Clifton had lied about the proportion of the waste to be approved. The Duchy Court confirmed the enclosure treaty in 1638, but Pilkington's opposition continued. Despite the fact that the Duchy Court accepted proof of Clifton's misrepresentation, it ordered compliance with the enclosure agreement becaue Clifton had secured the assent of another 250 tenants. Clifton undertook to pay for the cost of surveying and to suppress the rabbit warren, and agreed that he would not erect any cottages without providing each with ten acres of land so that the cottagers would not become a burden to the parish. Although only a quarter of the waste had been enclosed for Clifton's exclusive possession and the tenants were assured rights

---

[33] Sir Gervase Clifton was a close friend of Sir Thomas Wentworth and enjoyed the distinction of marrying seven heiresses and widows, of whom no fewer than four were the daughters of earls: C. V. Wedgwood, *Thomas Wentworth, First Earl of Strafford, 1593–1641: A Revaluation* (New York, 1962), *passim*; W. K. Jordan, *The Charities of Rural England, 1480–1660* (1961), 248 n.; *The Court Rolls of the Manor of Wakefield from October 1639 to September 1640*, ed. C. M. Fraser and K. Emsley (Yorks. Arch. Soc., Wakefield Court Rolls Ser. 1; 1977), pp. xii–xiii.

of common on the remainder, their access must have been hindered by Clifton's coal-pits which took up much of the unenclosed portion of the Outwood. Quite clearly, the Court of Duchy Chamber supported enclosures of waste even when such agreements were procured by deception and violated the court's earlier decrees. But Clifton compellingly argued that the enclosure scheme had originated with King James and that he could not keep up his payments to the duchy unless the enclosure agreement was carried through.[34]

In the far-northern counties the assault on border tenure or tenant right began after the Rebellion of the Northern Earls in 1569. On the estates of the Dean and Chapter of Durham, the Privy Council denied the claim by demesne farmers that they possessed their lands by tenant right, but upheld the heritability of customary tenancies. The need for military service on the Scottish border became redundant when the Crowns of England and Scotland were united in 1603. Border service was formally abolished in 1607. In 1618 Prince Charles concluded that the suppression of border service had voided manorial tenurial customs in the barony of Kendal, and tenants on the royal estates had to pay a composition of £2,700 to have their tenancies confirmed as estates of inheritance. The royal proclamation of 28 July 1620 extinguishing tenant-right tenure exhorted northern landlords to reduce their tenants to the status of leaseholders.[35]

The non-royal tenants of the barony of Kendal resisted by raising a common purse in order to initiate suits against their manorial lords, while Anthony Wetherell, vicar of Kirkby Stephen, drew up a remonstrance which defended tenant right in Westmorland by citing historical precedents. The attorney-general prosecuted Wetherell in Star Chamber for slander of justice for saying that the King's justice was 'not indifferent betwixte Lord and Tennant'. Samuel King, 'theire

---

[34] *Sir Edward Moseley, Attorney-General of the Duchy of Lancaster*, ex relation. *Sir Gervase Clifton, bart.* v. *Sir Arthur Pilkington, bart.*, PRO, DL 5/33, fos. 99ʳ&ᵛ, 298ᵛ–302.

[35] *TED*, i. 77–80; S. J. Watts, 'Tenant-Right in Early Seventeenth-century Northumberland', *NH* 6 (1971), 65–75; *Stuart Royal Proclamations*, ed. J. F. Larkin and P. J. Hughes (2 vols.; Oxford, 1973, 1983), i. *Royal Proclamations of King James I, 1603–1625*, no. 205; cf. Hoyle, 'Lords, Tenants, and Tenant Right in the Sixteenth Century', pp. 39–41; W. Butler, 'The Customs and Tenant Right Tenures of the Northern Counties, with Particulars of those in the District of Furness in the County of Lancashire', *Transactions of the Cumberland and Westmorland Antiquarian and Archaeological Society*, new ser. 26 (1926), 320–1; R. T. Spence, 'The Backward North Modernized? The Cliffords, Earls of Cumberland and the Socage Manor of Carlisle, 1611–1643', *NH* 20 (1984), 64–5.

captaine', read the libel to 100 persons who assembled in Stavely Chapel on 2 January 1621 and swore to maintain tenant right. Other copies were distributed elsewhere within the barony by James Smith, High Constable of Kendal, who gathered all the constables together under the guise of meeting to discuss repairs to bridges. The constables in turn met with householders to explain the issues and collect the common purse. The attorney-general prosecuted the leaders for sedition and unlawful assembly, but the Kendal tenants availed themselves of expert legal advice in their defence. They denied that border service was any part of their tenure and claimed that they possessed estates of inheritance by the customs of the country. Their strategy worked: the judges were compelled to accept their argument that the question of tenant right was not relevant, and that the royal proclamation of 28 July 1620 did not signify. The heritability of their holdings was to be decided in accordance with manorial custom.[36]

Tenants in Tudor and early-Stuart England fought long and hard to preserve or acquire estates of inheritance, and frequently took particular care to secure the rights of wards and widows and provide for female heirs. Some tenants apparently did lose their holdings during this period because mounting indebtedness prevented them from raising the capital to pay large entry fines or compositions, but not because manorial lords wished to be rid of them. On the Shropshire estates of the Earl of Bridgewater, where the Earl, by 1647, had increased entry fines to 30 times the level of 1602, every tenant or heir was offered a chance to renew his copyhold. Entry fines were abated in a few cases where labourers or cottagers pleaded poverty, but it is remarkable how readily tenants raised the money and how quickly the enhanced entry fines were paid. Most historians of English agriculture agree that the decline of the smallholder became pronounced only in the late seventeenth century—in corn-growing regions, while smallholders actually increased in many sylvan-pastoral regions.[37]

---

[36] *Sir Thomas Coventry, Attorney-General* v. *Anthony Wetherell, vicar of Kirkby Stephen*, PRO, STAC 8/34/4; Watts, 'Tenant-Right', pp. 75–8.
[37] D. G. Hey, *An English Rural Community: Myddle under the Tudors and Stuarts* (Leicester, 1974), 70–83; Thirsk, 'Seventeenth-century Agriculture and Social Change', pp. 156, 173–4; G. P. Jones, 'The Decline of the Yeomanry in the Lake Counties', *Transactions of the Cumberland and Westmorland Antiquarian and Archaeological Society*, new ser. 62 (1962), 211–12.

Fourteen case studies of manors or groups of manors troubled by resistance to enclosure agreements and by rent and tenurial disputes have been analysed in Chapters 5 and 6 because they illustrate the nature of these conflicts between lord and tenant and provide full details concerning formal agreements and equity-court decrees which attempted to resolve those conflicts. In most cases tenurial and rent disputes were settled to the advantage of the tenants: there is explicit evidence for ascertainment of entry fines in eight cases and probable evidence in a ninth case; in nine instances tenures were either confirmed or modified to the advantage of tenants.[38] Despite the large compositions levied for confirmation of tenants' estates and ascertainment of fines, those who could raise the money could usually recover their capital outlay by subleasing. In at least nine cases there is abundant evidence of impopulation and extensive subdivision and subleasing of tenements.

Eleven of the 14 examples are drawn from the west Midlands, Lancashire, and the West Riding of Yorkshire, while one case comes from Sussex and two from the east Midlands. Three of the 14 communities were exclusively agrarian in nature, but in two of these pastoral activities predominated. Of the 11 cases from Lancashire the West Riding, and the west Midlands, all but one reveal patterns of significant economic development and technological innovation. If we add to these ten proto-industrial communities the manor of Petworth, a tabulation of the variety of industrial pursuits reveals the presence of iron-founding and metal-working in three instances; clothing manufacture in another three communities; extensive use of water power for metal-working and cloth-fulling in six cases; and mineral extraction or peat-digging in seven instances. Impopulation led to subdivision and subleasing of wastes and messuages in nine instances, and this phenomenon was probably even more widespread. Sylvan-pastoral economies, where rural industrial development and impopulation occurred, displayed the most extensive alterations in land use and were especially prone to lengthy enclosure, rent, and tenurial disputes. In predominantly agrarian economies, tenurial and rent disputes were likely to occur on large estates where demesne

---

[38] However, for an example of the failure of the Council in the Marches and Principality of Wales to punish a tyrannical landlord, see J. Gwynfor Jones, 'Sir John Wynn of Gwydir and His Tenants: The Dolwyddelan and Llysfaen Disputes', *Welsh History Review* 11, 1–30, esp. 22–7.

leasing and the more extreme forms of fiscal seigneurialism were practised than on medium-sized estates where resident landlords more generally farmed their own demesnes and introduced new techniques in husbandry.[39]

[39] *VCH Stafford*, vi. 80.

PART II
Economic Crises and Social Protest

7

The Problem of Masterless Men

DURING the period from about 1586 to 1608 England was troubled by economic crises, political crises, social tension, and popular disorder. The crises were characterized by a sequence of harvest failures, dearth, and foot riots, as well as unemployment in the clothing trades; anti-enclosure riots occurred more frequently, and the government became more fearful of the problem of vagrants and masterless men. An epidemic of apprentices' riots, lasting nearly two decades, disturbed the peace of London, normally a well-governed city; an insurrection was attempted in Oxfordshire in 1596; and, finally, a rebellion spread across several midland counties in 1607.

To prevent the recurrence of popular disorder, the government undertook to establish a more ambitious programme of social and economic regulation. The Privy Council ordered magistrates to regulate the grain trade to ensure adequate supplies of corn at reasonable prices and to enforce the laws of apprenticeship in an attempt to provide fuller employment—especially in the depressed clothing industry. The Court of Star Chamber prosecuted landlords and farmers for enclosures which were alleged to be depopulating or were supposed to have caused a decline in the amount of land planted with grain. Parliament enacted a spate of laws intended to prevent the decay of tillage and houses of husbandry, the encroachment of illegal cottages upon commons, and to establish a rudimentary system of poor relief based upon the parish. This ambitious programme of social and economic regulation was codified in various Books of Orders issued between 1587 and 1631, and signalled a determination to compel magistrates and constables to enforce these regulative statutes. The recurrence of similar crises in 1623 and 1629–31 underlined the government's warnings about the need for social regulation and resulted in unwonted interference in local government and considerable resentment on the part of county magistrates.

The more immediate reaction to the late-Elizabethan and early-Stuart crises took the form of judicial severity in punishing crimes against public order, including sedition and the circumstances in which a riot could be construed as treason.[1] Increasingly, royal officials resorted to absolutist expedients to deal with the problem of masterless men, who were thought to have furnished many of the participants in popular disturbances.[2] Looking back on the century and a half that preceded the Restoration of Charles II, the antiquarian John Aubrey perceived that a loosening of the social bonds had cast many people adrift on a sea of change: 'whereby the meane people lived lawlesse, nobody to govern them, they cared for nobody, having on nobody any dependence. . . .' Aubrey was describing the phenomenon of masterless men, which he blamed on the disintegration of traditional agrarian society: the entailing of estates, enclosures of open fields and commons, the redistribution of monastic lands, the decline of aristocratic hospitality, and the poor example set by absentee gentry. In fact, the problem of masterless men was older and more complex than Aubrey realized. It was the product not only of agrarian change, but also of population growth and the development of rural industry.[3]

Masterless men represented the very antithesis of good order in a patriarchal society. Depending on no lord, recognizing no master, propertyless, and footloose, they inspired a fear of ungovernable multitudes which was out of all proportion to their numbers and actual potential for mischief. Two categories of masterless person

---

[1] Although historians generally are aware of the late-Elizabethan economic, social, and political crises, few have attempted to discuss them comprehensively. Among the most notable attempts to do so are to be found in Clark, *English Provincial Society*, chs. 7, 8, and 11; id., 'Popular Protest and Disturbance in Kent, 1558–1640', *Ec. HR*, 2nd ser. 29 (1976), 365–81; and Appleby, *Famine in Tudor and Stuart England, passim*. More recently, Peter Clark has edited a collection of essays which place the problem within a larger context: *The European Crises of the 1590s: Essays in Comparative History* (1985). The doubling of the frequency of enclosure riots during this period has been analysed in chs. 3 and 4. One aspect of the judicial reaction to popular criticism of the government is discussed in my essay, 'The Origins of the Doctrine of Sedition', *Albion* 12/2 (1980), 99–121. The extension of the law of treason to cover riots in certain circumstances is discussed in J. Bellamy, *The Tudor Law of Treason: An Introduction* (1979), 48, 78–81.

[2] A. L. Beier, *Masterless Men: The Vagrancy Problem in England, 1560–1640* (1985), 152–8, discusses the 'inventions of absolutism' employed to control and punish vagrancy.

[3] Jackson, *Wiltshire: The Topographical Collections of John Aubrey*, p. 9. For a discussion of the connection between the decline of aristocratic hospitality and the problem of poverty, see F. Heal, 'The Idea of Hospitality in Early Modern England', *P. & P.*, no. 102 (Feb. 1984), 66–93.

are to be discussed in this chapter: vagrants, who were largely but not exclusively an urban problem, and cottagers and squatters upon wastes and commons, who crowded into sylvan, pastoral, and proto-industrial regions. Both categories included considerable numbers of unemployed or underemployed artisans belonging to either decaying trades or developing industries. Vagrants and cottager-artisans were also highly mobile, and the law made little distinction between labour mobility and vagabondage.[4]

So great was the fear of vagrants and masterless men in Tudor and early-Stuart England that the government resorted to methods of social control of questionable legality. Between 1531 and 1597 Parliament enacted vagrancy laws which varied from the savage to the merely repressive. Although whipping was the most frequently applied punishment for ordinary vagrants, at various times branding, mutilation, hanging, slavery, transportation, and perpetual servitude in the galleys were tried out as remedies for incorrigible rogues. The employment of provost-marshals to round up vagrants, the use of general search warrants, and, after 1597, the summary whipping of vagrants, were some of the emergency measures that were advocated or, at least, acquiesced in during the late-Elizabethan and early-Stuart crises.[5]

i. *Vagrancy*

By statutory definition, a vagrant was a person able to labour who possessed neither land nor master, who worked at no recognized trade, and who refused to accept such employment as might be offered to him. Almost invariably this meant working as a servant-in-husbandry or agricultural labourer. Unless a person owned property worth 40s. *p.a.*, was an heir to property of that value, or possessed goods worth £10, or belonged to certain specified callings (i.e., gentlemen, clergy, scholars, miners, and colliers), he was not free

---

[4] P. A. J. Pettit, *The Royal Forests of Northamptonshire, 1558–1714* (Northants. Rec. Soc. 23; 1968), 162–3; Davies, *The Enforcement of English Apprenticeship*, p. 7; Hill, *The World Turned Upside Down*, pp. 32–5.

[5] W. K. Jordan, *Philanthropy in England, 1480–1660: A Study of the Changing Pattern of English Social Aspirations* (New York, 1959), 79; P. Williams, *The Tudor Regime* (Oxford, 1979), 199–204. The emergency measures used against recusants and seminary priests in the 1580s and 1590s were similar to some of those employed to apprehend and punish vagrants. Cf. my 'Elizabethan Recusancy Commissions', *HJ* 15/1 (1972), 23–36.

to dispose of his own labour. Those who were under 30 years of age and had completed apprenticeships might be compelled to work for any master of the same trade who asked for their labour. All other persons between the ages of 12 and 60, who were neither bound apprentices nor practised a craft, were obliged to work as farm labourers. To refuse to do so brought punishment for vagrancy.[6]

These strictures, as embodied in the Statute of Artificers of 1563 and the Vagrancy Act of 1572, were by no means new. They had originated in the fourteenth-century Statutes of Labourers, which had attempted to prevent labourers from wandering about seeking better wages and conditions of unemployment by prohibiting labourers leaving their hundreds without written passes or hiring themselves out for less than one year. An exception to the rule of annual hiring was harvest work, which even artificers from occupations other than husbandry could be compelled to undertake. Enforcement of the provisions of the Statutes of Labourers of 1388 relating to annual hirings appears to have lapsed in the favourable labour market of the fifteenth century, but resumed again in the 1530s and continued until the enactment of the Statute of Artificers in 1563. That law codified earlier legislation and added two new provisions: regulation of conditions of apprenticeship by the state rather than by guilds, and the fixing of local wage rates periodically by the Justices of the Peace.[7]

There did exist a small hard core of 'sturdy beggars' and 'lusty rogues' whom no law could compel to do honest labour. Thomas Harman's *A Caueat or Warening for Commen Cursetors vulgarely called Vagabones* (1567) distinguishes betwen 24 categories of professional vagabonds, and his list is not exhaustive. But the economic crises of the 1590s swelled the numbers of vagrants who sought work or relief in London, Salisbury, Norwich, and other towns. Gradually, the governors of Tudor England came to perceive that vagrancy and poverty were two distinct problems. Poverty was

---

[6] Statute of Artificers of 1563 (5 Eliz. I, c. 4), *TED* i. 338–49; Vagrancy and Poor Relief Act of 1572 (14 Eliz. I, c. 5), *Select Statutes and other Constitutional Documents Illustrative of the Reigns of Elizabeth and James I*, ed. Sir G. W. Prothero (4th edn.; Oxford, 1913), 67–72.

[7] Statutes of Labourers of 1388 (12 Rich. II, cc. 3, 7), *SR* ii. 56, 58; PRO, STAC 2/10, fo. 88; ibid., SP 12/19/43, printed in *TED*, i. 334–8; Davies, *The Enforcement of English Apprenticeship*, p. 7.

sharpest in the towns, and it was cities such as Norwich and London that first attempted to provide poor relief in a systematic manner. A category of deserving poor was discovered, but the deserving poor excluded all who could not establish a claim to residence. Therefore, one of the first concerns of any scheme of poor relief was to whip the wandering poor back to the parishes in which they were settled legally.[8]

In many English towns between one-quarter and one-third of the population were destitute because they did not receive regular wages. Most of the destitute poor were willing and able to work, but belonged to decayed crafts and depressed industries. A census of the poor in Norwich in 1570 revealed that women were half again as numerous as men and that poor families had an average of only two children each. The latter reflects the fact that children from poor households were compelled to take up service as apprentices in wealthier households. Most of the adult women and many of the children were able to spin thread or knit lace. But their wages were below the subsistence level and they frequently resorted to begging or asking for parish relief.[9]

Hardly better off than the destitute poor were the wage-earners, who were unable to set up even as small-scale independent craftsmen. They comrpised a little less than half of the urban taxpayers. Living close to the subsistence level, high food prices or even a brief illness could reduce a wage-earner's family to destitution very quickly. During the crisis of 1623 half of Salisbury's population was considered to be impoverished. Together, the destitute poor and the wage-earners made up between half and three-quarters of English urban populations. Economic crises could cause them to start begging or

[8] *TED* iii. 407–15; Williams, *The Tudor Regime*, pp. 175–6; J. Pound, *Poverty and Vagrancy in Tudor England* (1971), 25–6; P. Slack, 'Poverty and Politics in Salisbury, 1597–1666', in P. Clark and P. Slack (eds.), *Crisis and Order in English Towns* (Toronto, 1972), 168–71; E. M. Leonard, *The Early History of English Poor Relief* (repr. 1965), 61–6. J. Hadwin, 'The Problem of Poverty in Early Modern England', in T. Riis (ed.), *Aspects of Poverty in Early Modern Europe* (Alphen aan den Rijn, 1981), 219–51, provides both an introduction to the problem and a survey of the relevant literature.

[9] Pound, *Poverty and Vagrancy in Tudor England*, pp. 25–6; D. C. Coleman, 'Labour in the English Economy of the Seventeenth Century', *Ec. HR*, 2nd ser. 8 (1956), 280–95; A. D. Dyer, *The City of Worcester in the Sixteenth Century* (Leicester, 1973), 166; A. L. Beier, 'The Social Problems of an Elizabethan Country Town: Warwick, 1589–90', in P. Clark (ed.), *Country Towns in Pre-industrial England* (New York, 1981), 60.

wandering. Thus, not only the destitute poor but even wage-labourers thrown out of work were potential vagrants.[10]

Poverty was less of a problem in rural areas than in towns. The problem was least acute in those sylvan–pastoral regions where the poor still retained access to the resources of wastes—especially when rural industries suffered trade depressions. The poor did not require extensive public relief in Myddle or in other parts of North Shropshire until the late seventeenth century because abundant wastes and woodlands remained for squatters. Early-Stuart Myddle was still able to absorb immigrants and willingly dispensed charity to the poor. Most of the poor in Myddle were farm labourers who constituted about 20 per cent of the population of the parish at the beginning of the seventeenth century and about one-half at the end of that century. Nor were there to be found in Myddle the sharp contrasts between poor cottagers and prosperous farmers that were so evident in the villages of Essex and Suffolk. The tensions between these two groups were especially pronounced in early seventeenth-century Terling, an almost purely agricultural community where the commons had long been enclosed. Although woodland-pasture regions with their more diversified economies generally remained able to absorb the wandering poor until the seventeenth century, there were some exceptions. The broadcloth districts of Wiltshire, Somerset, and Gloucestershire were especially vulnerable to harvest failure, economic depression, and unemployment, and might spew out their marginal inhabitants during crisis years. Woodland areas were characterized by high rates of emigration as well as immigration. Moreover, town-dwellers especially feared vagrants from woodland areas because of the latter's reputation for lawlessness.[11]

The savage punishments meted out to vagrants testify to the deep and persistent fear of masterless men. This fear was out of all proportion to the actual numbers of vagrants; official estimates often

---

[10] Pound, *Poverty and Vagrancy in Tudor England*, pp. 25–6; Slack, 'Poverty and Politics in Salisbury, 1597–1666', p. 171; Beier, *Masterless Men*, pp. 15, 29–30.

[11] Jordan, *Philanthropy in England, 1480–1660*, pp. 67–71; Hey, *Myddle*, pp. 171, 178, 188; K. Wrightson and D. Levine, *Poverty and Piety in an English Village: Terling, 1525–1700* (1979), 175; P. Slack, 'Vagrants and Vagrancy in England, 1598–1664', *Ec. HR*, new ser. 17 (1974), 374–5; V. H. T. Skipp, 'Economic and Social Change in the Forest of Arden, 1530–1649', *Ag. HR* 18 (1970), 107–9; Beier, *Masterless Men*, pp. 37–40.

exaggerated their numbers, but they were unlikely to have exceeded 2 per cent of the population in 1603. Vagabonds were thought to travel in bands and lurk in woods and on heaths, and to be capable of offering much violence—a supposition natural enough in a culture which still relished tales of Robin Hood. But such outlaw bands had disappeared from even the frontiers of England and Wales by the middle of the sixteenth century.[12]

Vagrants were also feared because they were thought to have rebelled against the patriarchal authority of family and household; many of them had, in fact, deserted husbands or wives, or had run away from masters. Their very idleness was thought to constitute another act of rebellion. They were rootless and without visible ties of kinship. They did not enter into durable marital or familial relationships. Because vagrants were highly mobile they were regarded as spreaders of seditious rumours and also of disease. Vagrants were also considered to be prone to disorder, and Tudor statesmen assumed that they furnished the bulk of those who participated in rebellions and riots. It was not unusual for complainants in enclosure-riot cases in the Court of Star Chamber to allege that the defendants had hired vagrants out of alehouses for the work of levelling hedges.[13]

Fairs and market days were essential to the economic health of pre-industrial towns. Yet fairs and markets also attracted vagrants, who took advantage of these occasions to look for work or fence stolen goods. Some vagabonds might make the rounds of a dozen or more fairs in the course of a year. During the growing season vagrants roamed the highways of fielden areas looking for harvest work and other opportunities; they preferred to spend the winter months in woodland areas, where a bit of poaching might be done, or to take lodgings in alehouses in towns. Vagrants were thought to be incorrigible rumour-mongers and, indeed, their confabulations

[12] Id., 'Vagrants and the Social Order in Elizabethan England', *P. & P.*, no. 64 (1974), 6; id., 'The Social Problems of an Elizabethan Country Town: Warwick, 1589-90', pp. 57-8. The penalties of the criminal law were applied more harshly to indicted felons who were also strangers in early-Stuart East Sussex: C. B. Herrup, 'Law and Morality in Seventeenth-century England', *P. & P.*, no. 106 (Feb. 1985), 117-18.

[13] Slack, 'Vagrants and Vagrancy in England, 1598-1664', pp. 360-77; P. Clark, 'The Migrant in Kentish Towns, 1580-1640', in P. Clark and P. Slack (eds.), *Crisis and Order in English Towns, 1500-1700* (Toronto, 1972), 152-3; PRO, STAC 5/H76/17.

at fairs and festivals did spark disorder. Hence, local authorities often conducted sweeps of vagabonds during such times.[14]

The proliferation of illegal alehouses and lodging houses is a measure of the problem of masterless men in both rural and urban areas. In some towns as many as one in ten houses functioned as alehouses; perhaps 20 per cent of urban households contained lodgers. People who brewed ale and kept alehouses and lodging houses were themselves poor and needed to supplement meagre incomes. Alehouses were regulated by justices of the peace after the passing of the Licensing Act of 1552 (5 and 6 Edw. VI, c. 25); taking in lodgers was prohibited by a variety of late-Elizabethan enactments (31 Eliz., c. 7 and 35 Eliz., c. 6) and municipal ordinances. As alehouses came to be patronized almost exclusively by the poor and scorned by the more respectable members of the community, they also came to be viewed as havens for vagrants and centres for sedition. The poor depended on alehouses for bread as well as drink, and the latter constituted a significant part of their diet. Magistrates were frequently lax about suppressing illegal alehouses; some alehouse keepers had no other source of income and might otherwise have become public charges. But in times of dearth, most alehouses were usually suppressed because they consumed precious supplies of barley, the most common source of bread for the poor.[15]

The distinction between the 'impotent' poor—the aged, the sick, and the physically handicapped—and the 'impudent' poor was clear enough in Tudor England, but it was not until 1576 that English law distinguished between incorrigible vagabonds and those who were able and willing to labour but could find no work. The Statute of 1576 (18 Eliz., c. 3) ordered local magistrates to purchase stocks of wool, hemp, flax, and iron to provide work for the poor and to keep them from idleness. Although more elaborate schemes for poor relief were enacted subsequently, the main rationale for all vagrancy and poor laws remained the preservation of public order. Hence,

---

[14] Beier, *Masterless Men*, pp. 73–6; id., 'Vagrants and the Social Order in Elizabethan England', pp. 3–29; Hist. MSS Comm., *Salisbury*, xi. 170.

[15] P. Clark, 'Introduction: English Country Towns, 1500–1800', in P. Clark (ed.), *Country Towns in Pre-industrial England* (New York, 1981), 11; Beier, 'The Social Problems of an Elizabethan Country Town: Warwick, 1589–90', p. 61; PRO, STAC 8/40/9; K. Wrightson, 'Alehouses, Order and Reformation in Rural England, 1590–1660', in E. and S. Yeo (eds.), *Popular Culture and Class Conflict, 1590–1914: Explorations in the History of Labour and Leisure* (Brighton, 1981), 4, 11.

there was always a greater emphasis upon punishment of idleness than upon poor relief. The medieval Statutes of Labourers had been content to punish vagrancy by confining culprits in the stocks. It was an Act of the Reformation Parliament (22 Hen. VIII, c. 12) that provided a statutory basis for the whipping of vagrants until their backs 'be bloody'—a practice authorized the previous year by royal proclamation. The infamous Edwardian Vagrancy Act of 1547 (1 Edw. VI, c. 3), which proposed to inflict branding and slavery upon sturdy beggars, proved to be too severe and was repealed within two years. This restored whipping as the statutory punishment for vagrants.[16]

The enforcement of the vagrancy laws was sporadic and probably reflected the degree of official concern about threats to public order at any given moment. Between 1569 and 1571 the Privy Council ordered JPs to organize searches for vagrants. The effectiveness of these sweeps varied from county to county; those rounded up were subjected to a whipping campaign. The correspondence between Lord Burghley and Henry, Earl of Huntingdon, president of the Council in the North, indicates how apprehensive the government continued to be in the wake of the Rebellion of the Northern Earls of 1569. As late as 1572 Huntingdon was still flogging vagabonds in order 'to stay the spreading of false and seditious rumours and the sending of messages from the late rebels. . . .'[17]

It may have been alarm at the number of vagrants swept up after the 1569 rebellion that prompted the enactment of the Vagrancy and Poor Relief Act of 1572 (14 Eliz., c. 5)—the most repressive vagrancy law of the Elizabethan period. First offenders were to be imprisoned until the next quarter sessions or gaol delivery and upon conviction were to be whipped and burnt in the ear unless some worthy householder accepted them into service for one year. Second offenders were to be adjudged felons unless a householder took them into service for two years. A second offender who ran away was to be hanged. Two women were sentenced to be hanged as incorrigible vagrants at the Middlesex Sessions in October 1576; one was executed and the other spared because of pregnancy. Another woman

---

[16] *TED* ii. 331–4; Tawney, *The Agrarian Problem*, pp. 279–80; Pound, *Poverty and Vagrancy in Tudor England*, pp. 103–4; Williams, *The Tudor Regime*, pp. 196–8; C. S. L. Davies, 'Slavery and Protector Somerset: The Vagrancy Act of 1547', *Ec. HR*, 2nd ser. 19 (1966), 533–49.

[17] Leonard, *The Early History of English Poor Relief*, pp. 81–3.

was apparently hanged at Warwick in 1582 for the same offence. The Act of 1572 also established a national scheme for poor relief by authorizing appointment of overseers of the poor and making payment of parish poor rates compulsory.[18]

By the late 1590s the problem of vagrancy threatened to overwhelm the courts and summary punishment replaced more formal court proceedings. Whereas the Vagrancy Act of 1572 required that persons accused of vagrancy be convicted at the quarter sessions before corporal punishment was administered, the Vagrancy Act of 1597 (39 Eliz., c. 4), which repealed and superseded all previous laws against vagrancy, allowed two JPs (one of whom must be of the quorum) to hear and determine cases of vagrancy out of sessions. In practice, Dalton thought that one justice might authorize the flogging of vagrants. Where town or hundredal constables caught a person actually engaged in begging, they might inflict whipping at the cart's tail without reference to a magistrate. Vagrants who were strangers were given testimonials of punishment and sent back to their native parishes or parishes of last settlement. The law encouraged repeated whippings, and if a vagrant person's place of birth or last settlement could not be determined, then the last parish which had not whipped the vagrant was to bear the responsibility and cost of maintaining that vagrant. Finally, the Act also authorized the JPs at the quarter sessions to banish incorrigible rogues from the realm or condemn them to perpetual servitude in the galleys.[19]

Evidence concerning the enforcement of the Vagrancy Act of 1597 is scarce but, if the case of Salisbury is at all representative, another whipping campaign began almost immediately. Between 1598 and 1638 more than 650 vagrants were flogged out of Salisbury. Of these no fewer than 96 were punished and expelled during the first year — an indication of the severity of the crises of the 1590s in Salisbury. This first group did not consist of the sturdy beggars and perpetual wanderers of more normal times, but rather were predominantly

---

[18] *Select Statutes*, ed. Prothero, pp. 67–72; *Middlesex County Records*, ed. J. C. Jeaffreson (6 vols.; 1886), i. 102–3; Beier, 'Vagrants and the Social Order in Elizabethan England', p. 15 n; id., *Masterless Men*, p. 160. The death penalty for the second offence of vagrancy was renewed by three subsequent Acts of Parliament, but was rescinded in 1593 by 35 Eliz. I, c. 7: Leonard, *The Early History of English Poor Relief*, pp. 72–3.

[19] *Select Statutes*, ed. Prothero, pp. 100–2; cf. Dalton, *The Countrey Iustice*, p. 108; Williams, *The Tudor Regime*, p. 211 and n.

single women from within 20 miles of Salisbury. In London during the month of February 1598 between 25 and 50 vagrants were brought before the Court of Bridewell Hospital almost every day and punished by whipping.[20] The punishment of rogues was a prerogative that municipal corporations guarded jealously; the possession of stocks and pillory were the symbols of a well-ordered commonwealth. When Lord William Howard purchased Barnstaple Priory he tried to appropriate these symbols of authority; this provoked a clash between his servants and the mayor and bailiffs of the borough who claimed that as a consequence vagabonds went unpunished. Sir Edward Herne, a Lincolnshire justice of the peace, thought that flogging was a sovereign remedy for all beggars—even when they possessed licences from the lord chancellor. When Herne whipped a merchant of Rye who had obtained letters patent under the great seal authorizing him to take up a collection for the repair of Rye haven, he was prosecuted in Star Chamber, imprisoned in the Fleet Prison, fined £200, and ordered to pay £50 in damages.[21]

In London, the punishment of vagrants by whipping was first recorded in 1547, but probably began earlier. At first vagabonds were tied to a cart's tail and flogged through the streets, but during the reign of Elizabeth it became usual for parish officers to set up permanent whipping posts and stocks and to hire assistants to administer the punishment. The vestry-men of St Peter Cornhill and St Andrew Undershaft shared the costs of erecting a cage in which to confine vagrants until they could be whipped and passed on to the next parish.[22]

However conscientiously the churchwardens might apply themselves to their duties, they were not equal to the task of whipping every vagrant in London. The punishment of vagrants was taken over by Bridewell Hospital, a former royal palace, which was given to the city of London by the crown to serve as a 'Workhouse for poore and idle persons'. It was one of several specialized charitable institutions founded in London during the mid-Tudor period. The

---

[20] Slack, 'Poverty and Politics in Salisbury, 1597–1666', p. 166; id., 'Vagrants and Vagrancy in England, 1598–1664', pp. 360–1; London Guildhall Library, Bridewell Royal Hospital, Court Books, microfilm reel 512, unfol.; Beier, *Masterless Men*, p. 160.
[21] PRO, STAC 3/3/9; *Historical Collections*, ed. Rushworth, ii/2, app. 19.
[22] C. Pendrill, *Old Parish Life in London* (1937), 200–3.

Bridewell Court of Governors operated as a tribunal which could hand out summary punishment to runaway servants and incorrigible apprentices, as well as masterless men. More rarely, it dealt with masters who mistreated servants. The Bridewell Court of Governors also infringed upon the jurisdiction of the ecclesiastical courts in so far as it heard and determined cases involving prostitution, procuring for prostitution, adultery, fornication, carnal knowledge, bigamy, slander, and swearing.[23]

A. L. Beier's analysis of the court books of Bridewell demonstrates a large increase in the number of vagrants arrested and punished in late-Elizabethan and early-Stuart London. Sixty-nine vagrants were committed for punishment by the Court of Governors in 1560–1; 555 in 1600–1; and 815 in 1624–5. This suggests that during a period when London's population quadrupled, the vagrancy rate increased twelvefold. While it is true that vagrants were rounded up in a more systematic manner after the appointment of provost-marshals in 1588, the main reasons for the increase in vagrancy were the influx of population and the inability of the economy to absorb the immigrants. Whereas most of those arrested for vagrancy in the earlier part of the Elizabethan period came from outside London, by the late 1590s half of the vagrants claimed to have been born in the London area. Thus the slums of London perpetuated the problems of vagrancy and poverty by breeding more vagrants. Vagrants in London were predominantly young men and were typically domestic servants or apprentices who had run away from their masters or had been laid off during trade depressions.[24]

The function of Bridewell Hospital was to correct masterless persons who had claimed to have been born in London and to remove from London vagrants whose legal settlement was elsewhere. Inmates of Bridewell were required to work at the spinning and fulling of wool and nail-making; the most difficult rogues were sent to mills and lighters on the river or to the hospital bakehouse. There were various ways that inmates could be delivered from Bridewell: they

---

[23] Stow, *Survey of London*, ii. 44–5; A. L. Beier, 'Social Problems of Elizabethan London', *Journal of Interdisciplinary History*, 9/2 (1978), 203–21; *TED* iii. 439; Leonard, *The Early History of English Poor Relief*, pp. 34–6; London Guildhall Library, Bridewell Royal Hospital, Court Books, microfilm reel 512, unfol.

[24] Beier, 'Social Problems of Elizabethan London', pp. 203–221; Clark and Slack, *Crisis and Order*, pp. 35–6; R. Finlay, *Population and Metropolis: The Demography of London, 1580–1650* (Cambridge, 1981), 51.

could express penitence and a desire to enter service, provided they could find masters and sureties; and males could be discharged if they expressed a willingness to be impressed as soldiers. A group of Irish beggars were shipped back to Ireland in 1587, and after 1622 the practice began of transporting inmates to Virginia or the West Indies. Persons passing through the city with valid passports were routinely discharged, but were whipped first if they had tarried too long; those who lacked passports were punished and passed on to their native parishes. Very rarely a 'pore lame fellow' might be sent to St Thomas's Hospital instead of being punished, but most persons appearing before the Court of Governors were discharged only after they had been whipped. By the late 1580s Bridewell was so overcrowded that its function was limited to punishment rather than correction. Yet houses of correction, or 'bridewells' as they were commonly called, were built in many other parts of England in the seventeenth century despite the fact that the original model had been the least effective of all the charitable institutions of Tudor London.[25]

The failure of the city authorities to keep the streets cleared of vagrants frequently provoked interference by the Crown. Early in January 1582, towards the end of Christmastide, the Queen was riding through Islington when her carriage was surrounded by a great crowd of beggars. The incident must have alarmed her, because William Fleetwood, recorder of London, was ordered to begin a sweep of masterless men the same day. The campaign lasted about ten days and netted several hundred vagrants—100 being taken in a single day. The beggars in Islington were easily located because they were wont to huddle together for warmth among the brick kilns in the village. Other masterless persons were discovered through searches of private premises under the authority of general warrants which were issued routinely by the Privy Council to ferret out recusants as well as vagrants. Recorder Fleetwood often led these 'privy searches' in person; with the backing of Lord Burghley Fleetwood did not hesitate to extend his searches into the liberties and special jurisdictions of Middlesex and Surrey, and even invaded the Savoy Hospital and carried away inmates. Most of those apprehended were

---

[25] London Guildhall Library, Bridewell Royal Hospital, Court Books, microfilm reel 512, unfol.; CLRO, Rep. 21, fo. 429ᵛ; *TED* iii. 431, 439; Beier, 'Social Problems of Elizabethan London', p. 217.

bestowed upon Bridewell; some were committed to Newgate Prison to await general gaol delivery; and a few were released after being warned to return home to their masters.[26]

Although the lord mayor and other city magistrates were frequently admonished to be more vigorous in sweeping up masterless men, the Crown gave little help in eliminating the places where vagrants congregated. Henry VIII had agreed to the suppression of the stews, or licensed brothels, of Southwark in 1546, but Elizabeth turned a deaf ear to pleas from the city authorities to close the theatres built on the south bank of the Thames during periods of popular disorder. Only when epidemics of the plague raged did the government close the playhouses. Attempts were made to control the growth of London by parliamentary statute and royal proclamation, but courtiers and wealthy citizens who illegally subdivided dwelling houses, built cottages, and encroached upon scarce commons went unpunished. Under Charles I the Crown enforced these laws more rigorously — but only as a means of raising revenue.[27]

ii. *Cottagers and Squatters*

The movement of population from fielden to pastoral and sylvan regions, together with the growth of rural industries, led to an increase in the number of cottagers and squatters upon wastes and commons, in forests and fenlands, and on heaths and mosses. By the early seventeenth century there were clear signs of a reaction to this phenomenon among the smallhold tenants of sylvan and pastoral communities, who wished to preserve their own use-rights against the depredations of squatters. This often led to sharp conflict within

---

[26] J. Stow, *Survey of the Cities of London and Westminster*, ed. J. Strype (2 vols.; 1720), ii. 436–8; *Original Letters Illustrative of English History*, ed. Sir Henry Ellis (11 vols.; 1824–46), 1st ser. ii. 283–8; CLRO, Rep. 23, fo. 552ᵛ; D. J. Johnson, *Southwark and the City* (1969), 225–6. Aubrey tells the story of a group of highwaymen who resolved to be avenged upon Fleetwood for his severity towards some of their colleagues. They waylaid him near Tyburn Hill on the Oxford Road as he was returning from his country house in Buckinghamshire. The highwaymen bound his hands behind back, put a halter around his neck, and left him sitting on his horse beneath the Tyburn gallows tree. The steadiness of his horse kept him unharmed until another traveller could cut the rope: *Aubrey's Brief Lives*, ed. Dick, p. 107.

[27] Ibid., 67, 223–4; E. J. Davis, 'The Transformation of London', *Tudor Studies Presented . . . to Albert Frederick Pollard* (repr. 1970), 308–9; Stow, *Survey of London*, ii. 72; T. Birch, *The Court and Times of Charles I* (2 vols.; 1848), ii. 170.

such communities because certain individuals stood to profit from the impopulation of wastes: clothiers, coal-mine and quarry owners, and iron-masters desired pools of cheap, casual labour while some landlords found it more profitable to subdivide tenancies and rent cottages than to invest in agricultural improvement. On the royal estates crown officials were more interested in discovering squatters and collecting rents from them than they were in preventing encroachments on royal demesne or halting the erosion of the common rights of crown tenants.

Cottages were distinguished from houses of husbandry by the fact that they lacked sufficient land to support a household by agriculture alone. Consequently, cottagers hired themselves out as farm labourers or worked at by-employments. These occupations were seasonal and helped to define cottagers as underemployed and casual workers. Their work habits were often 'task-oriented', that is, they worked only so long as was necessary to obtain a certain sum of money. Where use-rights were allowed to all inhabitants and not limited to tenants, and where the resources of wastes continued unstinted, cottagers might subsist with very little labour. All of these characteristics were taken to be evidence of the 'idleness' of cottagers.[28]

Cottages originated in different ways. Some were built on land assarted, or cleared from the forest, under seigneurial licence; others were erected on approvements of waste undertaken by manorial lords and, perhaps, leased to old tenants on favourable terms in order to secure the latter's assent to enclosure agreements. Such cottages and their meagre parcels of land might be leased to subtenants or subdivided among daughters and younger sons in areas of partible inheritance. Others originated as squatters' huts built on illegal encroachments upon the waste, but were subsequently detected by surveyors or manorial officers and their occupants compelled to pay rent. In many communities cottages were furnished to paupers as a form of poor relief. In some woodland areas entirely new settlements of squatters sprang up; dispersed in isolated hamlets, distinct from older village communities, and remote from the influence

---

[28] A. Everitt, 'Farm Labourers', *AHEW* iv. 409 and n.; I. Blanchard, 'Labour Productivity and Work Psychology in the English Mining Industry, 1400–1600', *Ec. HR*, 2nd ser. 31/1 (1972), 4–7; Hill, *The World Turned Upside Down*, p. 35.

of manor house and parish church, their way of life was thought to display all of the dangerous tendencies of masterless men.[29]

In the earlier part of the sixteenth century the interests of small-holders and cottagers were not sharply distinguished, but the process of social differentiation together with the pressure of population on the diminishing resources of pasture, fuel, and living space widened the gulf between these social groups. Nor were all cottagers and labourers poor. The more prosperous members of this group, who were able to hold on to their use-rights and who took up some profitable trade, were sometimes able to rise into the ranks of the yeomanry. But between 1530 and 1640 most cottagers and labourers suffered from declining real wages, loss of use-rights on commons and wastes, and trade depressions. Increasingly, in the early seventeenth century, smallholders were prepared to co-operate in attempts to exclude cottagers and squatters from commons by means of enclosure agreements, disafforestation, fen-drainage schemes, or by simply destroying cottages that offended them.[30]

There were a number of Tudor statutes that dealt with the subject of cottages. The popular understanding of these laws, together with certain rather persistent myths, encouraged the belief that the poor had a moral claim to encroach upon wastes and commons and, indeed, might even obtain legal recognition of squatters' rights. The Vagrancy Statute of 1547 (1 Edw. VI, c. 3) authorized the building of cottages for the impotent poor. This clause was reenacted in 3 & 4 Edw. VI, c. 16. The Act of 1549–50 for the improvement of wastes and commons (3 & 4 Edw. VI, c. 3) permitted cottages with under three acres of ground, already standing upon wastes, to continue to remain with their enclosures. This, in effect, confirmed squatters' rights. The Statute of 1589 (31 Eliz., c. 7) was intended to control the proliferation of poor cottages and squatters' hovels on commons by requiring that each cottage built must have not less than four acres of land laid to it and forbidding more than one family per cottage. But excepted from this act were cottages within one mile of mineral works, coal-mines, quarries, brick, tile, and lime kilns, as well as cottages within one mile of the sea and dwellings on the

[29] Everitt, 'Farm Labourers', pp. 411–12; J. Porter, 'Encroachment as an Element in the Rural Landscape', *Local Historian* 2 (Aug. 1974), 141–7.
[30] A. Everitt, 'Social Mobility in Early Modern England', *P. & P.*, no. 33 (1966), 56–8; Smyth, *The Berkeley Manuscripts*, iii. 327–8.

banks of navigable rivers. Again, the Act did not apply to dwellings erected for the aged, sick, and impotent poor. The Poor Law of 1598 (39 & 40 Eliz., c. 3) authorized the overseers of the poor to pay for such cottages out of the poor rates.[31] Moreover, there existed a popular belief, widespread in the West of England and parts of Wales at least, that if a man succeeded in erecting a cottage on the waste overnight and smoke could be observed coming from the chimney with the first light of dawn, he might enjoy possession of the same. With the passage of a couple of decades his possession might even be recognized as constituting a title. In Montgomeryshire squatter settlements planted in this fashion lasted until the time of parliamentary enclosure in the nineteenth century.[32]

On the royal manor of Slaidburn in the West Riding of Yorkshire, encroachments by squatters were especially noticeable between 1519 and 1624. During this period some 90 acres of land were alienated from the waste, while presentments to the manorial court revealed that 198 buildings had been erected without licence, of which no fewer than 64 were dwelling houses. The population of the four townships within the manor probably doubled during this period as a consequence of squatters' settlements. Because they had a financial interest in doing so, the Duchy of Lancaster officials exerted themselves to detect such encroachments in order that punitive fines might be levied and rents collected. By 1586 the freehold and copyhold tenants were complaining about the loss of pasture land to squatters' encroachments. In 1587 the Court of Duchy Chamber imposed an enclosure agreement upon the cottagers and tenants whereby the former were allotted 20 acres and the latter as much as they cared to enclose in severalty at 4*d.* an acre p.a. Because of the cottagers' poverty, and in consideration of the improvements which they had made, they were to be granted 21-year leases of their parcels free of rent, with a promise of renewal for another 21 years at 4*d.* an acre. The continuing influx of squatters necessitated another and more extensive enclosure in 1624.[33]

[31] Leonard, *The Early History of English Poor Relief*, p. 57; *SR* iv/1. 102–3, iv/2. 804–5; *Select Statutes*, ed. Prothero, pp. 96–100.

[32] Everitt, 'Farm Labourers', p. 411 n; W. G. Hoskins and H. P. R. Finberg, *Devonshire Studies* (1952), 327–9; Hoskins, *Provincial England*, pp. 137–8; id., 'The Reclamation of the Waste in Devon, 1550–1800', p. 87; Slater, *The English Peasantry and the Enclosure of Common Fields*, pp. 119–20.

[33] Porter, 'Encroachment as an Element in the Rural Landscape', pp. 141–7; *TED* i. 81–4. Grindleton, one of the four townships of Slaidburn Manor, was the

Squatters' encroachments on Enfield Chase, a royal hunting preserve of more than 7,000 acres in Middlesex, swelled the population of the manor and parish of Enfield—especially after the 1580s. In 1572 the population had reached something like 2,200 and continued to grow in the early seventeenth century. Forty-six new cottages were built between 1615 and 1635; 25 of these dwellings had been erected by the occupiers, but the remainder were built for profit by local landowners, the parish clerk, and an alehouse keeper. The crowded conditions that prevailed in squatters' settlements are indicated by the fact that 665 inhabitants of the parish of Enfield died from the plague in 1625. Tenants sued in the Duchy of Lancaster Court to exclude the squatters from the commons and presented illegal cottages at the manorial court—all to no effect. By 1650 Digger colonies had established themselves at Enfield and in the nearby village of Barnet in Hertfordshire. The Diggers were accused of cultivating the commons, killing deer, and assaulting a game keeper. The sale by parliamentary commissioners of half of Enfield Chase provoked anti-enclosure rioting in 1659. Many of the purchasers were army officers, and a pitched battle followed in which lives were lost and the rioters declared themselves for King Charles. Enfield Chase, only 14 miles north of London, was still a scene of lawlessness and poaching affrays in the 1720s.[34]

The movement to deny common rights to cottagers seems to have gained momentum during the crises of the 1590s. In the fenland village of Willingham, Cambridgeshire, earlier in the century, many cottagers could survive with little or no arable land because, unlike their counterparts in upland villages, they could depend upon grazing and dairying, fishing and fowling. In 1575 between 40 and 50 per cent of the villagers were virtually landless but lived in commonable cottages. The appearance after 1603 of considerable numbers of non-commonable houses is indicative of the stinting of pasture rights and the growth of poverty. By the 1720s one-third of the households of Willingham fell into this category. In Cottenham, Cambridgeshire

---

place of origin of the radical religious sect known as Grindletonianism: cf. Hill, *The World Turned Upside Down*, pp. 65–8.

[34] Pam, *The Fight for Common Rights in Enfield and Edmonton, 1400–1600*, pp. 6–8; id., *The Rude Multitude: Enfield and the Civil War* (Edmonton Hundred Hist. Soc., new ser. 33; 1977), 7–13; Hill, *The World Turned Upside Down*, p. 101; E. P. Thompson, *Whigs and Hunters: The Origin of the Black Act* (New York, 1975), 169–74.

the tenants purchased the seigneurial rights from the lord of the manor and then concluded an enclosure agreement among themselves in 1596. The effect of this agreement must have been to expel many of the cottagers, because all existing cottages on the waste were to have been pulled down and no new ones erected.[35]

In some areas, the reaction against the influx of squatters and the proliferation of landless cottages was encouraged by the enforcement of the Books of Orders and the written articles of inquiry at quarter sessions and assizes beginning in the 1590s and reinforced by the increasing costs of poor relief. It also signified that many woodland communities, normally more open to immigration than those of fielden regions, were reaching the point of demographic saturation. In Staffordshire, popular complaints against householders harbouring masterless persons almost reached the proportions of a petitioning movement. The inhabitants of Wolverhampton complained in 1592 about a painter and his wife who took in lodgers suspected of being vagrants. In 1599 the inhabitants of Little Sandon addressed a petition to the quarter sessions about a yeoman who had erected five illegal cottages on a freehold parcel that was not adequate to pasture two animals. Twenty-eight persons crowded into these dwellings. One was a man accused of being a receiver of stolen goods to whom the inhabitants of Weston-upon-Trent had paid £4 to leave their parish. Petitions from several parts of Staffordshire in 1601 made complaint to the Council in the Marches of Wales that the village of Areley was a haven for persons who were 'little better than outlawes'.[36]

In Worcestershire in the early years of the seventeenth century the grand jury began to display the same kind of hostility towards squatters and vagrants. Instead of waiting for other officials to press for indictments, the grand jurors took the initiative in presenting offences for indictment. Constables were presented for failure to prevent begging or for allowing vagrants to pass through their jurisdictions unpunished; persons building illegal cottages, selling ale without licence, or accepting lodgers were dealt with in like fashion.

---

[35] Spufford, *Contrasting Communities*, pp. 136–54; J. R. Ravensdale, *Liable to Floods: Village Landscape on the Edge of the Fens, AD 450–1850* (Cambridge, 1974), 125; 'Common Rights at Cottenham and Sletham in Cambridgeshire', ed. W. Cunningham, *Camden Miscellany* 12 (Camden Soc., 3rd ser. 18, 1910), 183. For a discussion of *Gateward's Case*, cf. ch. 4.

[36] *Staffs. Q. S. R.*, ii. 194, iv. 95–6; *Acts PC*, xxxii. 102–4.

In the North Riding of Yorkshire, harassment of poor cottagers and lodgers was clearly motivated by the unhappiness of ratepayers with the increasing costs of poor relief. In the West Riding the justices of the peace had to restrain the campaign that parish officials mounted to drive paupers out of their communities and thus prevent them from obtaining a settlement.[37]

Considerable confusion existed concerning who might authorize the construction of new cottages. Many manorial lords continued to make intakes from the waste under the provisions of the Statutes of Merton and Westminster of 1235 and 1285, and to build and rent cottages for profit. Lord Chandos was accused of erecting more than 60 cottages on the waste shared by the manors of Purton and Blunsdon St Andrew, Wiltshire, and then letting the other ratepayers carry the costs of poor relief. It was difficult to prevent a manorial lord from exercising his seigneurial rights, but the Worcestershire grand jury repeatedly presented and indicted Sir Edmund Wheeler of Martin Hussingtree for not providing his cottages with the statutory four acres and for building cottages in the middle of public highways. The parishioners of 'the Rocke' in the same county petitioned the justices of the peace to restrain Sir William Welch from erecting any more cottages without the assent of the parish officers. The Statutes of 1589 (31 Eliz., c. 7) and 1598 (39 and 40 Eliz., c. 3) were not clear about the apportioning of authority among manorial lords, overseers of the poor, and justices of the peace concerning the building, continuance, or razing of cottages on the waste. However, because of the many complaints from ratepayers about the costs of poor relief, in practice the building of new cottages came to require the consent of the overseers and the licence of justices granted in open quarter sessions.[38]

In the Forest of Feckenham in Worcestershire, the erosion of common rights, the enclosure of woodland pasture, and the building

[37] *Calendar of the Quarter Sessions Papers*, 1591–1643, ed. J. W. Willis Bund (Worcs. Hist. Soc., 1900), i. 38–9, 58–62, 67, 106–10, 374; Leonard, *The Early History of English Poor Relief*, pp. 168–70 and nn.

[38] Hist. MSS Comm., *Various Collections*, i. (1901). Quarter Sessions Records, Worcs. and Wilts., 95, 292, 296, 301; *Calendar of the* [Worcestershire] *Quarter Sessions Papers, 1591–1643*, ed. Willis Bund, i. 226; *Quarter Sessions Records, County Palatine of Chester, 1559–1676*, ed. J. H. E. Bennett and J. C. Dewhurst (Rec. Soc. of Lancs. and Ches. 94; 1940), 107; *Quarter Sessions Records for the County of Somerset*, i. 1607–25, ed. H. E. Bates (Somerset Rec. Soc. 23; 1907), 331; Sharp, *In Contempt of All Authority*, pp. 160–1; *SR* iv/2. 804–5; *Select Statutes*, ed. Prothero, p. 98.

of new cottages were all closely linked and precipitated numerous disputes between lords, old tenants, and cottagers. This longstanding conflict undoubtedly influenced the decision to disafforest in 1629. The royal manor of Feckenham was granted, in succession, to several courtiers who appear to have sought quick profits from enclosure schemes. Sir John Throckmorton's attempts to build cottages in the forest was the cause of 500 tenants and commoners suing him in the Court of Requests in 1573. At that time they claimed that the Forest of Feckenham contained 5,000 inhabitants. In 1578 several of the tenants were imprisoned in the Marshalsea Prison for riotously pulling down the timber frame of a cottage. In 1579 the Privy Council ordered Throckmorton not to enclose any more of the forest common until the suit was determined. A petition addressed to the quarter sessions in 1605 claimed that the Forest of Feckenham was a refuge of burglars, horse thieves, and game poachers. No industry had developed in Feckenham to provide employment for the cottagers and squatters. Many of the newer cottages were noncommonable. Yet the economic reality was that their inhabitants remained dependent upon the pasture and fuel resources of the forest. The disafforestation and enclosure settlements of 1629–30 clearly demonstrated the cleavage between smallholder and cottager.[39]

In the seventeenth century the practice of erecting paupers' cottages on the waste at public expense was much more widespread than the building of bridewells or parish workhouses. Where the assent of tenants as well as manorial lords and overseers of the poor was obtained, there was rarely trouble. The parish clergy frequently exerted a beneficial influence in securing agreement in these matters, and smallholders were usually compassionate towards poor persons whom they regarded as neighbours and whom they deemed to be deserving. Failure to secure the assent of tenants or the perception that pauper cottagers presumed to take more from the commons than the charity of their more fortunate neighbours was prepared to allow them could precipitate violent protests.[40] William Andrewes, lord of the manor of Asthall, was ordered by the JPs of Oxfordshire to

[39] *VCH Worcester*, iii. 111–12; Everitt, 'Farm Labourers', *AHEW* iv. 410; *Acts PC*, x. 375–6, xi. 191; Sharp, *In Contempt of All Authority*, pp. 138, 149, 169.

[40] *Quarter Sessions Order Book, 1625–1637*, ed. S. C. Ratcliff and H. C. Johnson (Warwick County Records 1; 1935), 182; Hist. MSS Comm., *Various Collections*, i. 81–2, 294, 296; *Quarter Sessions Records for the County of Somerset*, vol. i, p. xxxvi.

build a cottage for a widow. Not only did he fail to obtain the consent of his copyhold tenants, but the widow's son, daughter-in-law, and two small children also moved into the cottage. They had no employment and were accused of consuming building timber for firewood. The tenants destroyed the cottage and admitted doing so—saying that they could not afford lawsuits; they added that it was such an insubstantial hovel that very little effort was required to pull it down.[41] At North Brewham, Somerset, in the Forest of Frome and Sellwood, Sir Charles Berkeley built a cottage for a poor family on the manorial waste against the will of his tenants, who burned it down in 1625. As in the previous case, the tenants admitted the deed, but defended themselves by complaining that the cottager was:

a man vehemently suspected to intertayne bad and lewd companie and haueinge fowre smalle children which in respect of his povertye are like to be not only a great burden to the parish but allsoe a greate destroyer of his Maiesties woodes and game as many other such like cottagers are.[42]

Disagreements concerning the amount of waste to be allotted to cottagers in the enclosure of Cold Ashby, Northamptonshire in 1624 led to litigation by the overseers of the poor that continued in the Court of Chancery until 1663.[43] Very clearly, there were limits to the amount of charity that smallholders were willing to allow to pauper cottagers in the seventeenth century.

iii. *Provost-marshals*

Of all the emergency measures employed to deal with vagrants, none aroused more controversy than the use of provost-marshals. John Selden and a number of other participants in the parliamentary debate preceding the Petition of Right of 1628 viewed the appointment of provost-marshals as a dangerous extension of the royal prerogative; lawyers believed that the domestic use of martial law threatened to subvert the common law. The reactions of justices of the peace were more mixed: magistrates of port towns and maritime counties from Norfolk westwards to Cornwall, struggling to control mutinous soldiers on their way overseas during the period 1624–8,

[41] PRO, STAC 8/44/16. Cf. ibid., STAC 8/104/9.
[42] Ibid., STAC 8/76/5.   [43] Ibid., C. 78/662/16.

had asked the Privy Council for help. This assistance came in the form of commissions of martial law which drew the JPs into the administration of military government and threatened the militarization of county government. Other justices interpreted the appointment of provost-marshals as a reproach for their own failure to catch thieves and punish vagrants. And, finally, provost-marshals, appointed as they were after 1585 by lord lieutenants, incurred some of the resentment directed at the growth of the lieutenancy during the numerous military emergencies of the 1590s and the reign of Charles I.[44]

Officers known as provost-marshals had been charged with maintaining discipline in English military expeditions since the beginning of the sixteenth century. In the reign of Elizabeth it would have been considered imprudent to muster companies of the county militia without the presence of a provost-marshal appointed by the lord lieutenant. During the suppression of the mid-Tudor rebellions between 1536 and 1569, popular rumour had depicted provost-marshals such as Sir Ralph Ellerker, Sir Anthony Kingston, and Sir George Bowes as travelling about the countryside with wagon-loads of halters for dealing out summary justice to rebels. During such emergencies few people were prepared to argue that a provost-marshal ought to be anything but a hangman; even mid-Tudor lawyers did not dispute the rule that martial law supplanted common law when the King's banner was unfurled.[45]

The first well-documented example of the use of provost-marshals against civilians who were not rebels was in Ireland in 1556, when martial law was employed to sweep up and punish vagrants, but both Bishop Rowland Lee, first President of the Council in the Marches of Wales, and Lord Herbert of Cherbury spoke as if martial law was

---

[44] L. Boynton, 'Martial Law and the Petition of Right', *EHR* 79 *(1964), 255–84;* Beier, *Masterless Men*, pp. 152–3; T. G. Barnes, *Somerset, 1625–1640: A County's Government during the 'Personal Rule'* (Cambridge, Mass., 1961), 104–5. The commission to execute martial law, directed to the Mayor of Dover in 1624, is printed in *Select Statutes*, ed. Prothero, pp. 398–9.

[45] L. Boynton, 'The Tudor Provost-Marshal', *EHR* 77 (1962), 437–55. Just how far, in terms of distance, this suspension of common law by martial law was effective is unclear. It certainly included the vicinity of battlefields and places where rebellions were being suppressed after the royal heralds had offered some form of royal pardon. It also included the verges (i.e. within 12 miles) of all royal palaces: cf. my 'The Origins of the Doctrine of Sedition', pp. 105–9, and M. H. Keen, 'Treason Trials under the Law of Arms', *Trans. R. Hist. Soc.*, 5th ser. 12 (1962), 85–103.

used routinely against 'Rebells, Thieves and Outlaws' in parts of Henrician Wales. Nowhere were provost-marshals given more extensive powers than in Elizabethan Ireland. Since Ireland was where the pattern of English colonial government was first developed and refined before being transplanted across the Atlantic, it should cause no surprise that a provost-marshal was regarded as an officer necessary for the government of early seventeenth-century Virginia, and that the royal governors of Barbados and Jamaica relied upon them to maintain order.[46]

Mary Tudor also ordered the use of martial law against rogues and vagabonds in England when, by royal proclamation dated 12 April 1558, she authorized the Marquess of Winchester to appoint provost-marshals in several towns and counties. Sir Giles Poole acted as provost-marshal in London and led his tipstaffs against rioters at St James's Fair on 9 August. Nor did Elizabeth hesitate to use martial law against civilians. In 1573, when Sir John Hawkins was stabbed by a man who mistook him for Sir Christopher Hatton, the Queen issued orders that the culprit was to be executed under martial law. Her legal advisers had to remind the Queen that martial law might be used only 'in camps' and 'during turbulent times' and that otherwise the common-law courts were capable of punishing crime. Shortly after the London Apprentices' Insurrections of June 1595 Elizabeth commanded Sir Thomas Wilford, the newly-appointed royal provost-marshal, to sweep up vagrants and those participating in unlawful assemblies and to hang, in summary fashion, those whom he thought were incorrigible rogues. Once more, wiser counsel prevailed and Wilford, an old soldier, was instructed by the Privy Council to co-operate with the magistrates of London and adjoining counties and boroughs by turning over to them the persons arrested by his mounted patrols.[47]

A reaction against the indiscriminate use of martial law began as early as the Northern Rebellion of 1569. The motive at first was

---

[46] Boynton, 'The Tudor Provost-Marshal', pp. 440–2; *The Life of Edward, First Lord Herbert of Cherbury*, ed. J. M. Shuttleworth (1976), 4–5; J. Bellamy, *The Tudor Law of Treason*, p. 233; R. A. J. Tyler, *Bloody Provost* (1980), 52–7; S. S. Webb, *The Governors-General: The English Army and the Definition of the Empire, 1569–1681* (Chapel Hill, NC 1979), 110–11, 179, 440–1, *et passim*.

[47] Bellamy, *The Tudor Law of Treason*, p. 233; *Select Statutes*, ed. Prothero, p. 176; Thomas Rymer, *Foedera, Coventiones, Literae, et cujuscunque generis Acta publica* (1742 edn.), vii. 166–7.

purely fiscal. This was because conviction under martial law caused the culprit to forfeit only his goods to the Crown. In order to obtain forfeiture of a traitor's lands, he had to be indicted and convicted under common or statute law. Otherwise, if a man of property were to be executed under martial law, the Crown would have to secure passage of an act of attainder in Parliament in order to obtain his lands. Despite Elizabeth's personal preference for summary punishment, the Crown's policy was to use martial law only against the propertyless. The difficulties in controlling mutinous or discharged soldiers and vagrants led to the appointment, after 1588, of provost-marshals all over southern England. The provost-marshal remained a part of local government and poor-law administration until the end of the reign. In 1589 provost-marshals did hang several soldiers picked out of a crowd of 500 or so who had menaced the royal palace in Westminster. Thereafter the royal judges grew jealous of their power and attempted to reassert the supremacy of common and statute law. In the *Case of Soldiers* (1601) the judges were asked to render an opinion concerning whether some soldiers, who had been impressed for service in Ireland and had subsequently deserted before leaving England, might be dealt with by martial law. The judges decided that the statutes of 7 Hen. VII, c. 1 and 3 Hen. VIII, c. 5 were perpetual acts that made desertion a capital felony and that the offence was determinable by justices of oyer and terminer in the counties where the desertion occurred.[48]

The appointment of provost-marshals reflected both official and popular perceptions that magistrates and constables were not zealous enough in punishing vagrants. William Lambarde, delivering a charge to the grand jury at the West Kent quarter sessions in Maidstone in September 1591, stated that the Queen and council were compelled to appoint provost-marshals 'to rake our rogues together' because of the 'slothfulness of jurors' who failed to present and indict constables for negligence in arresting vagrants. In 1631 the grand jury of Worcestershire peititoned the justices of the peace to secure the appointment of provost-marshals in each hundred 'for the better suppressing of rogues and vagabonds'. Four of the justices endorsed

[48] Bellamy, *The Tudor Law of Treason*, pp. 234–5; Stow, *Annales* (1601 edn.), p. 1264; Coke, *6 Reports*, fo. 27; Dalton, *The Covntrey Ivstice*, pp. 255–6; *SR* ii. 549–50; A. Hassell Smith, *Country and Court: Government and Politics in Norfolk, 1558–1603* (Oxford, 1974), 130–3.

the principle, but, significantly, delayed making the order until the next sessions. The author of the anonymous interlude, *The Pinder of Wakefield*, repeated a rumour that the justices of Halifax and the West Riding of Yorkshire had been given commissions of martial law to employ against the thieves and robbers who were thought to swarm over the county, but failed to use these powers. The stories of how George the Pinder and his company had to resort to vigilante action to protect the property of smallholders were intended as a reproach to magistrates who failed to do so.[49]

Provost-marshals, whether appointed by the Queen or by lord lieutenants, were maintained out of county rates collected by the JPs. In East Kent and the city of Canterbury, where Thomas Nevinson of Eastry in 1589 combined the functions of provost-marshal, scoutmaster for the trained bands, and captain of a troop of horse, the tax was collected monthly at the rate of 2*d.* per £ of valuation, based upon assessments made when the last parliamentary subsidy was collected.[50] It cost 10*s.* a day for each provost-marshal and an additional 2*s.* per diem for each horseman who assisted him. The provost-marshal of Middlesex maintained a patrol of 25 horsemen until February 1601, when the number of under-provosts was reduced to 16; at the same time the mounted provosts' patrols for Essex, Hertfordshire, Surrey, and Kent were cut from 20 to 12 men each. Justices had to keep an eye on costs because, like the payment of poor-rates, contributions towards the support of provost-marshals were resisted, and recalcitrant individuals had to be summoned before the Privy Council. Provost-marshals were supposed to be appointed for three months at a time, but appear to have been retained until the end of the 1590s in most counties.[51]

Just as population pressure and economic distress compelled the city of London to develop more elaborate forms of poor relief, so also the city's methods for repressing vagrancy became more highly

[49] *William Lambarde and Local Government: His 'Ephemeris' and Twenty-nine Charges to Juries and Commissions*, ed. C. Read (Ithaca, NY, 1962), 107; *Calendar of the* [Worcestershire] *Quarter Sessions Papers, 1591–1643*, ed. Willis Bund, ii. 485; *The Pinder of Wakefield: Being the Merry History of George a Greene the Lusty Pinder of the North*, ed. E. A. Horsman (1632; English Reprints Ser. 12, Liverpool, 1956), 1, 29, 44.

[50] Hist. MSS Comm., *Finch*, i (1913), 29; photograph of the tombstone of Thomas Nevinson, esq. in Eastrey Church, in Tyler, *Bloody Provost*, plate 2. A scoutmaster was a staff officer charged with gathering intelligence.

[51] *Acts PC* xviii. 222, 267, xxxi. 164, 188.

organized during the second half of the sixteenth century. In 1569 the mayor and the governors of Bridewell and the other municipal hospitals ordered the 16 beadles employed by the Court of Governors to conduct patrols and to station themselves at the city gates in order to take up beggars and vagrants. The beadles, whose functions supplemented those of the parish constables and surveyors of the poor, were also employed by the recorder of London for apprehending suspected felons. It quickly became clear that the Bridewell beadles were not adequate for all of the tasks thrust upon them, and in 1570 the Corporation of London appointed two city marshals, who were to be paid 12*s.* per diem each to furnish themselves with horses, arms, and six tipstaffs apiece. The city marshals were granted the discretionary authority either to commit the vagrants to the appropriate city hospital or to hand out summary corporal punishment.[52]

Although provost-marshals were appointed in surrounding counties in 1588, London was left alone during the early 1590s because the city already possessed a rudimentary constabulary. The royal provost-marshal, Sir Thomas Wilford, was appointed early in July 1595 because the lord mayor, Sir John Spencer, feared he could not restore order after the Apprentices' Insurrections without a proclamation of martial law. Wilford's commission seems to have expired early in November 1595. Sometime during the next few months a committee of aldermen was formed to oversee the activities of the two city marshals. After Wilford's commission had expired, the two city marshals were given the powers of provost-marshals and their patrols were strengthened and equipped for dealing with crowds, but they remained under the control of the committee appointed by the Court of Aldermen. The borough of Southwark, one of the 26 wards of the City of London, was also ordered to appoint and pay for its own provost-marshal to patrol the south bank. The two city marshals henceforth were referred to as provost-marshals.[53]

The enhanced powers and increased activities of the provost-marshals caused numerous problems. The patrols of the two marshals

[52] Stow, *Survey of London and Westminster*, ii. 431–3; B. R. Masters, 'The Mayor's Household before 1600', in A. E. J. Hollaender and W. Kellaway (eds.), *Studies in London History Presented to Philip Edmund Jones* (1969), 114; Leonard, *The Early History of English Poor Relief*, p. 98.
[53] CLRO, Rep. 23, fos. 426, 513, 517ʳ&ᵛ; William Maitland, *The History of London* (2 vols.; 1756), i. 258–9; Johnson, *Southwark and the City*, p. 325.

on the north bank of the Thames cost £35 monthly to maintain and the aldermen were obliged to provide for this out of their own pockets. In April 1596 the provost-marshals impressed 1,000 men for military service from among the vagrants detained, and the aldermen and the city chamberlain had to find the impressment money. The arrogant behaviour of the provost-marshals bred unpopularity and the Court of Aldermen directed the committee of oversight to seek legal opinions concerning how far the provosts' powers extended. Constables complained that they were made to perform the work of beadles or under-provosts by marshals who ordered them to carry vagrants to Bridewell. During the month of May, 16 constables were fined and imprisoned for disobeying or abusing the marshals or allowing prisoners to escape. In the same month 'some of the gentlemen of the Temple' assaulted provost-marshal John Read and rescued a 'lewd woman' whom he had arrested. During the spring and summer of 1596 there were several other confrontations with constables and courtiers and instances where crowds verbally abused the provost-marshals—especially on those occasions when the provosts raided brothels and unlicensed alehouses.[54]

The use of provost-marshals appears to have lapsed during the first years of James I's reign. Local authorities did not like the extra expense and neglected to reappoint provosts in the absence of pressure from the Privy Council. But renewed threats to public order and fear of vagrants led to their reappearance in London, Middlesex, and Sussex in 1616 and 1617. During the crisis of 1623 provost-marshals were widely employed to sweep up vagrants and their use was extended into the North Country. Although the use of martial law was objected to in the Petition of Right and associated with arbitrary government, provost-marshals continued to be used through the 1630s in campaigns against vagrancy in Worcestershire, Sussex, and Somerset, and enjoyed considerable local support. When confined to enforcing the poor laws, the employment of provost-marshals did not require the use of martial law. In the case of Sussex it is clear that the provost-marshals in each of the six rapes were persons acceptable to the county JPs and were supervised by them. However, the JPs of Essex and Hampshire

---

[54] CLRO, Rep. 23, fos. 524, 526ᵛ–527, 529ᵛ, 532ᵛ, 538ᵛ, 546ᵛ, 548ʳ&ᵛ, 573.

resisted the appointment of provosts and preferred to rely upon constables.[55]

The vagrancy and labour statutes, the statutes known collectively as the Elizabethan Poor Law, and the Books of Orders were enacted and promulgated during the mid-Tudor, late-Elizabethan, and early-Stuart crises because the governors of England attributed the origins of public disturbances to the problem of masterless men. In so far as these laws were punitive and socially-regulative in effect, they reveal a tendency to enhance concepts of property and a determination to protect property rights. Many smallholders were in complete agreement with this approach. But some of these same laws also provided for positive remedies such as the regulation of food supplies and prices, housing for impotent paupers, and other forms of poor relief. These latter provisions came in response to the appeal that the poor made to traditional concepts of justice and paternal duty by means of petitions or violent demonstrations. The Books of Orders appear to have been enforced quite effectively in several localities in the 1630s, and county magistrates expressed satisfaction that vagrancy was being brought under control. Although most of the contents of the Books of Orders possessed a statutory basis, the Puritan lawyer John Hawarde complained that enforcement, especially in the Court of Star Chamber, depended 'on the proclamation and not the statute'. Thus the enforcement of social regulation and poor relief by the use of royal proclamations, orders-in-council, general warrants, and provost-marshals strengthened the royal prerogative at the expense of common and statute law. These were the instruments of government that Elizabeth bequeathed to the early-Stuart monarchs.[56]

The poor-relief and social-regulatory measures necessitated much expense and effort for both rural and urban communities. They also tended to aggravate existing social divisions within local communities and to produce tension between the leaders of these communities, such as overseers of the poor and constables, and magistrates, and

[55] Johnson, *Southwark and the City*, p. 326; *Middlesex Sessions Records*, ed. W. Le Hardy (new ser., 4 vols.; Middx. County Records, 1935–41), iv. 121; BL, Add. MSS, 12,496, fos. 260–1; A. Fletcher, *A County Community in Peace and War: Sussex, 1600–1660* (1975), 167, 199–200; Barnes, *Somerset, 1625–1640*, pp. 105, 127; *Cal. SP, Dom., 1637*, pp. 556–7.

[56] Leonard, *The Early History of English Poor Relief*, pp. 296–300.

between JPs and the Privy Council. In Salisbury during the parliamentary election of 1625 the issue of poor relief led the aldermen to reject the nominees of their usual patrons and to choose candidates more sensitive to their problems. Salisbury's imaginative, Puritan-inspired experiments in social rehabilitation broke down during the 1630s and only the punitive and regulative aspects of poor relief—the whippings, workhouses, and settlement—survived the Civil Wars. Moreover, the fiscal exigencies of Charles I, such as disafforestation and fen-drainage, bore harshly on the poor and provoked a new wave of disorder in the 1620s and 1630s. Another example of how fiscal feudalism perverted social justice was the commission established in 1637 to fine or compound with cottagers whose dwellings lacked the statutory four acres; a clerical commentator said that it 'vexeth the poor mightily, [and] is far more burthensome to them than ship-monies, all for the benefit of Lord Morton and the Secretary of Scotland, Lord Stirling'. However well-intentioned some of this legislation had been, it was enforced in a most sordid manner under Charles I.[57]

---

[57] Slack, 'Poverty and Politics in Salisbury, 1597–1666', pp. 186–7, 192–4; *The Fairfax Correspondence: Memoirs of the Reign of Charles the First*, ed. G. W. Johnson (2 vols.; 1848), i. 216.

8

Apprentices' Riots in London

No part of England was troubled by popular protest to such a degree as London. Between 1581 and 1602, the city was disturbed by no fewer than 35 outbreaks of disorder. Since there were at least 96 insurrections, riots, and unlawful assemblies in London between 1517 and 1640, this means that more than one-third of the instances of popular disorder during that century-and-a-quarter were concentrated within a 20-year period. The only comparable epidemic of disorder in the London area occurred between May 1626 and June 1628, when 15 riots and unlawful assemblies protesting the disastrous policies of the Duke of Buckingham broke out. It was not the harvest failures of the 1590s that precipitated outbreaks of disorder in London so much as the effects of war and the extraordinarily rapid population growth.[1] The city companies could afford to buy grain from overseas and so reduce the likelihood of rioting on that account. But between about 1580 and the end of the century the population of London and its environs doubled, as the thousands of new apprentices, discharged mariners and soldiers, deserters, and vagrants who arrived each year added to the overcrowding and confusion of the city and its burgeoning suburbs.[2]

Tudor London was an orderly city until the early 1580s, but the rapid growth of population thereafter produced serious problems of maintaining public order in both the city and the suburbs. Under Elizabeth these problems were exacerbated by the frequent interference of the Queen and the Privy Council in the city's affairs. Something like two out of every three riots in the London area during the reign

---

[1] Cf. Table 8.1; Finlay, *Population and Metropolis*, p. 51.
[2] Cf. Table 8.2. The suburbs consisted of the Liberties, which were exempt jurisdictions and manorial franchises forming islands within the city's outer boundaries (marked by the bars rather than the walls), the 'out-parishes', and the 'distant parishes'. For boundaries, names, and locations of parishes, city wards, and the extent of settlement about 1600, see Finlay, *Population and Metropolis*, pp. 58, 168–71, 169 (maps); and Stow, *Survey of London*, vol. ii, map at end.

of Elizabeth occurred within the city and many were protests against harsh punishments imposed by city magistrates at the Crown's insistence. In the next reign, public order was restored within the city's jurisdiction—thanks to James's lack of interest in the city of London—but the problem of governing the suburbs remained intractable. Royal interference became a problem again during the reign of Charles I when the Privy Council placed pressure upon the city government to incorporate the suburbs in order to deal more effectively with problems such as building regulations. The city of London resisted annexation of the suburbs and so lacked authority to punish breaches of the peace, except where individual mayors and aldermen were members of the Middlesex commission of the peace. The city's magistrates were not unmindful of the desirability of seeking enhanced jurisdiction over the disorderly populations of the suburbs, but they hesitated to assume the almost full-time responsibilities which such authority would have imposed. They were, after all, businessmen and not gentlemen of leisure. The migration of vagrants, runaway apprentices, discharged soldiers and sailors, unemployed or underemployed artisans was directed into the suburbs, and the magistrates of Middlesex were not equal to the task of keeping the peace.[3]

It is not surprising, then, that most of the riots after 1603 occurred in the suburbs—although many participants still came from the city. The pattern of settlement in the suburbs increasingly revealed segregation between wealthy and poor parishes, and the distinction grew up about this time between the fashionable West End and the impoverished slums of the East End. Moreover, it was from the crowded riverside parishes of the suburbs that the plague spread to other parts of London.[4]

A striking development of the early seventeenth century is a gradual shift in focus of popular protests from localized grievances to issues of national importance. We do not know much about how this happened, but presumably the influence of Puritan preaching and

---

[3] V. Pearl, *London and the Outbreak of the Puritan Revolution: City Government and National Politics* (Oxford, 1964), 30–44; R. Ashton, *The City and the Court, 1603–1643* (Cambridge, 1979), 163–71.

[4] M. J. Power, 'The East and West in Early Modern London', *Wealth and Power in Tudor England: Essays presented to S. T. Bindoff*, ed. E. W. Ives (1978), 167–85; Finlay, *Population and Metropolis*, pp. 15–16, 121–2; J. F. D. Shrewsbury, *A History of Bubonic Plague in the British Isles* (Cambridge, 1970), 157.

the spread of radical ideas in city parishes, such as St Stephen's, Coleman Street, and in the suburbs had formed an urban 'crowd', which could be manipulated to demonstrate against favourites and ministers associated with unpopular royal policies.[5]

i. *The London Crowd*

The population of London stood at 50,000 persons at the beginning of Henry VIII's reign and had risen to only 70,000 by 1550. The drop in London's population from 90,000 to 70,000 during the plague year of 1563 only momentarily checked demographic expansion. Likewise the major epidemics of plague in 1593, 1603, and 1625, as well as the minor outbreak of 1636, produced mortality crises which had no lasting effects in the face of continuing immigration. Indeed, over a longer period of time, endemic diseases claimed a higher toll than sporadic epidemics. The growth of population from 100,000 in 1580 to 200,000 in 1600 was startling and unusually rapid, but the population doubled again by 1650. The inward flow of people came from all over England, but especially from the Midlands and the North. By 1600 something like one-twentieth of the population of England lived in London. Nearly half of the metropolitan population of 1600 resided in the Liberties and the out-parishes. Here also clustered the aliens—mostly from France and the Low Countries—who came in large numbers towards the end of the sixteenth century.[6] The rapid expansion of London frightened monarchs and their ministers from Henry VIII to Charles I, but

---

[5] V. Pearl, 'Change and Stability in Seventeenth-century London', *London Journal* 5 (May 1979), 5; ead., *London and the Outbreak of the Puritan Revolution*, pp. 37–44; P. Burke, 'Popular Culture in Seventeenth-century London', *London Journal* 3 (1977), 149–51.

[6] Finlay, *Population and Metropolis*, pp. 15, 51; E. A. Wrigley and R. S. Schofield, *The Population History of England 1541–1871* (Cambridge, Mass., 1981), 208–9; G. D. Ramsay, *The City of London in International Politics at the Accession of Elizabeth Tudor* (Manchester, 1975), 33; Wilson, *England's Apprenticeship*, pp. 45–6. Prof. Pearl's view that the population of the suburbs did not exceed that of the city until sometime between the 1650s and the 1670s is probably too cautious: 'Change and Stability in Seventeenth-century London', pp. 6–7. Dr Finlay's most recent calculations about the increase in the population between 1580 and 1600 are more conservative: cf. R. Finlay and B. Shearer, 'Population Growth and Suburban Expansion', in A. L. Beier and R. Finlay (eds.), *London, 1500–1700: The Making of the Metropolis* (1986), 37–57. For an up-to-date discussion of metropolitan epidemics, see P. Shack, *The Impact of Plague in Tudor and Stuart England* (1985), ch. 6.

John Stow, who had helped interrogate the leaders of a conspiracy who planned to raise an insurrection against aliens in 1586, believed that a large population need not lead to unrest so long as the city was well governed. In circumspect language Stow implied that left to its own devices London could maintain public order.[7]

Stow was excessively optimistic about the ability of the Corporation of London to keep the peace without royal interference. The rapid growth of population, the tension resulting from increasing social differentiation within the livery companies, and the growth of oligarchy in Tudor London would probably have caused trouble in any case. The seventy or so craft guilds or livery companies were, by the beginning of the sixteenth century dominated by the twelve great companies,[8] which began to assimilate the lesser companies. These incorporated bodies became increasingly hierarchical in structure and oligarchical in government. As the greater companies came to subsume the lesser ones, merchants tended to become pre-eminent over craftsmen; promotion through the various ranks of the great companies, the path to citizenship and municipal office-holding, required wealth and came only by co-option. Technological innovation led to the emergence of new crafts and to the subdivision and specialization of labour in older crafts such as cloth-making. Manufacturing expanded in the suburbs as London handicraft workers moved outside the old walls, while the immigration of aliens introduced important new skills and provoked deep resentment among London craftsmen. Although the problem of enforcing apprenticeship and regulating trade and manufactures in the suburbs obliged the great companies to acquire expanded powers of jurisdiction, they were in fact becoming primarily social clubs and philanthropic organizations for wealthy merchants. The cloth trade, controlled by the Merchant Adventurers, still remained the foundation of London's economy and was vulnerable to fluctuations in the overseas market.[9]

---

[7] CLRO, Rep. 21, fo. 330ᵛ; Stow, *Survey of London*, ii. 205-6.

[8] These were the Mercers, Drapers, Taylors, Clothworkers, Haberdashers, Skinners, Goldsmiths, Ironmongers, Salters, Grocers, Vintners, and Fishmongers. The Merchant Adventurers, whose jurisdiction extended throughout the realm, were not a London company, and most members of the Merchant Adventurers belonged to the Mercers' Company.

[9] G. Unwin, *Industrial Organization in the Sixteenth and Seventeenth Centuries* (Oxford, 1904; 2nd edn., 1957), 41, 74; id., *The Gilds and Companies of London* (repr. 1966), 243-5; Ramsay, *London in International Politics*, pp. 34-5.

The pre-emption of the livery companies and the regulation of London's economy by great merchants was paralleled by the growth of oligarchy in the city's government. The Court of Common Council, elected by liverymen who were 'free' of the city, still retained legislative power, but exercised it at the sufferance of the Court of Aldermen. The twenty-six aldermen, representing each of the city's wards, had to meet a high property qualification, which had risen to £10,000 in the early seventeenth century, and were often liverymen of the great companies. The Court of Aldermen, presided over by the lord mayor, governed the city. From the ranks of senior aldermen came the lord mayor and the two sheriffs; along with the recorder, they acted as justices of the peace and of oyer and determiner for the city, and the more experienced ones were also magistrates for Middlesex. Responsible as they were for a host of courts, municipal institutions for relieving social distress, and the preservation of the peace, aldermanic office had become very burden-some with the growth of the metropolis; those refusing to accept election could be fined heavily.[10]

The government of London had been tending towards oligarchy for over a century, but popular disorder became a serious problem only after 1580. Not only was this the period during which the most rapid growth in population occurred; it was also a time when the proportion of apprentices in the total population was two or three times that of normal times.[11] The popular disturbances that are so prominent a feature of the late Elizabethan period were usually attributed to 'apprentices', for lack of a better term to describe the

---

[10] Ibid.; S. L. Thrupp, *The Merchant Class of Medieval London* (repr. Ann Arbor, Mich., 1962), 14–16, 27–32; Pearl, *London and the Outbreak of the Puritan Revolution*, pp. 53–62; Ashton, *The City and the Court*, pp. 6–11, 34–6. Although the government of London was oligarchical at the top, political participation at the bottom appears to have been more widespread than has been supposed. Dr Steve Rappaport has argued recently that citizenship was more widespread among the adult male population in London than in other English cities. Whereas no more than half of the adult inhabitants obtained citizenship in Tudor York, Norwich, and Bristol, between two-thirds and three-quarters of adult males were granted the freedom of the city of London. However, the average age for completing apprenticeship and being admitted as a freeman in Elizabethan London was 28: 'Social Structure and Mobility in Sixteenth-century London, Part I', *London Journal* 9/2 (winter 1983), 111–15. Cf. R. M. Wunderli, *London Church Courts and Society on the Eve of the Reformation* (Speculum Anniversary Monographs 7; 1981), 28–31.

[11] Bound apprentices constituted 15% of the population of London in 1600 as contrasted with 5% in 1700: Finlay, *Population and Metropolis*, pp. 66–7.

amorphous London 'crowd' of these tumultuous decades. The complex composition and motivation of apprentices' riots was vividly described by John Strype:

The Apprentices of London are so considerable a Body, that they have sometimes made themselves formidable by Insurrections and Mutinies in the City, getting some Thousands of them together, and pulling down Houses, breaking open the Gates of Newgate, and other Prisons, and setting the Prisoners free. And this upon Occasion sometimes of Foreigners, who have followed their Trades in the City, to the supposed Damage of the Native Freemen, or when some of their Brotherhood have been unjustly, as they have pretended, cast into Prison and punished. But they have been commonly assisted, and often egged on and headed by Apprentices of the Dreggs of the Vulgar, Fellows void of worthy Blood, and worthy Breeding; yea, perhaps not apprentices at all, but forlorn Companions, masterless Men, and Tradeless, and the like. Who prying for mischief, and longing to do it, have been the very authors of all that is vile, discourteous to *honourable* Strangers, . . . rude towards Natives, seditious among their own, and villainous every where.[12]

Steven R. Smith has argued that London apprentices constituted a distinct adolescent 'subculture'. Shrove Tuesday was the apprentices' special holiday, when traditionally they performed their ancient rituals of justice by sacking theatres and destroying bawdy houses. In fact, this kind of Shrove-Tuesday apprentices' riot is not known to have occurred outside the years 1606–41; Elizabethan apprentices were concerned with less frivolous grievances and showed a clear preference for midsummer rioting. Later, during the impeachment proceedings of 1640–1 against Strafford and Laud, London apprentices, procured and manipulated by John Pym and Alderman Isaac Penington, are supposed to have played a significant role in circulating libels throughout London, presenting petitions to Parliament, and excluding members from both houses in order to secure passage of bills of attainder.[13]

---

[12] John Stow, *Survey of the Cities of London and Westminster*, ed. John Strype (2 vols.; 1720), ii. 332–3.
[13] S. R. Smith, 'The London Apprentices as Seventeenth-century Adolescents', *P. & P.*, no. 61 (Nov. 1973), 149–61; id., 'The Social and Geographical Origins of London Apprentices, 1630–1660', *The Guildhall Miscellany* 4/4 (Apr. 1973), 195–206; id., 'Religion and the Conception of Youth in Seventeenth-century England', *History of Childhood Quarterly* 2 (1974–5), 493–516; cf. S. Brigden, 'Youth and the English Reformation', in P. Slack (ed.), *Rebellion, Popular Protest and the Social Order in Early Modern England* (Cambridge, 1984), 77–91, and K. Thomas, 'Age

Any attempt to attribute apprentices' riots to the existence of an adolescent subculture raises problems about the homogeneity of age and occupational status of members of the London crowd. Contemporaries used the term 'apprentice' loosely and generically: there is difficulty in attempting to distinguish apprentices from servants, vagrants, and discharged soldiers and sailors. The term 'apprentice' was also used as a synonym for 'boy'. The largest single population group identified in London parish registers are servants. This category does not distinguish between domestic servants and apprentices learning a craft or a trade. There were at least 30,000 indentured apprentices in London in 1600, but domestic servants probably formed an even larger proportion of the population. Discharged and runaway servants and apprentices made up two-thirds of the vagrants punished by Bridewell Court between 1597 and 1608. Servants were frequently discharged on short notice when gentry or citizen households had to reduce expenditure; even bound apprentices were prone to lay-offs during slumps in the cloth trade such as occurred in 1586–7 and after 1614.[14] A very large number of indentured apprentices simply ran away. The proportion of gentlemen's sons among the apprentices was increasing in the late sixteenth and early seventeenth centuries to close to one-fifth of those bound. To contemporaries, gentlemen apprentices were associated with riotous living.[15] If the early career of John Lilburne is any indication, these discontented younger sons of the gentry added an articulate and politically-sophisticated leaven to the London crowd.[16] Discharged soldiers and sailors also formed a prominent part of the London crowd in the late Elizabethan and Caroline periods. Between 1585 and 1602, 10,560 men were pressed for soldiers from London and Middlesex—a conscription rate twice that

and Authority in Early Modern England', *Proceedings of the British Academy* 62 (1976), 218–19. Dr Keith Lindley has counted 24 Shrove-Tuesday riots between 1603 and 1641: 'Riot Prevention and Control in Early Stuart London', *Trans. R. Hist. Soc.*, 5th ser. 33 (1983), 109–10 and n.

[14] Beier, *Masterless Men*, p. 23; id., 'Social Problems of Elizabethan London', pp. 203–11; Finlay, *Population and Metropolis*, pp. 66–7; Rappaport, 'Social Structure and Mobility in Sixteenth-century London, Part I', p. 117.

[15] Smith, 'The Social and Geographical Origins of London Apprentices, 1630–1660', pp. 195–206. For examples of gentlemen apprentices punished for such behaviour, see London Guildhall Library, Bridewell Royal Hospital, Court Books, microfilm reel 512, unfol.

[16] *DNB*, s.v. John Lilburne; H. Shaw, *The Levellers* (New York, 1968), 28.

for the rest of the country. Both the Crown and the city agreed that impressment was an expedient solution to the problem of masterless men, but after discharge they usually found their way back to London.[17] They played a conspicuous part in riots in 1592 and 1595. Thirteen of the 33 riots between 1626 and May 1640 arose from naval mutinies or protests of discharged soldiers and sailors. That the distinction between apprentices and mariners could be blurred is illustrated by the career of John Taylor, the 'Water Poet', who, having been apprenticed to a waterman, was impressed into and discharged from naval service several times before he was twenty years of age.[18] Altogether, the evidence concerning the composition of the London crowd suggests that they were a mixed crew. The participants in the Evil May-Day Riots of 1517, for example, included, besides apprentices, domestic servants, women, watermen, husbandmen, labourers, priests, 'Courtiers', and servants of the royal household.[19]

When one considers that the various elements of the London crowd in the 1590s probably totalled not less than 100,000, the scale of London riots—although very much larger than rural enclosure riots of the same period—was clearly exaggerated by Strype. On only four occasions—in 1584 and 1618 and twice in 1595—did crowds of more than 1,000 persons participate in riots. In seventeen other cases where contemporary estimates of the size of crowds of rioters are known, only five numbered more than 500 persons, and 12 were smaller than 500. Yet London crowds were more difficult to control, because, in contrast to rural protests, the size of the crowd could grow very quickly if participants called upon sympathetic bystanders for assistance. Moreover, during the Tudor and early-Stuart periods, London rioters were more likely to offer personal violence than rural protesters.

When John Strype stressed that dislike of alien craftsmen caused many apprentices' riots, he was merely following the explanations offered by contemporary observers from Edward Hall to John Stow and William Fleetwood, recorder of London from 1571 to 1592. Actually, protests against the administration of justice were three

[17] C. G. Cruickshank, *Elizabeth's Army* (2nd edn.; 1968), 26–9, 36–40, 238, 256, 291; Beier, *Masterless Men*, pp. 93–5.
[18] *DNB*, s.v. John Taylor (1580–1653); R. J. Mitchell and M. D. R. Leys, *A History of London Life* (1958), 123.
[19] *Hall's Chronicle*, pp. 589–90.

times more numerous during the sixteenth century and much more menacing, but anti-alien riots received greater prominence because of the enduring notoriety of the Evil May-Day Insurrection of 1517, regarded as the archetype of apprentices' riots. However, it would be a mistake to underestimate the problem of xenophobia in London, which was longstanding and deep-seated. Parliamentary statutes in the fifteenth century placed numerous restrictions upon foreign merchants and artisans, and many of these laws were revived during the reign of Elizabeth. Lord Burghley conceived a dislike for foreign merchants because he thought that they exported their profits in the form of plate and bullion instead of reinvesting them in the English economy.[20] Tudor England's chief export remained woollen cloth, largely produced in rural areas, but shipped through the port of London to the international wool mart at Antwerp. The Company of Merchant Adventurers possessed the monopoly for the export of wool; it was not a London company but a national company governed from Antwerp. Although the city of London dominated the English economy to a considerable degree, G. D. Ramsay reminds us that Tudor London was merely a 'satellite city' of Antwerp, and foreigners controlled half of the wool-export trade to Antwerp. Moreover, these foreign merchants also handled more than half of England's imports.[21]

Since medieval times the influx of alien craftsmen had brought new methods of manufacturing and merchandising and sometimes higher standards of craftsmanship. Alien craftsmen were especially numerous among weavers of wool, silk, and linen and in the brewing and printing trades. The London leather-working industry had long since passed into the hands of strangers and was a grievance even before Evil May Day. The manufacture of the cheaper type of cloth known as 'bays' by foreign craftsmen was thought to be the cause of chronic unemployment in the cloth trade during the reign of Elizabeth. Foreign craftsmen tended to congregate in the suburbs where the absence of municipal taxation and the difficulty in enforcing apprenticeship regulations spawned appalling conditions

---

[20] Stow, *Survey of London and Westminster*, ed. Strype, ii. 295; Cf. I. Scouloudi, 'Alien Immigration into and Alien Communities in London, 1558–1640', *Proceedings of the Huguenot Society of London* 16 (1938), 27–49; T. Wyatt, 'Aliens in England before the Huguenots', ibid. 19 (1952–8), 74–94.

[21] Ramsay, *London in International Politics*, pp. vii, 37–41.

of sweated labour.[22] Prior to 1531, every citizen of London, when granted the freedom of the city, had to swear an oath that he would employ no child of a foreign-born craftsman; after that date a parliamentary statute allowed aliens to become apprentices. In 1576 the Court of Aldermen took seriously the complaint that strangers brought their pregnant wives over to London in order 'to wyne to those children the libertye that other Englyshemen do enioye. . . . '[23]

Roger Finlay has shown that, in proportion to the total population of London, the alien community 'reached' its most significant size in the last third of the sixteenth century'—rising from 4.7 per cent of the total London population in 1567 to 5.3 per cent in 1573, and declining to 3.6 per cent in 1593 and 1 per cent in 1635.[24] Although the population of aliens declined significantly in the early seventeenth century, various London companies continued to blame the slowness of trade upon alien craftsmen and frequently petitioned the Crown either to exclude them from the crafts in which they worked or to subject them to guild regulations.[25]

London had a long history of violent protest against aliens. During the Great Revolt of 1381, Wat Tyler's followers had attacked the Flemish occupants of Southwark's 'stews', or bawdy houses, before crossing the river into the city.[26] Even foreign ambassadors were not spared. The servants of the French ambassador were assaulted in 1599 after an exchange of insults with a butcher and a brewer provoked a riot. A brawl in which the Venetian ambassador's servants were alleged to have slain a butcher caused a crowd to besiege the ambassador's house in 1635.[27]

The Evil May-Day Riots were caused by widely-circulated rumours expressing the popular perception that when Englishmen brought

[22] Stow, *Survey of London and Westminster*, ed. Strype, ii. 295 ff.; Unwin, *Gilds and Companies of London*, pp. 245–9; Pearl, *London and the Outbreak of the Puritan Revolution*, pp. 14–16.

[23] Ead., 'Social Policy in Early Modern London', in H. Lloyd-Jones (ed.), *History and Imagination: Essays in Honour of H. R. Trevor-Roper* (New York, 1981), 117–19; Rappaport, 'Social Structure and Mobility in Sixteenth-century London, Part I', p. 112; CLRO, Rep. 19, fo. 38ᵛ.

[24] Finlay, *Population and Metropolis*, pp. 67–8.

[25] *Seventeenth-century Economic Documents*, ed. Thirsk and Cooper, pp. 716–21.

[26] Johnson, *Southwark and the City*, p. 70.

[27] Hist. MSS Comm., *Salisbury*, ix. 191; *Cal. SP, Dom., 1635*, p. 323.

complaints against foreigners in royal or municipal courts, they could not obtain justice because aliens enjoyed the special protection of the Crown. A London broker, John Lincoln, procured a clergyman named Dr Bele or Beal to preach a sermon during Easter week of 1517 against the unfair competition of foreign merchants and artisans which only served to increase the popular resentment of foreigners. The first riot occurred on 28 April when a number of young men attacked several foreigners and were subsequently arrested by the lord mayor and committed to Newgate and various other prisons. Another rumour, to the effect 'that on May daye next, the citie would rebell and slaye all aliens', reached the ears of Cardinal Wolsey, who demanded of the mayor and aldermen what they meant to do about the threat. The city fathers rejected the idea of mounting a special watch as an unwonted provocation, but did declare a curfew for May Day and ordered all servants and apprentices to be kept indoors. An attempt by an alderman to enforce the curfew against a group of young men playing games in Cheapside was resisted and the cry was uttered for 'prentyses and clubbes!' Several crowds of from 300 to 700 persons assembled in more than a dozen places within the city. First they went to Newgate and the Counter Prisons and released those imprisoned following the riot of 28 April; then they proceeded to attack and loot the homes and workshops of strangers—especially in the vicinity of Leadenhall and Cornhill, and the homes of house-holders in St Martin Ludgate who had thrown stones and poured boiling water on the rioters. The disturbances were over by 3.00 p.m. and the crowds dispersed by the Earls of Shrewsbury and Surrey and other noblemen. The lieutenant of the Tower, 'no great frende to the citie', lent his assistance by randomly discharging the garrison ordnance into the city. Altogether 278 prisoners were taken—mostly young apprentices—but Edward Hall's narrative emphatically states that they were not representative of the composition of the crowd.[28]

The punishment of the rebels formed part of a carefully-rehearsed drama played before the entire city. The military occupation of the city by the harnessed retainers of the Duke of Norfolk and the other peers was humiliating and meant to remind the governors and citizens of London that they had shown themselves incapable of preserving good order. Hall's highly-coloured account of the treason trials

---

[28] *Hall's Chronicle*, pp. 586–91; Stow, *Survey of London*, ed. Strype, i. 152, 156–8.

contrasts the harsh initial treatment of the defendants by Norfolk, Surrey, and Shrewsbury with the subsequent clemency of Henry VIII. The first batch of prisoners were tried on 4 May; 13 were executed in 11 different locations, and the knight marshal, Lord Edmond Howard, was especially cruel to the younger ones. The second group of five or six more prisoners were tried and condemned on 7 May, but after the execution of John Lincoln, a message from the King halted the executions and signalled the unfolding of the King's clemency. That was the cue for the recorder and aldermen to go before the King at Greenwich and beg for mercy; the King chastised them because they 'dyd wyncke' at the disorders and replied that he would refer the matter to the lord chancellor, Cardinal Wolsey. The final act of the drama was performed in Westminster Hall on 22 May when the prisoners, trussed up with ropes and halters, were led before the King and council; 400 men and boys and 11 women received the royal pardon.[29]

The consequences of Evil May Day were several. May-Day festivities in London were thereafter officially discouraged and ceased to be kept from the beginning of the Elizabethan period until their revival in the early-Stuart period.[30] Ten years after the event, a group of citizens attempted to prevent the election of Thomas Semer as mayor because of his behaviour as sheriff during the suppression of the riots.[31] The London companies turned the riots to their advantage by lobbying Parliament to enact a Statute (14 and 15 Hen. VIII, c. 2) in 1524 extending their jurisdiction over alien craftsmen into the suburbs. They used the new powers to enforce monopolies and to compel the strangers to share the burden of loans and taxation. The extension of jurisdiction solved no problems but only intensified social conflict in a system where craftsmen became increasingly alienated from merchants who restricted the right of the former to sell directly to the consumer and made it difficult for craftsmen to purchase raw materials or even find employment. Hence many craftsmen, some of whom were technically apprentices, but did not live in the households of masters, were considered vagrants and masterless men.[32]

[29] *Hall's Chronicle*, pp. 586–91; R. R. Sharpe, *London and the Kingdom* (3 vols.; 1894), i. 355–60.
[30] Lindley, 'Riot Prevention and Control in Early Stuart London', pp. 110–11.
[31] Sharpe, *London and the Kingdom*, i. 359–60.
[32] Unwin, *Gilds and Companies of London*, pp. 245–9.

The memory of Wolsey's arrogant behaviour towards London's governors in 1517 probably contributed to the latter's resistance to the collection of the Amicable Grant in 1525. The Cardinal had proposed to levy a sixth part of every man's money, plate, and goods in order to finance the French war. When the mayor and aldermen objected, the Cardinal began summoning individual groups of citizens to meet with him in an attempt to persuade them to contribute. The outrage against extra-parliamentary taxation was so vocal that several citizens 'were sent to ward'. Seditious bills were posted in several places, unlawful assemblies in individual wards organized popular resistance, while the Court of Common Council proposed paying a smaller benevolence instead of Wolsey's forced loan. Resistance to the Amicable Grant was also widespread in the south-eastern counties—especially East Anglia—and Archbishop Warham and the Dukes of Norfolk and Suffolk were unwilling to support Wolsey. The King rescinded the loan and pardoned those who had resisted.[33]

But the memory of Evil May Day also fostered vigilance in the city's rulers and London remained remarkably quiet during the rebellions of 1549. The rebel leaders in East Anglia and the West Country, busy as they were besieging their own provincial capitals, failed to march on London as the Cornish rebels had done in 1497, yet a dangerous situation existed in the city during the summer of 1549. The city authorities took determined action both to prepare London for siege and to preserve public order. Guns from the Tower Armoury were mounted on hastily-repaired walls. News of rebel activities and the frequent passage of soldiers through the city were disruptive. A curfew was imposed, watches strengthened, and plays and interludes suppressed. In order to halt rumour-mongering martial law was proclaimed, and 14 persons were summarily executed at various places throughout London and the suburbs as a warning to potential trouble-makers.[34] During the Rebellion of 1554, Sir Thomas Wyatt was convinced that he had many sympathizers within the city. Although he gained access to Southwark, London Bridge was secured against his entry after Queen Mary rallied her supporters at the Guildhall instead of fleeing to Windsor. Wyatt's forces marched to

---

[33] *Hall's Chronicle*, pp. 694–702; A. F. Pollard, *Wolsey* (1953 rev. edn.), 141–8.
[34] Beer, *Rebellion and Riot*, ch. 7.

Kingston to cross the Thames before doubling back on Ludgate—
only to find that it was too strongly held.[35]

The preservation of stability and public order in mid-Tudor
and early-Elizabethan London was also assisted by the specialized
institutions that the governors of the city developed for relief of
the deserving poor. The livery companies laid in stocks of grain
and coal for periods of distress. The aged and sick were sent to
St Bartholomew's or St Thomas's Hospitals, the insane to Bedlam,
and orphans and beggar children to Christ's Hospital. Help was also
provided in securing apprenticeships for orphans and relieving
unmarried daughters of deceased freemen, poor householders,
artisans, and shopkeepers who suffered periods of financial distress.
Bridewell Hospital was established for the correction of unruly
apprentices and sturdy beggars, but, by the 1580s, was so over-
whelmed by numbers that little was attempted beyond the punishment
of vagrants. The county of Middlesex, by contrast, did not possess
a house of correction until Hicks Hall, or New Bridewell, was erected
in St John's Street, Clerkenwell in 1614. The deserving poor included
only those who had some demonstrable connection with guilds or
individual merchants or could claim to be natives of London.
Outsiders and vagrants could make no such claim. They were
rounded up by the city marshals or provost-marshals, whipped, and
sent on their way. Most of the London poor belonged to the latter
category.[36]

ii. *The Late-Elizabethan Epidemic of Disorder*

The mounting problem of vagrants and masterless men in late-
Elizabethan London would have caused trouble in any case, but the
difficulty of preserving public order was exacerbated by frequent

---

[35] D. M. Loades, *Two Tudor Conspiracies* (Cambridge, 1965), 66–73.

[36] F. F. Foster, *The Politics of Stability: A Portrait of the Rulers in Elizabethan
London* (R. Hist. Soc., Studies in Hist., 1977), 4, 90–1, 118–20; Pearl, *London and
the Outbreak of the Puritan Revolution*, pp. 16–17; ead., 'Change and Stability in
Seventeenth-century London', p. 5; Beier, 'Social Problems of Elizabethan London',
pp. 217–18; CLRO, Rep. 23, fos. 479ᵛ–480. More recently, Prof. Pearl has had
second thoughts on the question of whether vagrants were excluded from poor relief
and suggests that in the seventeenth century relief was not denied to persons who
could not meet the residence requirements: 'Social Policy in Early Modern London',
p. 123.

conflicts with officers of the Crown. The authority of the knight marshal to punish transgressions within the verge of the royal court superseded both common law and the customs of London.[37] It was never very difficult to incite a mob to break into the Marshalsea Prison in Southwark and rescue prisoners. The Marshalsea Court, exercising the royal prerogative of purveyance, could requisition provisions, carts, and horses to supply the royal household.[38] The Lieutenant of the Tower, ever sensitive to violations of the liberties of the Tower, actually assaulted the lord mayor's men while the latter was attempting to suppress the Apprentices' Insurrection of 29 June 1595—perhaps the most dangerous urban uprising of the century.[39] Nor was the task of preserving the peace made easier by the official protection sometimes given to disorderly royal servants.

Elizabeth interfered in the government of London in other ways as well. She and the Privy Council were quick to reprimand the mayors and sheriffs for laxity in rounding up vagrants, suppressing popular disturbances, and punishing rioters. Crown officials, such as the attorney-general and the master of the Rolls, frequently interfered in investigations of popular disturbances and on several occasions interrogated prisoners under torture.[40] The Crown also arrogated the right to appoint the city recorder, who became the principal liaison between the Crown and the corporation. William Fleetwood, recorder from 1571 to 1592, obtained the office through the patronage of the Earl of Leicester. Edward Coke, who briefly held the office in 1592 before becoming attorney-general, owed his appointment to Lord Burghley.[41] The exercise of the prerogative of impressment to demand levies of soldiers and sailors for the late-Elizabethan wars undoubtedly caused less offence to the city's rulers than to the vagrants who were impressed. But compelling the city

---

[37] When the monarch was in residence at Greenwich or Westminster, the verge of the royal household, extending for a radius of seven miles, would have included parts of, or even much of, the London area.

[38] Johnson, *Southwark and the City*, p. 70.

[39] R. B. Manning, 'The Prosecution of Sir Michael Blount, Lieutenant of the Tower, 1595', *BIHR* 57 (Nov. 1984), 216–24.

[40] G. Norton, *Commentaries on the History, Constitution and Chartered Franchises of the City of London* (1829), 203–8; *Acts PC*, xxiii. 342, xxiv. 187; Hist. MSS Comm., *Salisbury*, v. 248; Stow, *Survey of London and Westminster*, ed. Strype, ii. 436–8.

[41] Foster, *Politics of Stability*, p. 141.

to accept royal provost-marshals was resented by the citizens, who were assessed for their maintenance.[42]

My argument that royal interference in the affairs of the city of London not only complicated the problem of preserving public order, but also provoked popular protests is supported by an analysis of the 35 outbreaks of popular disorder between 1581 and 1602.[43] At the very most, 12 of these riots and unlawful assemblies can be attributed to economic distress. The two instances of popular market regulation and the two protests against monopolies clearly belong in this category, but it is less easy to be confident about the inclusion of the four riots and conspiracies directed against aliens. The largest category of popular disorder consists of the 14 insurrections and riots which protested the administration of justice. This category includes symbolic acts such as rescuing prisoners from pillories and prisons, a riot at an execution, an assault upon constables, and violent demonstrations that directly challenged the authority of the mayor. Of the nine remaining instances of disorder during this period, four riots were directed against gentlemen and lawyers.

The first outbreak of the late-Elizabethan epidemic of disorder occurred on 7 September 1581, when prisoners rioted in Ludgate Prison in response to the attempts of a crowd outside to rescue them.[44] This incident may be related to a large-scale sweep of vagrants and masterless men which recorder Fleetwood was leading at about this time.[45] Fleetwood's letters are full of accounts of riots, brawls, and sweeps of beggars. In one letter to Lord Burghley he describes three large-scale riots that occurred during Whitsuntide 1584.[46] The first riot began on Monday evening when a gentleman did a pirouette on the stomach of an apprentice who had been sleeping on the grass at the entrance to a theatre. During the brawl that followed the former 'exclaimed . . . that he was a gentleman, and that the apprentice was but a rascal, and some there little better than roogs, that tooke upon them the name of gentlemen, and saide the prentizes were but the skumme of the worlde'. The next day a crowd of 500 apprentices attempted to rescue imprisoned companions. On Wednesday a riot, provoked when a serving-man wounded an

[42] *Acts PC*, xviii. 222, 267.   [43] See Table 8.1.
[44] CLRO, Rep. 19, fo. 23.
[45] Stow, *A Survey of London and Westminster*, ed. Strype, ii. 436–8.
[46] Wright, *Queen Elizabeth and Her Times*, ii. 227–31.

apprentice with his sword at a theatre door, drew a crowd of 'near a thousand people'. In the evening of the same day a fight between a tailor and a clerk of the Court of Common Pleas resulted in an attack upon the attorneys and gentlemen living in Lyon's Inn in Fleet Street. Continuing disorders, including a riotous rescue of an apprentice imprisoned in a cage in Aldersgate Street, led to the closing of theatres.[47]

In late September 1590, a crowd of apprentices, seeking revenge for an insult allegedly offered them by a lawyer, sacked Lincoln's Inn. The lord mayor and the sheriffs of London and Middlesex were reprimanded for failing to supply the names of the culprits to the Privy Council.[48] Elizabeth clearly doubted the ability of the governors of London to control the unruly London crowd and feared for her own personal safety. In December 1592 she once again admonished the lord mayor for not acting more quickly to prevent an unlawful assembly of 200 or 300 discharged mariners who 'assembled themselves together at Paule's cross with the sounde of a dromme' and began marching towards Hampton Court to claim their arrears of pay from the Queen.[49]

The anti-alien riots of late Elizabethan London were precipitated by the traditional popular belief that employment of foreign craftsmen caused unemployment of native artisans. As such these disturbances signified hard times. But the harsh punishments meted out to the culprits almost invariably triggered further popular protests against the lord mayor and the administration of justice. In early September 1586, when the city was already unnerved by the discovery of the Babington Conspiracy, the Privy Council uncovered another plot by a number of plasterers to raise an insurrection against French and Dutch artisans. The plot, which was revealed to the city government by the lord chief justice, may have represented nothing more than loose talk, but the Crown demanded a response from the city magistrates that made the conspiracy appear more serious than it probably was. A curfew was imposed, a standing watch set, and a sweep of vagrants begun.[50] The rigorous interrogation of the leaders,

[47] Ibid. [48] *Acts. PC*, xix. 476–7, xx. 63, 85.
[49] Ibid., xxiii. 342.
[50] Wright, *Queen Elizabeth and Her Times*, ii. 308–9; BL, Lansdowne MSS, 49, fo. 22, printed in *Original Letters Illustrative of English History*, ed. Ellis, ii. 306–8; Stow, *Survey of London and Westminster*, ed. Strype, ii. 301, 333; CLRO Rep. 21, fo. 330ᵛ.

who, Fleetwood pointed out, all came from Northamptonshire and Derbyshire, continued for several weeks. Sympathizers protested by throwing a seditious libel under the mayor's gate.[51] Some, at least, of the governors of London shared the dislike of foreigners. William Webbe, lord mayor in 1591–2, and the Common Council had spoken out against the employment of alien artisans when qualified native craftsmen were without work. Foreigners were also accused of causing higher food prices by exporting commodities. But when the agent for the United Provinces complained to the Privy Council in early June 1592 that Dutch candle-makers were being prosecuted for violating parliamentary statutes regulating that trade, the Privy Council stayed the legal proceedings against them.[52] Riots protesting the administration of justice broke out in Southwark and lasted through June and July, and revived again in the autumn.

The following spring seditious bills threatening violence against strangers were posted in several parts of the city. This time the mayor moved quickly and a conspirator was apprehended. The Privy Council ordered the use of torture to compel him to reveal the names of the author and his accomplices.[53] On May Day 1593, groups of apprentices made menacing speeches against foreigners, and it is not surprising that foreign craftsmen should reply in kind. Peter Coale, an immigrant 'painter-drawer' who lived in Aldersgate Street, was prosecuted in Star Chamber for threatening to set the city on fire.[54]

Food riots probably constitute the most unequivocal evidence of serious economic distress. Only two such protests are known to have occurred in London—both during the tumultuous month of June 1595. The evidence suggests that the problem was temporary and consisted primarily of high prices rather than serious shortages. In both instances groups of apprentices took upon themselves the power to determine the prices at which provisions were to be sold. On 12 June the rioters sold fish at popularly-established prices, and on the following day, in Southwark, a group of apprentices compelled the sale of butter at 3*d.* a pound where the butter-women had been asking 5*d.* per pound. The butter rioters were punished on 27 June by whipping, pillorying, and imprisonment. Their punishment set off another riot in which their fellows destroyed the pillories in

---

[51] Ibid., Rep. 21, fos. 334ᵛ, 337ᵛ–338.
[52] *Acts PC*, xxii. 506, 549.   [53] *Acts PC*, xiv. 187.
[54] *Attorney-General* v. *Peter Coale*, PRO, STAC 5/A14/31.

Cheapside and Leadenhall.[55] The punishment was carried out by the Court of Star Chamber, despite the fact that an inquest by the mayor into the butter riot in Southwark had determined that there was 'nothing ells but a great concourse & presse of people for buying of butter & other victuals without any force or other disorder'.[56] One can only conclude that there was a serious disagreement between the Crown and the mayor concerning the handling of this alleged disorder, and that the Privy Council had demanded exemplary punishment—even of innocent men. The city government were careful to avoid pretexts for further food riots, and Common Council authorized the purchase of rye from Danzig for distribution through the livery companies and ordered the companies in future to maintain larger stocks.[57]

As in the countryside, the pressure of population in late Elizabethan London strained the resources of pasture land on the outskirts of the city. The farmers of crown lands in the vicinity of Westminster had made enclosures of land upon which the parishioners of St Martin-in-the-Fields and St Margaret's, Westminster claimed common of pasture after Lammas Day. The parishioners had petitioned the lord treasurer, Lord Burghley, for redress, but becoming impatient, and perhaps emboldened by the news of riots in the city and suburbs during the summer of 1592, they exerted pressure on the authorities by breaching a number of closes in the vicinity of Chelsea and Westminster on 1 August. Their behaviour was disciplined and peaceful, and the presence of parish constables was intended to legitimize their actions. The Crown was responsive to this protest, and the following year Parliament enacted a Statute prohibiting enclosures within three miles of London. The Middlesex JPs were still enforcing this Act as late as 1631, when the names of those making enclosures in Chelsea were reported to the Council.[58]

The Crown's practice of selling monopolies and patents to courtiers and special-interest groups in order to raise revenue also provoked popular disturbances and pitted one London company against another. Edward Darcy, on behalf of the Glovers, had obtained a patent

[55] Hist. MSS Comm., *Salisbury*, v. 249; Stow, *Annales*, pp. 769–70; PRO, SP 12/252/94; Williams, *The Tudor Regime*, p. 330.
[56] CLRO, Remembrancia, ii, no. 98.
[57] Stow, *Annales*, p. 769; CLRO, Rep. 23, fos. 424ᵛ–425.
[58] Williams, *Tudor Regime*, pp. 335–6; 35 Eliz., c. 6, SR iv. 852–3; *Cal SP, 1631–1632*, p. 73;

granting him the authority to inspect all skins at Smithfield Market. This was opposed by the Leathersellers, who made it a practice to compel leather-workers to accept bad skins along with the good in each consignment. A confrontation occurred in the Court of Aldermen in 1592 in which Darcy struck an alderman in the presence of the mayor. The news of the insult provoked an unlawful assembly of apprentices, who were prevented from exacting retribution only by the mayor's intervention. Most city companies found their privileges infringed upon by monopolists and patentees at one time or another.[59] On another occasion, in October 1595, a group of apprentices riotously seized a cart-load of starch in Milk Street, Cheapside, belonging to the Queen's patentee of the much-hated starch monopoly.[60]

All of these examples of popular protest can be taken as symptoms of the economic problems of the 1590s, but they also suggest a decline of popular confidence in the ability of the city magistrates to dispense justice in an even-handed manner. Another example of this crisis of confidence in the governors of the city is provided by a conspiracy, organized by the parson of St Mildred Poultry, to resist payment of the fifteenth voted by the Parliament of 1601. Thomas Sorocold, a popular Puritan preacher, objected not to paying the tax, but rather to the unfair and inequitable assessments of individuals and the secretive manner in which the assessments were made. He and his supporters were accused of riotously breaking open the parish chest — presumably to get at the records of the assessment.[61]

Although I have classified 12 of the 35 instances of popular disorder in late-Elizabethan London as protests arising from economic distress, it is evident how difficult it sometimes is to distinguish this category of protest from the 14 disturbances which more directly challenged the mayor's administration of justice. Nor did the royal judges always attempt to make such a fine distinction. Although the butter-rioters of June 1595 were actually punished by the Court of Star Chamber for the misdemeanours of riot and sedition, a conference of judges in 1597, following the Enslow Hill Rebellion

---

[59] Unwin, *Gilds and Companies of London*, pp. 256–7.
[60] *Acts PC*, xxv. 16; *Analytical Index to the Series of Records Known as the Remembrancia, Preserved Among the Archives of the City of London, A.D. 1579–1664* (1878), 450–1; CLRO, Remembrancia, ii, no. 110.
[61] *Attorney-General* v. *Thomas Sorocold, clerk*, PRO, STAC 5/A44/10; *DNB*, s.v. Thomas Sorocold.

of 1596, decided in retrospect that the defendants should have been tried for treason. They reasoned that any popular attempt to regulate prices constituted an attempt to alter the laws of the realm by force. The majority of judges agreed that this was no different from rescuing prisoners or attempting to kill the lord mayor: all were construed as levying war against the Queen.[62]

The popular disturbances of the 1590s in London wore a more menacing face, and the Crown legal officers made the most of the situation. The trials of Thomas Cartwright and a number of other Puritan leaders for their supposed authorship of the *Marprelate* tracts excited popular sympathy; a conspiracy was uncovered in which William Hacket and a number of others were accused of planning to rescue the Puritan leaders from prison. Hacket's followers had proclaimed him the Messiah in Cheapside on 16 July 1591, and, once again, the lord mayor was reprimanded for failing to suppress the tumult. Hacket and his followers were interrogated under torture. Hacket's execution for treason took place in Cheapside on 28 July.[63]

The riots of 1592 reveal continuing friction between Londoners and crown officials. Moreover, William Webbe, lord mayor during that year, did not hesitate to condemn the arbitrary actions of the knight marshal which, Webbe complained to Lord Burghley, had provoked a battle between the knight marshal's men and the felt-makers' apprentices in which several persons were killed. The trouble began when the deputies of the knight marshal arrested and imprisoned a felt-maker in a particularly violent manner. On Sunday, 11 July 1591, under pretext of attending the theatre, a large group of felt-makers made plans to break into the Marshalsea Prison and rescue him. As they approached the Marshalsea, the knight marshal's men sallied forth and attacked the felt-makers with cudgels and daggers.[64] When the Privy Council heard rumours of further disturbances planned for Midsummer Eve and Midsummer Night, orders were issued to close the theatres, impose a curfew, and mount a watch. The felt-makers were deterred only momentarily: early in

---

[62] Hale, *The History of the Pleas of the Crown*, i. 144; Sir John Popham, *Reports and Cases* (1656), 122–3.

[63] *Acts PC*, xxi. 293, 297, 299–300, 319, 325; P. McGrath, *Papists and Puritans under Elizabeth I* (1967), 302.

[64] BL, Lansdowne MSS, 71, fo. 28; Johnson, *Southwark and the City*, pp. 277–8.

208 Economic Crises and Social Protest

July they seized Levenson, a knight marshal's man accused of killing a rioter, and carried him to Newgate to demand justice. A coroner's inquest determined that Levenson should be charged with manslaughter. Since this was a bailable offence, Levenson was bound over to appear at the Surrey Assizes and set at liberty.[65] Londoners probably perceived that a different standard of justice was applied in the case of the man convicted of homicide for killing an 'officer': a large riot broke out at his execution in Holborn in early October. The mayor arrested the leaders of this tumult, committed them to Newgate, but released them on bail the next day. The Privy Council reprimanded the mayor and ordered him to reapprehend the accused persons and hold them without bail for questioning. A few days later examinations of prisoners in the Marshalsea revealed that they talked freely of rebellion and killing the Queen.[66]

The London riots and rebellions of 1595 constituted the most dangerous and prolonged urban uprising in England between the accession of the Tudor dynasty and the beginning of the Long Parliament. There were at least 13 insurrections, riots, and unlawful assemblies that year in a dozen different parts of London and Southwark, of which 12 took place between 6 and 29 June. It was not merely the number and duration of the disorders that made this uprising so dangerous, but also the explicit attack upon the authority of the lord mayor: the attorney-general, Edward Coke, charged that the apprentices had intended 'to take the sworde of Aucthoryte from the magistrates and gouernours Lawfully Aucthorised and there vnto appointed. . . .'[67]

Sir John Spencer—'Rich' Spencer, as he was called for his great wealth—at first glance might seem the sort of mayor that the Queen and Privy Council had long desired.[68] In popular estimation he was a stern magistrate: a husbandman from Knightsbridge complained that 'where the Council had punished two, the lord mayor punished

---

65 *Acts PC* xxii. 549–50, xxiii. 19–20, 28–9. This reminds us that constables and officers of the Crown possessed no legal immunity and were not automatically held blameless when someone was slain during the suppression of a riot. When one of the Provost-Marshal's men killed a rioter at St James's Fair in 1558, a coroner's inquest examined evidence in the form of written depositions: ibid., vi. 370).

66 Ibid., xxiii. 242; PRO, SP 12/243/45.

67 PRO, STAC 5/A19/23.

68 Sharpe, *London and the Kingdom*, i. 533; Ashton, *The City and the Court, 1603–1643*, pp. 39–40.

seven'.[69] Ironically, the Privy Council thought that Spencer's negligence in not acting more decisively or working more closely with his fellow magistrates was one of the main causes of the riots.[70] But the rebels saw the mayor as a symbol of harsh justice: speeches were made against him threatening to kill him and burn his house, and a gallows was erected in front of his door.[71] A serving-maid, who claimed to be able to read the future in the coals of her kitchen fire, also predicted the Queen's death and declared her intention to go to Spain.[72]

The troubles began on 6 June when a silk-weaver and citizen appeared at the mayor's house and used 'some hard speeches in dispraise of his government'. The mayor assumed that the man was mad, and ordered him committed to Bedlam. Before the silk-weaver could be confined, a crowd of 200 or 300 persons gathered and effected his rescue.[73] On 12 June there were anti-alien riots in Southwark and elsewhere; on the same day and again on 13 June the two instances of popular market regulation occurred. Once again, the crowd attempted to prevent prisoners from being taken. On the 15th more crowds attacked the Counter Prison, and rescued prisoners on their way to the Counter. On 16 June leaders of the apprentices conferred with some discharged soldiers in the vicinity of St Paul's and, after discussing the assassination of the mayor, agreed to join forces.[74]

Thereafter, the crowd became larger and displayed more discipline. On 27 June another attempt was made to break into the Counter and release prisoners. Twenty rioters were arrested on this occasion. The largest gatherings occurred in Cheapside and Leadenhall, where a crowd of 1,800, protesting the whipping of the butter-rioters, tore down the pillories and then proceeded to the lord mayor's house, where they erected a gallows in front of the mayor's door and dared him to come out.[75] On Sunday afternoon, 29 June, 1,000 persons gathered on Tower Hill. The crowd was led by a man named Grant

[69] *Cal. SP Dom., 1595–1597*, p. 63; PRO, SP 12/252/94.ii–iii.

[70] Hist. MSS Comm., *Salisbury*, v. 250.

[71] Ibid., v. 249–50; Hale, *Pleas of the Crown*, i. 144; PRO, SP 12/252/94.ii–iii.

[72] PRO, SP 12/252/94.i.

[73] Hist. MSS Comm., *Salisbury*, v. 249.

[74] Stow, *Survey of London and Westminster*, ed. Strype, ii. 303; Stow, *Annales*, pp. 769–70; Hist. MSS Comm., *Salisbury*, v. 249.

[75] PRO, SP 12/252/94.ii–iii; MSS Comm., *Salisbury*, v. 250.

from Uxbridge and included shoemakers, girdlers, silk-weavers, and husbandmen, besides the apprentices, discharged soldiers, and vagrants. The Crown prosecution stated that they had intended to break open the city armouries, rescue prisoners, and kill the lord mayor.[76] An attempt by the watch of Towerstreet Ward to disperse the crowd failed: the rioters, displaying a banner and 'hartened thereunto by sounding of a trumpet . . . the trumpetter hauing bene a souldier', drove the militia back into Tower Street. The attorney-general claimed that the rioters were armed with 'halberdes, bills, goonnes, daggs, maine pikes, poll axes, swordes, daggers, staves and such lyke'.[77] Later in the afternoon the sheriffs were on the scene making arrests. The mayor, Sir John Spencer, did not arrive until seven o'clock, when the proclamation to disperse again was read. At this point 100 retainers of Sir Michael Blount, lieutenant of the Tower, who all the while had refused to lend assistance in suppressing the rebellion, objected to the mayor's sword of justice being borne up within the Liberty of the Tower, and assaulted and beat the sword-bearer and the mayor's servants. Another contingent of the Tower garrison actually released prisoners who were in the custody of the mayor's officers. An investigation into Blount's activities subsequently uncovered a conspiracy to hold the Tower and its armoury against the Privy Council in the event of the Queen's death and to support the Earl of Hertford's claim to the throne.[78]

The evidence suggests that several days were required to restore order. The Queen ordered the proclamation of martial law on 4 July and commanded the provost-marshal to carry out summary executions. Fortunately, the provost-marshal ignored the latter instruction; mounted patrols swept up vagrants and brought them before city magistrates. The next day, Saturday, 5 July, a double watch was mounted and stood to arms through Sunday night. The treason trial of the leaders of the rebellion was held at Guildhall on 22 July. Two days later Grant and four companions were drawn on hurdles from Newgate to Tower Hill and executed.[79]

[76] Stow, *Annales*, pp. 769–70; PRO, SP 12/252/94; Hale, *Pleas of the Crown*, i. 144.

[77] PRO, STAC 5/A19/23.

[78] Manning, 'The Prosecution of Sir Michael Blount, Lieutenant of the Tower, 1595', pp. 216–24.

[79] Stow, *Annales*, pp. 769–70; CLRO, Rep. 23, fo. 416ᵛ; PRO, SP 12/253/48; Hale, *Pleas of the Crown*, i. 144.

iii. *The Problem of the Suburbs*

Following the suppression of the riots and rebellions of June 1595, popular disorder declined within the walls and bars marking the corporate limits of the city, but remained an intractable problem in the suburbs. Of the 55 insurrections, riots, and unlawful assemblies which occurred between 1606 and May 1640 all but nine of them took place in suburban parishes of Westminster, Middlesex, Surrey, and the Liberties. The governors of the city became more vigilant: watches were mounted and trained bands mustered on holidays, and the presence of provost-marshals grudgingly accepted. But like nineteenth-century police forces, they could not eliminate disorder; they could only try to confine it to certain areas.[80]

The 22 riots that occurred between 1606 and 1623 are very different from the popular disturbances of the 1580s and 1590s. Most of the Jacobean riots broke out in the northern suburbs between Clerkenwell and Shoreditch, and 15 happened on Shrove Tuesday. The participants appear to have consisted largely of apprentices, and their activities were mostly limited to sacking or pulling down the theatres and bawdy houses that clustered together in the area between Clerkenwell and Shoreditch, an area crowded with taverns, brothels, and theatres. On two occasions, in 1617 and 1618, the unruly apprentices rescued or attempted to rescue prisoners from New Bridewell Prison in St John's Street, Clerkenwell and Finsbury Prison. The rioting of 1617 caused great alarm because it spread outside this area to St Katharine's, Wapping, Lincoln's Inn Fields, and Drury Lane. The riot that disturbed St James's Fair in Westminster on 12 July 1614 can also be classified as an example of festive misrule.[81]

This description of the popular disorders of the Jacobean period is based on the letters of John Chamberlain and the records of the Middlesex Sessions. There are also a number of allusions to Shrove-Tuesday apprentices' riots in the plays of Jacobean dramatists,

[80] Lindley, 'Riot Prevention and Control in Early Stuart London', pp. 110, 126. Prof. Pearl argues that the amount of popular disorder in London has been exaggerated: 'Change and Stability in Seventeenth-century London', pp. 3–5. Cf. Rappaport, 'Social Structure and Mobility in Sixteenth-century London, Part I', pp. 107–8.

[81] *Middlesex County Records*, ed. Jeaffreson, ii. 26, 86; *Middlesex Sessions Records*, ed. Le Hardy, vols. i, ii, iii, and iv, *passim*; R. Ashton, 'Popular Entertainment and Social Control in Late Elizabethan and Early Stuart London', *London Journal* 9 (1983), 14; *Letters of John Chamberlain*, ed. N. E. McClure (2 vols.; Philadelphia, 1939), i. 339; ii. 59–60, 74, 142; *Cal. SP Dom., 1611–1618*, p. 449.

of which the most familiar is John Taylor's amusing caricature in *Jack a Lent* (London, 1630):

Then Tim Tatters, a most valiant villain, with an ensign made of a piece of bakers mawkin fixed upon a broom staff, he displays his dreadful colors, and calling the ragged regiment together, makes an illiterate oration, stuffed with the most plentiful want of discretion, the conclusion whereof is, that somewhat they will do, but what they know not. Until at last comes marching up another troop of tatterdemalions, proclaiming wars against no matter who, so they may be doing. Then these youths . . . put play houses to the sack, and bawdy houses to the spoil, in the quarrell breaking a thousand quarrels (of glass I mean) . . . tumbling from the tops of lofty chimneys, terribly untilling houses, ripping up the bowels of feather beds.[82]

E. K. Chambers assumed that these annual rituals of violence were 'but a traditional Saturnalia of apprentices at Shrovetide'.[83] But a search of the Elizabethan State Papers, the Middlesex Sessions, and the London Corporation records has failed to turn up anything remotely resembling the Jacobean Shrove-Tuesday apprentices' riots in the Elizabethan period.[84] This raises the question whether the Jacobean Shrove-Tuesday assaults on theatres and bawdy houses were really traditional survivals from the Elizabethan period, revivals of rites from an earlier period, like the rural sports and festivals of Robert Dover, or inventions of the Jacobean playwrites, which the London apprentices emulated. One wonders to what extent dramatists such as Thomas Dekker, Joseph Cooke, and Beaumont and Fletcher may have encouraged the rowdy behaviour of apprentices on their holidays by ridiculing the customs and values of their masters, the citizens of London, and treating the Shrovetide antics of the apprentices in a jocular vein.[85] John Taylor knew from personal

---

[82] C. L. Barber, *Shakespeare's Festive Comedy: A Study of Dramatic Form and its Relation to Social Custom* (Princeton, 1959), 38. The play is reprinted in *The Old Book Collector's Miscellany*, ed. C. Hindley (1872), vol. ii. Other examples of allusions to Shrove-Tuesday apprentices' riots have been gathered together in Norton, *Commentaries*, pp. 205 n–206 n. For a brief discussion of the association of Shrove Tide with the public chastisement of sexual offences, cf. A. Yarborough, 'Apprentices as Adolescents in Sixteenth-century Bristol', *Journal of Social History* 13/1 (1979), 70–1.

[83] E. K. Chambers, *The Elizabethan Stage* (4 vols., Oxford, 1923), i. 265 n.

[84] The earliest example I have found occurred in 1602 when two yeomen of Tottenham, Middlesex, were accused of 'pullinge downe bridges gates styles and breakinge glasse wyndowes on Easter daye last in the night': *Middlesex County Records*, ed. Jeaffreson, i. 280.

[85] Cf. Norton, *Commentaries*, pp. 205 n.–206 n.

experience how apprentices were exploited by their masters and had little love for the 'fur-gowned money-mongers' of the city. Taylor was very much a royalist and showed contempt for Puritans.[86] Although James I favoured traditional calendar customs, it would be too much to say that he encouraged Shrove-Tuesday riots; but, on the other had, he did not keep a vigilant eye on the policing of London and Middlesex until the Shrove-Tuesday riots of 1617 gave him a bad fright.[87]

It appears that as long as Shrove-Tuesday antics remained within the accepted limits of attacking only the stews and playhouses of the Clerkenwell-Shoreditch area, the rioters might expect relatively lenient punishments. Although individual groups of rioters might include as many as 200 persons, the magistrates were usually able to bring only between two and ten persons to trial. Whippings were administered to ten persons involved in two separate riots in 1607; in 1612, 1613, 1614, 1616, 1620, and 1623 indicted rioters paid recognizances of £20–£40. The riots of 1617 went beyond the accepted limits of Shrovetide rituals; John Chamberlain saw them as distinctly more dangerous and described the official reaction:

On the 4th of this present [March 1617] beeing our Shrove Tewsday the prentises or rather the unruly people of the suburbs played theyr parts, in divers places, as Finsburie fields, about Wapping by St. Katharines, and in Lincolns Ynne fields, in which places beeing assembled in great numbers they fell to great disorders in pulling downe of houses and beating the guards that were set to kepe rule, specially at a new play house (sometime a cockpit) in Drurie Lane, where the Quenes players used to play. Though the fellowes [i.e. the actors] defended themselves as well as they could and slew three of them [apprentices] with shot and hurt divers, yet they entered the house and defaced yt, cutting the players apparell all in pieces, and all other theyre furniture and burnt theyre play bookes and did what mischiefe they could: in Finsburie they brake the prison and let out all prisoners, spoyled the house by untiling and breaking downe the roofe and all the windowes and at Wapping they pulled downe seven or eight houses and defaced five times as many, besides many other outrages as beating the sheriffe from his horse with stones and dooinge much other hurt too long to write. There be divers of them taken since and clapt up, and I make no question but we shall see some of them hanged this next weeke, as yt is more then time they were.[88]

---

[86] Mitchell and Leys, *History of London Life*, p. 123.
[87] *Cal. SP Dom., 1611–1618*, p. 449.
[88] *Letters of John Chamberlain*, ed. McClure, vol. ii, pp. 59–60.

The defendants were evidently charged with felony-riot, one of but two instances that have come to light of attempts to apply the statute of 1559, but the jury refused to convict them on that charge. At least two were found guilty of misdemeanour-riot, fined, and imprisoned.[89]

Thereafter, the trained bands of Middlesex and London were regularly mustered on Shrove Tuesday and May Day. Watches were also mounted and the provost-marshal's men turned out in full force. On Shrove Tuesday 1636, the Middlesex trained bands alone mustered 120 horse and 1,461 foot. The last known Shrove-Tuesday riot took place in 1641. The apprentices, together with students of Gray's Inn, attempted a midsummer riot in June 1638 when the office of the sheriff of Middlesex in Holborn was attacked. A particularly nasty disturbance occurred on 10 July in Fleet Street and the Strand, when a group of army officers resisted arrest. They were joined by students from Lincoln's Inn and the Temple. Together, they took on the mayor, sheriffs, and the city trained bands, and slew a militia captain. One or two others were also killed and several wounded. Two army officers were hanged as a consequence, but their funeral occasioned further disturbances.[90]

The popular disorders of Charles I's reign reveal a growing political awareness on the part of the London crowd. In contrast to the Jacobean period the riots could no longer be contained and spread throughout the London area: eight happened in the city; six in the eastern riverside parishes; at least 18 in the northern and western suburbs, the Liberties, and Westminster; and two on the south bank of the Thames. Some of the forms of protest are quite familiar: two instances of prisoners rescued and an attack upon the Venetian ambassador's servants.[91] Of the 33 instances of popular disorder between 1626 and May 1640, 16 can be classified as protests against the Duke of Buckingham and Archbishop Laud and their policies. The focus of popular protest was moving dangerously close to the throne.

The disturbances of 1626–8 consisted mostly of naval mutinies occasioned by the disastrous military expeditions against Cadiz in

---

[89] 1 Eliz., c. 16, *SR* iv. 377; *Letters of John Chamberlain*, ed. McClure, ii. 66. See also chs. 3 and 9 (ii).

[90] *Cal. SP Dom.*, *1611–1618*, p. 449; *1635–1636*, p. 196; *1637–1638*, p. 209; Lindley, 'Riot Prevention and Control in Early Stuart London', p. 115.

[91] *Cal. SP Dom.*, *1635*, p. 323.

1625 and the Isle of Rhé in 1627. Ill-fed and poorly equipped while overseas and confined to stinking hulks upon return, the sailors awaited satisfaction of their arrears of pay with increasing restlessness. They were easily persuaded that the royal favourite, the Duke of Buckingham, was to blame for their troubles. The inhabitants of the London area sympathized with the plight of the sailors and protested the unparliamentary exactions levied to pay for Buckingham's policies.[92]

The protests began on 16 May 1626 at the Fortune Playhouse, Whitecross Street in the Clerkenwell-Shoreditch area when a crowd, consisting mostly of sailors, assaulted a constable and attempted to rescue some of their mates who had been arrested. One sailor, Thomas Alderson, 'beinge charged in the Kinges name to yeelde and keepe the peace . . . saide hee cared not for the Kinge, for the Kinge paide him no wages' and vowed to 'bringe the whole Navy thither to pull downe the playhouse'. Further examination of Alderson revealed that the sailors planned an assembly at the Bear Garden to seek revenge for an injury done to a sailor; they were to be led by a captain and a drummer.[93] On 13 June, Dr John Lambe, the Duke of Buckingham's astrologer—known to the London populace as the 'Duke's devil'—was attacked and murdered by a crowd in the parish of St Margaret Lothbury. The mayor and sheriffs of the city were called to account by the Council. A double watch was mounted, and when a man was caught holding a libel against Buckingham he was hanged even though he claimed that he had only removed it from the wall to read it.[94] There was much resistance in the city and suburbs to extra-parliamentary taxation—some of it led by merchants of the highest standing. The parishioners of St Clement Temple Bar and the inhabitants of the Liberties, incited by 'the Prophet Ball', a tailor who quoted scripture 'mightily', rioted in early October against the forced loan, and said they stood 'ready for a press groat rather than yield a jot'. Freeholders who refused to pay actually were impressed for soldiers.[95]

Another wave of violence began in late November over arrears of pay. Three hundred sailors attacked the houses of the commissioners

[92] Pearl, *London and the Outbreak of the Puritan Revolution*, p. 76.
[93] *Middlesex County Records*, ed. Jeaffreson, iii. 161–2.
[94] Birch, *The Court and Times of Charles I*, i. 364–8; Pearl, *London and the Outbreak of the Puritan Revolution*, p. 76.
[95] Birch, *The Court and Times of Charles I*, i. 154.

of the navy breaking windows and doors, and would have done the same to the house of Sir William Russell, treasurer of the navy, if he had not calmed them with 'fair words'. When six captains recently returned from service in Ireland broke into Buckingham's apartment in Whitehall, he reminded them of the proclamation of martial law against soldiers or mariners violating the precincts of the palace. The officers said that they were ready to hang; Buckingham became alarmed and promised them their back-pay.[96] Several hundred sailors in Portsmouth also left their ships and marched to Whitehall to demand their wages. By the time they arrived on 1 February 1627, the gates were shut fast, but a message from the King promised them their pay on 3 February if they would proceed to Tower Hill. The sailors were easily appeased at this point with promise of payment and cheered the King. Charles immediately wrote to the lord mayor to call out the trained bands to prevent the sailors returning to Whitehall and commanded the lieutenant of the Tower to fire on them if they offered resistance. The sailors, having arrived at Tower Hill, vowed that if they were not paid the Duke 'should loose his head'. Another group attempted to march on Whitehall in late August, but were intercepted by provost-marshals.[97]

By December the situation in the navy had become desperate. The mariners at Portsmouth had been ten months without pay and complained to one of the navy commissioners about their tattered clothes. When it was learned that they intended to march on Whitehall again, the mayor of Portsmouth and the commander of the garrison were ordered to mount strong guards to intercept them. The Portsmouth sailors mutinied again on 14 January 1628. By the end of January the ships anchored in the Thames had run out of provisions and their crews also mutinied. They were given billeting tickets and dispersed among the eastern suburbs. The trained bands of London and surrounding counties were held in readiness should the mariners attempt to assemble.[98]

Many felt that the King's assent to the Petition of Right on 7 June 1628 had eased the tension, and lit bonfires in celebration. But a group of boys who gathered on Tower Hill the same evening were of a contrary mood. They tore down the scaffold, made a bonfire

[96] Birch, *The Court and Times of Charles I*, i. 175, 177; *Cal. SP Dom., 1627–1628*, p. 47.
[97] Birch, *The Court and Times of Charles I*, i. 189, 194; *Cal. SP Dom., 1627–1628*, pp. 44, 47, 314.
[98] Ibid., pp. 469–70, 516, 536, 568.

of it, and said 'they would have a new one built for the Duke of Bucks'. When Buckingham was assassinated in Portsmouth by John Felton, a disillusioned naval officer, the latter was acclaimed a hero, while the escort for the Duke's body had to proceed through the streets at night under heavy guard for fear of popular tumult.[99]

The other major outbreak of disorder in pre-revolutionary London came in May 1640. A major depression in trade, beginning about 1633, had caused widespread unemployment in the clothing industry as well as among seamen idled by the decline in exports to European markets.[100] Although the economic crisis furnished fertile ground for the seeds of popular discontent, the demonstrations against Archbishop Laud were more directly the consequence of the remarkable spread of Puritan opinions among the populace during the preceding decade by means of pulpit and printing press. Moreover, the vocal defiance of John Lilburne and other victims of the Court of Star Chamber effectively focused attention upon the evils of arbitrary rule when they were publicly pilloried or whipped through the streets of London for the crime of seditious libel.[101]

When the Short Parliament, summoned in April 1640, was dissolved abruptly in early May, popular rumours blamed Laud. Libels posted in the Exchange and other parts of London exhorted apprentices to free the commonwealth from prelatical rule and to join in hunting 'William the Fox'. The placards appointed St George's Fields in Southwark, early in the morning of 11 May, as the place of assembly. The trained bands were sent there to prevent mischief, but the crowd, consisting of sailors, glovers, and tanners, waited until the militia had retired for the day. A little before midnight 500 persons marched to Lambeth and besieged the Archbishop's Palace, which he had fortified earlier before the King had ordered him to withdraw across the river to the safety of Whitehall Palace. During the night of 14–15 May a group of apprentices broke open the White Lion Prison in Southwark and rescued prisoners; another offered to free Thomas Atkins, one of the four aldermen imprisoned for resisting a forced

---

[99] Birch, *The Court and Times of Charles I*, i. 362; Pearl, *London and the Outbreak of the Puritan Revolution*, p. 77.

[100] Supple, *Commercial Crisis and Change in England*, pp. 120–5; Wilson, *England's Apprenticeship*, p. 52.

[101] W. Haller, *The Rise of Puritanism* (New York, 1938; repr. 1957), ch. 7; B. Manning, *The English People and the English Revolution* (1976), ch. 4.

loan. Atkins declined, and the King ordered him released the next day in an effort to appease the crowd.[102] Only two rioters were captured in the attack on Lambeth Palace. The first, John Archer, a glover from Southwark, had marched before the crowd with a drum and was supposed to be the leader. He was cruelly, but vainly, tortured for information—the last use of the rack in England. The other was a sixteen-year-old sailor from Rochester named Thomas Bensted. The latter was executed for treason at the end of May. The examination of two apothecary's apprentices who had taken part in the assault on the White Lion Prison revealed a strong anti-Catholic bias on the part of the crowd: plans were discovered to attack the Queen Mother's house, Somerset House Chapel, and the Earl of Arundel's house, where the Earl was rumoured to have mounted guns to fire upon the apprentices in St George's Fields. The Privy Council's intervention in the suppression of the rioting revealed not only panic, but also a distrust of the London magistrates. They ordered the trained bands of Essex, Kent, and Hertfordshire to furnish 6,000 foot to keep order after parts of the London and Middlesex militia declined to serve. Royal provost-marshals were again forced upon the London authorities.[103]

The most significant categories of popular disturbance in Tudor and early-Stuart London were festive misrule, anti-alien riots, protests against unjust punishments, and the demonstrations against royal ministers during the Caroline period. As stages in the process of historical change they display a progression from traditional rituals of social inversion through attempts to blame economic distress upon outsiders and efforts to recall magistrates to traditional standards of justice, finally emerging as cohesive and politically-conscious attempts to influence royal policies by removing evil ministers and supporting the summoning of a Parliament.

---

[102] S. R. Gardiner, *History of England from the Accession of James I to the Outbreak of the Civil War, 1603–1642* (10 vols.; repr. New York, 1965), ix. 132–5; H. R. Trevor-Roper, *Archbishop Laud, 1573–1645* (2nd edn.; 1962), 388–9; Pearl, *London and the Outbreak of the Puritan Revolution*, pp. 107–8, 311–12.

[103] *Cal. SP Dom., 1640*, pp. 174–5, 184, 201, 221; Lindley, 'Riot Prevention and Control in Early Stuart London', pp. 124–5. For a discussion of popular anti-Catholicism, cf. R. Clifton, 'The Popular Fear of Catholics during the English Revolution', *P. & P.*, no. 52 (Aug. 1971), 23–55.

Xenophobia persisted as an element in crowd behaviour to the very end and coloured accounts of apprentices' riots by Edward Hall and John Strype, although neither attempted to hide popular dissatisfaction with the harshness and partiality of justice. The crown's frequent interference in the preservation of public order and the administration of justice reveals a fear of the London populace that contrasts with the generally more lenient treatment of anti-enclosure rioters in the countryside. It is clear that Elizabeth and her councillors believed that most London apprentices were little better than rogues, and this view was shared and articulated by courtiers and lawyers, which provoked additional instances of violent social conflict.

The Shrove-Tuesday riots do not fit neatly into this analytical model. Something of a reaction seems to have set in against Elizabethan attitudes towards festive misrule. Perhaps encouraged by Jacobean courtiers and dramatists, the antics of apprentices were tolerated, or at least lightly punished by magistrates, so long as they were confined to the Clerkenwell-Shoreditch area and directed only against actors and prostitutes. Only when these unwritten rules were broken in 1617 and 1618 was a more severe official reaction forthcoming.

Between 1626 and 1628 wealthy citizens protesting forced loans and poor sailors, many of them serving on ships requisitioned from London and commanded by Admiral Penington, brother of Alderman Isaac Penington, found common cause in protesting the extra-parliamentary taxation and fiscal irresponsibility of Buckingham. The popular protests in May 1640 against Laud's breaking of Parliament took the form of an anti-popery demonstration, which masked aldermanic fears of more forced loans. City politicians had developed techniques for manipulating London mobs for their own purposes. These they would continue to exploit for the next century and more.

9

The Rebellions of 1596 and 1607

THE food riots of the late-Elizabethan and early-Stuart periods were confined to areas of clothing manufacture in Kent, East Anglia, and the West of England, which were especially vulnerable to a combination of dearth and unemployment resulting from trade depressions. In other parts of the realm—especially the Midlands—popular protests against grain shortages and high prices were more likely to take the form of anti-enclosure riots. This was the case with both the Oxfordshire or Enslow Hill Rebellion of 1596 and the Midland Revolt of 1607. In the areas affected by these two revolts it was generally held that enclosures withdrew land from tillage and thus caused grain shortages and high prices. While most violent enclosure disputes were caused by enclosures of commons and wastes, there is good evidence that in certain parts of Oxfordshire, Northamptonshire, Warwickshire, Lincolnshire, and Leicestershire there were extensive enclosures of arable land in the late 1580s and 1590s that caused depopulation. Although the government first responded by hanging the rebel leaders, the rebellions of 1596 and 1607 were also followed by new parliamentary legislation and by prosecutions for causing the decay of tillage. Professor Kerridge and others have demonstrated that in many of these cases the landowners who were prosecuted were not converting to permanent grassland but rather were introducing the new techniques of convertible husbandry which alternated nitrogen-fixing leys with corn in order to restore fertility to the soil and increase yields. That Professor Kerridge may be describing the more typical phenomenon does not gainsay the existence of very real grievances in the areas disturbed by these two rebellions. Agrarian conditions varied considerably from one local community to another, just as each farming country displayed distinct characteristics.[1]

[1] E. F. Gay, 'The Midland Revolt and the Inquisitions of Depopulation, 1607', *Trans. R. Hist. Soc.* 18 (1904), 212 and n.; Walter and Wrightson, 'Dearth and the Social Order in Early Modern England', pp. 26 n., 27, 30; Thirsk, 'The Local History of Enclosing and Engrossing', *AHEW* iv. 228–32; Kerridge, *Agrarian Problems*, ch. 6.

i. *The Enslow Hill Rebellion of 1596*

The Enslow Hill Rebellion was a poorly-organized and abortive conspiracy. It alarmed the government because the leaders uttered threats of violence against the gentry and had planned to march on London to join up with the apprentices. The events began peaceably in the early autumn of 1596 when a group of between 40 and 60 men went to see Henry, Lord Norris, the lord lieutenant of Oxfordshire, at his seat at Rycote, near Thame, and petitioned him to provide corn for the poor and to order that illegal enclosures be thrown down. It appears that Lord Norris did not respond and the meeting got out of hand; some of the petitioners threatened to level the hedges themselves and knock down a few gentlemen as well. Lord Norris's failure to exercise his paternal and magisterial responsibilities led one of his own servants, Bartholomew Steere, to plan an uprising.[2]

Steere, a carpenter, began to organize the conspiracy while still in Lord Norris's employ. Steere thought that the servants of Lord Norris and other Oxfordshire gentry could be persuaded to join a rising because 'they were kept like dogges'; he subverted several of Lord Norris's servants and those of other gentry who visited Rycote. Steere later confessed that he began making plans in mid-September and started recruiting followers from the middle of October. Two of Steere's lieutenants, the brothers Richard and James Bradshaw, were millers and since their occupations required them to travel frequently, they were able to help Steere with the recruiting. When Steere visited his home at Hampton Poyle in the Cherwell Valley, he persuaded his father, also a miller, and his father's servants to join him (see Map 9.1). His brother John, a weaver of Witney, said he could recruit cloth-workers from that centre of broadcloth manufacture, while others promised support from Bicester and Yarnton. Two gentlemen, John Harcourt of Cogges and a Mr Pudsey of Elsfield, were reported to be sympathetic and willing to act as leaders, but, if true, they subsequently changed their minds. Steere had expected at least 300 men to meet him on Enslow Hill, in the parish of Bletchingdon, in the evening of Sunday, 21 November. Only between 10 and 20 men actually showed up. After waiting two hours they dispersed, but were quickly apprehended by Sir William Spenser of

---

[2] PRO, SP 12/261/10, 262/4; *Cal. SP Dom., 1595–1597*, pp. 342 ff.; Hist. MSS Comm., *Salisbury*, vii. 49–50.

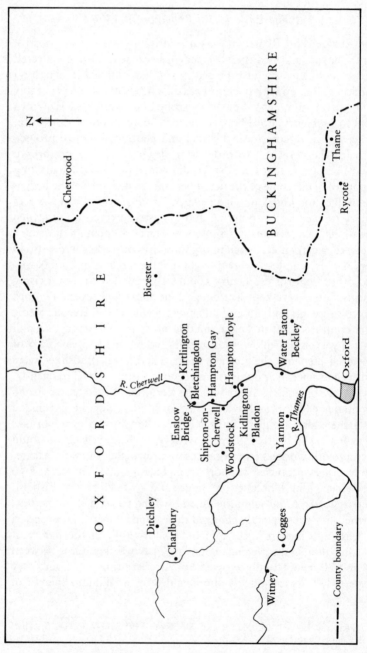

MAP 9.1 The Enslow Hill Rebellion of 1596

Yarnton, a deputy lieutenant. They had been betrayed by Roger Symonds, a poor carpenter of Hampton Gay whom Steere had taken pity upon and wished to help after he learned that Symonds was hard-pressed to feed his wife and seven sons.[3] Steere and his adherents were aware that the London apprentices had recently rebelled and that their leaders had been hanged. The Oxfordshire insurgents had planned to march on London and join up with the apprentices whom they assumed were ready to rise again. Steere's choice of Enslow Hill, overlooking the River Cherwell, as a place of assembly was a dramatic gesture because local tradition held that 'there was ons [once] a rising at Enslow by the commons, and they were persuaded to goe downe [i.e., to lay down their arms] and after were hanged like doggs'.[4] As soon as his army was gathered together Steere had intended to level the hedges belonging to Francis Poure in Bletchingdon, and those of other enclosing landlords in the Cherwell Valley, and appropriate horses, armour, weapons and provisions from various gentry seats. One house the

---

[3] Ibid.; PRO, SP 12/262/4; Hist. MSS Comm., *Fourth Report*, ii (1843): Calendar of the Baga de Secretis, pp. 289–90; *Acts PC* xvi. 365.

[4] PRO, SP 12/262/4; SP 14/287/64, mistakenly calendared in *Cal. SP Dom.*, *1603–1610*, p. 373, printed in Gay, 'The Midland Revolt and the Inquisitions of Depopulation of 1607', pp. 238–9. Bartholomew Steere's reasons for the choice of Enslow Hill are reminiscent of those which were said to have determined the choice of Mousehold Heath by Robert Ket's followers in 1549. In both instances particular places of assembly were thought to have been hallowed by the protests of ancestors. Modern-day revolutionaries sometimes still share the same superstition. A. Vere Woodman thought that Enslow Hill might have been the location of the last resistance of the Oxfordshire rebels in 1549, but the more recent research of Barrett Beer states that they established their final camp at Chipping Norton in the Cotswolds before Lord Grey's army attacked them. Some of the confessions extracted from Steere's adherents give Enslow Bridge as the place of assembly. There were good reasons for choosing the latter: this was where the main road from Chipping Norton to London crossed the Cherwell and it was also the junction of three local roads. Most of Steere's followers came from the parishes of Hampton Gay, Hampton Poyle, Kirtlington, and Bletchingdon on the east side of the river, but they were to be met by men from Yarnton, Witney, and Woodstock on the west side. There is now a railway bridge of the former Great Western Railway on the site of the ancient bridge. There would also have been good reasons for choosing Enslow Hill, which consists of the high ground east of the bridge and is regarded locally as a landmark. Enslow Hill had been an Anglo-Saxon *Spelleburge*, or 'Speech Hill', which had long been a traditional outdoor meeting place. It was also located within the parish and manor of Bletchingdon, where the enclosures of the Poure family, who were the manorial lords, had been the occasion of great popular outrage. Steere's adherents had intended to level these enclosures: A. Vere Woodman, 'The Buckinghamshire and Oxfordshire Rising of 1495', *Oxoniensia* 12 (1957), 80; *VCH Oxfordshire*, vi. 2, 56–7, 64; Beer, *Rebellion and Riot*, pp. 149–51; PRO, SP 12/261/10.i; *Cal. SP, Dom. 1595–1597*, pp. 316 ff.

rebels meant to visit was that owned by the aged Sir Henry Lee at Ditchley, near Charlbury; he had become notorious as a 'great sheep-master' and the man who had profited from selling villeins their freedom.[5] The main objective before marching on London was to have been Lord Norris's house at Rycote, which had been sacked in 1549. Here, Steere had arranged with fellow servants to seize two brass cannons and mount them on carriages after the coach bodies had been removed.[6]

Steere appealed to popular dislike of the gentry when recruiting his followers. He told them that the world 'would never be well untill some of the gentlemen were knockt downe' and 'that the commons long sithens in Spaine did rise and kill all gentlemen . . . and sithens that time have lyued merrily there.' He thought that 'yt was but a monethes work to overrunne England'. The leader of the Oxfordshire rebels told his followers that they would possess an advantage because they would be helped by 'a mason who could make balls of wild-fire', which could be hurled at their enemies by means of a sling. Steere assured a weaver of Witney that his supporters 'were no base fellows, but husbandmen who possessed plough lands of their own'; he himself 'stood in no need, but meant to have risen to help his poor friends and other poor people who lived in misery'. Steere probably was in a state of euphoria when he told Roger Symonds that he cared 'not for work, for we shall have a merrier world shortly. . . . I will work one day and play the other.'[7]

Attorney-general Coke thought that the Oxfordshire rebels' declared intention of levelling hedges and helping the poor was merely a pretence, and that they actually meant to kill the gentry and spoil their houses. However, there is evidence of extensive enclosures in the Cherwell Valley and we know that Steere's followers attributed the high corn prices to depopulating enclosures and the decay of tillage. The harvest of 1596 was the most disastrous of the Tudor and early-Stuart periods, and the evidence clearly indicates that prices were especially high in Oxfordshire. Whereas the average price of wheat was somewhat above 50s. a quarter generally and nearly 63s.

---

[5] *DNB*, s.v. Sir Henry Lee (1530–1610).
   [6] PRO, SP 12/261/10, 261/15.ii–iii, 262/4; SP 14/28/64; *Cal. SP Dom.*, *1595–1597*, pp. 316, 318; *Acts PC*, xxvi. 398; Hist. MSS Comm., *Salisbury*, vii. 49–50.
   [7] *Cal. SP Dom.*, *1595–1597*, pp. 316, 342–5; PRO, SP 12/261/15.ii; SP 14/28/64; Hist. MSS Comm., *Salisbury*, vii. 49–50.

at Exeter, the price at Oxford rose from 64s. a quarter in late September 1596 to 72s. by late March 1597. James Bradshaw discovered that the price in Bicester had already reached 72s. in the autumn of 1596, and he had wondered how the poor would live. William Darbley, baker to Sir William Spencer, who had recently enclosed the common fields of Yarnton, thought that the price of corn would remain high until enclosures were cast down. Richard Bradshaw blamed the high cost of food in Oxfordshire on gentlemen and rich farmers who engrossed corn and enclosed commons. The Oxfordshire justices had attempted to prevent the export of corn from the country, but were overruled by the Privy Council, who were more fearful of renewed outbreaks of popular rebellion in London.[8]

Other gentlemen also were identified as being culpable: William Frere was accused of depopulating the whole hamlet of Water Eaton. The greatest anger was directed at Francis Poure of Bletchingdon whose lands included Enslow Hill and bordered on the parishes of Hampton Gay, Hampton Poyle, and Kirtlington, where Bartholomew Steere, the Bradshaws, and several other ringleaders had their homes. The antipathy towards the Poure family very likely dated back to the time of Francis Poure's father, Vincent, who had inherited Bletchingdon manor in 1526. He enclosed demesne arable and waste on a considerable scale, altered the copyhold tenures to his advantage, and allied himself with a few tenants in order to force the remainder to sell out. Francis Poure continued the same policies and enclosed and engrossed a further 780 acres during the reign of Elizabeth. An especially large enclosure was made on the eve of the Enslow Hill conspiracy when Poure acquired a freehold belonging to Thomas Rathbone and consisting of 96 acres. This enclosure particularly angered Richard Bradshaw; the Rathbone family had been the last yeomen farmers in the neighbourhood, but for the last two generations had been consolidating their position as gentry with purchases of land in the adjoining parishes of Bletchingdon and Shipton-on-Cherwell. The other houses of husbandry had already decayed and been reduced to cottages with only three acres or so of land attached to them. Thus, the village of Bletchingdon in 1596

---

[8] *Cal. SP Dom., 1595–1597*, pp. 319–20; Hoskins, 'Harvest Fluctuations and English Economic History, 1480–1619', p. 46; *VCH Oxfordshire*, ii. 194–5; PRO, SP 12/261/15. iv, 262/14; J. Walter, 'A "Rising of the People"? The Oxfordshire Rising of 1596', *P. & P.*, no. 107 (May 1985), 97–8.

consisted of 'nothing but poor people'.[9] The growth of poverty was becoming a serious problem in Oxfordshire.

Lord Norris responded belatedly to the petitioners' complaints and finally asked for a commission on 16 December to investigate enclosures in the county. Lord Norris still could not comprehend that Bartholomew Steere had begun planning the rebellion under his own roof because of his inaction; he persisted in believing that 'this stir' began in the western part of Oxfordshire. Francis Poure and several other gentlemen of Oxfordshire were summoned before the Privy Council on 30–31 January 1597. Poure was then sent to the attorney-general for examination and may have been prosecuted for causing the decay of tillage. If so, little was changed, because the remainder of the parish of Bletchingdon was enclosed in 1623.[10]

Bartholomew Steere and his lieutenants were subjected to nearly two months of rigorous interrogation. Between 23 November and 14 December they were examined by Lord Norris and the deputy lieutenants of Oxfordshire. Steere at first refused to confess anything. Roger Ibell, a servant at John Steere the elder's mill in Hampton Poyle, where the final stages of planning had taken place, provided some information that corroborated evidence deposed by the informer Roger Symonds but refused to give any names. After intensive cross-examination Bartholomew Steere also confirmed the basic outline of the conspiracy, but he too betrayed no names. Interrogation of other prisoners proved more fruitful, but Lord Norris complained that he could not extract even 20 names, so he recommended to the Privy Council that the prisoners be examined under torture. In mid-December Lord Norris's son and heir, Sir Henry Norris, conducted Bartholomew Steere, Roger Ibell, and the Bradshaw brothers to London; they were escorted under guard with 'their hands pynnioned and their legs bound under the horse[s'] bellys', and were kept apart so that they could not 'have conference one with another'. The four prisoners, plus Robert Burton, a bricklayer-mason of Beckley, were

[9] Ibid., pp. 110–11; *VCH Oxfordshire*, ii. 195, vi. 62–4; PRO, SP 12/261/15.iii. The adjoining manor of Kirtlington, parcel of the Duchy of Lancaster, appears to have been more tranquil. However, the manorial court ceased to be the place for resolving conflict and handling petty litigation after 1593 and the proportion of labourers and cottagers in the population grew steadily: M. Griffiths, 'Kirtlington Manor Court, 1500–1650', *Oxoniensia* 14 (1959), 269–70, 276–7.

[10] Ibid.; *Acts PC* xxvi. 398, 455; *Cal. SP Dom., 1595–1597*, p. 316; *VCH Oxfordshire*, vi. 64.

each lodged in a different prison in the city to keep them from sending messages one to another. They were tortured and examined at Bridewell Prison by attorney-general Coke, solicitor-general Francis Bacon, and the recorder of London. Coke regarded Steere as the main organizer of the conspiracy and had obtained a full confession from him by the second week of January. Yet Bartholomew Steere was not hanged with his lieutenants in June; one suspects that he died in prison, quite possibly from the effects of torture. Coke thought that he had enough evidence to convict Steere, the Bradshaw brothers, Robert Burton, and Edward Bompas, a fuller of Kirtlington, of treason.[11]

Although Sir Edward Coke was ready to proceed to trial by the middle of January 1597, the trial was delayed until 11 June—despite the attorney-general's frequent memoranda to the Council stating that the Treason Act of 1571 (13 Eliz., c. 1) required that the defendants be indicted within six months after the crime had been committed. The trial was held at Westminster before a jury impanelled in Oxfordshire. The attorney-general argued that the conspirators were guilty of compassing or conspiracy to levy war against the Queen by presuming to 'take upon them [selves] royal authority, which is against the King'. The argument that they had usurped royal authority by attempting a general reformation of enclosures rested upon a distinction between public and private protest. The defendants were accused of going from place to place and, in general terms and public manner, advocating the destruction of enclosures. This was to be distinguished from an ordinary anti-enclosure riot which was regarded as a private dispute between one lord and his tenants. Since the defendants had confessed that they meant to procure arms from gentlemen's houses in order to carry out their conspiracy, this was taken to be proof of the public and general nature of their protest. On the basis of Coke's ingenious argument, Richard Bradshaw and Robert Burton were attainted of treason and executed on Enslow Hill. That the conviction was obtained under the Treason Act of 1571 three months after the statutory limitation specified in that Act shows how expedient the judges had become during the crises of the 1590s. Sir Matthew Hale later remarked that

---

[11] *Acts PC* xxvi. 373–4; *Cal. SP Dom., 1595–1597*, pp. 316, 318; PRO, SP 14/28/64; Hist. MSS Comm., *Salisbury*, vii. 49–50; id., *Fourth Report*, p. 289–90. James Bradshaw also did not stand trial.

no conviction could have been obtained under the Great Treason Statute of 1352, still widely employed at that time, 'because no war was levied, and that statute [of 1352] extended not to a conspiracy to levy war'. Indeed, if the case had been tried before more impartial judges, Coke probably would have had trouble proving that as much as a riot had been committed.[12]

In the 1530s the need to secure compliance with the Henrician succession and settlement of religion had been used to justify extending the Tudor law of treason to comprehend words as well as actions. The widespread fear of popular disorder in the 1590s was behind a further extension of the doctrine of treason: conspiracy to levy war against the King could now be construed as actually levying war against the King even if the accused persons meant no harm to the King, but had merely combined in a public manner to level hedges, to alter prices or wages, or to change laws established by Parliament. Since there were no accessories but only principals in high treason, all participants in protests that extended beyond the village community were to be regarded as being guilty of treason.[13]

Edward Coke listed 15 persons who were implicated as leaders and participants in the Enslow Hill conspiracy. Eleven were identified as pursuing a trade other than husbandry; one was a husbandman and another was a servant in husbandry. The remaining two were probably also agricultural servants. Yet there are good reasons for thinking that this was not entirely an artisans' rising. Several of the defendants' confessions—especially those of Bartholomew Steere and the Bradshaw brothers—emphasize that they identified with the interests of smallholders who were suffering from the consequences of enclosure. The attorney-general agreed that most of the conspirators lived in comfortable circumstances and had no plausible excuse for

---

[12] Hist. MSS Comm., *Salisbury*, vii. 49–50; PRO, SP 14/28/64; Coke, 3 *Institutes*, pp. 9–10; Hale, *The History of the Pleas of the Crown*, i. 145; Bellamy, *The Tudor Law of Treason*, pp. 78–9; *Select Statutes*, ed. Prothero, pp. 57–60; Walter, 'A "Rising of the People"? The Oxfordshire Rising of 1596', pp. 129–30. The modern crime of conspiracy originated in Star Chamber practice and shows the tendency, which was especially pronounced at this time, for law originating in that court to permeate the common law. In his report on the *Poulterers' Case of 1611*, Coke asserted the principle, based on Star Chamber practice, 'that a false conspiracy betwixt divers persons shall be punished, although nothing be put in execution': T. G. Barnes, 'Star Chamber and the Sophistication of the Criminal Law', *Criminal Law Review* (1977), 325.
[13] Coke, 3 *Institutes*, pp. 9–10.

rebelling. While two of the conspirators, including Bartholomew's brother John, were weavers living in Witney, the conspiracy notably failed to recruit cloth-workers. The identification of the Steeres and James Bradshaw, an apprentice miller living in Chetwood, Buckinghamshire, with the apprentices of London was probably a reflection of the fact that they were still serving out their own apprenticeships in households other than those presided over by their fathers. Despite the universal terms in which they denounced the gentry, Bartholomew Steere and his followers blamed the shortage of corn and consequent high prices upon particular gentlemen who were notorious in the neighbourhood for enclosures that decayed and depopulated houses of husbandry. Several other conspirators were tenants or servants of these offending gentlemen, and most likely would have agreed with this explanation for the high price of corn. At the same time, such an explanation probably had little appeal to the cloth-workers of central and western Oxfordshire. Thus it appears that Bartholomew Steere's followers had selected the particular culprits for their rituals of popular justice carefully and never intended to go on the wild rampage that Coke had imagined. Likewise, the participants in the Midland Revolt of 1607 also chose the victims of their anti-enclosure protests with a view to making examples of the worst offenders.[14]

ii. *The Midland Revolt of 1607*

The series of agrarian risings, known collectively as the Midland Revolt, began on the last day of April 1607 in Northamptonshire, spread next to Warwickshire, and then to Leicestershire. In Northamptonshire the rioters assembled first at Rushton, Pytchley and Haselbech, where they proceeded to level hedges and fill in ditches, working by night and day. Some of the enclosure rioters evidently came from outside these communities, because Edmund Howes points out that they were equipped only with bills and pikes, until the local inhabitants came to their assistance with 'many Carts laden with victuall' and 'also good store of spades and shovells'. Crowds

---

[14] PRO, SP 12/262/4, SP 14/28/64; Hist. MSS Comm., *Salisbury*, vii. 49–50. For different interpretations, cf. Sharp, *In Contempt of All Authority*, pp. 20–1, 38–9, and Walter, 'A "Rising of the People"? The Oxfordshire Rising of 1596', pp. 118–19, 122–3.

of up to 1,000 persons, including women and children, were said to have gathered in these villages, yet they remained remarkably orderly and well disciplined. Howes stresses the fact that they kept to their work of levelling enclosures 'without exercising any manner of theft, or violence upon any man's person, goods or cattell.'[15]

Sometime later, in May, as many as 3,000 persons gathered at Hillmorton, just across the boundary in south-eastern Warwickshire.[16] They were met by the sheriff and justices of Warwickshire, who, avoiding any provocation in the face of so many people, attempted to show the rioters the danger in which they had placed themselves in the eyes of the law, and urged them to return to their homes. The protesters replied 'that the cause of theyr rising was oute of no vndutifull mynde to his Maiestie but only for reformation of thos late inclosures which made them of the porest sorte reddy to pyne for wante.' They made it clear that they would not depart until they had the King's promise to redress their grievances.[17] It may have been the same spokemen for the Hillmorton protestors, who also issued the manifesto of the so-called 'Diggers of Warwickshire to all other Diggers', proclaiming themselves to be the King's 'most true harted communality' who 'doe feele the smart of these incroaching Tirants which would grinde our flesh upon the whetstone of poverty . . . so that they may dwell by themselves in the midst of theyr heards

---

[15] Gilbert, Earl of Shrewsbury, in a letter to Henry, Earl of Kent, dated 2 June 1607, gives the date for the beginning of the riots as 'May eve': BL, Lansdowne MSS 90, no. 23, printed in Gay, 'The Midland Revolt and the Inquisitions of Depopulation of 1607', pp. 240–1; Edmund Howes, who continued John Stow's narrative in the 1615 and 1631 editions of the *Annales, or a General Chronicle of England*, says that the riots began about the middle of May: Stow, *Annales* (1631 edn.), p. 890.

[16] The estimates of the sizes of these crowds are recorded by Edmund Howes: ibid. However, the Earl of Shrewsbury's letter of 2nd June (BL, Lansdowne MSS 90, no. 23, printed in Gay, 'The Midland Revolt and the Inquisitions of Depopulation of 1607', pp. 240–1) makes it clear that the Privy Council assumed that they were dealing with crowds of approximately 1,000 persons. I am sceptical of Howes' estimates that give the number of persons involved in the Midland Revolt as 3,000 at Hillmorton and 5,000 at Cotesbach (which he misread as 'Tottlebich'). The largest crowd known to have gathered in London during the sixteenth and early seventeenth centuries was that of 1,800 persons, who rioted in Cheapside on 27 June 1595: cf. ch. 8 above. Nor is it clear whether the crowds which gathered at the six principal locations of the Midland Revolt were stationary or moved from place to place. I am inclined to believe that they were on the move, since the six villages, although located in three different counties, are within 20 miles of one another: Thirsk, 'The Local History of Enclosing and Engrossing', *AHEW* IV. 232.

[17] BL, Lansdowne MSS 90, no. 23, printed in Gay, 'The Midland Revolt and the Inquisitions of Depopulation of 1607', pp. 240–1.

of fatt weathers'.[18] The Privy Council, wrote Gilbert, Earl of Shrewsbury, thought it 'very strange to expostulate with suche insolent, base and rebellilous people'; rather the Warwickshire magistrates should 'have vsed force, and . . . set vppon them and vsed them as rebells and traytors.' However, Shrewsbury later admitted that the Northamptonshire trained bands were found to be disaffected. Very likely the Warwickshire justices could see no alternative but to negotiate until a more reliable armed force could be gathered together.[19]

Towards the end of the same month 5,000 people were reported to have assembled at Cotesbach in the very southern part of Leicestershire, where they began levelling hedges. On 1 June they were joined by supporters from Leicester whom the Privy Council accused of bringing 'weapons and other means of assistance'. A royal proclamation dated 30 May was prepared to be used against the 'levellers', as they had begun to call themselves.[20] However, this proclamation was not received in Leicester until 6 June and probably was the same one that was read at Newton on 8 June, the day of the final débâcle. The proclamation told the levellers that they were slandering the King's government (which was a species of seditious libel) by saying that the King did not punish those who made illegal enclosures since the first Parliament of the King's reign had enacted a law (1 Jac. I, c. 25) against depopulating enclosures. The levellers were also told that if they did not return to their homes, they would be crushed by 'force of armes'.[21]

---

[18] BL, Harley MSS 787, art. 11, printed in J. O. Halliwell, *The Marriage of Wit and Wisdom* (1846), 140–1.

[19] BL, Lansdowne MSS 90, no. 23, printed in Gay, 'The Midland Revolt and the Inquisitions of Depopulation of 1607', pp. 240–1; J. Nichols, *The History and Antiquities of the County of Leicester* (4 vols.; 1795–1815), iv/1. 83.

[20] L. A. Parker, 'The Agrarian Revolution at Cotesbach, 1501–1612', *Trans. Leics. Arch. Soc.* 24 (1948), 41; *Records of the Borough of Leicester, 1603–1688*, ed. H. Stocks (Cambridge, 1923), 59; Martin, *Feudalism to Capitalism*, p. 192; *Stuart Royal Proclamations*, ed. Larkin and Hughes, i, no. 71. The Privy Council Order to the Deputy Lieutenants of Leicestershire commanding them to suppress 'unlawful assemblies got up for the purpose of laying open enclosures' is dated Whitehall, 29 May: Hist. MSS Comm., *Twelfth Report*, i. 405. Edmund Howes says that proclamations were read to the rebels on 27 May: Stow, *Annales*, p. 890.

[21] *Stuart Royal Proclamations*, ed. Larkin and Hughes, i, no. 71. For a discussion of 'slander of justice' and other forms of seditious libel, see my 'The Origins of the Doctrine of Sedition', pp. 99–121.

Another crowd of approximately 1,000 levellers had gathered at Newton, Northamptonshire in early June to cast down Thomas Tresham's enclosures.[22] On this occasion they were prepared for battle, being armed with bows and arrows and stones, as well as pikes and long bills. If the digger manifesto accurately reflects their intentions, they were resolved to 'manfully dye' rather than 'be pined to death for want of that which these devouring encroachers do serue theyr fatt hogges and sheep withall'.[23] The gentry of Northamptonshire, 'fynding great backwardnes in the trained bands', were constrained to form themselves into a troop of horse and to recruit infantry from among such 'of their owne servants and followers as they could trust'. Commanded by Sir Edward Montagu, a deputy lieutenant, and Sir Anthony Mildmay, this irregular force of gentry retainers confronted the levellers at Newton on 8 June. Shrewsbury's terse description of the battle says that Montagu and Mildmay

first read the proclamacion twice unto them, using all the best persuasions to them to desist that they could devise; but when nothing would prevail, they charged them thoroughlie both with their horse and foote. . . . The first charge they stoode, and fought desperatlie; but at the second charge they ran away, in which theare weare slaine som[e] 40 or 50 of them, and a verie great number hurt.[24]

Thomas Cox, a Northamptonshire parson who died in 1640, wrote a brief account of the battle of Newton in his parish register. He said that 'many were taken prisoners, who afterwards were hanged and quartered, and their quarters set up at Northampton, Oundle, Thrapston and other places.'[25] That some of the prisoners were summarily executed under martial law is confirmed by the royal proclamation dated 28 June. However, the distribution of carcasses may refer also to the executions that followed the treason trial at Northampton on 21 June before special commissioners of oyer and terminer.[26]

---

[22] This was Thomas Tresham of Newton (d. 1636), not to be confused with his cousin Sir Thomas Tresham of Rushton (d. 1605).

[23] Nichols, *The History . . . of the County of Leicester*, iv/1. 83; BL, Harley MSS 787, art. 11, printed in Halliwell, *The Marriage of Wit and Wisdom*, pp. 140–1.

[24] Nichols, *The History . . . of the County of Leicester*, iv/1. 83.

[25] Peter Whalley, *The History and Antiquities of Northamptonshire* (Oxford, 1791), ii. 206; *Northamptonshire Notes and Queries*, i (1886), no. 62.

[26] *Stuart Royal Proclamations*, ed. Larkin and Hughes, i, no. 72; Stow, *Annales*, p. 890.

Among the persons executed following the Northampton treason trial was John Reynolds, commonly known as 'Captaine Powch' because of the supposedly magical contents of the leather pouch that he carried by his side. Although he emerged as a popular leader only after the enclosure riots had begun, he was able to impart to the levellers a remarkable degree of discipline and determination. Since the gentry and yeomanry had refused to be drawn into the popular rebellions of the late-Tudor and early-Stuart periods, the poorer commoners were forced to provide their own leadership.[27] Edmund Howes called Reynolds a 'base fellow' and described him as a pedlar or tinker by trade. As for Captain Pouch's prodigious purse, 'in which . . . he affirmed to his company . . . there was sufficient matter to defend them against all comers . . . ', Howes mockingly reported that after Reynolds was captured and his pouch searched, the contents consisted of 'onely a peece of greene cheese'. Yet Howes conceded that Reynolds kept his followers under control:

Hee told them also, that hee had authority from his maiestie to throwe downe enclosures, and that he was sent of God to satisfie all degrees whatsoever; and thereupon they generally inclined to his direction, so as hee kept them in good order; hee commaunded them not to sweare, nor to offer violence to any person, but to ply their businesse, and to make faire worke, entending to continue this worke, so long as God should put them in mind. . . .[28]

The treatment meted out to the Midland rebels was not nearly as brutal nor as vindictive as that alloted to the leaders of the Enslow Hill conspiracy. While Robert Wilkinson's assizes sermon reveals the official fear of continuing social conflict and popular disorder that preceded the trial at Northampton, he rebuked not only the 'rebellion of the many' but also the 'oppression of the mighty'—especially that of the 'pasturemen', or enclosing landlords, who denied the poor their bread.[29] Although Sir Edward Coke and the royal judges had laid it down in 1597 that conspiracy to commit treason constituted high treason and that all conspirators were to be regarded as principals, the defendants in the Northampton trial were dealt with under the

[27] Ibid.; K. Wrightson, *English Society, 1580–1680* (1982), 178.

[28] Stow, *Annales*, p. 890.

[29] R. Wilkinson, *A Sermon preached at North-Hampton the 21. of June Last Past, before the Lord Lieutenant of the County, and the Rest of the Commissioners there assembled upon Occasion of the late Rebellion and Riots in those Parts committed* (1607) sigs. A3ʳ⁻ᵛ, Flᵛ⁻2ʳ, in B. Stirling, *The Populace in Shakespeare* (repr. New York, 1965), 126–7.

three categories of high treason, felony-riot, and misdemeanour-riot — despite the fact that Sir Edward Coke, now chief justice of the Court of Common Pleas, was the presiding judge. According to Edmund Howes' account, 'some of them were indicted of high treason, and executed for leauying warre against the King, and opposing themselues against the King's forces; Captaine Powch was made exemplary'. But others were indicted for 'fellonie in continuing together by the space of an houre, after proclamation to cease and depart according to the statute'. The remainder of the defendants 'were indicted for Ryots, vnlawfull assemblies and throwing downe of hedges and ditches'.[30]

Soon after the Northamptonshire rebels were crushed at Newton, other disturbances were reported to have broken out in Derbyshire and Bedfordshire. A Lincolnshire man, writing from Staple Inn in June 1607, told his corrrespondent that 'the Grantham men were up again on Friday'. At Caistor, Lincolnshire in late July a libel, entitled 'The Poor Man's friend and the gentlemen's plague', was thrown into the parish church.[31] When the Earl of Huntingdon, lord-lieutenant of Leicestershire, ordered a gibbet to be erected in the market place of Leicester to discourage the inhabitants from joining the anti-enclosure rioters in Cotesbach, a crowd, consisting

[30] Coke, 3 *Institutes*, pp. 9–10; Hale, *Pleas of the Crown*, i. 145; Stow, *Annales*, p. 890. The source of authority for prosecuting some of the defendants in the Northampton trials for the offence of felony-riot is found in the Elizabethan statute (1 Eliz. I, c. 16, *SR* iv. 377), which revived the Marian Statute (1 Mary, st. 3, c. 12, *SR* iv. 211–21). The Act Against Unlawful Assemblies made it felony for 12 or more people assembled together to remain for the space of one hour after a magistrate, by proclamation, had ordered the rioters to disperse. The Elizabethan statute continued the Marian statute during the natural life of Queen Elizabeth until 'thende of the Parliament then next following' (i.e., until the end of the first Jacobean Parliament, which was dissolved in 1611). Although Holdsworth (*A History of English Law*, iv. 497) is unclear concerning when this statute lapsed, the Crown's law officers and the members of Parliament participating in the debate concerning the Midland Revolt on 1–2 July 1607 agreed that the Elizabethan Act against Unlawful Assemblies was still in effect. Sir Francis Bacon and the other law officers favoured making the Act perpetual, but the motion to do so was defeated: *The Parliamentary Diary of Robert Bowyer, 1606–1607*, ed. D. H. Willson (Minneapolis, 1931), 363–7. John Chamberlain (*Letters of John Chamberlain*, ed. McClure, ii. 59–60, 66) says that the Crown attempted to prosecute the leaders of the Shrove Tuesday, 1617 riots in London for felony-riot, but the jury refused to convict them. Two of the leaders were subsequently found guilty of misdemeanour-riot, fined, and imprisoned in irons: above, ch. 8.

[31] Hist. MSS Comm., *Twelfth Report*: Rutland MSS, i. 405–6; Gay, 'The Midland Revolt and the Inquisitions of Depopulation of 1607', p. 243; J. W. F. Hill, *Tudor and Stuart Lincoln* (Cambridge, 1956), 139.

largely of children, tore it down. Huntingdon blamed the mayor for failure to stop the protest and placed him under arrest; he also reproved the mayor for failing to remove his hat in the Earl's presence. Thirty-two inhabitants of Leicester were named as having marched out of town to join Captain Pouch. The mayor was ordered to pick eight of them to be impressed for military service. The mayor of Northampton and the sheriff and magistrates of Northamptonshire were prosecuted in the Court of Star Chamber for their negligence in not dealing more expeditiously with the popular disorders in their jurisdictions.[32] The attorney-general, Sir Henry Hobart, tried to depict enclosure riots at Gnosall, Staffordshire and Cherry Burton, Lincolnshire as being sympathetic responses to the Midland Revolt. This legal ploy of trying to discredit defendants by attempting to represent them as 'levellers' or 'diggers' was used in a number of enclosure-riot cases in the Court of Star Chamber.[33]

One should avoid the temptation to view the Midland Revolt of 1607 merely as a series of enclosure riots. Not only did the protest break out of the confines of the local community and become more generalized; like the rebellions of 1549 the Midland Revolt also was distinguished by the absence of gentry leadership and by the more explicit articulation of social conflict. In his sermon preached at the Northampton trials on 21 June, Robert Wilkinson emphasized that the rumours which circulated among the participants in the Midland Revolt contained threats of violence against both gentry and clergy: 'They will accompt [i.e. settle accounts] with clergie men, and counsell is given to kill up Gentlemen, and they will levell all states [i.e. estates, or social distinctions] as they levelled bankes and ditches.' Wilkinson also attempted to depict the Northamptonshire rebels as displaying behaviour usually characteristic of adherents of millenarian movements: the belief that their leader, Captain Pouch possessed magical powers, that they no longer were bound by the law, and that they no longer needed to labour.[34]

[32] *Records of the Borough of Leicester, 1603-1688*, ed. Stocks, pp. 59-64; Martin, *Feudalism to Capitalism*, pp. 172-3.
[33] PRO, STAC 8/12/7, 18/19; Hill, *Tudor and Stuart Lincoln*, p. 142 n.; cf. the discussion of such legal tactics in ch. 4 above.
[34] *A Sermon preached at North Hampton the 21. of June Last Past* (London, 1607), sigs. F2ᵛ-F3, quoted in H. C. White, *Social Criticism in Popular Religious Literature of the Sixteenth Century* (repr. New York, 1973), 119.

At the same time one must avoid the mistake of assuming that all enclosure riots occurring in the late spring of 1607 were part of the Midland Revolt. Historians should not be deceived by assertions made by the attorney-general or lawyers representing landowners in the Star Chamber that such was the case. Some disturbances, such as the enclosure riots at Chilvers Coton, Warwickshire and Belton, Leicestershire probably were sympathetic responses to the main disturbances. In the case of Withybrook, Warwickshire, the rioters did include artisans from Leicester. However, in the case of Ladbroke manor, Warwickshire, while Dr Martin is able to show that some of the rioters came from 20 different villages, he fails to demonstrate that the Ladbroke tenants, who were substantial smallholders and knew how to use the courts, considered their protest to be part of the Midland Revolt, which was a rising of desperate artisans and labourers. That the Ladbroke riots were organized and led by gentlemen ought to be a sufficient warning against attempts to link the two disturbances together. The Ladbroke tenants aimed their protest at only one farmer's hedges and never advocated levelling all hedges. But, the most telling reason is that the Ladbroke protesters were never accused of treason; they were prosecuted for riot in a private suit in Star Chamber rather than by means of an attorney-general's information.[35]

In his account of the Midland Revolt, Edmund Howes reported that a number of rumours had circulated to the effect that the insurrection was precipitated by religious factionalism. Howes added that this explanation was not supported by the evidence gleaned from the examinations of captured rebels. Edwin Gay, Joan Thirsk, and John Martin have followed Howes in rejecting religious animosity as a significant cause, and instead have emphasized agrarian grievances.[36] Although there is abundant evidence of rapid agrarian change in the Midlands prior to the rebellion of 1607, several remarkably thorough studies of Tudor and Stuart Northamptonshire suggest that it may not be so easy to separate religious strife from agrarian protest in the north-eastern part of the county, where most of the risings occurred.

---

[35] Martin, *Feudalism to Capitalism*, pp. 165, 168–70, 190–1; cf. ch. 4 above for a discussion of the Ladbroke riots.

[36] Stow, *Annales*, p. 890; Gay, 'The Midland Revolt and the Inquisitions of Depopulation of 1607', pp. 214–15 n.; Thirsk, 'The Local History of Enclosing and Engrossing', *AHEW* iv. 232–6; Martin, *Feudalism to Capitalism*, pp. 182–5; cf. *Cal. SP Dom., 1611–1618*, p. 532.

Dr W. J. Sheils has shown how religious factionalism in North-amptonshire caused Puritans and Catholic recusants to take up exceptionally hostile positions towards one another. Early in James I's reign the Catholic gentry had attempted to make their way back into the magistracy, while the Puritans were rebuffed in their efforts to prevent the deprivation of several of their ministers. Although there was no danger of the Puritan gentry being displaced, Puritans among the commonalty imagined that the threat of a popish conspiracy in Northamptonshire was very real. The latter tended to focus their fears upon Sir Thomas Tresham of Rushton. In 1605, following an outbreak of the plague in Northampton, Henry Godly, who had been the brother-in-law of John Penry, was accused of circulating rumours to the effect that Sir Thomas Tresham and Lord Mordaunt had planned to massacre the Protestants of Northampton. Later in the same year, Francis Tresham, son and heir of Sir Thomas Tresham of Rushton, who had previously been caught up in the Essex Revolt of 1601, was implicated in the Gunpowder Plot along with a number of other Catholic gentlemen whose families were associated with Northamptonshire and Warwickshire.[37] It was something more than a coincidence that of the four Northamptonshire townships where violent disorders broke out in the spring of 1607, in three of them—Rushton, Haselbech, and Newton—the rioting was directed against enclosures made by members of the Tresham family.

Furthermore, Dr P. A. J. Pettit has demonstrated how this ming-ling of agrarian protest, religious factionalism, and dislike of the Treshams in particular provoked an anti-enclosure riot at Brigstock in Rockingham Forest in 1603. Sir Robert Cecil had been granted the farm of Brigstock Parks, and he, in turn, had appointed Sir Thomas Tresham of Rushton the keeper of Brigstock Little Park. The economic causes of the protest included Cecil's ruthless destruction of timber and Tresham's overgrazing of the commons. But there were other reasons that explain why there was so much opposition to

[37] W. J. Sheils, *The Puritans in the Diocese of Peterborough, 1558–1610* (Northants. Rec. Soc. 30; 1979), 10, 70–1, 110–11, 115–16, 126; *Cal. SP Dom., 1603–1610*, p. 200; Hist. MSS Comm., *Salisbury*, xvii. 572; *DNB*, s.v. Francis Tresham. Although Sir Thomas Tresham was never reinstated in the commission of the peace, James I did make him and Lord Mordaunt commissioners for forest causes for the bailiwick of Kingscliffe in Rockingham Forest: Anstruther, *Vaux of Harrowden: A Recusant Family* (Newport, Monmouthshire, 1953), 263–4. Cf. my discussion of the enclosure disputes at Ladbroke and Great Wolford, Warwickshire in ch. 4 above.

Sir Thomas Tresham. He was considered 'most odious in this country' because of 'his hard and extreme usage of his tenants and his countrymen'. Moreover, Brigstock was a Puritan community—as were most of the villages of Rockingham Forest, and Tresham's servants offended local sensibilities by causing mass to be celebrated in Brigstock Little Park Lodge and at Lyveden in the adjoining parish of Aldwinkle.[38]

Although the Midland Rebels expressed their hatred of the gentry in general terms, their protests were aimed at particular landlords. It is no exaggeration to say that the main thrust of the Midland Revolt in Northamptonshire was directed at the Treshams of Rushton. Their considerable estates, extensive ties of kinship and lavish hospitality dispensed in the setting of a feudal household made them one of the most eminent Catholic families in Jacobean England. At the same time Sir Thomas Tresham's financial troubles tempted him into ruthless schemes of fiscal seigneurialism that made him perhaps the most hated landlord in the Midlands. It was not merely the accumulation of recusancy fines, the ambitious building programme at Rushton and Lyveden, or the household of 52 servants that undermined the family's financial position and ultimately brought ruin; Sir Thomas had to pay £3,000 in fines and bribes to secure a pardon for Francis Tresham after the Essex Revolt. Moreover, the Treshams and their numerous progeny and relations had the nasty habit of perpetually bringing lawsuits against one another. Although Francis died in the Tower before trial for his part in the Gunpowder Plot, the Crown treated him as a traitor and was prevented from seizing the family estates only by a legal technicality that diverted them to Lewis, a younger brother.[39]

In truth, Sir Thomas Tresham was a grasping landlord even before the extraordinary behaviour of his family and his long imprisonment began to weigh so heavily upon him. In the 1570s he increased the rent of his Great Houghton tenants fivefold and began compelling

---

[38] Pettit, *The Royal Forests of Northamptonshire*, pp. 173–4. For an example of an enclosure riot directed against Lord Vaux at Irthlingborough, Northants., in 1590, see Anstruther, *Vaux of Harrowden*, pp. 217–18.

[39] Finch, *The Wealth of Five Northamptonshire Families*, pp. 76–83; DNB, s.v. Sir Thomas Tresham (1543?–1605); A. Morey, *The Catholic Subjects of Elizabeth I* (1978), 161–7; J. H. Hexter, *Reappraisals in History* (New York, 1963), 160–1. Glapthorn, a forest village four miles east of Lyveden, had been the scene in 1548 of popular disorders arising from the advanced Protestant opinions of the inhabitants: Beer, *Rebellion and Riot*, p. 151.

tenants at Haselbech to exchange their copyholds for leases. Between 1580 and 1597 he began engrossing and enclosing both tenants' holdings and demesne lands on a large scale and eventually built up flocks of sheep that totalled nearly 7,000 head.[40] When offending landlords were prosecuted in the Court of Star Chamber in 1608 following the returns of the commissioners for inquiring into depopulations, the attorney-general stated that Sir Thomas Tresham had depopulated 11 farms and houses of husbandry on his principal estate at Rushton, engrossed and enclosed 670 acres taken from these tenancies, and converted 288 acres from tillage to pasture. The houses were let to poor cottagers. The largest part of his sheep flock was kept at Rushton, and 300 acres were devoted exclusively to a huge rabbit warren where Sir Thomas bred conies for the London market.[41]

At Haselbech, the location of the second leveller demonstration in 1607, the attorney-general charged that Sir Thomas Tresham had decayed 14 of 16 ploughs and engrossed 1,600 acres including church glebe lands.[42] The attorney-general's allegations are compatible with Dr Finch's investigation of the Tresham estates. Sir Thomas already possessed 960 acres, or 24 yardlands, which was half of the lordship before he compelled the other freeholders, who held 17 yardlands, to agree to enclosure in severalty of the open fields of Haselbech in the late 1590s. Tresham immediately raised the rents of his tenants in the midst of the years of dearth. None could pay the new rents and all left or were evicted. Excluding the persons evicted by the other freeholders of Haselbech, 60 persons lost their livelihood. The negotiations for enclosure dragged on between 1596 and 1599, and even before the agreement was concluded, popular

---

[40] Finch, *The Wealth of Five Northamptonshire Families*, pp. 72–5.
[41] PRO, STAC 8/18/12. Dr Finch provides independent evidence for the Star Chamber allegations. She found evidence for the decay of nine farms at Rushton and the engrossing of 810 acres during the periods 1581–8 and 1598–1604. Tresham was prosecuted in the Court of Queen's Bench in 1597 for violating the tillage statutes. In this case it was alleged that he had converted 1,000 acres at Rushton to pasture. He was fined £1,000. Dr Finch found portions of the 1607 returns of the commissioners of depopulation for Northamptonshire (PRO, C. 2055/5) to be illegible. She was not aware of the Star Chamber prosecutions and her evidence comes from a wide variety of sources. Indeed, she states that the returns of the depopulation commissioners underestimate the extent of enclosures, since the returns specify only enclosures of arable land and not common pasture: *The Wealth of Five Northamptonshire Families*, pp. 74–5 n., 87–8 n.
[42] PRO, STAC 8/18/12.

opinion blamed Tresham for the high price of corn. In 1596, Tresham's servant, Thomas Vavasour, told him that 'the common people exclayme exceedingly . . . upon inclosures and you are not forgotten for Hasselbiche, although it be beforehand'. However much Sir Thomas Tresham suffered for his recusancy, he remained quite insensitive to the plight of his tenants.[43]

Since Sir Thomas Tresham spent much of his time in prison, the actual management of the family estates fell to his son and heir Francis, who also did not scruple at extorting money from tenants. Francis's scheme for improving the rents paid by his father's tenants at Orton, part of the manor and hundred of Rothwell which Tresham leased from the Crown, led those tenants in July 1603 to petition the King not to renew Tresham's lease. Sir Thomas, during one of his rare moments of freedom, rode out to Rothwell Church to browbeat the tenants into disclaiming their petition. But Sir Thomas also backed down and gave up his plans to improve the rents at Orton. In any case the lease was not renewed, and many of the lands at Great Houghton and Haselbech were sold off between 1601 and 1605.[44]

Newton, the scene of the bloody encounter between the levellers and the Northamptonshire gentry on 8 June, was the property of Thomas Tresham, esq., a cousin of Sir Thomas Tresham. It was located only three miles east of his cousin's house at Rushton. Thomas Tresham of Newton's estates were more modest in scale, but were evidently managed in the same ruthless manner. The attorney-general alleged in 1608 that he had engrossed four farms at Newton, converted 150 acres of arable to pasture, destroyed two houses of husbandry, and let the remaining two houses to poor cottagers. Altogether 12 persons were displaced. On a second estate at Pilton, purchased from his cousin c.1599, Thomas Tresham of Newton was said to have decayed five farms and converted 135 acres of arable to sheep pasture.[45]

---

[43] Finch, *The Wealth of Five Northamptonshire Families*, p. 87. The enclosure agreements, which were negotiated by Francis Tresham, are printed in Kerridge, *Agrarian Problems*, pp. 174–84.

[44] Finch, *The Wealth of Five Northamptonshire Families*, p. 88. However, Fernando Bande and the other four purchasers of the manor of Great Houghton were accused of destroying 31 houses of husbandry and driving 260 people out of the village: PRO, STAC 8/18/12.

[45] Ibid., STAC 8/18/12; Finch, *The Wealth of Five Northamptonshire Families*, pp. 75 n., 90.

Sir Euseby Isham's hedges at Pytchley, south of Kettering, were the only enclosures attacked by the Northamptonshire levellers in 1607 which did not belong to the Tresham family. Sir Euseby Isham was a cousin of John Isham of Lamport, who was notorious for replacing tenants with sheep on his own lands. The Ishams were an old Northamptonshire gentry family who had been making careers in London as mercers and lawyers for over a century. Sir Euseby Isham (fl. 1580–1626), the builder of Pytchley Hall, was accused of converting 140 acres on the manor of Pytchley from arable to pasture, suppressing nine ploughs, pulling down five houses of husbandry, and placing cottagers in the other four. Forty-five persons were displaced by Sir Euseby's improvements.[46]

Although parts of Northamptonshire, Warwickshire, and Leicestershire where the Midland Revolt occurred are now devoted to dairying and grazing, this area was once the heartland of the classic commonfield system of agriculture and one of the great corn-growing regions of the Midlands. The inhabitants of the region did not give up the old ways of farming without a struggle. Yet rapid agrarian change was forced upon these communities and land was withdrawn from cultivation during years of dearth in an area already suffering from shortages of fuel and common pasture. The difficulties of transporting grain to market in the east Midlands contributed to the conversion to grass and intensified distress in isolated areas.[47] The Warwickshire levellers had complained of the high price of grain in 1607 and again in June 1608, when William Combe, a Warwickshire JP, reported that high corn prices were causing people to grumble about the failure of magistrates to punish violations of the tillage statutes.[48] The grievances of the Midland Rebels were consistently explicit about the connection between converting arable land to grass and high corn prices. Sir Edward Montagu, MP for Northamptonshire, had warned

---

[46] Ibid., pp. 14–16; *VCH Northamptonshire*, iv. 208–13; PRO, STAC 8/18/12; G. D. Ramsay, *John Isham: Mercer and Merchant Adventurer* (Northants. Rec. Soc. 21; 1962), *passim*. Although Pytchley had no associations with the Treshams, the manor had belonged to the Treshams' kinsmen, the Vauxes of Harrowden, until sometime in the latter part of the 16th century: Anstruther, *Vaux of Harrowden*, p. 54.

[47] *AHEW* iv. 89, 232; W. E. Tate, 'Inclosure Movements in Northamptonshire', *Northamptonshire Past and Present*, i/2. 19–33; Leonard, 'The Inclosure of Common Fields in the Seventeenth Century', pp. 138–9; Hoskins, 'Harvest Fluctuations and English Economic History, 1480–1619', p. 46.

[48] *Cal. SP Dom., 1635–1636*, p. 22; PRO, SP 14/34/4, printed in E. I. Fripp, *Shakespeare: Man and Artist*, (2 vols.; repr. 1964), ii. 706.

Parliament about the problem of population exceeding resources in his county as early as 1604.[49]

The withdrawal of these lands from corn production seems to have had an especially severe impact upon the villages of Rockingham Forest which lay cheek by jowl with the estates of the two branches of the Tresham family at Rushton, Brigstock and Lyveden (Rushton branch), and Newton and Pilton (Newton branch). Over half of the known Northamptonshire levellers (or 78 out of 143) came from villages, such as Corby, Weldon, and Benefield, which were within the bounds of the forest (see Map 9.2).[50] The population of the nearby fielden villages remained stable or actually declined, but many of the forest communities where the levellers dwelled were increasing in population quite rapidly. Moreover, cottagers, wage labourers, and paupers constituted nearly half of the people in the forest villages. Unlike many woodland areas, the economy of Rockingham Forest was not sufficiently developed to absorb the excess population from nearby fielden areas. Hence many inhabitants resorted to stealing wood and poaching. Moreover, the topography of the Rockingham Forest region suggests that the large forest villages were especially dependent on corn supplies from nearby non-forest villages such as Rushton, Newton, Pilton, Haselbech, and Pytchley, which probably sold their corn in the market town of Kettering (where another 27 of the rebels resided). If the occupational breakdown of this group of levellers is indicative, the Midland Revolt in Northamptonshire was essentially a rising of propertyless cottagers from forest communities. Of the 143 persons who sought a royal pardon, 55 were artisans, 62 were labourers, and 5 were shepherds, but only 21 described themselves as husbandmen.[51] It is curious that Buchanan Sharp omitted mention of the Midland Revolt, since the occupational

---

[49] Hist. MSS Comm., *Montagu of Beaulieu* (1900), 42.

[50] On 24 July 1607 the King proclaimed a pardon for those rebels who submitted by Michaelmas of 1607: *Stuart Royal Proclamations*, i, no. 74. In Northamptonshire 143 persons appeared before Sir Edward Montagu, Deputy Lieutenant, whose seat at Boughton was on the edge of Rockingham Forest, and begged for a pardon: Hist. MSS Comm., *Buccleuch and Queensberry*, iii. (1926), 118. In addition to the 78 persons from Rockingham Forest, a further 20 persons came from the fielden villages of Harrowden, Broughton, and Cransley, where the Vaux estates were located: Anstruther, *Vaux of Harrowden*, p. 54. There is an excellent detailed map of Rockingham Forest in Pettit, *The Royal Forests of Northamptonshire*, at end.

[51] Ibid., pp. 143-4, 173 n.; 200-3; Hist. MSS Comm., *Montagu of Beaulieu*, pp. 107-9; id., *Buccleuch and Queensberry*, iii. 118.

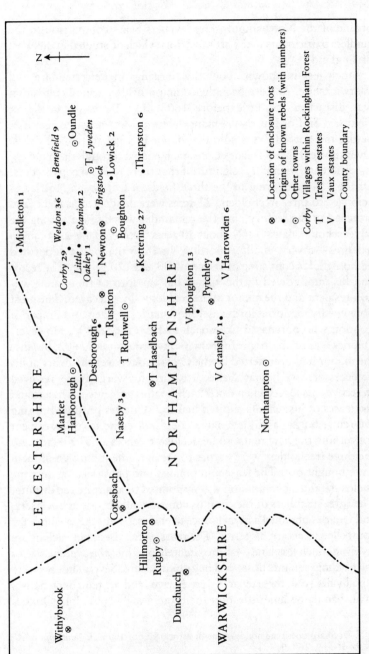

MAP 9.2 The Midland Revolt of 1607

profile of the Northamptonshire levellers bears comparison to the landless participants in the artisans' riots which he studied in the West of England.[52]

Much less is known about the uprisings in Leicestershire and Warwickshire. At Cotesbach the common-field system of cultivation was disturbed but little before 1603. The Devereux family of Chartley, Staffordshire were manorial lords for nearly two centuries before the Earl of Essex sold the manor in 1591 to pay off debts. Over the next three decades Cotesbach passed through the hands of six different owners. It is significant that there were no copyholders. Of the 854 acres lying in the three fields of Cotesbach, 152 acres belonged to three freeholders, 22 acres were designated as glebe land attached to the rectory, and the remainder was divided among the 13 leasehold tenants. Only about 50 acres were available as common pastures—a very small proportion. In 1603 the manor supported 18 households consisting of between 100 and 120 people. The rector and his family lived in the village but the lord of the manor was non-resident and the manor house had long since decayed. The most noteworthy manorial lord was John Quarles, citizen and draper of London who purchased Cotesbach in 1596 for £6,000. However, Quarles was unable to profit from his investment until 1602, because the manor had been seized by the Crown to recover the debts of his predecessor, Sir Thomas Sherley, treasurer for war. Quarles resolved to recover his losses when Cotesbach finally came into his hands and the leases of his tenants expired in 1602. Quarles proposed raising the rents, but he and his tenants could not come to an agreement concerning the new rents, so he decided to enclose. The rector and the three freeholders were parties to the agreement but two of them were bought out. The leasehold tenants had petitioned against the enclosure and a commission was appointed to arbitrate the dispute. The three members of the commission were all notorious enclosers, and Quarles obtained a royal licence to enclose. Thus the tenants were compelled to accept his terms. The rents were raised, but each house received much less land—approximately one-half the average size of the holdings tenants possessed before enclosure. Several houses were literally decayed, three tenants were evicted, and the remaining houses of husbandry became little more than cottages. By 1607, John Quarles

---

[52] Dr Sharp does take notice of the Brigstock Riot of 1603: *In Contempt of All Authority*, pp. 168–9, 171.

had enclosed and converted to grass 420 acres of arable, which was approximately two-thirds of the arable land previously lying in the common fields. The population declined by some 80 persons—most choosing to depart rather than remain in such impoverished circumstances. Quarles probably doubled his income, but it was not sufficient to stave off bankruptcy. The manor changed hands several more times over the next 20 years. By 1622 Cotesbach was largely given over to sheep grazing.[53]

As in the county of Leicester, the Warwickshire justices had failed to enforce the tillage statutes prior to the Midland Revolt. At Hillmorton, where the Warwickshire 'diggers' did their work in 1607, the depopulation returns made after the rising revealed that 15 houses of husbandry had been destroyed and 250 acres enclosed.[54] An undated document summarizing the grievances of the Warwickshire diggers of 1607 suggests that in addition to the anti-enclosure riots at Hillmorton, Dunchurch, Withybrook, Chilvers Coton, and Coventry, there were also attacks upon parks and chases elsewhere in the county. Their complaints specified a variety of agrarian problems besides enclosure: absentee landlords, excessive rents, decay of tillage, depopulation, both the engrossment and the subdivision of tenancies and the renting of cottages without four acres of land attached. All were equated with increases in the prices of grain. Once again we are reminded of the complicated motivation that lies behind the symbolic act of destroying enclosures.[55]

The rebellions of 1596 and 1607 were the most serious outbreaks of rural disorder during the late-Elizabethan and early-Stuart crises. In both instances, the local magistrates were caught off guard at first because the protesters employed the traditional ritual and symbolism of the familiar anti-enclosure demonstration, but interrogations of the Enslow Hill conspirators, as well as the events of early June 1607, suggested to the alarmed authorities a more menacing aspect of these stirs. The lawyers were ready at hand to argue that by advocating the

---

[53] Parker, 'The Agrarian Revolution at Cotesbach, 1501–1612', pp. 41–76; id., 'The Depopulation Returns for Leicestershire in 1607', *Trans. Leics. Arch. Hist. Soc.* 23 (1947), 237, 286–7.

[54] M. Beresford, 'The Deserted Villages of Warwickshire', *Trans. Birmingham Arch. Soc.* 66 (1945–6), 59 and n., 62; *VCH Warwickshire*, vi. 108–14; Martin, *Feudalism to Capitalism*, pp. 188–9. The lady of the manor of Hillmorton in 1607 was Mary, widow of Sir Isaac Astley, bart.

[55] PRO, SP 16/307/2; *Cal. SP Dom., 1635–1636*, p. 22; Martin, *Feudalism to Capitalism*, pp. 165–6.

general levelling of hedges the rebels had crossed that line dividing misdemeanour-riot from high treason, while the threats which both groups of rebels had uttered against the gentry lent credibility to the fears of the Crown officials responsible for repressing the disturbances. We do not know how Bartholomew Steere's followers would have behaved if his conspiracy had not been stillborn, but the actions of the Midland Rebels were restrained and disciplined and popular justice was visited only upon the hedges of a few of the most egregious enclosers. Members of the gentry and yeomanry were conspicuously absent from these two risings and the leaders, who were predominantly rural artisans and labourers, showed a disturbing glimmer of political awareness in wishing to involve urban artisans and apprentices in their protests. The Oxfordshire conspirators failed in this last objective, but the people of Leicester came to the aid of the Midland Rebels and the Mayor of Northampton was unable to prevent a sympathetic demonstration in that town. There may have been similar reverberations in other midland towns at the same time.[56]

iii. *Prosecutions for Decay of Tillage*

Of the many reasons which may be advanced to explain the rebellions of 1596 and 1607, the most significant cause of both risings was the popular perception that, in times of high corn prices, the magistrates in the affected counties failed to heed the commonalty's pleas to enforce the tillage statutes. These statutes, as well as the late-Elizabethan Book of Orders, had repeatedly defined depopulating enclosures, the conversion of tillage to pasture, the engrossment of tenancies, and the displacement of husbandmen by landless cottagers as grave social evils.[57] Such notions had been axiomatic during the

---

[56] Martin, *Feudalism to Capitalism*, pp. 170–3; 'The Journal of Sir Roger Wilbraham', ed. H. S. Scott, *Camden Miscellany* 10 (Camden Soc., 3rd ser. 4; iv 1902), 90–1.

[57] The Tillage Act of 1593 (35 Eliz., c. 6) had modified some of the more stringent provisions concerning enclosure and caused much confusion. The belief that the partial removal of restraints had led to an increase in the rate of enclosure of arable land during the 1590s and had contributed to the grain shortages of that period led to the hasty re-enactment in 1597 (39 Eliz., cc. 1 & 2) of the most important parts of the earlier Tudor tillage laws: *Select Statutes*, ed. Prothero, pp. 93–6; Leonard, 'The Inclosure of Common Fields in the Seventeenth Century', pp. 123–5; Beresford, 'Habitation Versus Improvement', pp. 40–69, esp. 64–5. 39 Eliz., cc. 1 & 2 were continued by 43 Eliz., c. 9 and 1 Jac. I, c. 25.

Tudor period because the maintenance of a sturdy and substantial husbandry was thought to be necessary both for the defence of the realm and the prevention of disorder. This official social policy was still being voiced when the attorney-general prosecuted a number of Lincolnshire gentlemen in January 1608.

. . . The strength and preseruacon of your Maiesties Imperial Crowne consisteth principallie in the breeding, preseruacon and increase of able people in such a condicon of wealth and estate, as may mayntayne them both in hart and courage to serve your Maiestie in tyme of warres for the Defence and honor of your kingdoms and also in sufficyent meanes and abilitye to beare and sustayne in tyme of peace any such charge as is necessarie for the publique Weale and benefite of the Estate; . . . the mayntenance of the ploughe and tyllage is one most necessarie and effectuall meane to preserue and increase people, and namelie people of that qualitye, as are both in bodye strengthened and hardened by Labor, and also in condicon of life not oppressed with pouertie and necessitye; And . . . contrarywise the decaye and depopulacon of houses and ffarmes of husbandrye and turning of them to cottags doth of necessitye breede great Multitudes of poore and needye people wherevpon infinite Inconvenyence may ensue, and is a thing that doth so generallie discontent, as many tymes it is the occasion of Insurrecon and Commotions in the State.[58]

These same assumptions concerning military necessity and the preservation of public order had been articulated in the preamble to the Tillage Act of 1597 (39 Eliz., c. 2), when Parliament, fearing that high corn prices would lead to more popular disorders like the Enslow Hill conspiracy, yielded to popular pressure and reinstated the older, more uncompromising official hostility to enclosures of arable land. Even in that statute a significant breach was made, since 15 northern and south-western counties were excluded from its provisions because their sandy or clayey soils were more suited to grazing and dairying than grain production. Another clause exempted the practice of convertible husbandry provided an amount of land was ploughed up that was equal to the number of acres laid down to grass.[59]

In June 1607, immediately following the suppression of the Midland Revolt, Parliament once again considered the question of

---

[58] PRO, STAC 8/17/24;

[59] *SR* iv/2. 893; Beresford, 'Habitation Versus Improvement', pp. 46–8; Walter, 'A "Rising of the People"? The Oxfordshire Rising of 1596', pp. 130–7.

new legislation against enclosures. But on this occasion a more critical approach to the problem of enclosure was evident in the parliamentary debates. In the first place, the proponents of military necessity had changed their tune. Somerset, a largely enclosed county, was thought to be able to support a much larger trained militia than Northamptonshire, still mostly champion country even in 1607. Somerset was also said to yield much more revenue in the form of parliamentary subsidies. Moreover, it was reasoned that 'Foreign invaders . . . cannot so easily march, spoil and foray in an enclosed country as in champion'. Care must be taken in correcting the evil of depopulation to avoid giving the impression that enclosure invariably results in depopulation, which had furnished the 'pretended cause of this last tumult' as well as the pretext for Ket's Rebellion in 1549. The unenclosed commons of fens and forests were decried as 'nurseries of beggars', whereas enclosed regions were supposed to produce 'wealthy people' and furnish labourers with employment planting hedges and digging ditches. In fielden regions the resulting hedgerows would be quite adequate to supply the peoples' fuel needs.[60]

Not all of the arguments in favour of regulated enclosure were as specious as these. The main drift of the debate was to identify engrossing as the real cause of depopulation rather than 'converting', i.e. convertible husbandry. If the questions of enclosure and agricultural innovation were left to negotiations between landlord and tenant, as in the case of those counties excluded from the Tillage Act of 1597, then 'the poor man shall be satisfied in his end—habitation, and the gentleman not hindered in his desire—improvement'. The fallacy of this argument is that in areas such as the Midland Plain, where there had existed an imbalance between pasture and arable, conversion to up-and-down husbandry necessarily reduced the proportion of land used for corn growing at any given time—even while increasing yields. The resulting agricultural system was less labour-intensive and consequently had a depopulating effect.[61]

Opinion among the landowners in Parliament concerning land use and agricultural innovation was divided, but all agreed that depopulation and the engrossing of farms was intolerable and

---

[60] 'A Consideration of the Cause in Question before the Lords touching Depopulation', printed in Kerridge, *Agrarian Problems*, pp. 200–3.

[61] Ibid.; Beresford, 'Habitation Versus Improvement' pp. 44–8; Kerridge, *Agrarian Problems*, p. 121.

ought to be punished. Moreover, the government could not ignore popular complaints about violations of the tillage statutes and the Books of Orders and found it necessary to make examples of some of the depopulators. Consequently, the Crown sought to identify and prosecute culprits after the rebellions of both 1596 and 1607. In neither case was official enforcement of the tillage laws very successful.[62]

The attorney-general prosecuted at least 18 persons from the counties of Norfolk, Suffolk, and Kent in the Court of Star Chamber during the summer and autumn of 1597. Probably more prosecutions were initiated, or at least intended. The few informations which have survived are remarkably vague and imprecise; only in a few instances did the attorney-general specify how many houses of husbandry had been decayed. Whereas the Star Chamber informations of 1608, despite questions about their legality, were based upon the returns of royal commissioners sitting in each of the affected counties, those of 1597 appear to have been based almost entirely upon hearsay evidence and the allegations of informers, which the attorney-general had not verified. One Norfolk man, accused of engrossing three houses of husbandry, pleaded that three cottages had been thrown together 50 years earlier and that altogether their lands totalled a mere ten acres, which was hardly sufficient to support his household. He also farmed five acres from an adjoining cottage, which he had rented to an 80-year-old woman for the previous 50 years. Sir Edward Coke was usually more careful about verifying his evidence; he may have halted prosecutions when he discovered how distorted some of the accusations were.[63] Some informations were also brought against offending landlords in Queen's Bench. In 1600 Sir Thomas Tresham was fined £1,000 in the latter court for violating the Tillage Act of 1597.[64]

Following the suppression of the Midland Revolt, royal commissioners were appointed to gather evidence concerning depopulations

---

[62] J. Martin, 'Enclosure and the Inquisitions of Depopulation of 1607: An Examination of Dr. Kerridge's article "The Returns of the Inquisitions of Depopulation"', *Ag. HR* 30 (1982), 45.

[63] PRO, STAC 5/A2/40, A13/18, A16/32. Although the Elizabethan Star Chamber Proceedings badly need rearranging, I did search all of the 'A' files, which include attorney-general's informations, without discovering any subsequent prosecutions of landowners in other counties.

[64] Finch, *The Wealth of Five Northamptonshire Families*, p. 88 n.

and other offences against the tillage laws in Northamptonshire, Warwickshire, Leicestershire, Buckinghamshire, Bedfordshire, Huntingdonshire, Nottinghamshire, Lincolnshire, Yorkshire, and possibly other counties.[65] Whereas the 1597 proceedings caught only a few small fry, the royal commissions, sitting from late August to October of 1607, netted a number of big fish. Among those presented were Henry, Earl of Lincoln, accused of depopulating 31 houses of husbandry, and Sir Robert Cotton, the antiquarian, who displaced the households of seven husbandmen at Connington, Huntingdonshire. Several commissioners also were presented: the Earl of Kent and Sir Robert Conquest, commissioners for Bedfordshire, and Sir Oliver Cromwell, the Lord Protector's royalist uncle, who represented Huntingdonshire in Parliament. Members of the leading families of Northamptonshire were presented by the enclosure commissioners and later prosecuted in Star Chamber: Sir Richard Knightley, who had sheltered the Marprelate press, and his son, Sir Valentine, both Members of Parliament; Sir Roger Wilbraham, a master of requests; and Sir Walter Montagu, son of Sir Edward Montagu, the senior deputy lieutenant and a depopulation commissioner. Sir Walter stood accused of depopulating six houses of husbandry and displacing 40 persons at Hanging Houghton.[66]

The official efforts to enforce the tillage statutes and punish depopulators following the 1607 rebellion were not much more successful than had been the case following the 1596 rebellion. To begin with, the commissions authorizing the inquiries in 1607 were defective because they granted only the authority to inquire and not to hear and determine. For this reason a man accused of depopulating enclosures was denied the opportunity to traverse the charge and clear himself; the judges held that he was thereby defamed. Furthermore, the evidence, whether collected by the depopulation commissioners from common informers seeking profit or from people who possessed genuine grievances, frequently displayed a lack of technical knowledge concerning how the land was actually employed. A number of defendants in the Star Chamber prosecutions successfully defended

---

[65] Parker, 'The Depopulation Returns for Leicestershire in 1607', p. 232; Leonard, 'The Inclosure of Common Fields in the Seventeenth Century', p. 125; J. D. Gould, 'The Inquisition of Depopulation of 1607 in Lincolnshire', *EHR* 67 (1952), 392–6.

[66] PRO, STAC 8/15/21, 17/16, 17/17, 18/12; Gay, 'The Midland Revolt and the Inquisitions of Depopulation of 1607', p. 226 n.

themselves by pleading the convertible husbandry clause in the Tillage Act of 1597.[67]

As a result of the returns of the commissioners for depopulation, prosecutions were begun not only in Star Chamber, but also in the Court of Exchequer and at the assizes and quarter sessions. When Sir Edward Coke was on the Western Assizes circuit in 1609 he ordered 26 houses of husbandry to be repaired and two engrossed farms to be redivided into their original four parts. The lord chief justice also took a strong stand against William Combe in the Welcombe enclosure dispute in Warwickshire in 1616–17 and ordered the latter to maintain tillage. Yet there was little political support for rigorous enforcement of the tillage statutes, and the attorney-general was given the authority to compound for fines in cases of depopulation. Some of the defendants, such as John Quarles of Cotesbach and Lewis Tresham purchased royal pardons. The latter paid a mere £10 for his pardon.[68]

Sporadic efforts to enforce the tillage laws continued until 1619 when corn prices fell and the government felt obliged to help the farmers more than the poor. By 1621 the activities of common informers had caused the courts to be clogged with 2,000 cases involving accusations of depopulation, and royal commissioners were appointed to grant pardons in such cases. In 1624 most of the tillage laws were repealed, but when corn prices rose again during the crisis of 1629 the government once again became concerned to prevent depopulating enclosures and conversions from tillage to pasture. The partial repeal of the tillage laws was no obstacle to reviving the depopulation commissions and prosecuting offenders during the years 1632–6, since Sir Edward Coke had argued that depopulation had become a crime in common law.[69]

---

[67] E. Kerridge, 'The Returns of the Inquisitions of Depopulation', *EHR* 70 (1955), 222–5; id., *Agricultural Revolution*, pp. 189–90. John Martin ('Enclosure and the Inquisitions of 1607', pp. 43–4) has discovered convictions for violating the tillage laws that Dr Kerridge missed and also sharply disagrees with his conclusions about the reliability of the inquisitions of depopulations.

[68] Leonard, 'The Inclosure of Common Fields in the Seventeenth Century', p. 126; Beresford, 'Habitation Versus Improvement', pp. 48–9, 59 n; Chambers, *William Shakespeare*, ii. 145; Hist. MSS Comm., *Salisbury*, xx. 299; Finch, *The Wealth of Five Northamptonshire Families*, p. 88 n.

[69] Leonard, 'The Inclosure of Common Fields in the Seventeenth Century', pp. 126–9, 133; Beresford, 'Habitation Versus Improvement', pp. 49–55; id., 'The Common Informer, the Penal Statutes and Economic Regulation', *EHR*, 2nd ser. 10 (1957), 235; *Seventeenth-century Economic Documents*, ed. Thirsk and Cooper,

In contrast to the fairly strict administration of the regulations in the Books of Orders concerning the marketing of corn, the tillage laws were never enforced effectively and appear to have deterred very few landlords. These contrasting practices in local government during the seventeenth century tended to shift the blame for grain shortages and high prices in the midland counties from the enclosing activities of peers and gentlemen, upon which popular outrage had focused in the rebellions of 1596 and 1607, to corn merchants, who increasingly became the victims of popular protests concerning food shortages.[70] Such laxity in the enforcement of the tillage statutes was undoubtedly encouraged by the Courts of Chancery and Duchy of Lancaster Chamber, which in the seventeenth century came to favour enclosure agreements as a means of settling enclosure disputes.[71] Moreover, agricultural practice had become too complex a business for effective regulation by statute or the law courts. In any case the enforcement of the tillage laws was rendered obnoxious by the activities of common informers and by the exercise of the suspending and dispensing powers under the royal prerogative to grant landlords pardons for offences against the tillage statutes or licences to enclose in return for monetary compositions. (It appears that there was always a sordid side to Stuart paternalism.)[72] Critics of the tillage laws were left wondering if they served any useful purpose except to provide those who protested agrarian improvement by levelling hedges with a moral justification for their actions.

pp. 121–2; PRO, STAC 8/27/1; *Historical Collections*, ed. Rushworth, vol. ii/2, app., pp. 106–8; PRO, SP 16/499/10, printed in Kerridge, *Agrarian Problems*, pp. 198–9.

[70] G. C. F. Forster, 'The North Riding Justices and Their Sessions, 1603–1625', *NH* 10 (1975), 115–19; Parker, 'The Depopulation Returns for Leicestershire in 1607', p. 59 n.; W. J. Shelton, *English Hunger and Industrial Disorder: A Study of Social Conflict during the First Decade of George III's Reign* (Toronto, 1973), 113; Thompson, 'The Moral Economy of the English Crowd in the Eighteenth Century', pp. 108–9.

[71] Above, ch. 5.

[72] Beresford, 'Habitation Versus Improvement', pp. 50–1.

PART III
Social Protest in Pastoral and Sylvan England

10

Pastoral and Sylvan Society

THE forests and fens of England were the scene of especially sharp conflict in the early seventeenth century. The very rapid population increase in these regions had already placed heavy demands upon land resources when agricultural improvers, led by the Crown, launched an assault upon wastes and forests with schemes for disafforestation and land reclamation by drainage. By curtailing the formerly abundant use-rights that attracted cottagers and squatters to heaths, moors, forests, and fens, they intended to bend the idle poor to labour and subject them to gentry control. The improvers and speculators did not perceive that where they converted pastoral economies into arable ones they also altered the societies in ways that increased the problems of poverty, underemployment, and disorder in pastoral and sylvan regions.[1]

At the same time that these woodland–pasture communities were compelled to adjust to agrarian innovation, some of them also experienced rapid development of rural industries. Labour-intensive industries such as nail-making and other metal-working trades sought out pools of cheap labour in the forest areas of the west Midlands. Coal-mining expanded in areas such as the Severn basin and the Staffordshire plateau to provide fuel for these secondary metal-working trades as well as to satisfy a general increase in domestic and industrial consumption. Because coal-mining scarred the wastes and impinged upon a variety of property- and use-rights, it was conducive to social conflict and litigation. Several primary metallurgical industries, most notably the new indirect method of iron-smelting, made especially heavy demands upon water power and timber for charcoal, and conflicted with the fuel and energy requirements of older industries such as cloth-making. The location of mining and primary metallurgical production, which were capital-intensive industries, was determined by the availability of natural resources rather than cheap labour, but when established they tended to

[1] Thirsk, 'Seventeenth-century Agriculture and Social Change', pp. 167–8.

attract persons whom the indigenous communities regarded as alien and disorderly.

It is well known that disafforestation and fen-drainage schemes and other forms of fiscal seigneurialism provoked a number of large-scale forest and fen riots in the reign of Charles I. Less well known but more numerous are the instances of violent social protest provoked by the influx of population into woodland areas and the development of newer and technologically-innovative industries which brought more intensive land use and proved to be more damaging to the natural environment. These problems and the conflict which they caused will be studied in this chapter. Altogether, agrarian improvement, economic development, and the growth of rural industries undermined common rights and communal control of the land and generally worked against the interests of the older inhabitants of woodland and pastoral districts.

i. *Economic Diversity*

The conditions that gave rise to the growth of rural industry are usually to be found in the diversified economies of pastoral-sylvan regions. Although there were limits upon how far industrial development could proceed in pastoral areas such as the fenlands, the forest regions of Shropshire and Staffordshire were subsequently the scene of the earliest stages of the first and only spontaneous industrial revolution. This unique achievement was preceded by an extended pre-industrial period, when certain agricultural activities and traditional crafts flourished in a symbiotic relationship.[2]

Woodland-pasture regions possessed characteristics that champion areas and arable economies generally lacked. Although not necessarily wooded, forest areas usually contained abundant wastes and commons, which long continued to provide unstinted grazing where stock-rearing and dairying flourished on small family farms. This type of agriculture did not make heavy demands upon the farmer's time and left him and his family free to pursue secondary occupations. If timber was not plentiful, alternative fuels such as peat and coal were usually available. Over half of Staffordshire consisted of forests,

---

[2] Ead., 'Industries in the Countryside', pp. 70–88, esp. 86–7; ead., 'Horn and Thorn in Staffordshire: The Economy of a Pastoral County', *North Staffs. Journal of Field Studies* 9 (1969), 6–9.

heaths, and wastes which prejudiced lowlanders considered 'for the most part barren'. Since these were upland regions, they were usually well supplied with watercourses and fall lines which furnished the power so necessary for further industrial development.[3] Except for mining and primary metallurgical industries which needed to be near the minerals extracted, the most important consideration in the location of rural industries was the availability of cheap and plentiful labour. A surplus of labour beyond what was needed for agriculture generally resulted from the existence of partible inheritance as well as the influx of population attracted by abundant wastes. Such proto-industrial communities were often characterized by free or heritable copyhold tenures, decaying manorial organiz- ation, and dispersed settlement, which weakened the influence of the gentry and parochial clergy.[4]

There was necessarily a close connection between industry and agriculture in pre-industrial society. This was especially true in the proto-industrial economies of woodland regions. Most industrial activities consisted of processing the products of forest and farm in order to provide food and fuel, housing, and clothes. The seasonal nature of most industries, caused by the variability of water power, the casual nature of labour, chronic underemployment, or the requirements of labour for harvest work made it necessary for most artisans to engage in some sort of agricultural activity in addition to plying their trades. This was true even of virtually landless cottagers, but most artisans combined agriculture and craftsmanship by preference.[5]

Almost all of the local agrarian economies in early seventeenth- century England had responded to regional, or in a few cases, national market opportunities. Many had specialized and ceased to be self-sufficient — especially with regard to grain supplies. Special- ization, whether in agricultural produce such as butter and cheese, or industries such as cloth-making, allowed sylvan–pastoral regions

---

[3] *AHEW* iv. 99; P. Frost, 'Yeomen and Metalsmiths: Livestock in the Dual Economy in South Staffordshire', *Ag. HR* 29 (1981), 30; Hey, *Myddle*, p. 8.

[4] Thirsk, 'Horn and Thorn in Staffordshire', pp. 3–4; ead., 'Industries in the Countryside', pp. 70–2; E. L. Jones, 'The Agricultural Origins of Industry', *P. & P.*, no. 40 (July 1968), 63; E. Kerridge, *The Farmers of Old England* (1973), 59–61; Aubrey, *The Natural History of Wiltshire*, p. 11.

[5] D. C. Coleman, *Industry in Tudor and Stuart England* (Ec. Hist. Soc., 1975), 12.

to support a larger population, but made such communities vulnerable to grain shortages as well as fluctuations in the markets of the commodities in which they specialized.[6] Thus pastoral and proto-industrial communities in the West of England suffered from the crises of 1629–32 as well as disafforestation projects, and were the scenes of much disorder. Ultimately, the shortages of one region stimulated production in neighbouring regions. Staffordshire presents the classic example of a well diversified economy, which may help to explain why both the agricultural and industrial revolutions took hold at a very early date. Although stock-rearing was the dominant agricultural occupation and exposed the county to grain shortages early in the seventeenth century, convertible husbandry was practised within the county from the early years of the century and relieved Staffordshire of dearth well before the century was over. The metallurgical and mineral-extractive industries were also important in Elizabethan and early-Stuart Staffordshire: Cannock Chase was the location of the first blast furnace in the Midlands, while Wednesbury was where Thomas Savery first tried out his vacuum-steam pumping engine in 1698.[7]

The Forest of Dean also displayed a wide variety of economic pursuits even before the introduction of blast furnaces and hydraulic forges brought an expansion of the iron industry. This diversity of occupations is demonstrated by the survey of men fit for military service drawn up in 1608 by John Smyth of Nibley. Of the 831 men listed for the hundred of St Briavels, which was contained entirely within the forest, only 159 individuals (or 19 per cent) were classified as landowners and smallholders. Artisans made up 45 per cent of the adult male population, while servants and labourers, who comprised 34 per cent, were probably divided between agriculture and industry. Of the artisan population, 36 per cent were miners, metal-workers and stone-workers; 30 per cent laboured in the wood-working crafts or processed animal products (the latter were mostly tanners, cobblers, and glovers); 25 per cent were cloth-workers; and the remainder (13 per cent) were distributed among a variety of miscellaneous crafts. These statistics may not be entirely reliable since

---

[6] J. Thirsk, 'The Peasant Economy of England in the Seventeenth Century', *Studia Historiae Oeconomicae* 10 (1975), 5–7.

[7] Sharp, *In Contempt of All Authority*, pp. 63–7, 82–96; Thirsk, 'Horn and Thorn in Staffordshire', pp. 6–7; G. M. Cockin, 'The Ancient Industries of Cannock Chase', *Trans. Burton-on-Trent Nat. Hist. Arch. Soc.* 5 (1906), 126–43.

only 30 individuals were described as miners, whereas there were probably a hundred households dependent upon mining in Dean Forest ten years later. Some of the miners may be concealed among the smallholders, since anyone born within the forest might claim the right to be a miner. Certainly, some of the miners were freeholders. Moreover, cottagers appear to have been left out of the survey, since there is evidence that several hundred men, women and children worked at making wooden trenchers and cooperage. After 1612 the numbers of foundry and forge workers as well as woodcutters and colliers must have increased, while the number of cloth-workers undoubtedly declined.[8]

The siting of rural industries was determined by a number of considerations which varied from one industry to another. The location of the iron industry in the Kentish Weald was dictated by the iron ore lying in the sandstone ridge only a few feet deep. The source of charcoal fuel was also an important consideration, since charcoal was so fragile that it could be carried no more than about fifteen miles without reducing it to a heap of dust. Transportation was not quite as important originally, but the muddy Wealden roads—among the worst in England—did prove to be a disadvantage in the long run. The Weald was thickly populated, but the iron-works employed comparatively few workers; most of the labour surplus found employment in the clothing industry. It was not the depletion of timber supplies that caused the Wealden iron industry to decline in the seventeenth century, since the charcoal fuel was obtained from young coppice-grown trees. Rather, it was a combination of poor transport, rainfall that was insufficient to supply the millponds all year round, and intense competition for wood fuel and water power.[9]

Whereas iron-founding was still largely concentrated in the Weald of Kent, Sussex, and Surrey in the middle of the Elizabethan period, by the beginning of the seventeenth century more than a third of the iron furnaces in the realm were to be found in South Wales and the west Midlands. Gunfounding had consumed a significant part of the Wealden iron production and it made sense to be near the

[8] Sharp, *In Contempt of All Authority*, pp. 184–8; C. E. Hart, *The Free Miners of the Royal Forest of Dean and the Hundred of St. Briavels* (Gloucester, 1953), 164.

[9] C. W. Chalklin, *Seventeenth-century Kent: A Social and Economic History* (1965), 113–17, 130–2; M. W. Flinn, 'Timber and the Advance of Technology: A Reconsideration', *Annals of Science* 15/2 (1959), 117.

royal dockyards on the Thames and the Medway; but the iron industry of the west Midlands was called into existence to serve the needs of the secondary metal-working trades of Worcestershire, Staffordshire, and Warwickshire, which in turn had sought out the cheap and plentiful supply of labour in the upland stock-rearing regions of those counties. Coal and iron were both important to secondary metal crafts such as nail-, bridle-bit- and spur-making, but the location of coal-pits and finery forges did not necessarily determine where nailers and lorimers located their trades.[10]

Although the Severn opened up markets for Shropshire coal and Forest of Dean iron ore, the west Midlands were not otherwise very well served by waterways in the seventeenth century. The metal-working trades spread across three counties despite the lack of good transport. The amount of coal sold by land still exceeded the quantity carried by water. The Staffordshire coalfield was not near navigable rivers, but because of its quality the coal was hauled overland into Worcestershire and and Warwickshire. Cannel coal from Beaudesert Park, on the edge of Cannock Chase, was especially choice and was transported as far east as Leicester, where it competed with local coals. Birmingham smithies fetched their coal and iron out of South Staffordshire by ox-drawn wains, while Staffordshire whirlers obtained the iron for drawing wire all the way from the Forest of Dean.[11]

Thus underemployment resulting from overpopulation in the diversified economies of certain sylvan-pastoral regions, together with the availability of cheap labour, usually including women and children eager to supplement incomes derived from stock-rearing, stimulated the development of rural industry and technological innovation.

ii. *Influx of Population*

Forest villages were regarded as being more open than those of fielden areas, and the excess population of champion regions, cast adrift

[10] G. Hammersley, 'The Charcoal Iron Industry and its Fuel, 1540–1750', *Ec. HR*, new ser. 26 (1973), 595; R. A. Pelham, 'The Establishment of the Willoughby Ironworks in North Warwickshire in the Sixteenth Century', *Birmingham University Historical Journal* 4/1 (1953), 18–29; M. B. Rowlands, *Masters and Men in the West Midlands Metalware Trades before the Industrial Revolution* (Manchester, 1975), ch. 1.

[11] Trinder, *The Industrial Revolution in Shropshire*, p. 8; Court, *The Rise of the Midland Industries*, pp. 4, 24, 29, 35, 81; Frost, 'Yeomen and Metalsmiths', p. 32; Nef, *The Rise of the British Coal Industry*, vol. i, pp. 66, 103.

by agrarian improvement, economic crises, natural increase, and impartible inheritance, migrated to these communities. So rapidly did the populations of sylvan communities increase during the period between 1530 and 1640 that the demands placed upon natural resources exceeded what could be satisfied by an extension of traditional crafts and economic activities.[12]

Very rapid population increases in sylvan communities were especially noticeable in the early seventeenth century, and were often followed by the appearance of new industries. In sixteenth-century Whittlewood and Rockingham Forests in Northamptonshire agriculture remained the principal occupation but was supplemented on a seasonal basis by the felling, dressing, and transport of firewood and timber. The influx of surplus population in the seventeenth century stimulated a more diversified wood-working industry that produced ship's spars and hurdles for fences as well as the burning of lime and charcoal and potash production. The processing of oak bark also served a tanning industry that grew up on the forest's edge. The medieval crafts of the Forest of Arden in North Warwickshire included tanning, coopery, weaving, tile-making, and wood-working—all practised on a part-time basis by smallholder-craftsmen. Beginning in the 1590s, at the end of a period of demographic pressure, new crafts appeared that were practised by landless cottagers; these included shoe-making and glove-making as well as the processing and weaving of flax and hemp. There followed a demographic crisis in the first quarter of the seventeenth century when deficient local harvests caused a decline in fertility and an increase in mortality rates; emigration probably exceeded immigration. Wooded areas were cleared, wastes ploughed up, and convertible husbandry introduced during this time of distress. This was also the period during which metal-smithing first appeared in Arden. The wood-working crafts also became more specialized, as substantial smallholders and farmers rebuilt and refurnished their homes. Carpenters and coopers were supplemented by sawyers, joiners, turners, and wheelwrights. These agrarian and industrial adaptations permitted the population of Arden to achieve a rate

[12] R. G. Wilkinson, *Poverty and Progress: An Ecological Perspective on Economic Development* (New York, 1973), 21–2, 76–80; V. Skipp, *Crisis and Development: An Ecological Case Study of the Forest of Arden, 1570–1674* (Cambridge, 1978), 9–10.

of natural increase of 62 per cent during the second quarter of the seventeenth century.[13]

Similar developments are observable in the fenlands. In the Isle of Axholme, on the large manor of Epworth with its dispersed hamlets, 100 new cottages were built between 1590 and 1630. The surplus population was encouraged to engage in the labour-intensive cottage industries of growing and processing hemp and flax and weaving it into rope, netting, canvas, sackcloth, and linen. Population increases also occurred in the south Lincolnshire and Cambridgeshire fens. Poor fenmen in Cambridgeshire and the Isle of Ely dug peat and gathered sedge and deadwood to supply fuel to upland parishes and towns. By-employments had become economically significant in seventeenth-century Willingham and probate inventories reveal that social and economic status no longer depended entirely on the possession of land.[14]

Although it did much to lessen demographic pressure, the growth of industry in sylvan and pastoral areas was never sufficient to absorb all surplus labour. A survey of the Forest of Dean in 1610 reported that the iron industry attracted far more persons than could be hired; employment in iron-founding was sporadic at best. Consequently, the newcomers resorted to stealing wood and poaching. In 1615 340 persons were discovered living in 79 huts illegally erected within coppices enclosed for timber; they lived by wood-carving, turnery, and coopery. Duffield Frith in Derbyshire, one of the smaller royal forests, contained in 1587 a population of 1,800 souls, not counting squatters, within an area of 70 square miles. Lead-smelting and coal-mining inadequately supplemented stock-rearing; the former was severely limited by a lack of water power, which had already contributed to the decline of iron-founding. Although lacking the clothing industry of the Kentish Weald, Wealden villages in Sussex were more populous that downland villages. Several in north-west Sussex contained as many as 500 and 600 inhabitants on the eve of the Civil War. The villages adjoining the Forests of Frome Selwood, Blackmore, and Chippenham along the Wiltshire–Somerset border

---

[13] Pettit, *The Royal Forests of Northamptonshire*, pp. 158–61; Skipp, *Crisis and Development*, pp. 13, 23, 42–5, 54–64.

[14] J. Thirsk, *English Peasant Farming: The Agrarian History of Lincolnshire from Tudor to Recent Times* (1957), 114; ead., *AHEW* iv. 13, 204; K. Lindley, *Fenland Riots and the English Revolution* (1982), 10; Spufford, *Contrasting Communities*, p. 157.

must have been among the most crowded in England. The broadcloth industry was quite depressed in the early seventeenth century and unemployment was chronic. Frome, Somerset possessed more than 6,500 inhabitants in 1631, of whom 500 had been receiving poor relief ten years earlier. Conditions in Leicester Forest, Braydon Forest in Wiltshire, Feckenham Forest in Worcestershire, and the Forests of Westward and Inglewood in Cumberland, where no significant industries were established, were probably no better. All had experienced substantial population increases, and were crowded with virtually landless cottagers who appear to have lived entirely by commoning.[15]

The expansion of the west Midlands metal-working trades illustrates some of the problems of rural industrial development. Metalworkers were still only a small part of the population of South Staffordshire at the end of the sixteenth century, but by the third quarter of the seventeenth century they constituted one-third of the population and were as numerous as agriculturalists. The craftsmen comprehended by the metal-working industries included cutlers, scythesmiths, lorimers, spurriers, and locksmiths. Nailers made up two-thirds of all metalsmiths. The nail-making trade was easy to enter without serving an apprenticeship; few tools were required and the region was remarkably free of guild regulations. The industry offered the prospect of fuller employment for the households of poor cottagers, since women and children also worked at nail-making. At first most metalsmiths owned a few cattle, but by the end of the seventeenth century only about 40 per cent of them possessed cattle, although most still kept pigs. Poor nailers tended to become perpetually indebted to ironmongers and corn merchants who engrossed local supplies of food. These obnoxious middlemen began the practice of paying the nailers in truck, by giving them food and iron rods in exchange for finished nails, a practice that parliamentary bills unsuccessfully sought to regulate in 1604 and

---

[15] Pettit, *The Royal Forests of Northamptonshire*, pp. 161-2; Hart, *The Free Miners of the Royal Forest of Dean*, pp. 174-5; Sharp, *In Contempt of All Authority*, pp. 160-9, 181; Fletcher, *A County Community in Peace and War*, pp. 3-4, 165; Supple, *Commercial Crisis and Change in England*, p. 6; J. C. Cox, *The Royal Forests of England* (1905), 181-201; C. M. L. Bouch and G. P. Jones, *A Short Economic and Social History of the Lake Counties, 1500-1830* (Manchester, 1961; repr. New York 1967), 77-8; Appleby, 'Common Land and Peasant Unrest in Sixteenth-century England, A Comparative Note', pp. 209-23.

1621. Little wonder that nailers were attracted to radical religious groups![16]

Like most crafts, mining remained a part-time occupation that was usually combined with agriculture until the early seventeenth century. Ian Blanchard has noted that artisans, whether in mining or other trades, were 'task-oriented', that is, the artisan worked only so long as it took to earn a sum of money sufficient to pay the rent or buy what he could not produce. Various developments caused the landless cottager-miner to supplant the smallholder-miner. Population pressure and declining real wages compelled many miners to work longer hours in the Cornish Stannaries and in the Derbyshire Peak lead mines. The advent of joint-stock companies, such as the Mines Royal and the Mineral and Battery Works (both chartered in 1568), with their heavy investments in new processes and equipment, tended to put pressure upon miners to devote more time to their crafts and pushed out independent miners. Yet spending more time at their digging did not eliminate the problems of underemployment and poverty for these artisans.[17]

While agrarian innovations and the development of new industries permitted the Forest of Arden to support a population increase of 50 per cent, approximately one-third of the population lived in a state of poverty. The poor were characterized by landlessness, by exemption from the hearth tax of 1663, or by the fact that they received poor relief at some time in their lives and did not pay poor rates. Although landless cottagers may be regarded as full-time artisans, it does not follow that they were fully employed. Their poverty was a consequence of their landlessness and underemployment. Thus, the development of rural industries in sylvan-pastoral communities in the early seventeenth century was not sufficient to keep pace with population increases.[18]

[16] Court, *The Rise of the Midland Industries*, pp. 61–2, 100–1; Frost, 'Yeomen and Metalsmiths', pp. 29, 34, 38–40; Thirsk, 'Horn and Thorn in Staffordshire', pp. 6–8; *Seventeenth-century Economic Documents*, ed. Thirsk and Cooper, pp. 188–9, 208–10.

[17] Blanchard, 'Labour Productivity and Work Psychology in the English Mining Industry, 1400–1600', pp. 4–7, 9–13; A. Raistrick and B. Jennings, *A History of Lead Mining in the Pennines* (1965), 182–4; J. W. Gough, *The Mines of Mendip* (Oxford, 1930), 129–30.

[18] Skipp, *Crisis and Development*, pp. 78–80; Pettit, *The Royal Forests of Northamptonshire*, pp. 161–2.

The parish and manor of Condover, Shropshire provides a detailed case study of a woodland community that went through the stresses of agrarian change, rapid population growth, and the development of a clothing industry—all during the second half of the sixteenth century. Wooded land was still being cleared in the sixteenth century and it remained easy to assart woodland and waste and to secure confirmation of these approvements from the lax manorial administration, which was a legacy of the days when Condover had been a crown estate. All of this ended when Sir Henry Knyvett became lord of the manor and took up residence in 1533. He attempted to tighten manorial administration and control the assarting of woodland and waste and the alienation of demesne land. His successor, Robert Longe, a London mercer, who purchased the manor in 1544, continued the policy of fiscal seigneurialism by ruthlessly cutting down timber, attempting to raise entry fines, to eliminate copyholds of inheritance, and to revive long-forgotten seigneurial fees. In 1550 Longe secured a Star Chamber decree permitting the total enclosure of the two principal wastes, Buriwood and Radmore, which, together, appear to have contained more than 1,000 acres. The implementation of this enclosure agreement was delayed for another generation by an anti-enclosure riot in the same year.[19]

The manor passed to Longe's son-in-law, Henry Vynar, who was also a London mercer, in the 1560s. Vynar tripled the income of the manor and attempted to carry out the enclosure decree in 1577 by severing and enclosing 700 acres of Buriwood Waste. Again, there was resistance in the form of several riots and numerous other instances of hedge-breaking between 1577 and 1579. Whereas the manorial tenants appear to have presented a united front against the improvement of rents and total enclosure in 1550, there was now a cleavage between Vynar, supported by a number of 'old-hold' tenants who had been promised allotments of enclosed waste, and a large number of less substantial tenants and cottagers, who stood to lose much by the extinction of their common rights. There were also other sources of contention: many of the cottagers and smaller tenants were part-time cloth-workers who were apparently forced to sell their cloth to Vynar in exchange for grain grown by Vynar on the enclosed waste and then ground in his mills. The smaller

[19] *VCH Shropshire*, viii. 28–47; PRO, STAC 3/4/80; C. 78/85/15a.

tenants and cottager-weavers were supported in their opposition to
Vynar by Thomas Owen, a powerful lawyer, judge, and member
of the Council in the Marches of Wales. Owen, who represented
the interests of the Shrewsbury Drapers, eventually obtained the
manor through extensive litigation and struck a bargain with the
tenants confirming their copyholds of inheritance and completing
the enclosure of waste and woodland. The agreement was embodied
in a Chancery decree of 1586. Although the Vynar family lost the
seigneurial jurisdiction, some land in Condover did pass to Vynar's
son, Henry the younger, who continued to be harassed by the cloth-
workers and smaller tenants. His hedges were levelled in
1593—blown up by gunpowder.[20]

Thomas Owen, his son Roger, and their descendants prospered
in the seventeenth century. They pacified their tenants through a
policy of completing the enclosure of the manorial wastes and buying
out the trouble-makers among the copyholders. Thomas built the
finest Elizabethan stone house in Shropshire, while his son enclosed
a park of over 300 acres and purchased several manors.[21]

The influx of population into sylvan-pastoral regions in the early
seventeenth century proved to be very disruptive. The older inhabitants suffered the loss or diminution of their use-rights and means
of livelihood. Moreover, in no instance did the growth of rural
industries provide sufficient employment to absorb the population
increases. Poverty increased and so did the cost of poor relief. Many
underemployed, or 'idle' persons as they were called, were alleged
to have turned to petty crime as a consequence, while increased
consumption of the resources of woodland and waste became a
perpetual source of intercommoning disputes and litigation. Critics of
the disorders of sylvan and pastoral communities, such as John Smyth
of Nibley, argued that social regulation had to precede improvement;
this meant carrying out schemes of fen drainage, disafforestation,
enclosure, and division in severalty as the only means of controlling
the ungovernable multitudes of cottagers and squatters.[22]

---

[20] Ibid., STAC 5/V6/17, V8/12, V8/37; V9/23; C. 78/85/15a; *VCH Shropshire*, viii. 46–7; *DNB*, s.v. Thomas Owen (d. 1598); T. C. Mendenhall, *The
Shrewsbury Drapers and the Welsh Wool Trade in the XVI and XVII Centuries*
(Oxford, 1953), 19 n., 126, 130, 142.
[21] *VCH Shropshire*, viii. 37–47.
[22] Smyth, *The Berkeley Manuscripts*, iii. 327–8; Pettit, *The Royal Forests of
Northamptonshire*, pp. 156–8.

iii. *Technological Change and Land Use*

Most economic historians today maintain that Professor Nef exaggerated the degree of economic development, industrial growth, and technological innovation in Tudor and Stuart England. Yet it cannot be denied that the mining and metallurgical industries made heavy demands upon the resources of timber, fuel, and water power of certain sylvan communities. A lively debate has developed concerning whether or not there was a timber famine that led to a fuel revolution which in turn sparked such inventions as the steam engine and the substitution of coke for charcoal in iron-smelting. One must be careful about generalizing, since poor inland transport could produce shortages of timber within 20 miles of abundant supplies. So far, historians have given little consideration to how the exploitation of water power, timber, and fuel in sixteenth- and seventeenth-century England conflicted with the use-rights of sylvan communities and provoked protests from those who wished to maintain alternative uses of natural resources. The remainder of this chapter will consider the effect of economic change and technological innovation in the coal-mining and metallurgical industries upon land utilization in sylvan and pastoral communities.[23]

Wind- and water-mills provided the only supplement to human and animal muscle power. Windmills depended on a source of power which, even in eastern England, was notoriously fickle. The municipal windmills of Lincoln could not grind corn for five weeks in 1555 because the wind had failed. Horse-mills and querns were pressed into service, but the poor still suffered from a shortage of bread. Most water-mills required extensive ponds, and very few locations would have possessed water supplies adequate for year-round operation. Water-mills might be shut down by summer drought, winter ice, and spring floods. The blowing-mills used for lead smelting in Duffield Frith were operated by overshot water-wheels; the water supply was sufficient to power each wheel only one day

---

[23] Nef, *The Rise of the British Coal Industry*, i. 19–22, 158–64; id., 'The Progress of Technology and the Growth of Large-scale Industry in Great Britain, 1540-1640', in E. M. Carns-Wilson (ed.), *Essays in Economic History* (3 vols.; 1954), i. 88–107; A. D. Dyer, 'Wood and Coal: A Change of Fuel', *History Today* 26 (Sept. 1976), 598–607; Coleman, *Industry in Tudor and Stuart England*, pp. 15–16; J. A. Chartres, *Internal Trade in England, 1500-1700* (Ec. Hist. Soc., 1977), 31–5; Flinn, 'Timber and the Advance of Technology', pp. 109, 113; Hammersley, 'The Charcoal Iron Industry and its Fuel, 1540-1750', pp. 602–8.

a week, except during a summer drought when the works closed down altogether. Indeed, the seasonal variations in the availability of wind and water power was a major cause of underemployment in pre-industrial societies.[24]

Water power was gradually applied to more and more uses in the Tudor and Stuart period. Water power was used for operating the bellows of blast furnaces, trip hammers in forges, and was applied to slitting mills in the west Midlands for the first time in the 1620s. It was used for drainage operations in coal-mines with mixed success, while hydraulic paper-mills first appeared in 1588. Most of the new applications of water power in England were actually medieval in origin or were introduced from the continent. The only significant application of water power to a labour-saving device in the woollen-textile industry, still the most important of all English industries, was the water-powered fulling or tucking mill. Many manorial grist-mills were converted to this use. English industry remained technologically conservative, but even a slight increase in the use of water power was bound to cause conflict over water rights, since the area affected extended well above and below the mill-race.[25]

Prime mill sites were already in short supply by the middle of the sixteenth century. When the Company of Mineral and Battery Works was looking for sites for its proposed wire-drawing mills in the 1560s, its surveyors scoured the tributaries of the Severn estuary for 40 miles around Bristol searching for suitable locations. They found these water courses already crowded with grist- and fulling-mills. Not until the surveyors crossed into Monmouthshire did they find a site—in a remote valley next to Tintern Abbey where the Angidy flows into the Wye.[26]

The proliferation of water-mills increased the competition for water rights. John Norden pointed out that the damming of streams to make ponds could be highly profitable for the landlord. Ponds not only furnished power for all kinds of mills but also provided

[24] Hill, *Medieval Lincoln*, p. 337; Coleman, 'Labour in the English Economy of the Seventeenth Century', pp. 280–95; Cox, *The Royal Forests of England*, pp. 181–201.
[25] Nef, *The Rise of the British Coal Industry*, i. 240, 355–8, ii. 449–51; Coleman, *Industry in Tudor and Stuart England*, pp. 16, 38; *A History of Technology*, ed. C. Singer *et al.* (7 vols.; New York, 1957–), iii. 50, 324–34.
[26] M. B. Donald, *Elizabethan Monopolies: The History of the Company of Mineral and Battery Works from 1565 to 1604* (Edinburgh, 1961), pp. 87–8.

a harvest of fish that was much in demand on the London market. However, landlords found it difficult to keep the millers' servants from helping themselves to the fish in the mill ponds while neighbouring landlords and tenants were frequently inconvenienced by the alteration of watercourses and flooding, and protested by destroying the heads of offending mill-ponds. In the Isle of Purbeck in Dorsetshire, Morden Heath had been considered a quagmire before the farmer of the manor of Morden dug several drainage ditches which led into a pond constructed to serve a new mill. The commoners could no longer water their cattle on the heath and the miller had enclosed the millpond with hedges to deny them access. The tenants of Morden, stirred up by a gentleman who also operated a mill in the neighbourhood which no longer had adequate water power, hired vagrants to help them destroy the dam, level the hedges, and raze cottages built upon the waste. William Vaughan, the new lord of Morden, saw himself as an agricultural improver who was making better use of Morden Heath, but his tenants kept up their violent protests for many months between 1597 and 1599. On lands belonging to Henry, Lord Berkeley in Stone, Gloucestershire, the opening of a second grist-mill made it necessary to increase the height of a weir gate. This raised the level of the millpond by a mere six inches but flooded 16 acres of meadow previously worth 30s. an acre annually. Several tenants took to a boat and chopped the new weir gate to pieces while a suit in Common Pleas was pending. When Lord Paget built his new blast furnace and hydraulic forges on Cannock Chase in the 1570s, he altered the watercourses in such a way that the existing grist- and fulling mills were deprived of power. When the furnace and forges operated, the discharge of water was so effusive that houses and barns were flooded and his tenants were deprived of pastures that they customarily used at that time of year.[27]

From the late sixteenth century until the early nineteenth century the rivers Stour and Tame in Staffordshire and their tributaries came to be the most exploited watercourses in England as the metal-working industries of the Black Country grew. Although nail-making remained a primitive operation in the nailers' cottages, the industry's

---

[27] John Norden, *The Surveyor's Dialogue* (1607), 218–20, printed in *Seventeenth-century Economic Documents*, ed. Thirsk and Cooper, p. 115; PRO, STAC 5/V8/24, V6/18, V9/5; STAC 8/81/8; STAC 5/P63/16.

expansion was facilitated by several technological innovations: water-powered blast furnaces and forges replaced bloomsmithies and increased the output of iron, coal was substituted for charcoal in the metal-smith's forges, and the introduction of water-powered slitting mills in the 1620s automated the production of rod iron. The Tame and Stour were swift enough to turn water-wheels without the expense of dams and millponds, and grist-mills and blade-mills for edged tools already lined their banks when the multifarious metal-working mills as well as paper-mills crowded in amongst the older mills. All remained busy until the coming of steam.[28]

Next to the erosion of common-pasture rights, the loss of common of estovers, firebote, and housebote was the most frequent cause of agrarian protest. The wood-fuel shortage cannot be blamed entirely on the consumption of iron furnaces and the growth of rural industry. The supply of firewood was also threatened by the need for more agricultural land as well as the widespread seigneurial assault upon wastes and commons in the search for quick profits. The common right of gathering wood for fuel or for the construction and repair of dwellings was usually regulated by licence of the manorial lord, which generally had to be purchased. Timber stealing had not yet been defined as the statutory crime of larceny, but rather was punished in manorial courts under the heading of 'committing waste' or was actionable in the royal courts as a trespass. Wood stealing was not confined to cutting and taking trees in the usual sense of the phrase, but could also extend to cutting furze or gorse on heathlands or pillaging hedgerows—which shows how desperate the poor were for fuel.[29] What is called wood stealing by the authorities often consisted of attempts by tenants, cottagers, or even squatters to revive traditional common rights of gathering fallen wood. The latter had probably never possessed such rights; yet their claim, however specious, lent an air of legitimacy to their endeavours.

Large-scale disputes about timber use-rights, where the commoners organized themselves and carried off 20 or 30 cart-loads of timber or turves, became common after the middle of the sixteenth century. Since the manorial lords were usually attempting to improve the fees for licences to exercise all use-rights, such instances of carrying off

[28] Court, *The Rise of the Midland Industries*, pp. 100–3, 110–13.
[29] Hammersley, 'The Charcoal Iron Industry and its Fuel, 1540–1750', p. 608; Emmison, *Elizabethan Life: Home, Work, and Land*, pp. 250–8.

wood, peat, and coal were often combined with disputes about common of pasture, as in the case of Wychwood Forest, Oxfordshire, where the tenants of Langley Manor kept up a running battle with their lords, the Untons, for more than 40 years. The attempt by William, third Earl of Worcester in 1587 to increase the fees charged for common of pasture and estovers on the manor of Tretower, Brecknockshire caused his tenants to protest by carrying away 40 wains of oak timber. When the Earl brought an action of trespass against the Tretower tenants at Hereford Assizes, the jury found for the tenants. The women of Enfield in April 1603 stayed carts attempting to carry wood from Enfield Chase to the King's palace at Theobalds saying that by custom the wood should either be burnt in the royal hunting lodge at Enfield or given to the poor. As was the case with the shipment of grain, there was a strong popular prejudice against exporting firewood from a local community, and a large riot broke out in Brigstock Park in May 1603 when the inhabitants of Stanion and several other towns in Rockingham Forest protested Sir Robert Cecil's sale of wood from the forest.[30]

The shortage of fuel was especially acute in early-Stuart Leicester. Neighbouring landowners claimed that wood-stealing was rife. The mayor of Leicester perceived that the preservation of public order required him to be alert to anything that might disrupt the supplies of wood and coal for the market. In 1617 the mayor complained to the Earl of Huntingdon, lord lieutenant and chief forester of Leicester Forest, that the latter's kinsman, Sir Henry Hastings of Kirby, was extorting money from the carters who carried coal through the forest to Leicester market. This practice threatened to deprive the poor of their fuel, which the borough corporation subsidized.[31]

While shortages of timber did not significantly retard the expansion of the English iron industry in the long run, heavy cutting of timber did cause hardship and conflict in several sylvan communities. This was certainly the case in the Forest of Dean in the first half of the seventeenth century, where the new blast furnaces had a larger

---

[30] PRO, STAC 3/1/86; DL 1/81/A20; STAC 5/U1/27, U3/35, W57/13; SP 14/1/25, 65, 76. There was a regulation in the Forest of Essex, known as the Loughton Rule, which forbade the selling of firewood outside the forest: W. R. Fisher, *The Forest of Essex: Its History, Laws and Ancient Customs* (1887), 256.

[31] L. Fox and P. Russell, *Leicester Forest* (Leicester, 1948), 99–100; *Records of the Borough of Leicester, 1603–1688*, ed. Stocks, pp. 121, 135, 168.

capacity than those of the Weald. Between the 1590s and the 1620s, 11 blast furnaces and 13 forges were crowded into an area of 50 square miles, and at the peak of production turned out 7,500 tons of pig- and bar-iron a year—an output that would have required the replanting of 60,000 acres of timber a year to sustain it. The spoliation of Dean Forest contributed to several popular uprisings and even outraged crown officials. The third Earl of Pembroke lost his lease for a time and Sir Edward Winter, a local landowner and Queen Henrietta Maria's secretary, was prosecuted. The number of ironworks in Dean Forest also was curtailed.[32]

Richard de Burgh, Earl of Clanricarde was another courtier who ruthlessly destroyed timber resources for iron-founding. He acquired the manor of Ross Foreign in Herefordshire by right of his wife Frances, widow of the second Earl of Essex. The Earl of Essex had established a furnace in Bishop's Wood in about 1592, and by 1604 the tenants of the adjoining manor of Walford claimed that Clanricarde had cut down 30,000 oaks and beeches and that if the felling continued at the same rate the timber would be depleted in another three of four years. The tenants of Walford, fearing that Clanricarde meant to deprive them of their common pasture and estovers, collected a common purse, retained legal counsel, and petitioned the King to restrain Clanricarde and remove the illegal cottages in Bishop's Wood. The sheriff was ordered to remove the cottages, in which lived Clanricarde's wood-cutters, charcoal-burners, and foundry-workers—amounting to 100 men, women, and children altogether—but the Walford tenants riotously anticipated the execution of the order. There were at least four separate riots directed at Clanricarde's workmen in 1603.[33]

By the end of the sixteenth century it was the usual practice for land-owners to lease their furnaces and forges to iron-masters. Landlords were dismayed to discover that iron-workers frequently cut so much wood that insufficient cover remained for breeding game. Often the game was removed as well. When Lord Abergavenny's servants

---

[32] Hammersley, 'The Charcoal Iron Industry and its Fuel, 1540–1750', pp. 607–8; Sharp, *In Contempt of All Authority*, pp. 191–2, 199. Henry, second Earl of Pembroke's tenants on his Usk Valley estates in Monmouthshire also obstructed his efforts to make charcoal and smelt iron at his Monkswood furnace for a decade in the 1570s and 1580s: PRO, STAC 5/P66/5, P45/16, P51/22, P28/11, P12/19, Y3/15; Donald, *Elizabethan Monopolies*, pp. 98, 110, 113.

[33] PRO, STAC 8/84/18.

attempted to compel the iron-masters who leased his Rotherfield, Sussex works to honour their contract with respect to cutting wood and preserving game, the latter menaced them with shovels full of red-hot coals. The use of woodland for both game parks and charcoal fuel was clearly incompatible.[34]

Tenants suffered even greater losses from iron-founding and the mining of minerals. The lord of the manor usually possessed the mineral rights throughout the manor and could dig for coal or iron-ore on his tenants' lands. On the manor of Petworth, the seventh Earl of Northumberland's servants, when excavating ore or cutting timber for charcoal upon tenants' lands, were disregardful of the tenants' hedges and fences, and cattle fell into the pits. At first the ironstone pits were filled in, but the reclaimed land would not sustain corn-growing and bore little if any grass. It was generally agreed in the neighbourhood that it took reclaimed land 40 years to recover.[35]

The small bloomery furnaces of medieval times had disturbed the environment but little. In the Weald of Sussex, Kent, and Surrey it was not difficult to travel upon the forest roads by horse in the fifteenth century, but by the seventeenth century the heavy traffic introduced by the larger-scale methods of iron-founding associated with blast furnaces and hydraulic forges had reduced Wealden roads to an impassable mire, which coaches could navigate only when drawn by teams of oxen. The primary consideration in the location of blast furnaces and hydraulic forges was water power; large mills required separate ponds and had to be spread out along watercourses. The iron-ore and charcoal had to be hauled to the furnaces; the cast-iron sows and pigs had to be drawn from furnaces to forges or to gun foundries. Thus the Wealden clay was continually churned up on the forest roads. This and the destruction of timberland caused soil erosion and the silting up of harbours and navigable rivers, which contributed to the decline of several Sussex and Kentish ports.[36]

The more primitive bloomery was a small furnace equipped with hand bellows, which could smelt about two hundredweight of iron

[34] E. Straker, *Wealden Iron* (repr. New York, 1969), 346; PRO, STAC 5/A2/25.

[35] Jerrome, *Cloakbag and Common Purse*, pp. 67–8; Straker, *Wealden Iron*, p. 428.

[36] Ibid. 182–6; C. Thomas-Stanford, *Sussex in the Great Civil War* (1910), 6–7; R. B. Manning, *Religion and Society in Elizabethan Sussex: A Study of the Enforcement of the Religious Settlement, 1558–1603* (Leicester, 1969), 4–8.

blooms in about 12 to 14 hours. The bloom or spongy mass of iron was worked by hand immediately, without reheating, in order to produce wrought iron. Bloomsmithies could use bog iron and other inferior ores with high sulphur and phosphorus contents and still produce a pure grade of wrought iron. However, bloomery furnaces could not keep up with the increased demand of the sixteenth and seventeenth centuries nor could they be heated to a sufficiently high temperature to produce the cast iron which was needed by gun foundries. Thus blast furnaces gradually replaced bloomeries, first in the Weald, then spreading in the reign of Elizabeth to tributaries of the Severn in Glamorgan and Monmouthshire, and finally to the Forest of Dean, the west Midlands, and the Sheffield region. Blast furnaces could smelt two or three tons of cast-iron pigs at a time, but made heavier demands upon fuel and water power relative to the amount of iron produced. They burned more charcoal per unit of iron, and such was the consumption of water by blast furnaces and forge hammers that each required a separate millpond and therefore a separate location. Blast furnaces also needed higher grades of iron-ore which often had to be brought from a distance. Lead-smelting technology evolved in an analogous manner. Primitive furnaces called 'boles', which were open on the windward side, were later equipped with foot-powered bellows; in the sixteenth century hydraulic blast furnaces for copper and lead smelting spread through the Pennines and the Lake District. Again, the introduction of the new technologies increased the consumption of fuel and water power.[37]

In the Kentish Weald iron-masters competed for dwindling wood supplies with glass furnaces and cloth-dyers. During the war years of the 1590s the blast furnaces and gun foundries were operating at capacity, while the clothing industry was in the midst of a deep depression. Tension was especially acute in the populous parish of Cranbrook, which was the centre of the Kentish clothing industry and also the location of six ironworks. In an attempt to relieve unemployment, the Cranbrook clothiers had promoted parliamentary bills to preserve the woods and prohibit the erection of new furnaces

[37] Court, *The Rise of Midland Industries, 1600–1838*, p. 80; H. R. Schubert, *History of the British Iron and Steel Industry from c.450 B.C. to A.D. 1775* (1957), 152, 158; Hammersley, 'The Charcoal Iron Industry and its Fuel, 1540–1750', p. 595; Raistrick and Jennings, *A History of Lead Mining in the Pennines*, pp. 75–9, 118.

within eight miles of Cranbrook without success. By 1594 there were severe shortages of grain and domestic fuel. The clothiers attempted to fix the blame for the shortages and unemployment on the iron-masters, and conspiracies to attack a hammer mill in Cranbrook and a gun foundry in Horsemonden were uncovered. Ultimately, this competition for wood-fuel drove up the price and contributed to the decline of the Wealden iron industry.[38]

In the Forest of Dean the principal opposition to the introduction of large-scale iron-smelting came from the free miners of Dean. During the sixteenth century they were an integral part of an iron industry in which bloomsmithies supplied the needs of nailers and other metalsmiths. The ore was dug by the free miners, who were notoriously resentful of outsiders. Early in the reign of James I a number of courtiers expressed interest in exploiting the resources of Dean Forest for large-scale iron production, and in February 1612 William, third Earl of Pembroke, constable of St Briavels Castle and governor of the Company of Mineral and Battery Works, was granted exclusive rights to all minerals and woodland in the forest except naval timber. The miners' ancient privilege of free-mining, based upon custom and long usage rather than charter, was ignored when Pembroke was granted a monopoly on the digging of ironstone and coal. Moreover, Pembroke imported a number of labourers from the Sussex Weald. On 14 August 1612, 15 miners set fire to wood that Pembroke's servants had begun cutting and stacking on a Sunday morning when they thought the miners would be in church. The main cause of the riot was the infringement of the free-miners' privileges, but the miners were also alarmed by the rumour that Pembroke, already a much-hated man in the area, was to be allowed to take 12,000 cords of wood per year. Moreover, the miners continued to dig ore in spite of Pembroke's monopoly, and he brought suit against them in the Court of Exchequer in 1613. Because of the great poverty of the miners, who claimed that they depended almost entirely upon their digging for a livelihood, the court allowed the miners to continue digging limited amounts of minerals 'of charity and grace, not of right'. The Earl of Northampton expressed the opinion that

[38] Clark, 'Popular Protest and Disturbance in Kent, 1558-1640', pp. 371-3; Straker, *Wealden Iron*, pp. 125-6; C. W. Chalklin, *Seventeenth-century Kent: A Social and Economic History* (1965), 132-3; Hammersley, 'The Charcoal Iron Industry and its Fuel, 1540-1750', p. 596.

the miners of Dean were no better than 'Robin Hoods' and criticized the inability of the Gloucestershire magistrates to apprehend or restrain them. The miners refused to accept a settlement that so diminished their privileges, and were accused of binding themselves together by oaths and bonds to defy Pembroke. They continued to dig for minerals and shipped their ore to Ireland instead of selling it only to Pembroke at much-reduced prices. Some of the miners, who were freeholders and small farmers in Newnham parish, claimed that Pembroke's timber felling impinged upon their use-rights in the forest. They also maintained that they could not make a living if they were allowed to sell their ore only to Pembroke at his prices. Furthermore, it is clear that Pembroke exceeded the annual quota established for cord-wood and that his servants were also felling oaks marked for naval use.[39]

The introduction of blast furnaces to Cannock Chase in the reign of Elizabeth severely damaged the natural environment and precipitated open conflict between the Lords Paget and their tenants and neighbours. The iron industry was well established on Cannock Chase long before William, first Lord Paget acquired in 1546 numerous estates, formerly belonging to Burton College and the Bishops of Coventry and Lichfield, which surrounded that huge waste. Iron was still smelted in bloomery furnaces, although a water-powered forge hammer was operating as early as 1485. At first the Pagets farmed out their ironworks, but Henry, second Lord Paget began managing them himself in 1561. He soon erected the first blast furnace in the Midlands, and a total of three were in operation by 1578. There were also hammer mills and, later, a glass furnace. The alteration of watercourses was especially damaging, and, as in the Weald, the roads quickly deteriorated. Extensive wood-felling, coal-mining, and coppicing for future charcoal supplies consumed large amounts of woodland and grazing land, and provoked numerous protests.[40]

Henry, second Lord Paget and his brother, Thomas, the third lord, alienated the local gentry by their ruthless disregard of the common rights of the manorial communities surrounding Cannock Chase. In

[39] Hart, *The Free Miners of the Royal Forest of Dean*, pp. 165–74; id., *Royal Forest: A History of Dean's Woods as Producers of Timber* (Oxford, 1966), 86–93; *VCH Gloucestershire*, ii. 272.

[40] *VCH Staffordshire*, ii. 109–11, vi. 79; PRO, STAC 5/P60/40, P54/6, P63/16; S. M. Jack, *Trade and Industry in Tudor and Stuart England* (1977), 146–51.

1564 Thomas Rugeley, esq., of Hawksyard led several large poaching affrays against the second Lord Paget's game. Between August 1580 and February 1581 the hedges surrounding two large coppices and an enclosed pasture were attacked and burned under cover of darkness on five separate occasions by crowds of more than 30 persons. One of the leaders, Robert Chetwynd, belonged to a family who were lords of Brereton Manor and rival iron-masters, while another, Thomas Adams, was a constable. The protesters came from more than 15 villages surrounding Cannock Chase and most of them seem to have been Paget's own tenants from the manor of Rugeley. Their grievances were numerous and they complained of loss of common rights, the decay of grist- and fulling mills, the building of 50 illegal cottages, and, generally, the harmful consequences of Paget's iron-works. In August 1581 servants of Sir Walter Aston of Tixall, while cutting firewood on Cannock Chase, were attacked and beaten by 20 of Paget's servants, whose numbers were augmented by a dozen or so toughs brought up from London.[41]

The leaders of the Cannock enclosure riots were fined £40 by the Court of Star Chamber and the participants £20 each. All were ordered imprisoned in the Fleet. But Thomas, Lord Paget's triumph was brief. He was suspected of complicity in the Throckmorton Plot and fled to Paris in 1583. He was attainted and his estates and ironworks confiscated by the Crown and leased to Richard Bagot. Lord Burghley wished to continue the operation of the furnaces and forges, but at the same time expressed a desire not to exhaust the timber supply nor oppress the poor any further.[42]

James I restored the family estates to William, fourth Lord Paget, who was raised as a Protestant. He preferred to farm out his mines and ironworks on Cannock Chase and to compose the differences with his numerous tenants. A Chancery decree of 1606 ratified an agreement that ended tenurial disputes, confirmed common rights on Cannock Chase, and limited the practice of coppicing young trees

---

[41] PRO, STAC 5/P12/25, P7/7, P60/40, P54/6, P63/16, A13/1; Jack, *Trade and Industry in Tudor and Stuart England*, pp. 146–51.

[42] BL, Harley MSS, 2143, fo. 11; *Roman Catholicism in Elizabethan and Jacobean Staffordshire: Documents from the Bagot Papers*, ed. A. G. Petti (Collections for a History of Staffordshire, 4th ser. 159; 1979), 9–14; *VCH Staffordshire*, ii. 111.

for charcoal supplies to nine years, after which the enclosed coppices were to be thrown open to commoning.[43]

Coal-mining was an especially disruptive activity. Mining and agriculture necessarily coexisted, but the constantly shifting workings destroyed the fertility of the soil and impinged upon both property rights and common rights of tenants. Coal-mining was not subjected to special jurisdictions or peculiar customs, as was the case with the tin-miners of Cornwall or the lead-miners of the Mendip Hills. This was because coal-mining, unlike lead- and tin-mining, was widely dispersed and was an integral part of the economies and customs of many manorial communities in England and Wales. Manorial custom varied widely concerning whether copyhold tenants, or even freeholders, might dig for coal on their own holdings or refuse access to the lord. On the manorial waste, however, the lord possessed something approaching absolute control over minerals. In any case, manorial custom governing access to minerals was disintegrating as the coal-mining industry expanded. Hence, coal-mining was especially conducive to litigation and violent conflict. James Clifford, coal-mining entrepreneur and lord of the manor of Broseley in Shropshire, was accused of instigating 40 or 50 lawsuits against 50 or 60 persons in 1606.[44]

In many manorial communities where alternative fuels were unavailable, tenants had long claimed the right to take coal from the waste for household fuel. When the lord of the manor granted licences for commercial exploitation of coal, the tenants found themselves excluded from a resource which they had taken for granted, or discovered that the easily-gained coal near the surface was consumed quickly and that deeper workings required special skills and equipment. Tenants brought suits to re-establish their claims, but often discovered that they had to pay something approaching the commercial price for what they got. In parts of Lancashire the shortage of wood compelled the use of coal as a household fuel early in the sixteenth century. The Duchy of Lancaster's lease of mineral rights on the manors of Hindley and Ightonhill provoked large riots in

[43] PRO, C. 78/165/8; cf. ch. 6 above for a fuller discussion of the Chancery decree of 1606.
[44] Nef, *The Rise of the British Coal Industry* i. 286–9, 305–10; PRO, STAC 8/310/16.

the late 1520s when the crown farmers excluded the tenants from the manorial coal pits.[45]

Coal-mining considerably diminished the space and resources of the manorial waste and caused environmental damage. On the manor of Hindley, the relatively rudimentary coal-mining facilities, including pits, a dozen workmen's cottages, gardens, barns, and pastures for the miners' animals severed 20 acres of common grazing land. Tenants' animals frequently fell into unfenced, open pits, and undermined lands subsided. New excavations and tunnelling required a constant supply of pit-props. At Chilvers Coton, Warwickshire 12 acres of woodland were stripped for pit-props, and the area was then coppiced and enclosed for new growth. The colliery operator still had to purchase £150 worth of timber per year elsewhere. The Chilvers Coton works were deep enough to require a pumping engine, which was driven by a water-wheel powered by water from a dammed pool. The water-wheel was supplemented by a horse-mill in dry seasons. When workings went as deep as 22 yards, as was the case at Bradford, Lancashire, the pumping engines and other equipment represented a heavy capital investment and were vulnerable to machine-smashing riots by unhappy commoners, jealous rivals, and disgruntled workmen. Wooden railways, such as the one employed at Broseley early in the seventeenth century remained rare until the next century. Wains and pack-horses were the usual means of transportation and over-taxed the primitive roads. The 500 horses and 100 oxen which conveyed coal from Kingswood Chase to Bristol must have consumed a prodigious amount of grass and fodder. Yet other forms of mineral extraction were even more devastating than coal-mining. The mining and smelting of lead was an especially toxic activity because it poisoned streams and ponds and made it impossible to raise animals.[46]

The most important source of coal in the Midlands was the East Shropshire coalfield. James Clifford, lord of the manor of Broseley

[45] M. J. Ellis, 'A Study in the Manorial History of Halifax Parish in the Sixteenth and Early Seventeenth Centuries, Part II', *Yorks. Arch. Journal* 61 (1961), 421–2; Nef, *The Rise of the British Coal Industry*, i. 317; *Pleadings and Depositions in the Duchy Court of Lancaster*, ed. Fishwick, pp. 138, 161–71, 181–2.

[46] Ibid. 161–71; PRO, STAC 8/152/20, 106/7; *VCH Warwickshire*, ii. 219; Martin, *Feudalism to Capitalism*, p. 189; Nef, *The Rise of the British Coal Industry*, i. 355, 375 n., 383; ii. 15; Raistrick and Jennings, *A History of Lead Mining in the Pennines*, pp. 182–3; Gough, *The Mines of Mendip*, pp. 12, 70–1.

exploited this rich vein by tunnelling into the banks of the Severn Gorge and shipping the coal by river to Shrewsbury, Worcester, and Gloucester. As early as 1575 he was reprimanded for dumping his slag and rubbish into the river. In 1607, Clifford claimed that he had invested £2,000 in his mine works. He also built 25 cottages on the manorial waste for his colliers, whom the freeholders and tenants regarded as the 'Scumes & dreggs of many countreys'. Several of the freeholders and tenants, including Rowland Lacon, esq., and Richard Willcox, gent. also mined considerable quantities of coal on their own holdings, but lacked access to the river and were forbidden by Clifford to transport the coal across the waste to the Severn docks. Clifford had begun digging pits and shafts on tenants' lands and wanted especially to mine the rich deposits that lay under a close in the hands of Willcox. While each side waged law against the other, the dispute took a more violent turn during the years 1605–7. In May 1605 Lacon and Willcox procured the destruction of the miners' cottages and mining equipment on the manorial waste under pretence of reclaiming their common of pasture. Two people were seriously wounded. Lacon, Willcox, and the tenants then laid a wooden railway, one of the first in England, across the waste to the quayside. In November 1607 Clifford led a mob of his own workmen in the night-time and destroyed the railway. Willcox counter-attacked against the cottages which housed Clifford's workmen and the battle lasted for three days and three nights. Clifford paid his hired rioters 12*d.* for their labours and also provided them with 20*s.* worth of ale in a single night, which both amazed and horrified Willcox. None of the procurers of these riots seems to have been punished, but in 1611 the Court of Star Chamber did fine four of Lacon's servants in amounts ranging from £300 to 200 marks.[47]

In the North Riding a group of very obstinate Yorkshiremen succeeded in defending their commons and obstructing Sir Stephen Procter's efforts to mine coal for nearly two decades. Procter, the purchaser of Fountains Abbey, was attempting to reopen lead and coal mines formerly exploited by the monks in the Forest of Nidderdale. His digging of coal on Thorpe Moor, which the Earl of Derby and his tenants of Kirkby Malzeard claimed as commons,

[47] Trinder, *The Industrial Revolution in Shropshire*, pp. 5, 10; Nef, *The Rise of the British Coal Industry*, i. 144, 308–9; PRO, STAC 8/86/18, 310/16; BL, Stowe MSS, 397, fos. 22ᵛ–23.

provoked an attack in 1601 upon Procter's miners by 200 tenants led by the manorial bailiff and the town constable. The riot was a well-organized affair, procured by Derby's farmer with the Earl's consent. The watchword for the protesters to assemble and organize themselves into companies and march to Thorpe Moor was 'Arise and take a poke pudding in thy hand'. When Procter's colliers attempted to resume digging on Thorpe Moor in May 1607 they were assaulted and wounded by 'Captain Dorothy' and 37 women wielding coal knives and throwing stones. The attacks continued throughout the month of June. Procter claimed that although 'Captain Dorothy' Dawson and the other leaders were wives of substantial tenants and freeholders, most of the women were cottagers and paupers who were theatened with eviction, denial of alms, and banishment if they did not co-operate. After Procter got the female rioters bound over to keep the peace, they continued their attacks on the miners through October, but worked two at a time, thinking they could avoid prosecution for riot.[48]

Meanwhile, the Earl of Derby had begun surveying Thorpe Moor and other wastes intending to sever, enclose, and improve 3,100 acres of the 30,000 acres of waste that he claimed belonged to the manor of Kirkby Malzeard. His efforts to work out an enclosure agreement were halted by Procter's claim to the waste as parcel of Fountains Abbey; mediation by the Earl of Salisbury upheld Procter's claim. When Procter began to make enclosures, 200 tenants tore them down in October 1608. In order to be 'ridd of . . . Sir Stephen Procter whom they much feared', the tenants persuaded Elizabeth, Countess of Derby to purchase the 400 acres on Thorpe Moor for £500 in exchange for allowing the Earl of Derby to enclose one-third of the moor. When the Earl began to enclose 100 acres and convert to tillage, the tenants refused to honour their agreement. Roger Dawson, perhaps a kinsman of Captain Dorothy, led 40 disguised protesters in a midnight attack on Derby's enclosures in May 1615. Twice in 1616 the Earl attempted to rebuild the enclosures and twice they were torn down; cattle caught within the closes were killed or maimed.[49]

[48] Raistrick and Jennings, *A History of Lead Mining in the Pennines*, pp. 58–9; PRO, STAC 8/4/3, 227/3. In the 'Captain Dorothy' Riot case of 1607 it is significant that the Star Chamber regarded the husbands as principals and compelled them to answer Procter's bill of complaint.   [49] PRO, STAC 8/20/23.

Great difficulty was encountered in prosecuting the commoners who protested the intakes of commons made by Sir Stephen Procter and the Earl of Derby. When Procter complained that the villagers of Grantley, Winkesley, and Gawhay had destroyed his enclosures on the waste where they intercommoned, the latter secured his prosecution for forging a writ of distringas against them.[50] Three different attorney-generals prosecuted the Kirkby Malzeard tenants for riot in the Court of Star Chamber. It took Sir Edward Coke three years to gather enough evidence to bring the culprits in the Poke-Pudding Riot of 1601 before the Court because witnesses who attempted to testify were beaten up. Sir Francis Bacon observed that the Kirkby Malzeard tenants only observed 'Clubb lawe' in their land disputes. As late as 1617 Procter was still trying to obtain a conviction in the case of a riot that had occurred seven years earlier; the Star Chamber judges refused to sentence the defendants because several of them were still awaiting trial at common law on a charge of committing murder during the riot. The Court of Star Chamber refused to prejudice the cause of the defendants, even though the murder case was unlikely to go to trial because many of the witnesses had died.[51]

The tragic fate of the commons intensified poverty. As long as pasture- and fuel-rights remained adequate the community was able to carry the cost of poor relief without unwonted hardship to the ratepayers. But the demands of agricultural improvement, fiscal seigneurialism, fuel and water consumption by rural industries, and encroachment by squatters all diminished the space and resources of wastes and commons. Such communities continued to be torn by disorder during the period of the Civil Wars and the Interregnum and provided fertile ground for the growth of radical sects.[52]

The problem of poverty needs more study. No sylvan community developed enough industry in the seventeenth century to provide full employment. In many instances it was a pool of cheap labour that attracted entrepreneurs in the first place, and rural industrial development cannot be blamed for failing to eradicate a problem

---

[50] A writ of distringas would have compelled the villagers to pay the costs of rebuilding the fences.

[51] PRO, STAC 8/4/3, 16/120, 20/23; BL, Stowe MSS, 397, fos. 39ʳ&ᵛ.

[52] Thirsk, 'Seventeenth-century Agriculture and Social Change', pp. 172–3.

that already existed. There is reason to believe that those who could combine a trade with some agricultural activity were more prosperous than smallholders in fielden areas. But in the seventeenth and eighteenth centuries, Staffordshire metalsmiths kept fewer animals because of the declining resources of commons. Clearly, they were becoming more impoverished.[53]

[53] Frost, 'Yeomen and Metalsmiths', pp. 40–1.

11

Poaching

AT first glance, game-poaching appears to be a more primitive form of social protest than the anti-enclosure riot. Yet closer examination reveals that the authorities considered game-poaching to be a more explicit challenge to the concept of aristocracy. Poaching has its roots in that love of hunting and fishing that is to be found in all rural societies.[1] This most universal of sports was gradually transformed into a crime in late-medieval and early-modern England by Acts of Parliament which defined hunting as an exclusively aristocratic privilege and declared parks and ponds to be private property. Countrymen persisted in believing that wild places and bodies of water, and the beasts and fishes that dwelled therein, could not be appropriated by an individual. Like the seigneurial assault upon wastes and woodland, this attempt to restrict one of the principal forms of social intercourse to a privileged few provoked widespread violent protest. Most cases of poaching prosecuted at the assizes and quarter sessions appear to have arisen out of attacks upon the enclosed deer-parks of peers and the greater gentry. Beginning late in the reign of Elizabeth and continuing under the early Stuarts, the punishment of those who hunted deer was referred to the Court of Star Chamber. A more vigorous enforcement of the game laws went hand-in-hand with a more exalted view of the royal prerogative and a determination to impose a greater degree of social regulation upon servants, artificers, and masterless men.

Most late-Elizabethan and early-Stuart prosecutions for game-poaching involved taking deer or hares. Yet common law did not recognize deer and hares as game, strictly speaking, because they were wild beasts and thus belonged to no one. Such wild beasts were things of pleasure rather than profit and no price could be put upon them. Therefore one could not commit the common-law crime of grand larceny by stealing deer or hares, because an individual could

---

[1] Barnes, *Somerset, 1625–1640*, pp. 29–30; cf. also Bloch, *French Rural History*, p. 182.

not possess them and because the value of the thing stolen had to be specified in order to secure an indictment for felonious theft.[2] No statute ever made deer-stealing *per se* a crime. Yet between the fourteenth and the eighteenth centuries, Parliament succeeded in making every conceivable circumstance in which a commoner might hunt a deer or course a hare a crime. A crime was committed if a person without sufficient estate possessed dogs, nets, or weapons used for hunting, broke into a park, or hunted at night or in disguise. Indeed, Henrician and Edwardian legislation made some of these offences capital felonies, but such extreme measures were eschewed by Elizabethan and Jacobean parliaments. There was in the Tudor and early-Stuart periods a clear tendency to extend the doctrine of private property to enclosed deer-parks and fish-ponds and to protect the breeding-grounds of young animals for the purpose of preserving game for royal and aristocratic sport and pleasure. The effect was to partially domesticate wild animals and to assert that they could be stolen.[3]

Within the context of aristocratic culture hunting was not merely sport; it was also a rehearsal for war. Gentlemen poachers frequently wore helmets, corslets, and shirts of chain mail, and invariably carried offensive weapons. At the same time it was axiomatic that artificers and servants should not be allowed to hunt because it was 'under such Colour [that] they make their Assemblies, Conferences, and Conspiracies for to rise and disobey their Allegiance'. Thus, major rebellions were often followed by the enactment of more severe game laws. Following the Great Revolt of 1381 a statute of Richard II prohibited hunting for laymen who did not possess lands or tenements worth 40s. a year and for clerics who did not have an annual income of £10. Henry VII's first Parliament made hunting in disguise or hunting at night a felony in an attempt to suppress disorders which were said to be especially widespread in Kent, Sussex, and Surrey. The mid-Tudor rebellions were followed by similar legislation. The Henrician laws of 1539 and 1540 made it felony to break the head of a fish-pond or to enter the King's forest or anyone's park at night or in disguise with an attempt to hunt. These penalties were allowed

---

[2] *The Reports of Sir John Spelman*, ed. J. H. Baker (2 vols.; Selden Soc. 93–4; 1976, 1978), ii. 316–22; P. B. Munsche, *Gentlemen and Poachers: The English Game Laws, 1671–1831* (Cambridge, 1981), 3–4.
[3] Ibid.; 31 Hen. VIII, cc. 2, 12, *SR* iii. 718, 731; 32 Hen. VIII, c. 11, *SR* iii. 755–6; 5 Eliz. I, c. 2, *SR* iv. 449.

to expire upon the accession of Edward VI, only to be revived following the rebellions of 1549. It was also reasoned that hunting was not a fit activity for those who should be following the plough or working at a trade, because it encouraged idleness. By the beginning of the eighteenth century it was assumed that poaching led to a life of crime.[4]

It was not only the exclusion of the commonalty that made the game laws conducive to social conflict. Many members of the lesser gentry also were denied the right to hunt. An Act of 1544 specified that no person having an estate of less than £100 per year might possess, carry, or hunt with handguns or cross-bows. The Game Acts of 1603 and 1605 restricted the possession of hunting dogs, nets, and guns to armigerous gentry and their heirs, £10 freeholders, and £30 copyholders. The property qualifications for those taking partridges or pheasants were even higher. Qualified persons might confiscate cross-bows, guns, nets, setters, lurchers, and greyhounds found in the possession of unqualified persons. Thus younger sons and gentlemen tenants were frequently to be found in the company of yeomen, husbandmen, and the like, breaking into the game preserves of elder brothers, courtiers, and peers. In actual practice the sport of the chase was never confined only to qualified persons possessing hunting franchises; landowners cultivated support among tenants and neighbours with invitations to hunt or gifts of game. This was part of the traditional exercise of 'good lordship'. It also served to reinforce the distinction between the magnate who possessed the right to hunt by virtue of his considerable property, grant of free chase, or royal warrant and those who might hunt only by his sufferance.[5]

Even when a man was qualified by property and social rank to hunt he still needed permission to take game in a particular place. In some cases this might be secured from the manorial lord as lord of the soil, but the manorial lord's hunting rights might be abridged by the revival of the forest laws in the early-Stuart period, by the

[4] Thomas, *Man and the Natural World*, p. 183; Holdsworth, *A History of English Law*, iv. 505–6; Pettit, *The Royal Forests of Northamptonshire*, p. 43; Munsche, *Gentlemen and Poachers*, pp. 11, 180; 13 Rich. II, st. 1, c. 13, *SR*, ii. 65; 1 Hen. VII, c. 7, *SR* ii. 505; 31 Hen. VIII, cc. 2, 12, *SR* iii. 718, 731; 32 Hen. VIII, c. 11, *SR* iii. 755–6.

[5] 33 Hen. VIII, c. 6, *SR* iii. 832; 1 Jac. I, c. 27, *SR* iv. 1055; 3 Jac. I, c. 13, *SR* iv. 1088.

possession by others of the rights of free chase and warren (which did not necessarily belong to the lord if the manor had changed owners by sale and purchase), and by the issuing of royal game-keepers' warrants.[6]

The forests of sixteenth-century England were the remnants of vast hunting preserves established by the Norman kings for their recreation. A forest need not consist of thickly wooded land, but usually did include some woodland and pasture to provide cover and food for deer. Although not actually enclosed, a forest did possess definite boundaries and was subject to forest law, which was administered by Justices in Eyre and officers of the forest. The Tudor monarchs had not employed their prerogative powers to create new forests or to protect game. Indeed, the royal forests were neglected and much encroached upon, and the forest laws were regarded as obsolete by the end of the sixteenth century. Forest offices, however, remained an important source of Crown patronage.[7]

English kings had also rewarded their followers with grants of chase, park and free warren. Permission to hunt in these places could be granted only by the holders of such franchises. A chase was a large unenclosed area with definite boundaries intended to preserve deer for the exclusive sport of the subject to whom it was granted. Some chases, such as Cannock Chase, were formerly royal forests. A park was an enclosure held in severalty and surrounded by fences and hedges for the purpose of breeding and protecting deer. The grant of free warren on a subject's demesne lands gave him exclusive hunting rights over rabbits, hare, pheasants, and partridges. When parks and chases were established within royal forests they were protected by forest law; otherwise poaching was punished by the common-law courts.[8]

James I was obsessed with hunting and he was determined to revive the royal powers of protecting game. He persuaded Parliament to

---

[6] Munsche, *Gentlemen and Poachers*, pp. 9–10.

[7] J. Manwood, *A Treatise of the Lawes of the Forest* (1615; repr. Amsterdam, 1976), fos. 8–22; C. and E. Kirby, 'The Stuart Game Prerogative', *EHR* 46 (1931), 240.

[8] Cox, *The Royal Forests of England*, pp. 2–3; William Harrison, *Description of England* (1587) in Raphael Holinshed, *Holinshed's Chronicles*, ed. Sir Henry Ellis (6 vols.; 1807–8), i. 346; Manwood, *A Treatise of the Lawes of the Forest*, fo. 24^r&^{v}. The use of the term 'warren' to describe an enclosed place used for the breeding of conies or rabbits for the market is more recent: L. Cantor, 'Forests, Chases, Parks and Warrens', in L. Cantor (ed.), *The English Medieval Landscape*, (Philadelphia, 1982), 82.

increase the property qualification for hunting, and he told county magnates that he would hold them responsible for preserving game for his personal sport. The King also issued gamekeepers' warrants to noblemen and courtiers, granting them the necessary authority to enforce the game laws as well as conferring upon them special hunting privileges. Peers might be granted such powers over a whole county. Thus they were in a position to reward their own followers with licences to hunt. Such gamekeepers' warrants frequently conflicted with older rights of free chase and warren and provoked a number of violent encounters between rival hunting parties.[9]

Whereas forests sheltered populations who enjoyed diverse use-rights and supported themselves by a wide variety of agricultural and industrial pursuits, the establishment of parks and warrens had a harmful effect on local economies. Common rights were extinguished and all were excluded except gamekeepers. Because emparkment caused depopulation, it was considered one of the great evils of the age and one of the causes of what mid-Tudor social critics perceived as a decline in military resources. William Harrison thought emparkment was the curse of the Normans, 'who added this Calamatie . . . to the servitude of our nation'; along with other kinds of depopulating enclosure it drove men to rebellion and made it difficult to recruit soldiers so that 'King Henrie the eight . . . was constreined to hire forren aid, for want of competent store of souldiers here at home.' During the riots and rebellions of 1549 parks were attacked, the pales and fences levelled, and the game destroyed. Rumours of James I's proposal to enclose part of Enfield Chase as a deer-park so alarmed the commoners that they 'began to mutyne'; Sir Fulke Greville advised the King to back down because 'this tight sea of busie people is raysed up with every wynde'. Deer-parks had proliferated following the dissolution of the monasteries, and were still numerous in the early seventeenth century. There were as many as 100 of them in Sussex in the 1630s.[10]

---

[9] Kirby, 'The Stuart Game Prerogative', pp. 240–5; *Reports of Cases in the Courts of Star Chamber and High Commission*, ed. S. R. Gardiner (Camden Soc., new ser. 39; 1886), 145–8.

[10] Harrison, *Description of England*, i. 344–5; cf. J. Goring, 'Social Change and Military Decline in Mid-Tudor England', *History* 60 (1975), 185–97; *VCH Hampshire*, iv. 469; Fisher, *The Forest of Essex*, pp. 36–7; *VCH Wiltshire*, iv. 48–9; Fletcher, *A County Community in Peace and War*, p. 28. Cf. also *VCH Surrey*, iv. 430.

The conflicting claims of hunting franchises and game warrants, as well as the resentment of lesser gentry excluded from the right to hunt, contributed much to gentry feuding and manifested that tendency towards violence that was still inherent in aristocratic culture in the early-modern period. The poaching affrays of the aristocracy continued to breed disorder and to offer a corrupt example to their social inferiors. When John Trye of Hardwick, a Gloucestershire JP, went hunting partridges on a young neighbour's lands in 1579, his reason for wearing a corslet and leading 60 'meniall servants, reteyners and tenants' armed with swords and bucklers and halberds was not to protect himself against the sharp beaks of the birds, but rather to provoke a fight with the neighbour's guardian who had already complained against Trye for poaching on earlier occasions. The Lancashire gentry accused of hunting in the Forest of Amounderness in 1531 apparently enjoyed baiting gamekeepers as much as killing the King's deer. They defied the keepers who ordered them out of the forest and flung the heads of the deer they took at the gamekeepers' lodge. The eight days that John Hercy spent hunting deer on the lands of George Wastnes seems excessive, while his slaughter of 16 does and fawns in one day of poaching, in the company of the sheriff of Nottinghamshire, seems wanton. But then some contemporaries thought that it was immoderate for James I to spend one-third of every year hunting while others were disgusted with the delight that the King took in bathing in the gore of stags which he had killed. There seems little danger of over-emphasizing the sheer love of violence that aristocratic sportsmen displayed.[11]

When the Crown granted forest offices without any attempt to delimit overlapping jurisdictions, the consequences were bound to be disruptive. In 1560 Sir Edward Littleton, who claimed to be the forester of the royal hey of Teddesley in Cannock Chase, attempted unsuccessfully to stop Sir Henry Stafford, son and heir of Henry, first Lord Stafford, and his younger brothers and servants from hunting deer. On a subsequent occasion the underkeepers confiscated one of the Staffords' greyhounds, but the Stafford brothers attacked the keepers' lodge, broke down the door, and rescued their hound.

---

[11] PRO, STAC 2/23/52; STAC 5/V8/30; *Pleadings and Depositions in the Duchy Court of Lancaster*, ed. Fishwick, i. 228–9; G. P. V. Akrigg, *Jacobean Pageant, or the Court of King James I* (New York, 1967), 159; D. H. Willson, *King James VI and I* (London, 1963), 180–1.

When the Stafford brothers and 40 armed retainers were confronted on a third occasion by two justices, Sir Henry Stafford showed them a patent making his father deputy ranger for all royal forests in Staffordshire, with the right of taking three does a year. Although the Stafford brothers were allowed to continue hunting, the slight was not forgotten. At the next quarter sessions, Lord Stafford himself, accompanied by 20 armed retainers, attacked Littleton's two brothers-in-law and challenged Littleton to a fight. A brawl followed in the market-place, watched by a crowd of 500 people who had assembled after someone rang the church bells, and it was some time before the other magistrates could restore order. The very next day Lord Stafford's sons picked a quarrel with Sir Walter Aston and another riot broke out.[12]

Many justices of the peace could not be depended upon to punish poachers impartially because they themselves were involved in poaching. The brothers John and Richard Sherborne of Wolfhouse were minor Lancashire gentry but were well-connected. They were accused of killing a deer within the Forest of Bowland and assaulting a gamekeeper. When Sir Richard Houghton, bow-bearer of the forest and a JP, ordered a constable to arrest them, the widowed mother of the Sherborne brothers sent to Richard Sherborne of Stonyhurst, the chief of that clan. Although a JP himself, Sherborne was not wanting in familial loyalty and dispatched his bastard brother, sons, servants, and followers—amounting to 30 in all—to rescue his Sherborne kin from the constable. Richard Sherborne's sons then entered the Forest of Bowland and took deer on two separate occasions. Richard Sherborne of Stonyhurst's father, Sir Richard, had been steward of Bowland Forest, a Duchy of Lancaster office, and he may have wished to make the point that Sherbornes could hunt there whenever they pleased.[13]

In a similar case in Wiltshire in the late 1590s, John Thynne of Longleat used his authority as a justice to protect his friends and servants from prosecution for poaching deer in the Forest of Frome Selwood in Somerset. When royal gamekeepers discovered that Thynne's servants were luring royal deer into Longleat Park, which

[12] PRO, STAC 5/L24/18; BL, Lansdowne MSS, 639, fo. 73.
[13] PRO, STAC 8/15/15; R. B. Manning, 'The Making of a Protestant Aristocracy: the Ecclesiastical Commissioners of the Diocese of Chester, 1550–1598', *BIHR* 49 (1976), 68.

adjoined Frome Selwood, and threatened to make trouble, Thynne prosecuted them in Star Chamber for riot and unlawful hunting.[14]

A violent poaching affray contributed to a notorious feud in Caroline Sussex; the animosity of the two protagonists was subsequently reflected in their political allegiances during the Civil Wars. The extensive estates and political power of Sir Thomas Pelham II, bart. made him a magnate. His deer-park stretched past his mansion of Halland all the way from Laughton to East Hoathly, where it abutted the lands of the Lunsfords, a family which had declined since the reign of Elizabeth from office-holding to parochial status. Thomas, one of several sons of Thomas Lunsford the elder, together with some companions broke into Pelham's deer-park in January 1630 and killed several deer—more than they could carry away. There was also a fight in which two gamekeepers were severely wounded. The younger Lunsford repeated his forays into Pelham's deer-park several times. In June one of the Pelham hounds strayed on to Lunsford property and Thomas's brother Herbert killed it. Furious because Pelham prosecuted him, Thomas Lunsford the younger in August of the same year ambushed Pelham and his family and guests on the way to church and attempted to murder him. Thomas Lunsford was prosecuted in the Court of Star Chamber in 1632 for poaching and sentenced to three years' imprisonment in addition to paying a heavy fine and damages. He had fled in the meantime—probably to Ireland—and was outlawed. Eventually he submitted and was imprisoned in Newgate Prison in London where he lay for several years until he was pardoned in 1639. He entered the royal army and was made lieutenant of the Tower of London in 1641, but was removed from that post by means of a parliamentary address got up by Pelham. During all of these events Pelham, a Puritan, became the leader of resistance to Arminianism and extra-parliamentary taxation in East Sussex. Thomas Lunsford and two of his brothers served with distinction as royalist officers: Thomas and Herbert were knighted, while Henry was killed at the siege of Bristol.[15]

Gangs of poachers were frequently led by discontented small gentry such as Edward Lowe of Alderwaster, Derbyshire, who delighted

[14] PRO, STAC 7/15/41.
[15] *Historical Collections*, ed. Rushworth, ii. 47–8; Fletcher, *A County Community in Peace and War*, pp. 13, 29, 54–5, 241; *DNB*, s.v. Henry, Sir Herbert, and Sir Thomas Lunsford.

in attacking the parks of peers. Lowe and leaders of two other poaching bands were prosecuted in the Court of Star Chamber for killing deer belonging to Gilbert, Earl of Shrewsbury in five different parks in Yorkshire and Derbyshire. Sixty deer were slaughtered in Sheffield Park in one year alone. Sir Francis Bacon, the attorney-general, thought that since most of the deer were killed out of season when the meat, to his taste, was fit only for dogs, the deer-stealers' purpose must have been to destroy a peer's game out of malice and envy. However, some of the poachers were in the habit of feasting on venison at Lowe's house after their night-time forays, while one of the Sheffield Park poachers said that he had very little else with which to maintain his family except poaching. Bacon thought Lowe was a social leveller, 'grudging that your [Majesty's] nobles and statesmen should have any priviledges or ymunities more than they'.[16]

Poaching was more prevalent in counties where deer-parks were numerous. The vast majority of cases of poaching prosecuted at quarter sessions and assizes involved attacks upon aristocratic game preserves. Of four counties where the records permitted a quantitative assessment of the incidence of poaching, this species of social protest occurred much more frequently in Sussex and Staffordshire than in Kent and Essex. In Sussex between 1569 and 1624 there were 27 incidents of poaching prosecuted at the assizes involving 105 poachers. All but 3 occurred before 1588. Twenty-three of the 27 incidents (or 85 per cent) involved attacks upon the deer-parks of four peers: Henry Neville, Lord Abergavenny (7 instances), Henry Fitzalan, Earl of Arundel (4), Gregory Fiennes, Lord Dacre (7), and Anthony Browne, Lord Montague (5). In Staffordshire 41 instances of unlawful hunting were prosecuted at the quarter sessions between 1586 and 1609, resulting in indictments of 88 persons. Prosecutions for unlawful hunting at quarter sessions apparently involved a larger proportion of cases where the property of lesser persons was involved or where unqualified individuals were prosecuted, not for actually poaching, but for merely possessing guns, dogs, nets, or other 'engines' used for hunting. Ten out of 41 (or 24 per cent) of the Staffordshire cases fall into this category. Of the remainder, 24 (or 59 per cent) involved attacks upon the deer-parks, rabbit warrens, and fish-ponds of peers and gentry, while seven instances (or 17 per cent)

---

[16] PRO, STAC 8/20/32.

were directed against royal forests or parks. The apparent decline in the prosecutions of poachers at the assizes of the home circuit during the reign of James I probably reflects the policy of punishing attacks upon royal and aristocratic deer-parks in the Court of Star Chamber.[17]

Religious animosity also appears to have been part of the motivation for attacking aristocratic game preserves. Hostility between Catholics and Protestants was involved in more than one-fifth of the cases of poaching prosecuted at the Staffordshire quarter sessions. In Sussex, of the eight peers whose parks were attacked, the Earl of Arundel and Lord Montague were Catholics; Henry Neville, sixth Lord Abergavenny was a conservative who had been closely tied to the Marian regime in Kent, where his principal residence was located; the fortunes of his cousin Gregory Fiennes, tenth Lord Dacre of the South, who resided at Herstmonceux Castle in Sussex, seem not to have recovered from the execution of his father, Thomas, ninth Baron Dacre, for a murder committed during a poaching 'frolic' against a deer-park belonging to the Pelhams of Laughton. The tenth Lord Dacre, whom Camden thought was 'crack-brained', was a political non-entity, although he remained on the commission of the peace.[18]

The disproportionate number of Catholics whose game preserves were poached is to be explained by a popular misconception that most recusants were excommunicated and outlawed and therefore could not initiate prosecutions or complaints at law. A witness at the East Sussex sessions in 1641 testified that Thomas Bishe had bragged:

that he would have two brace of buckes and two of dowes out of Sir Richard Weston's ground yearely. And he had killed fower deere in one night there, besides the deere left killed by him and not carried away. And [Bishe] said also that Sir Richard Weston beinge a recusant convicted he cold have no remedy by law for itt.[19]

---

[17] *Calendar of Assize Records, Sussex Indictments, Elizabeth I* and *James I*, ed. J. S. Cockburn (1975), *passim*; *Staffs. QSR*, *passim*. Cf. T. G. Barnes, 'Star Chamber Litigants and their Counsel', *Legal Records and the Historian*, ed. J. H. Baker (R. Hist. Soc., Studies in History, 1978), 11.

[18] *DNB*, s.v. Thomas Fiennes, 9th Baron Dacre and Gregory Fiennes, 10th Baron Dacre of the South; Clark, *English Provincial Society*, pp. 86, 88, 105, 128; Manning, *Religion and Society in Elizabethan Sussex*, pp. 221–2; D. M. Loades, *Two Tudor Conspiracies* (Cambridge, 1965) 85 *et passim*.

[19] Quoted in Fletcher, *A County Community in Peace and War*, p. 29.

Anthony Maria Browne, second Viscount Montague was another Catholic aristocrat, whose large household and 1,100 acres of well-stocked deer-parks at Cowdray, near Midhurst, and Fernhurst excited envy and invited attacks from a number of neighbouring small gentry. He was obliged to bring no fewer than four Star Chamber prosecutions against these bold poachers before he was able to obtain a conviction. In 1609 Lord Montague complained of three attacks in the previous 14 months by a gang of a dozen poachers drawn from nearby villages in Sussex, Surrey, and Hampshire who evidently had been brought in by Owen Bray and Peregrine Chislethwaite of Fernhurst, where two of Lord Montague's parks were located. The gamekeepers were too terrified to resist. Between 1611 and 1616 the leadership of the poaching fraternity passed to Peter Bettsworth of Iping. Bettsworth, variously described as a yeoman and a gentleman, resented Lord Montague's social position and recusancy and invited the whole neighbourhood to make war upon Montague's deer and gamekeepers. Lord Montague complained that the Bettsworth gang killed more deer than they could carry away and carried away more than they could eat, so that they were forced to feed the excess to their 'menial servauntes'. All dined on venison 'with greate Jollitie'. In one of his answers, Bettsworth admitted exercising his greyhounds in Montague's parks, but did not know whether they had 'killed any thinge or not'. He boasted that he had been indicted at the Chichester sessions, but despite testimony from Montague's gamekeepers the jury had refused to find him guilty. Audaciously, he offered Lord Montague 'condicons of agreement' for ending the poaching war. After Bettsworth wounded two of Montague's gamekeepers in 1616 the Court of Star Chamber finally decided to punish him. Bettsworth seems to have made a submission and was fined 100 marks. Bettsworth was undoubtedly what was known in hunting circles as a 'thruster'. During the Interregnum he became a JP and a member of the county committee.[20]

Sir Thomas Fitzherbert's long imprisonment for recusancy left him exposed to predatory neighbours in Hamstall Ridware who were stirred up against him by his treacherous nephew, Thomas Fitzherbert of Norbury. Hamstall Ridware was just three miles east of Cannock Chase on the north side of the River Trent. The younger

---

[20] PRO, STAC 8/84/21, 22, 23, 24; Barnes, 'Fines in the High Court of Star Chamber', p. 175; Fletcher, *A County Community in Peace and War*, pp. 326, 349.

Fitzherbert had been imprisoned in Derby Gaol as a consequence of the Babington Conspiracy in 1586. He turned renegade to gain his freedom and betrayed the hiding-place of his father John, who subsequently died in prison. Thomas was the heir of his uncle until the latter disinherited him. He was determined to gain possession of his uncle's estates and, in the spring of 1587, he occupied his uncle's house by force. He and a dozen of his hunting cronies were convicted of unlawful assembly, forcible entry, and destroying a bridge. Whatever punishment the Staffordshire sessions imposed upon them proved to be no deterrent. Over the next two months, Fitzherbert's friends, who included the rector of Hamstall Ridware and his curate, three local gentlemen, and several other yeomen, husbandmen, and labourers, carried out no fewer than five poaching forays against Sir Thomas Fitzherbert's deer in Rowley Park. When Sir Thomas Fitzherbert died, his nephew, with the help of Richard Topcliffe, the notorious rack-master of the Tower of London, persuaded Archbishop Whitgift to suppress the uncle's will. Consequently, the younger Fitzherbert inherited his uncle's estates.[21]

The appearance of two new words in the English language reflects the attempt to construe the unlawful hunting and sale of game by unqualified persons as a crime. The word 'poacher' first occurs in 1611, while Sir Edward Coke, as attorney-general, employed the term 'deer-stealer' in a Star Chamber information in which he prosecuted several bands of Staffordshire poachers in 1599. Coke and others who used the words 'poacher' and 'deer-stealer' were describing the problem of an increase in organized poaching by gangs who were responding to the rising demand for game on the London market and in provincial markets. It was generally agreed that one of the first steps in preventing poaching was to make the traffic in game illegal. The sale of venison was already prohibited, and the Game Law of 1603 (1 Jac. I, c. 27) forbade the sale of partridges, pheasants, and hares.[22]

---

[21] J. C. Wedgwood, *Staffordshire Parliamentary History* (Wm. Salt Arch. Soc., 1917), i. 1213–1603, 399–400; *The House of Commons, 1558–1603*, ed. P. W. Hasler (3 vols.; History of Parliament Trust, 1981), ii. 125; W. N. Landor, *Staffordshire Incumbents and Parochial Records, 1530–1680* (Wm. Salt Arch. Soc., 1915), 112–14; *Staffs. QSR* i. 195–6, 206–8.

[22] *OED*; PRO, STAC 5/A12/38; Munsche, *Gentlemen and Poachers*, pp. 55, 177; *SR* iv. 1055.

Sir Edward Coke, when prosecuting the Staffordshire poachers in 1599, described them as:

beinge verie dissolute, riotous and vnruly persons, common nightwalkers and stealers of deare out of the fforests, chases and parkes of your maiestie and other your lovinge subiectes . . . betakinge themselves to no honest trade or course of lief but lyvinge of the spoyle & ravyne [ravin] of other your maiesties dutifull and industrious subiects combininge and confederatinge themselues with dyvers other of their companyons and adherents . . . whereof great multitudes doe swarm in that cuntrie.

The Staffordshire poachers, in bands of up to 21 persons, had made repeated attacks upon Tixall Great and Little Parks, just north of Cannock Chase and Birchwood Park, near Leigh and had taken deer belonging to Walter Aston, whose wardship Coke had purchased for £1,300 and later sold to his ward for £4,000. Significantly, Coke was unable to put a price on the deer that the culprits had taken; had he been able to do so they would have been prosecuted at the assizes for theft. Instead, the 'deer-stealers' were prosecuted in Star Chamber for unlawful assembly and riot, hunting at night and breaking a close.[23]

The leader of one poaching gang was Anthony Kymersley of Tapley, 'a gentleman of some countenance in the countrie'; another included a kinsman and servants of Sampson Erdeswick, esq., the antiquary. Two more gangs appear to have been encouraged by recusant gentry: one consisted of servants of Walter Fowler, esq. while another was led by Robert Wells of Hoarcross. Coke complained that Kymersley had so much venison that he had to salt it down and store it in barrels, and even fed it to menial servants.[24]

Kymersley became a JP at the beginning of the next reign. In 1610 Sir Henry Hobart, attorney-general, accused Kymersley of being 'himself a deerstealer and a procurer and abettor of deerstealers'. Kymersley was protecting a gang of professional poachers in Needwood Forest, located to the east of Cannock Chase, who were led by William Walton of Marchenton, gent. and included Peregrine Browne of Hanbury, esq. Walton and his companions were charged with five counts of hunting royal deer in Needwood Forest, assaulting

---

[23] PRO, STAC 5/A12/38; J. Hurstfield, *The Queen's Wards: Wardship and Marriage under Elizabeth I* (1958), 274–5.
[24] PRO, STAC 5/A12/38, STAC 7/10/10, STAC 8/12/2; *Staffs. QSR* iv. 365, v. 273, 320–1; Wedgwood, *Staffordshire Parliamentary History*, vol. i, p. 349.

and wounding several gamekeepers and maiming their cattle. On one occasion the keepers tracked Walton to his house in Marchenton, where they discovered him still in his night-shirt at noontime. The gamekeepers demanded to be allowed to search Walton's house but he refused, and spent the remainder of the day and part of the night, according to the gamekeepers' testimony, burning quantities of venison and deerskins for which he usually found a ready market. When darkness fell Walton and his friends escaped. Walton's aged father was also named a defendant by the attorney-general because he had accepted a gift of venison from his son and had offered him aid and comfort. The elder Walton was denounced by a neighbour who wanted to settle an old quarrel. William Walton remained in hiding for three months before being apprehended and committed to the Fleet Prison in London. A companion in the escape from the house in Marchenton, John Browne of Hanbury, was apprehended almost immediately by the keeper of Needwood Forest. Browne was a pardoned felon, who had already been bound to good behaviour for poaching. The keeper ordered Browne sent to Tutbury Castle, but, at this point, Kymersley intervened and, after pretending to examine Browne, ordered him released. Kymersley was also accused of intimidating other magistrates, attempting to bribe forest officials, and falsely accusing the gamekeepers of poaching and other crimes in an effort to shield his own protégés.[25]

There were other groups of poachers who were tempted by the many parks and warrens in the neighbourhood of Cannock Chase. The Lords Paget had claimed absolute rights of free chase and free warren over the parts of Cannock Chase that lay within the parishes of Cannock and Rugeley until Thomas, third Lord Paget fled overseas in 1587. With his attainder and the forfeiture of the Paget lands to the Crown, local sportsmen enjoyed a field day in Cannock Chase. Indictments at the Staffordshire sessions in the 1590s suggest that there were poaching fraternities at Rugeley, led by Nicholas Adey, vicar of Rugeley, whose vicarage house Puritans regarded as a gambling and drinking hell, and at Wolseley, near Rugeley, led by Edward Wolseley, gent. Such individuals were undoubtedly amateur poachers, but Thomas Elkin was an habitual criminal, who may have been associated with the Hamstall Ridware poachers at various times. In 1586 he was indicted for hunting at night in Sir James Croft's

[25] PRO, STAC 8/12/1, 2.

park at Wychnor and was outlawed for failing to appear at the quarter sessions. In February 1594 he was accused of breaking into Beaudesert Park on two occasions and carrying off six of the Queen's deer. In September he was accused of committing burglary on the house of Sir Thomas Fitzherbert—perhaps by the procurement of Sir Thomas's evil nephew. At the time that Elkin was indicted for this offence and for an unlawful entry committed in 1595, it was reported that he had escaped from gaol and could not be found.[26]

We know more about gentlemen poachers because many of them were prosecuted in the Court of Star Chamber where bills of complaint and informations described their misdeeds in detail. Lesser folk were generally dealt with at the assizes and quarter sessions where, by contrast, the indictments contained only terse statements of the name and social status of the accused and the time, place, and nature of the crime. Still, the number of gentlemen indicted for unlawful hunting at the assizes and quarter sessions is disproportionate. Historians generally estimate that the gentry made up only 5 per cent of the population of England in the seventeenth century. Yet 13 per cent of those indicted for poaching at the assizes in Elizabethan and Jacobean Sussex were gentlemen; at the Staffordshire quarter sessions between 1586 and 1609 gentlemen comprised 11 per cent of those indicted for unlawful hunting, clergy 8 per cent, yeomen and husbandmen 31 per cent, labourers 28 per cent, and artisans 19 per cent. Moreover, many of these persons of inferior social rank were accused of hunting deer in the company of gentlemen poachers; left to themselves, poachers of humble social rank seem to have preferred to take conies or fish.[27]

Poaching was the most violent of all forms of social protest other than armed rebellion. Gentlemen poachers went hunting armed to the teeth and apparently thought that knocking a gamekeeper on the head was half the fun of breaking into a magnate's deer-park. Considering this pervasive atmosphere of violence, it is not surprising that murders and fatal accidents were common. In 1608 John Armitage and 27 companions launched several attacks against Sir John Savile's park near Wakefield and killed the head gamekeeper. In Smeeth, Kent a battle in 1597 between William Richards, gent.

---

[26] Ibid., STAC 5/P12/25; *Staffs. QSR* i. 149, 183, 195–6, ii. 62–3, 124–5, 144; Landor, *Staffordshire Incumbents and Parochial Records*, p. 221.

[27] P. Laslett, *The World We Have Lost* (2nd edn.; New York, 1971), 62.

and seven fellow poachers and three of Thomas Scott's gamekeepers
left Scott's head gamekeeper dead. For their part, gamekeepers and
parkers often attacked 'nightwalkers' first and asked questions later.
In Knole Park, near Sevenoaks, on a dark night in August 1587,
two separate parties of gamekeepers each mistook the other for
deer-stealers and in the ensuing affray one of the keepers beat another
to death.[28]

Efforts to punish poaching were remarkably unsuccessful. Of the
105 persons indicted for unlawful hunting at the Sussex assizes
between 1569 and 1624 only 12 are known to have been caught,
tried, and found guilty (eight of them by confession); out of the 12
only four were sentenced to the three months of imprisonment
specified in the Game Act of 1563 (5 Eliz. I, c. 7), from which
sentence one was subsequently reprieved. In addition, one poacher
was tried and found not guilty, while the bill of indictment against
another three was endorsed 'ignoramus' by the grand jury because
of insufficient evidence.[29]

In Essex, another county well supplied with forests, parks, and
chases, most poachers probably went undetected, but the county's
magistrates seem to have pursued them a little more vigorously.
Nearly a third of those indicted at the assizes between 1570 and 1624
(22 out of a sample of 77) were brought to trial and found guilty.
Nineteen of the 22 persons against whom a guilty verdict was returned
had confessed. Two poachers were fined, five sentenced to three
months' imprisonment, and six were bound to good behaviour, while
in 12 cases the sentence of the court is not indicated. The verdict
is unknown in 32 of the 77 cases. Five persons were remanded on
bail to appear before the Court of Star Chamber while in another
five instances it was noted that the accused persons had fled from
justice. In the case of five labourers who confessed that they broke
into a warren in Stifford, Essex and took 12 rabbits with ferrets
and nets, the defendants threw themselves on the mercy of the court.
Four of them were also indicted for petty larceny for stealing a

---

[28] PRO, STAC 8/268/2; *Calendar of Assize Records, Kent Indictments,
Elizabeth I*, ed. J. S. Cockburn (1979), nos. 1806, 2545. Cf. *Calendar of Assize
Records, Essex Indictments, Elizabeth I*, ed. J. S. Cockburn (1978), no. 3338; *Calendar
of Assize Records, Hertfordshire Indictments, James I*, ed. J. S. Cockburn (1975),
no. 831.
[29] *Calendar of Assize Records, Sussex Indictments, Eliz. I and Jac. I, passim*; SR
iv. 449.

sheep. Three confessed to this crime and were whipped. The bill of indictment against the fourth labourer was returned 'ignoramus' by the grand jury. Another three rabbit-poachers were tried at the Brentwood Assizes in 1603 for the murder of a gamekeeper. Two were found guilty but allowed benefit of clergy, while the verdict on the third is unknown. In eight cases the records state that the indicted person was 'bailed to the next assizes'. Prior to the enactment of 60 Geo. III, c. 4, a defendant at the assizes or quarter sessions had the right in cases of misdemeanour to take issue with the chief matters of the indictment. The effect was to postpone trial until the next sessions. Although the defendant was obliged to find sureties for his appearance, one suspects that some of these persons disappeared and were eventually outlawed.[30]

While most poachers went unpunished, a very large proportion of them, when caught, chose to make confessions, despite the fact that grand juries could not always be counted upon to return true bills or petit juries guilty verdicts. This was because statutory enactments encouraged confession. The Act of 1485 (1 Hen. VII, c. 7), which made it felony to conceal the crime of hunting at night or in disguise by refusing to give evidence or to confess, was still in force. The same Act specified that if an individual accused of those crimes acknowledged his offences the charge could be reduced from felony to trespass, which was a misdemeanour punishable by fine. The Game Act of 1563 (5 Eliz. I, c. 21) went further and permitted the aggrieved party to release the poacher from his recognizance. The law taught that deference was the path to mercy and confession was good for the body as well as the soul. At the Devon assizes at Exeter Castle in 1638 six poachers who had 'offended in divers affronts and trespasses' by hunting in warrens belonging to Sir Edward Southcott and John Luttrell were discharged from their recognizances because they had made a humble submission. The Court of Star Chamber in 1624 reduced the sentences of two men accused of stealing royal deer from imprisonment for three years and fines of £100 each

---

[30] F. G. Emmison, *Elizabethan Life: Disorder, Mainly from Essex Sessions and Assize Records* (Chelmsford, Essex Record Office Publications 56, 1970), 234–5; *Calendar of Assize Records, Essex Indictments, Eliz. I*, ed. Cockburn, no. 3338 *et passim*; *Calendar of Assize Records, Essex Indictments, James I*, ed. J. S. Cockburn (1982), nos. 120–1 *et passim*; *Staffs. QSR*, vol. i, p. xxxix.

to fines of £20 each after they expressed 'their sorrow and contrition at the Bar'.[31]

Deer were royal animals. No one might hunt them but the King or those who enjoyed his licence. The Stuart monarchs, with their exalted notions of the powers of the royal prerogative, considered deer-stealing to be an especial affront to the royal dignity; that is why the Court of Star Chamber punished deer-stealers with increasing severity. 'The offence was the greater', declared the attorney-general when he prosecuted a brace of deer-poachers in that court in 1624, because 'the king had but one darling pleasure, and yet they would offend him in that'. To which the Lord President of the Council replied. 'Mr Attorney [General] was the best keeper the King had of his Parks, in regard he brings the Offenders into this Court to be punished'. Charles I punished deer-stealers even more severely than his father had done. Sir John York of Gowthwaite stubbornly claimed the right of free chase and free warren on his manor of Appletreewick, and whenever Francis, Earl of Cumberland's deer wandered out of the latter's chases of Skipton and Barden in Craven on to his land, Sir John hunted them down. Cumberland prosecuted York no fewer than four times in 15 years. When he became too old to take Cumberland's deer himself, Sir John entrusted that task to his son John. The judges of the Court of Star Chamber recognized that Sir John York might have a claim to free chase on his own lands, but left the question of title to be decided by the common-law courts, and confined themselves to punishing Sir John's affront to the dignity of the Earl of Cumberland. Whereas in 1616 the court had fined Sir John £20, in 1625, after the accession of Charles I, he was fined £200 and committed to the Fleet Prison for the same offence. The court dealt with other deer-stealers in similar fashion. Not content with that, Charles I, who was fond of taking pheasants and partridges with hawks, ordered the Court of Star Chamber also to punish persons who unlawfully hunted game birds with 'setting dogs' and nets.[32]

---

[31] *SR* ii. 505, iv, 449; *Western Circuit Assize Orders, 1629–1648*, ed. J. S. Cockburn (Camden Soc., 4th ser. 17; 1976), no. 634; Popham, *Reports and Cases*, p. 152; cf. *Cal. SP Dom., Add., 1580–1625*, p. 587.

[32] Manwood, *A Treatise of the Lawes of the Forest*, fos. 20, 25ʳ&ᵛ, 26; Popham, *Reports and Cases*, p. 152; PRO, STAC 8/85/19, 20; Barnes, 'Fines in the High Court of Star Chamber', p. 184; *Historical Collections*, ed. Rushworth, ii/2. 3, 8, 12, 43, 74–5; *Stuart Royal Proclamations*, ii. *Royal Proclamations of Charles I, 1625–1646*, ed. J. F. Larkin and P. J. Hughes (Oxford, 1983), nos. 188, 192.

Conies or rabbits, as distinct from hares, were not native to Britain and were probably introduced by the Normans. They multiplied rapidly and had practically no natural predator except man. Rabbits were extremely destructive to crops and to young seedling trees in enclosed coppices. It was nearly impossible to keep them out of coppices before the invention of wire fences. James I ordered all conies destroyed in royal parks and forests because they undermined the ground, caused injuries to deer, and threatened the King's safety when he hunted. Because of the damage that they caused in gardens, arable fields, and commons, commoners sometimes declared war on rabbits and slaughtered large numbers of them. One defendant argued in King's Bench in 1601 that rabbits were vermin like foxes and one might kill them with impunity. The judges disagreed and ruled that conies were beasts of warren and profitable to their owners, the lords of the soil. The Staffordshire grand jury frequently, but not invariably, placed a price upon stolen conies in their bills of indictment. It might seem that this would have made rabbit-poachers liable to charges of petty or grand larceny, but this never seems to have happened. At other times the Staffordshire grand jury simply presented rabbit-poachers for unlawful hunting because they did not meet the qualifications of property and rank.[33]

With regard to taking fish, the law distinguished between free fishing and several fishing. Fish might be caught by anglers in running water, provided the surrounding land was not enclosed. Fishing in ponds, or in still water, as where a river was dammed with a weir, was not free, even if access could be gained from a common or waste or the king's highway. Where the lord of the soil owned both sides of a river or an enclosed pond, he was said to possess several fishing. Judicial writers all agreed that fish which had been caught and placed in a cask or a basket were chattels and might be stolen; they also agreed that fish in open rivers and lakes were not chattels. Between these two extremes much doubt existed. The statute of 1539 (31 Hen. VIII, c. 2), which made fishing in ponds, moats, and stews on several ground at night or breaking the head of a fish-pond by

---

[33] *Cal. SP Dom., 1623–1625*, p. 425; D. Hay, 'Poaching and the Game Laws on Cannock Chase', in D. Hay *et al.* (eds.), *Albion's Fatal Tree: Crime and Society in Eighteenth-century England* (New York, 1975), 221–34; PRO, STAC 3/1/98, 6/91, 7/56, 8/26, STAC 5/S73/10, S8/24; Sir George Croke, *Reports*, part I. King's Bench and Common Pleas, Elizabeth (1669), p. 876; *Staffs. QSR* ii. 317, 362, iii. 152–3, iv. 291, v. 320–1.

day or night a felony, does not appear to have been enforced. Although the indictments of fish-poachers at the Staffordshire quarter sessions invariably gave the value of fish taken, it is fairly clear that the defendants were not tried for grand or petty larceny. Usually, the defendants were charged with other offences such as breaking a close or a pond or unlawful and riotous assembly.[34] Cunning poachers were able to exploit the ambiguities in the law, as the examination of John Partridge of Smethwick, tanner, indicates:

He and his brother Frauncis Partridge were cominge towardes Walsall vpon Saturdaie after twelfe deye laste [1602] about two of the clocke in the after noone . . . and his brother Frauncis rydinge out of a close of his before him into a lane called Jane Mille by reason that the said lane is stopped where they should have ridden by stoppinge the water in the right course and tourninge the water ofte tymes to a newe erected fordge, or Ironworke, where his brother said 'I cannot ryde for my horse treadinge vpon fishe. How shall wee doe to catche some of yt?' And this examinant said, 'Goe whome [home] and fetche a boarde to thruste ouer the Lane and I will steye here betweene the fishe and the streme and keepe them where they are till yow retourne', which his brother did, and . . . his brother brought back his table boarde, which they set ouer the Lane and filled yt vp . . . and sent for a little draught nett . . . wherwith they drewe out very neere six stricke of fish, which he assureth himselfe he might lawfullye doe consideringe yt was in no stue [stew], inclosed pounde or place inclosed, but out of the Ryver, either newe, or olde [course], and in her maiesties heigh waye, and his brother Frauncis haveinge and houldinge the groundes on [both] sides by lease.

John Partridge and two accomplices were indicted for breaking the head of a pond and taking six bushels of fish valued at £20. They were bound by recognizances to attend the next sessions, but subsequently failed to appear.[35]

The Staffordshire justices were indulgent towards a poacher who could tell a good fish story. Another examination, taken in 1591, provides a rare profile of a vagrant who earned a comfortable livelihood in Staffordshire by unlawful fishing.

---

[34] 'A Short Discourse by Way of Postscript, touching the Laws of Angling', appended to Izaak Walton, *The Compleat Angler* (1875), 212–14 (reference courtesy of Dr Mark Francis); *The Reports of Sir John Spelman*, ed. Baker, ii. 322; *SR* iii. 718; *Staffs. QSR* ii. 58, 117, 167, 345, iii. 77, iv. 421.
[35] Ibid., iv. 421, 437.

Henrie Davies taken at Lytle Loxley as a Roge or vagabonde person. Beinge examined, sayeth that he hathe now [no] dwelling place nor hath had theese two yeares past, but travellinge a brode as a tooth drawer. And abowte two yeares past he was within this countie and made his Reporte [i.e. boasted] boeth at Enston and at Geaton that in fyshinge in the waters he coulde be worthe his x *s.* or noble adaie. Alsoe at Loxley upon Mondaie the xvijth of Maie last, he reported to Marten of Loxley that in the snowe in wynter he took soe muche fyshe within three howres that he soulde for twelf shillinges reservinge the three beste peyces to himself; and further confesseth that abowte Candlemas laste he came to Robt. Buckley's howse in Waterfall, alkeeper, and contenewed with his wyffe and two children nine wickes and lived onely by stealinge of fyshe. At Loxley where he was taken he had contenewed three wickes at Hilles Howse, alkeper there, and soulde there carpe and other powle [pool] fishe besyde trowte and other ryver fyshe.

Davies was not indicted, but instead posted a surety of £100 that he would leave the county within the next ten days.[36]

Poachers like Henry Davies, who worked alone and turned to unlawful fishing out of poverty, did not constitute a challenge to royal dignity or aristocratic privilege, nor were they a threat to public order. However, fish-poaching sometimes accompanied violent attacks upon enclosed ponds, when smallholders were denied access to streams and ponds where they had customarily watered their animals. The law compelled manorial lords to surround ponds with enclosing hedges in order to establish a claim to several fishing. Evidently such a claim was incompatible with communal access to a stream or a pond for other purposes, such as watering stock.[37]

The late-medieval and Tudor game laws were enacted because poaching was seen as an activity that bred idleness, violence, and even rebellion. In the early-Stuart period any kind of unlawful hunting by unqualified persons was considered an offence against aristocratic privilege. The authorities perceived this as an especially serious matter during a time when the social hegemony and political influence of the aristocracy was being challenged or undermined in a variety of ways.[38] The breaching of enclosed parks, warrens, and fish-ponds was also an assault upon the emerging concept of the absolute rights of private property and was part of the larger protest

---

[36] Ibid. ii. 134–5.   [37] Cf. PRO, STAC 8/67/4, 126/4.
[38] Cf. Stone, *Crisis of the Aristocracy*, pp. 9–10.

against the extinction of ancient use-rights. Finally, because the early-Stuart monarchs were more interested in the sport of the chase than the heirs of Henry VIII and were also especially conscious of the symbols of divine-right monarchy, they determined to take steps to preserve the royal deer for their sport and to punish those who affronted the royal dignity by hunting the King's beasts.

With the exception of James I, Charles I, and a few courtiers and landowners, few people really believed that poaching was a crime. Even lawyers had to admit that the game laws took magistrates on to unsure ground. The enforcement of the game laws had the effect of pitting peers, courtiers, and other magnates not only against members of the commonalty, but also against the lesser gentry and even members of the office-holding county families. In other words, the social conflict produced by the game laws approximated the cleavage between 'court' and 'country'.[39]

[39] Cf. P. Zagorin, *The Court and the Country: The Beginning of the English Revolution* (1969), 32-9.

PART IV
Conclusion

12

Social Protest and the Sense of Community

BETWEEN 1549 and 1640 popular disturbances rarely showed any sign of developing from social into political protest. The essential characteristic of these village revolts was localism. During the late medieval popular revolts, by contrast, contact with the artisans of provincial towns and especially the inhabitants of London had produced a comparatively high degree of political awareness. In the rebellions of 1450 and 1536 the leadership provided by gentlemen also served to focus the attention of the protesters on larger issues, such as government policies initiated by unpopular royal ministers. During the Pilgrimage of Grace, the defence of traditional religious practices helped to shape an ideology of resistance, which, conceivably, could have led to civil war in the continental manner.[1] Dislike of the gentry was widely articulated during the rebellions and riots of 1549, but the resulting social conflict never entirely dissolved the habitual pattern of deference and obedience, and class warfare failed to materialize. The preoccupation of movements of protest between 1549 and 1640 with local issues arising from agrarian change, alterations in land use, and the seigneurial assault upon use-rights and customary tenures is one aspect of what some historians misleadingly call the 'decline of disorder'. The conflict between lord and tenant which characterized the seigneurial regime remained endemic, but the stability produced by the Elizabethan religious settlement and the Stuart succession to the Crown effectively removed political matters from the arena of popular dispute; aristocratic rebellions ceased to draw popular support, as is well illustrated by the failure of the Rising of the Northern Earls in 1569 and the Essex Revolt in 1601. Such popular conspiracies and rebellions as did occur in

---

[1] C. S. L. Davies, 'The Pilgrimage of Grace Reconsidered', *P. & P.*, no. 41 (Dec. 1968), 54–76, esp. 56, 76; id., 'Popular Religion and the Pilgrimage of Grace', in A. Fletcher and J. Stevenson (eds.), *Order and Disorder in Early Modern England, 1500–1700* (Cambridge, 1985), 58–88. For a different interpretation, see A. G. Dickens, 'Secular and Religious Motivation in the Pilgrimage of Grace', in G. J. Cuming (ed.), *Studies in Church History* 4 (1967), 39–64.

1596 and 1607 were easily contained, so long as nothing disrupted the unity of the political élite. At the same time social and economic forces were at work which divided and differentiated village and manorial communities, drawing smallholders into the gentry camp and politically isolating landless cottagers, artisans, and labourers. Clearly, there was a 'decline of disorder' only with respect to the larger regional revolts, and village revolts remained a problem throughout the early-modern period. Indeed, Professor Elton has suggested that 'the sum of hundreds of small affrays and quarrels year by year was a far more pressing problem to the government than the very occasional major risings.'[2] Yet one can exaggerate the danger of village revolts, since social protest rarely posed a threat to the political and social order. To put it into a larger context, peasant resistance, although it did not invariably take a violent turn, was 'part of the everyday life in the European states in the early-modern period.'[3]

The very nature of social protest limited its effectiveness under the political and social conditions of early-modern England. Social protest is a reactive rather than an active process. Its manifestations were directed against particular grievances within a local context and popular demonstrations were likely to remain static unless some powerful external force, widely-shared experience, or the commanding presence of a charismatic leader intervened to break down the barriers of localism. Popular protest, whether it began in the more politically fertile environment of town life or the ideologically barren environment of the village, was always more motivated by personal hatred than by class conflict. Even in the late-medieval urban revolts, this juxtaposition of political consciousness and localism is striking. Furthermore, whether the grievance arises within the community or comes from afar, popular discontent remains focused upon personalities rather than issues. Consequently, popular justice was selective and often vindictive. It was as much concerned with settling private feuds as it was with correcting public wrongs. The obsessive inability to forget or forgive an affront was characteristic of a society which still rested, in part, upon honour and ties of kinship. This

---

[2] Sir G. R. Elton, *England under the Tudors* (Cambridge, 1963), 59.

[3] W. Schulze, 'Peasant Resistance in Sixteenth- and Seventeenth-century Germany in a European Context', in K. von Greyerz (ed.), *Religion, Politics and Social Protest: Three Studies on Early Modern Germany* (1984), 62.

characteristic not only intensified neighbourhood quarrels, it also blunted the effectiveness of popular protest.[4]

Between the early-Tudor period and the eve of the Civil Wars, the anti-enclosure riot was the most common species of social protest. During this period one may discern several historical trends with regard to contemporary perceptions of such popular disturbances, as well as in their aims, leadership, and social composition. One is a change from official tolerance of violent enclosure disputes to a qualified disapproval. Enclosure riots in the early-Tudor period were unfocused expressions of social protest and, not infrequently, masked cases of forcible entry and gentry feuding, but became more specifically anti-aristocratic during the rebellions of 1548–9. Although we know that the leadership in these rebellions was drawn mostly from the level of society next below the gentry, magistrates and royal officials emphasized the participation of artisans and cottagers in such disturbances and the role of vagrants in spreading the rumours and prophecies, which, suffused with anti-gentry sentiment, caused village revolts to coalesce into major rebellions.

Changing official attitudes towards anti-enclosure demonstrations are evidenced in the Edwardian, Marian, and Elizabethan Acts against Unlawful Assemblies, which at first threatened prosecution for treason and then created the new crime of felony-riot to punish village revolts that got out of hand.[5] The death penalty may have been invoked infrequently against rioters, but Parliament allowed the Elizabethan Act against Unlawful Assemblies to lapse only after the suppression of the Midland Revolt. Following the discovery of the Enslow Hill conspiracy, the judges in the case of *R. v. Bradshaw* sharply delineated the distinction between public and private protests and decreed that no one might participate in an enclosure dispute who did not have a clear interest in the community's common rights.[6] The decision in *Gateward's Case* reiterated that rights of

---

[4] R. B. Dobson, 'The Risings in York, Beverley and Scarborough, 1380–1381', in R. H. Hilton and T. H. Aston (eds.), *The English Rising of 1381* (Cambridge, 1984), 113, 138–41; Morrill, *The Revolt of the Provinces*, pp. 19–20; A. Fletcher, 'National and Local Awareness in the County Communities', in H. Tomlinson (ed.), *Before the English Civil War: Essays on Early-Stuart Politics and Government* (New York, 1983), 154–8.

[5] 3 & 4 Edw. VI, c. 5, *SR* iv. 104–8; 1 Mary, st. 2, c. 12, *SR* iv. 211–12 1 Eliz. I, c. 16, *SR* iv. 377.

[6] Coke, 3 *Institutes*, pp. 9–10.

common were to be limited to tenants.[7] Cottagers, or mere inhabitants, were increasingly denied access to common wastes.

The government's attitude towards enclosure rioting remained curiously ambivalent. Although royal officials were capable of imposing the death penalty when sufficiently frightened, the fact remains that, with the exception of insurrections, enclosure rioting was almost invariably punished as a misdemeanour. Perhaps it was difficult for officials to maintain a consistently firm attitude towards something which might fairly be regarded as a national pastime. It is difficult to avoid the conclusion that magistrates continued to be indulgent towards gentry violence but grew nervous when artisans and labourers presumed to lead such disturbances.

Earlier in the period, the gentry often played a significant role in procuring and even leading anti-enclosure riots. Gentlemen were, of course, to be found on both sides of enclosure disputes. Moreover, the lesser gentry frequently stiffened the resistance of tenants to the enhancement of rents and the degradation of tenures. This cleavage between gentry-tenants and those possessing seigneurial jurisdiction, when taken together with evidence of frequent attacks of gentlemen-poachers upon the deer-parks of the greater gentry and peerage, is related to the growing discontent among 'younger sons' of the gentry in the seventeenth century so vividly described by Joan Thirsk.[8] There is abundant evidence of the violent proclivities of the gentry, who continued to set a bad example with their private feuding. At the same time, it must be remembered that many gentlemen led or procured enclosure riots out of a paternalistic regard for tenants and neighbours or were acting to protect their own rights of usufruct. In the long run, gentry leadership in enclosure disputes diminished and smallholders or artisans and cottagers were more likely to take the initiative in leading agrarian protests. This appears to be connected with several regional developments in the geographical distribution of enclosure riots.

One such trend is indicated by a shift in geographical emphasis after 1550 from the east Midlands to the west Midlands, in which the epicentre of tension moved from an open-field corn-producing region suffering from depopulation to an area of woodland pasture beset by problems of sustained demographic expansion and the rapid

---

[7] Id., 6 *Reports*, fo. 59ᵛ.
[8] J. Thirsk, 'Younger Sons in the Seventeenth Century', *History* 54 (1969), 358–77.

growth of rural industry. The gentry were supposed to have been busy colonizing the villages of England during this period, but their influence remained weaker in the areas of dispersed settlement of sylvan England than in the larger villages of fielden regions.[9]

The forest and fen disturbances in the period from 1626 to 1640 were comparatively large anti-enclosure riots—frequently involving more than 100 participants, and were traditional responses to drastic alterations in land use and the extinction of communal use-rights. There was little or no co-ordination of these protests between local communities, but there is evidence that some of the later riots were sympathetic responses to commonly-perceived grievances. The riots against disafforestation, collectively known as the Western Rising of 1628–31, (which occurred in the Midlands as well) were largely artisan and cottager revolts, and the minimal participation by smallholders signified serious social tension in the western and midland forest communities. Such social conflict is less evident in the fenland villages, where social cohesion appears to have remained stronger and some of the gentry were still prepared to play their traditional role of leading protests against injustice and outside interference.[10]

Most enclosure riots were circumscribed by the localism of their participants and by a prudent regard for the legal distinction between private disputes and public protest. The abortive Enslow Hill Rebellion of 1596 and the Midland Revolt of 1607 were more generalized protests which broke away from these traditional constraints because of adverse conditions in the east Midlands and east Oxfordshire. In this region extensive enclosures of arable land continued into the late-Elizabethan period, while expanding populations of artisans and labourers were exposed to exceptionally high corn prices. Isolated instances of dearth could result where certain villages were dependent on local supplies of grain in a region of notoriously poor transport. Such risings were more likely to become a menace in earlier periods before popular movements were cut off from gentry and yeomanry leadership and the participation of husbandmen. Like the Caroline Forest Riots and some of the larger

[9] Laslett, *The World We Have Lost*, p. 62.
[10] D. C. G. Allan, 'The Rising in the West, 1628–1631', *Ec. HR*, 2nd ser. 5 (1952–3), 76–85; Sharp, *In Contempt of All Authority*, pp. 126–8, 134; Lindley, *Fenland Riots and the English Revolution*, pp. 1, 253–5.

food riots, these protests displayed considerable evidence of sharp social conflict. The weakness of so many seventeenth-century agrarian protests was the fragmentation of popular protest. The gentry and yeomanry might still participate in the village revolts with which this book is concerned, but they were notably absent from protests such as the Enslow Hill Rebellion and the Midland Revolt which embodied the grievances of landless artisans and labourers. Poverty undoubtedly increased in England during the late-Elizabethan and early-Stuart crises, but the poor were losing their ability 'to translate discontent into rebellion'.[11]

Food riots in Tudor and early-Stuart England were neither as numerous nor as widespread as anti-enclosure riots. Between 1585 and 1660, approximately 40 cases of food riots came to the attention of the Privy Council. Research in local archives has revealed more instances. In the county of Essex, which possesses an unusually complete set of records, nine grain riots are known to have occurred during this same period. Food riots were largely confined to proto-industrial areas which specialized in cloth manufacture. Chronologically, most of these food riots occurred during the crises of 1586, 1594–7, 1622, and 1629–31, when scarcity of food and dislocation of supplies coincided with extensive unemployment in the clothing industry.[12] Despite the fact that the judges in *R. v. Bradshaw* had declared that a conspiracy to alter prices was levying war against the King,[13] local magistrates were generally lenient towards food rioters who confined themselves to the traditional rituals of popular market regulation and the harassing of badgers, the middlemen of the grain trade. Although food riots occurred less frequently than enclosure riots they were more likely to lead to threats against the governors and a breakdown of traditional deference and obedience. Because of the more prominent role that rumours played in food riots, they might more readily metamorphose into generalized protests than enclosure riots.[14] Some of the food riots

---

[11] Walter, 'A "Rising of the People"? The Oxfordshire Rising of 1596', pp. 108–22, 137–9.

[12] Sharp, *In Contempt of All Authority*, pp. 10–13; Walter and Wrightson, 'Dearth and the Social Order in Early Modern England', pp. 26–7; P. J. Bowden, *The Wood Trade in Tudor and Stuart England* (1962), p. xvi; G. D. Ramsay, *The Wiltshire Woollen Industry in the Sixteenth and Seventeenth Centuries* (2nd edn.; New York, 1965), ch. 6.   [13] Coke, 3 *Institutes*, pp. 9–10.

[14] *Acts PC* xxx. 386–7; *Cal. SP Dom., 1595–97*, p. 401; Clark, 'Popular Protest and Disturbance in Kent, 1558–1640', pp. 371–2; H. T. White, 'A Hampshire Plot',

of this period were probably caused more by fear of hunger than by the actual presence of famine. This would help to explain the presence of rumours in the more dangerous kinds of food riots, since rumours are more likely to feed upon fear and uncertainty than upon the disaster which is apprehended. The local governors also thought that food riots were more dangerous than enclosure riots because the participants were, again, mostly artisans and masterless men, who, by general agreement, were more intractable than husbandmen.

If the persistence of agrarian protests is any indication, a sense of community, as demonstrated by the organized defence of common rights and by tenant resistance to other forms of fiscal seigneurialism, remained strong well into the middle of the seventeenth century. However, in communities which saw a considerable influx of population, such as sylvan, pastoral, and proto-industrial areas, the question of common rights could prove socially divisive. There was a trend towards stinting in the exercise of common rights, and many manorial communities, backed by court decisions such as *Gateward's Case*, began to exclude cottagers and squatters from access to common wastes. An indication of the degree to which smallhold tenants had become differentiated from cottagers and labourers is seen in the tendency, beginning early in the seventeenth century and especially noticeable in the west Midlands, of grand jurors to present offences involving illegal cottagers or lodgers or of tenants to resort to vigilante action in destroying illegal cottages. Moreover, local governors and village notables did not hesitate to employ summary justice against vagrants.[15] Many of these problems stemmed from the movement of population into woodland-pasture regions. The development of industry in such areas probably reduced tension by offering employment to cottagers and squatters, but also exacerbated problems of land-use, as well as increasing conflicts over fuel resources and water rights.[16] Certainly, where industrial development did not follow impopulation, as in the Forest of Feckenham, social conflict

---

Papers and Proceedings of the Hampshire Field Club and Archaeological Society 12 (1934), 54–60; J. Walter, 'Grain Riots and Popular Attitudes to the Law: Maldon and the Crisis of 1629', in Brewer and Styles (eds.), *An Ungovernable People*, 48–9, 65–77; id., 'A "Rising of the People"? The Oxfordshire Rising of 1596', pp. 91–2.

[15] Beier, *Masterless Men*, pp. 155–8.

[16] For a revealing discussion of the latter problem, see P. F. Brandon, 'Land, Technology and Water Management in the Tillingbourne Valley, Surrey, 1560–1760', *Southern History* 6 (1984), 75–103.

was especially sharp. Many of these tendencies limited the sense of community to those who possessed property or had a legally-demonstrable claim to rights of common, but Keith Wrightson is surely mistaken in assuming that increased social differentiation invariably led to a decline in localism.[17] Quite the contrary, impopulation and the increase of poverty posed a threat to common rights and often caused tenants to rally together to protect those use-rights against outsiders.

Although poaching and enclosure riots were by far the most prevalent forms of popular protest in Tudor and early-Stuart England, royal officials and local magistrates appear to have feared masterless men far more than the smallholders who made hedge-levelling something of a national pastime. At first this paranoia focused upon vagrants and elicited the savage punishments of Tudor legislation, but by the early seventeenth century attention was also directed towards squatters and cottager-artisans, who were attracted to the more abundant commons of sylvan and pastoral regions. The fear that unenclosed wastes were becoming nurseries of beggars and thieves contributed to the movement to enclose commons and the motive of social regulation was probably more important than that of agricultural improvement. Increasingly, the old tenants became more amenable to enclosure schemes, as their fear of squatters and cottagers grew. Poor-relief measures, the appointment of provost-marshals, and the regulation of the grain trade all arose from the fear of paupers and masterless men and the concern to preserve public order. But the costs of poor relief and the maintenance of provost-marshals, as well as the encroachment of poor-law cottages upon the commons, increased the tension between ratepayers of whatever social rank and masterless men.

Poaching is difficult to categorize as a species of social protest because it is a complex phenomenon. In its most primitive manifestations poaching includes acts such as unlawfully removing fish or rabbits from ponds and warrens held in severalty for reasons of economic necessity. Vagrants also resorted to such acts because it was an easy way to make a living—especially in woodland regions such as Staffordshire, where there was good cover and a ready market for their catch in alehouses and among a numerous artisan

---

[17] K. Wrightson, 'Aspects of Social Differentiation in Rural England, c.1580–1660', *Journal of Peasant Studies* 5 (Oct. 1977), 40.

population. It appears that a commercial market for venison also was developing in Staffordshire, where the trade was facilitated by co-operation between a few justices and hardened criminals. The motivation for these varieties of unlawful hunting ranged from necessity to greed. Poachers who caught more than they could consume themselves, or killed animals wantonly or for mercenary motives, furnished their social superiors with evidence that poaching was the first step towards a life of crime.

In other circumstances, poaching is more clearly an expression of social protest. This was certainly the case where poaching was directed against the emparkment of common wastes and was accompanied by anti-enclosure rioting. The same can be said for taking fish out of ponds or breaking the heads of ponds, where such ponds flooded commonable meadows or conflicted with the water-rights of others. Protests of this kind were especially frequent in Wealden Sussex, where parks and ponds encroached upon commons to an unusual degree. Here, again, the growth of rural industry and impopulation intensified conflicts concerning land-use. Poaching and enclosure riots in forest regions were often on a larger scale than in champion areas because a dozen or more villages might share the same waste and because their populations contained a large admixture of under-employed cottager-artisans.

Poaching affrays led by the gentry, who felt that full harness was the only appropriate attire for breaking into a magnate's park, were the most violent of all forms of popular protest excepting only full-scale rebellions. Moreover, poaching of this kind constituted an explicit challenge to aristocratic privilege, if not to the social order. For this James I and Charles I and their supporters were partly to blame, because early-Stuart game laws and the royal practice of granting gamekeepers' warrants had the effect of pitting the parochial gentry, who often lacked sufficient estates to qualify for hunting, against the seigneurial gentry with their well-stocked parks. James I and Charles I were both obsessed with hunting and were determined to preserve royal beasts and to employ the Court of Star Chamber to prosecute those who offended royal and aristocratic dignity by poaching deer. The increasing time and attention devoted to prosecuting *pro rege* cases of seditious libel and poaching offences undoubtedly altered popular perceptions of that court as a place where smallholders might hope for protection against oppressive landlords. Star Chamber had become a court primarily concerned with buttressing royal dignity and aristocratic privilege rather than dispensing justice.

A comparison of popular disturbances in London with village revolts is useful for suggesting some of the conditions which might transform early-modern movements of social protest into political protest. Except for their localist concerns during much of the Tudor period and the reign of James I, the London apprentices' riots do not quite fit into the categories of social protest which I have discussed. Popular disorder in London reveals more violence against persons than one finds in village revolts. Londoners talked more openly about overthrowing their local governors and were more likely to utter speeches expressing disloyalty to the Crown than countrymen. Early in the reign of Charles I the London crowd began to display an awareness of royal policies and a hostility toward ministers of the Crown which is reminiscent of the central role that Londoners of all social ranks had played in the rebellions of 1381 and 1450. During the late-Elizabethan crisis discontent in London had become sufficiently generalized and diffused to unsettle the inhabitants of Middlesex villages, and a number of them participated in the London insurrections of June 1595. The artisans of east Oxfordshire, who participated in the Conspiracy of 1596, had also developed a fellow-feeling with the London apprentices and expressed a desire to join them in rebellion. It is significant that the late-Elizabethan and early-Caroline epidemics of disorder in the metropolis coincided with periods of military and naval mobilization. The experience of impressment, military service (sometimes overseas), and discharge, often without pay, did much to give veterans a sense of shared discontent and made them more disposed to take collective political action than most Englishmen. While acts of military indiscipline occurred elsewhere, the problem was especially acute in the metropolis where so many soldiers and masterless men masquerading as soldiers tended to congregate.

On the eve of the Civil Wars the forms of popular protest remained largely devoid of political content and employed rituals usually derived from the traditional expressions of popular justice and festive misrule. Undoubtedly, it was the persistent localism of village communities which reinforced the apolitical character of village revolts. In attempting to fathom the mentality of participants in social protest, one must be wary of accusations made against them by their enemies or crown advocates. Bills of complaint often insist that 'the

Defendants, in Contempt of All Authority, Combined together', that 'they cared neither for god nor the king', and that they were 'wicked and sedicious persons, being for the most parte of the basest and pooreste condicion, not fearinge God and maliciously envyinge the state and peaceable government of this lande'.[18] During and after the Midland Revolt of 1607, enclosure rioters frequently were depicted as 'levellers' who belonged to a widespread popular conspiracy. Christopher Hill warns us about the 'very special problems in attempting to trace continuities of underground ideas' and reminds us that the history of popular protesters is often written by their enemies.[19] It will not do to mistake the hyperbole of Star Chamber complaints or pamphleteers for evidence of the roots of radicalism or revolutionary behaviour. With very few exceptions, the men, women, and children who participated in social protest during the Tudor and early-Stuart periods were guided by tradition and custom and were vainly attempting to restore a lost world which may never have existed.

[18] Sharp, *In Contempt of All Authority*, p. ii; C. Holmes, 'Drainers and Fenmen: Political Consciousness in the Fenland', in A. Fletcher and J. Stevenson (eds.), *Order and Disorder in Early Modern England, 1500–1750* (Cambridge, 1985), 168; PRO, STAC 5/A9/23, printed in Manning, 'The Prosecution of Sir Michael Blount, Lieutenant of the Tower of London, 1595', p. 222; Lindley, *Fenland Riots and the English Revolution*, pp. 64–5.

[19] C. Hill, 'From Lollards to Levellers', in M. Cornforth (ed.), *Rebels and their Causes: Essays in Honour of A. L. Morton* (Atlantic Highlands, NJ, 1979), 49–50.

Appendix of Tables

Table 2.1: Analysis of Anti-Enclosure Riot Cases during the Reigns of Henry VIII and Edward VI (%) [a]

I. Type of Enclosure Destroyed
  1. Commons or waste — 33
  2. Arable — 12
  3. Emparking of woodland pasture — 5
  4. Enclosure and coppicing of woodland pasture — 8
  5. Pasture or meadow held in severalty — 15
  6. Enclosure of highway or common way — 7
  7. Breaking the head of a fish-pond — 1
  8. Pound breach for rescue of distrained cattle — 1
  9. Unspecified — 18

II. Destruction of Enclosure Procured by:
  1. Order of manorial court or municipal officials — 5
  2. Order of crown officials — 4
  3. Gentry (including peers) — 41
  4. Smallholders and craftsmen — 16
  5. Clergy — 7
  6. Townsmen — 5
  7. Dispute concerning commons shared by two or more villages — 3
  8. Social status unspecified — 19

III. Victims of Enclosure-riots
  1. Gentry resident — 27
  2. Gentry absentee — 8
  3. Smallholders and craftsmen — 19
  4. Outsiders (new owners and farmers of leases)[b] — 32
  5. Townsmen — 4
  6. Clergy — 1
  7. Dispute concerning commons shared by two or more villages — 2
  8. Social status unspecified — 5

[a] Based upon 75 Star Chamber Cases from PRO STAC 2, STAC 3.
[b] Includes a number of townsmen in this category.

Table 2.2: *Geographical Distribution of Enclosure-riot Cases during the Reigns of Henry VIII and Edward VI*

	No.	%
I. West of England Cornwall, Devonshire, Dorsetshire, Somersetshire	6	8
II. North of England Northumberland, Cumberland, Co. Durham, Westmorland, Lancashire, Cheshire, Yorkshire	12	16
III. West Midlands Shropshire, Staffordshire, Herefordshire, Worcestershire, Warwickshire, Gloucestershire	15	20
IV. East Midlands Lincolnshire, Derbyshire, Nottinghamshire, Leicestershire, Rutlandshire, Northamptonshire, Huntingdonshire, Bedfordshire	18	24
V. East Anglia Norfolk, Suffolk, Essex, Cambridgeshire	9	12
VI. Southern Counties Wiltshire, Hampshire, Berkshire, Oxfordshire, Buckinghamshire, Hertfordshire, Middlesex, Surrey, Sussex, Kent	15	20
VII. TOTAL	75	100

Table 3.1: Analysis of Anti-Enclosure Riot Cases during the Reign of Elizabeth I (%) [a]

I. Type of Enclosure Destroyed	
1. Commons or waste	36
[Cases where practice of convertible husbandry is evident]	[7]
2. Arable	1
3. Emparking of woodland pasture	8
4. Enclosure and coppicing of woodland pasture	19
5. Pasture or meadow held in severalty	26
6. Enclosure of highway or common way	3
7. Destruction of dams or hedges surrounding millponds	2
8. Pound breach for rescue of distrained cattle	1
9. Unspecified	4
II. Destruction of Enclosures Procured by:	
1. Order of manorial court or municipal officials	3
2. Order of crown officials	1
3. Gentry (including peers)	33
4. Smallholders (yeomen and husbandmen)	23
5. Craftsmen, cottagers, and squatters	9
6. Clergy	5
7. Townsmen	5
8. Dispute concerning commons shared by two or more villages	5
9. Social status unspecified	16
[Raising of common purse alleged]	[7]
III. Victims of Enclosure Riots	
1. Gentry resident	35
2. Gentry absentee	14
3. Smallholders	9
4. Craftsmen, cottagers, and squatters	5
5. Outsiders (new owners and farmers of leases) [b]	17
6. Clergy	—
7. Townsmen	—
8. Dispute concerning commons shared by two or more villages	5
9. Social status unspecified	15

[a] Based upon 105 cases, of which 75 are from the proceedings of the Court of Star Chamber (PRO, STAC 5, 7, 8) and the remainder from PRO, C. 78, DL 5; BL, Harley MSS 2143 and Lansdowne MSS 639, and the following printed sources: *Acts PC*; M. Eccles, *Shakespeare in Warwickshire* (Madison, Wisc., 1961); J. Hawarde, *Les Reportes del Cases in Camera Stellata, 1593 to 1609*, ed. W. P. Baildon (1894).
[b] A number of townsmen are included in this category.

Table 3.2: Geographical Distribution of Enclosure-riot Cases during the Reign of Elizabeth I

	No.	%
I. West of England Cornwall, Devonshire, Dorsetshire, Somersetshire	7	8
II. North of England Northumberland, Cumberland, Co. Durham, Westmorland, Lancashire, Cheshire, Yorkshire	8	9
III. West Midlands Shropshire, Staffordshire, Herefordshire, Worcestershire, Warwickshire, Gloucestershire	30	34
IV. Welsh Border Flintshire, Denbighshire, Montgomeryshire, Radnorshire, Brecknockshire, Monmouthshire	14	16
V. Wales (excluding border counties) Anglesey, Caernarvonshire, Cardiganshire, Carmarthenshire, Glamorganshire, Merionethshire, Pembrokeshire	2	2
VI. East Midlands Lincolnshire, Derbyshire, Nottinghamshire, Leicestershire, Rutlandshire, Northamptonshire, Huntingdonshire, Bedfordshire	3	4
VII. East Anglia Norfolk, Suffolk, Essex, Cambridgeshire	9	10
VIII. Southern Counties Wiltshire, Hampshire, Berkshire, Oxfordshire, Buckinghamshire, Hertfordshire, Middlesex, Surrey, Sussex, Kent	15	17
IX. TOTAL	88	100

Table 4.1: Analysis of Anti-Enclosure Riot Cases during the Reign of James I (%) [a]

I. Type of Enclosure Destroyed	
1. Commons or waste	49
[Cases where the practice of convertible husbandry is evident]	[3]
2. Arable	16
3. Emparking of woodland pasture	2
4. Enclosure and coppicing of woodland pasture	8
5. Pasture or meadow held in severalty	17
6. Enclosure of highway or common way	1
7. Destruction of dams or hedges surrounding millponds	2
8. Pound breach for rescue of distrained cattle	—
9. Unspecified	2
II. Destruction of Enclosures Procured by:	
1. Order of manorial court or municipal officials	—
2. Order of crown officials	1
3. Gentry (including peers)	39
4. Smallholders (yeomen and husbandmen)	43
5. Craftsmen, cottagers, and squatters	8
6. Clergy	—
7. Townsmen	5
8. Dispute concerning commons shared by two or more villages	1
9. Social status unspecified	4
[Raising of common purse alleged]	[19]
III. Victims of Enclosure Riots	
1. Gentry resident	30
2. Gentry absentee	20
3. Smallholders	12
4. Craftsmen, cottagers, and squatters	8
5. Outsiders (new owners and farmers of leases)	13
6. Clergy	1
7. Townsmen	8
8. Dispute concerning commons shared by two or more villages	2
9. Crown as lord of manor	3
10. Social status unspecified	3
[Religious factionalism also an issue]	[8]

[a] Based upon 119 cases, of which 97 are from the proceedings of the Court of Star Chamber (PRO, STAC 8), and the remainder from PRO, C. 78, DL 1, 5, 6, and Hawarde, *Les Reportes del Cases in Camera Stellata, 1593 to 1609.*

Table 4.2: *Geographical Distribution of Enclosure-riot Cases during the Reign of James I*

	No.	%
I. West of England Cornwall, Devonshire, Dorsetshire, Somersetshire	7	6
II. North of England Northumberland, Cumberland, Co. Durham, Westmorland, Lancashire, Cheshire, Yorkshire	21	17
III. West Midlands Shropshire, Staffordshire, Herefordshire, Worcestershire, Warwickshire, Gloucestershire	38	30
IV. Welsh Border Flintshire, Denbighshire, Montgomeryshire, Radnorshire, Monmouthshire	9	7
V. Wales (excluding border counties) Anglesey, Caernarvonshire, Cardiganshire, Carmarthenshire, Glamorganshire, Merionethshire, Pembrokeshire	—	—
VI. East Midlands Lincolnshire, Derbyshire, Nottinghamshire, Leicestershire, Rutlandshire, Northamptonshire, Huntingdonshire, Bedfordshire	25	20
VII. East Anglia Norfolk, Suffolk, Essex, Cambridgeshire	4	3
VIII. Southern Counties Wiltshire, Hampshire, Berkshire, Oxfordshire, Buckinghamshire, Hertfordshire, Middlesex, Surrey, Sussex, Kent	21	17
IX. TOTAL	125	100

Table 8.1: Analysis of Insurrections, Riots, and Unlawful Assemblies in London, 1517 to May 1640 (No.)

I. Type of Disturbance, 1517–58
Against aliens	2
Protesting taxation	1
Festive misrule	1
Conflict of jurisdiction	1
Social conflict	1
SUB-TOTAL	6

II. Type of Disturbance, 1581–1602
i. *Economic distress*	12
Against aliens	(4)
Against monopolies	(2)
Popular market regulation	(2)
Against enclosures	(1)
Protesting taxation	(1)
Soldiers and sailors demanding arrears of pay	(2)
ii. *Protesting administration of justice*	14
(including rescue of prisoners and mutiny of prisoners)	
iii. *Other categories*	9
Social conflict (against gentlemen and lawyers)	(4)
Festive misrule	(1)
Conflict of jurisdiction	(2)
Miscellaneous and unspecified	(2)
iv. SUB-TOTAL	35

III. Type of Disturbance, 1606–May 1640
i. *Festive misrule*	29
Shrove Tuesday apprentices' riots	(21)
Riots on other holidays	(8)
ii. *Against royal ministers*	16
Naval mutinies and riots by discharged soldiers and sailors	(9)
iii. *Protesting administration of justice*	7
(including rescue of prisoners and mutiny of prisoners)	
iv. *Other categories*	3
Against aliens	(3)
v. SUB-TOTAL	55

IV. TOTAL 96

Table 8.2: *Geographical Distribution of Insurrections, Riots, and Unlawful Assemblies in London and Middlesex, 1517 to May 1640 (No.)*[a]

I. Location of Disturbances, 1517–58	
City of London (including Southwark as the 26th ward)	3
Suburbs (including the borough of Westminster, the Liberties, and Middlesex)	4
Location unclear	—
II. Location of Disturbances, 1581–1602	
City of London	20
Suburbs	12
Location unclear	5
III. Location of Disturbances, 1606–May 1640	
City of London	9
Suburbs	41
Location unclear	6
TOTAL	100

[a] Some disturbances have been counted twice where they have spilled over boundaries.

Bibliography

This bibliography includes all manuscript collections cited, but only those printed works cited more than once in the footnotes. Consistent with the footnotes and the list of abbreviations, the place of publication of printed books is understood to be London unless otherwise indicated.

I. MANUSCRIPT COLLECTIONS

British Library
  Additional MSS
  Cotton MSS
  Hargrave MSS
  Harley MSS
  Landsdowne MSS
  Royal MSS
  Stowe MSS

Corporation of London Record Office
  Remembrancia
  Repertories of the Court of Aldermen

London Guildhall Library
  Bridewell Royal Hospital, Court Books (microfilm reel 512, unfol.)

Public Record Office
  C. 78 (Chancery, Decree Rolls)
  DL 1 (Proceedings, Duchy Court of Lancaster)
  DL 3 (Duchy of Lancaster, Commission and Deposition Books)
  DL 5 (Duchy of Lancaster, Entry Books of Decrees and Orders)
  DL 6 (Duchy of Lancaster, Draft Decrees)
  DL 37 (Duchy of Lancaster, Chancery Rolls)
  REQ 2 (Proceedings, Court of Requests)

SP 10 (State Papers, Domestic, Edward VI)
SP 12 (State Papers, Domestic, Elizabeth I)
SP 14 (State Papers, Domestic, James I)
SP 16 (State Papers, Domestic, Charles I)
STAC 2 (Proceedings, Court of Star Chamber, Henry VIII)
STAC 3 (Proceedings, Court of Star Chamber, Edward VI)
STAC 4 (Proceedings, Court of Star Chamber, Mary I, Philip, and Mary)
STAC 5 (Proceedings, Court of Star Chamber, Elizabeth I)
STAC 7 (Proceedings, Court of Star Chamber, Elizabeth I, Addenda)
STAC 8 (Proceedings, Court of Star Chamber, James I)

II. PRINTED SOURCES

Abstracts of Star Chamber Proceedings relating to the County of Sussex: Henry VIII to Philip and Mary, ed. P. D. Mundy (Suss. Rec. Soc. 16; 1913).

Acts of the Privy Council of England, ed. J. R. Dasent (32 vols.; 1890–1907).

Alcock, N. W., *Warwickshire Grazier and London Skinner, 1523–1555: The Account Book of Peter Temple and Thomas Heritage* (British Academy Records of Social and Economic History, new ser. 4; 1981).

Analytical Index to the Series of Records Known as the Remembrancia, Preserved among the Archives of the City of London, A.D. 1579–1664 (1878).

Aubrey, John, *Aubrey's Brief Lives*, ed. O. L. Dick (1950).

—— *The Natural History of Wiltshire*, ed. J. Britton (1874).

Calendar of Assize Records, Essex Indictments, Elizabeth I, ed. J. S. Cockburn (1978).

Calendar of Assize Records, Essex Indictments, James I, ed. J. S. Cockburn (1982).

Calendar of Assize Records, Hertfordshire Indictments, James I, ed. J. S. Cockburn (1975).

Calendar of Assize Records, Kent Indictments, Elizabeth I, ed. J. S. Cockburn (1979).

Calendar of Assize Records, Sussex Indictments, Elizabeth I, ed. J. S. Cockburn (1975).

Calendar of Assize Records, Sussex Indictments, James I, ed. J. S. Cockburn (1975).

Calendar of the Quarter Sessions Papers, 1591–1643, ed. J. W. Willis Bund (Worcs. Hist. Soc., 1900).

Calendar of State Papers, Domestic, 1547–1603 (12 vols.; 1856–72).

Calendar of State Papers, Domestic, 1603–1625 (4 vols.; 1857–9).

Calendar of State Papers, Domestic, 1625–1649 (23 vols.; 1858–97).

Clifford Letters of the Sixteenth Century, ed. A. G. Dickens (Surtees Soc. 172; 1957).

Coke, Sir Edward, *Reports* (1738 edn.)
—— *The Third Part of the Institutes of the Laws of England* (4th edn.; 1669).
'Common Rights at Cottenham and Sletham in Cambridgeshire', ed.
W. Cunningham, *Camden Miscellany* 12 (Camden Soc., 3rd ser. 18; 1910).
The Court Rolls of the Manor of Wakefield from October 1639 to September 1640, ed. C. M. Fraser and K. Emsley (Yorks. Arch. Soc., Wakefield Court Rolls Ser. 1; 1977).
Croke, Sir George, *Reports*, part I. King's Bench and Common Pleas, Elizabeth (1669).
Crompton, Richard, *Star-Chamber Cases* (1630; repr. Amsterdam, 1975).
Dalton, Michael, *The Countrey Ivstice* (1622; repr. New York, 1972).
The Duchy of Lancaster's Estates in Derbyshire, 1485–1540, ed. I. Blanchard (Derbys. Arch. Soc., Rec. Ser. 3; 1967).
The Fairfax Correspondence: Memoirs of the Reign of Charles I, ed. G. W. Johnson (2 vols.; 1848).
Hale, Sir Matthew, *The History of the Pleas of the Crown* (2 vols.; 1800).
Hall, Edward, *Hall's Chronicle* (1809; repr. New York, 1965).
Harrison, William, *Description of England* (1587), in Raphael Holinshed, *Holinshed's Chronicles*, ed. Sir Henry Ellis (6 vols.; 1807–8).
Hawarde, John, *Les Reportes del Cases in Camera Stellata, 1593–1609*, ed. W. P. Baildon (1894).
Historical Collections, ed. John Rushworth (2nd edn., 8 vols.; 1721–2).
Hist. MSS Comm., *Fourth Report*, ii (1843). Calendar of the Baga de Secretis.
—— *Twelfth Report*, i (1891). Rutland MSS.
—— *Thirteenth Report* (1907). Hereford Corp. MSS.
—— *Buccleuch and Queensberry*, iii (1926).
—— *Finch*, i (1913).
—— *Montagu of Beaulieu* (1900).
—— *Salisbury*, i–xv (1906 *et seq.*).
—— *Various Collections*, i (1901). Quarter Sessions Records, Worcs. and Wilts.
Holinshed, Raphael, *Holinshed's Chronicles of England, Scotland and Ireland*, ed. Sir Henry Ellis (6 vols.; 1807–8).
Jackson, J. E., *Wiltshire: The Topographical Collections of John Aubrey* (Devizes, Wilts., 1862).
'The Journal of Sir Roger Wilbraham', ed. H. S. Scott, *Camden Miscellany* 10 (Camden Soc., 3rd ser. 4; 1902).
Lambarde, William, *Eirenarcha, or of the Office of Iustice of Peace* (1602).
Lancashire and Cheshire Cases in the Court of Star Chamber, ed. R. Stewart-Brown (Lancs. and Ches. Rec. Soc. 71; 1916).
Letters and Papers, Foreign and Domestic of the Reign of Henry VIII, ed. J. S. Brewer *et al.* (23 vols. in 38 parts; 1862–1932).
Letters of John Chamberlain, ed. N. E. McClure (2 vols.; Philadelphia, 1939).

The Life of Edward, First Lord Herbert of Cherbury, ed. J. M. Shuttleworth (1976).

Manwood, John, *A Treatise of the Lawes of the Forest* (1615; repr. Amsterdam, 1976).

Middlesex County Records, ed. J. C. Jeaffreson (6 vols.; 1886).

Middlesex Sessions Records, ed. W. Le Hardy (new ser., 4 vols.; Middx. County Records, 1935–41).

Noy, William, *Reports and Cases Taken in the Time of Queen Elizabeth, King James and King Charles* (1656).

Original Letters Illustrative of English History, ed. Sir Henry Ellis (11 vols.; 1824–46).

The Parliamentary Diary of Robert Bowyer, 1606–1607, ed. D. H. Willson (Minneapolis, 1931).

The Pinder of Wakefield: Being the Merry History of George a Greene the Lusty Pinder of the North, ed. E. A. Horsman (1632; English Reprints Ser. 12; Liverpool, 1956).

Pleadings and Depositions in the Duchy Court of Lancaster, ed. H. Fishwick (3 vols.; Lancs. and Ches. Rec. Soc., 1896–9).

Popham, Sir John, *Reports and Cases* (1656).

Proceedings of the Court of Star Chamber in the Reigns of Henry VII and Henry VIII, ed. G. Bradford (Somerset Rec. Soc. 27; 1911).

Quarter Sessions Order Book, 1625–1637, ed. S. C. Ratcliff and H. C. Johnson (Warwick County Records i; 1935).

Quarter Sessions Records for the County of Somerset, i. 1607–25, ed. H. E. Bates (Somerset Rec. Soc. 23; 1907).

Quarter Sessions Records, County Palatine of Chester, 1559–1676, ed. J. H. E. Bennett and J. C. Dewhurst (Lancs. and Ches. Rec. Soc. 94; 1940).

Records of the Borough of Leicester, 1603–1688, ed. H. Stocks (Cambridge, 1923).

Reports of Cases Decided by Francis Bacon . . . Lord Chancellor in the High Court of Chancery, ed. J. Ritchie (1932).

Reports of Cases in the Courts of Star Chamber and High Commission, ed. S. R. Gardiner (Camden Soc., new ser. 39; 1886).

The Reports of Sir John Spelman, ed. J. H. Baker (2 vols.; Selden Soc. 93, 94; 1976, 1978).

Rymer, Thomas, *Foedera, Conventiones, Literae, et cujuscunque generis Acta publica* (1742 edn.), vii.

Selected Cases before the King's Council in Star Chamber (1477–1544), ed. I. S. Leadam (2 vols.; Selden Soc. 16, 24; 1903, 1911).

Select Statutes and other Constitutional Documents Illustrative of the Reigns of Elizabeth and James I, ed. Sir G. W. Prothero (4th edn.; Oxford, 1913).

Seventeenth-century Economic Documents, ed. J. Thirsk and J. P. Cooper (Oxford, 1972).

Smyth of Nibley, John, *The Berkeley Manuscripts*, ed. Sir John Maclean (3 vols.; Gloucester, 1885); vol. ii. *The Lives of the Berkeleys*; vol. iii. *A Description of the Hundred of Berkeley, in the County of Gloucester and its Inhabitants.*

The Staffordshire Quarter Sessions Rolls, ed. S. A. H. Burne (Wm. Salt Arch. Soc., 4 vols.; 1930–6).

'Star Chamber Proceedings, Hen. VIII and Edw. VI [Staffs.]', ed. W. K. Boyd, *William Salt Archaeological Society* (1912).

Statutes of the Realm (9 vols.; 1810–22).

Stow, John. *Annales, or a Generall Chronicle of England*, ed. E. Howes (1631).

—— *A Survey of London*, ed. C. L. Kingsford (2 vols.; repr. Oxford, 1971).

—— *Survey of the Cities of London and Westminster*, ed. John Strype (2 vols.; 1720).

Strype, John, *Ecclesiastical Memorials* (3 vols.; Oxford, 1816).

Stuart Royal Proclamations, ed. J. F. Larkin and P. J. Hughes (2 vols.; Oxford, 1973, 1983).

A Survey of the Duchy of Lancaster Lordships in Wales, 1609–1630, ed. W. Rees (Cardiff, 1953).

The Third Book of Remembrance of Southampton, 1514–1602, ed. A. L. Merson (2 vols.; Southampton, 1952, 1955).

Tudor Economic Documents, ed. R. H. Tawney and E. Power (3 vols.; 1924).

Tudor Royal Proclamations, ed. P. L. Hughes and J. F. Larkin (3 vols.; New Haven, 1964–9).

Western Circuit Assize Orders, 1629–1649, ed. J. S. Cockburn (Camden Soc., 4th ser. 17; 1976).

William Lambarde and Local Government: His 'Ephemeris' and Twenty-nine Charges to Juries and Commissions, ed. C. Read (Ithaca, NY, 1962).

The Works of Gerrard Winstanley, ed. G. H. Sabine (repr. New York, 1965).

Wright, Thomas, *Queen Elizabeth and her Times* (2 vols.; 1838).

Yorkshire Star Chamber Proceedings, ed. W. Brown *et al.* (4 vols.; Yorks. Arch. Soc., Rec. Ser. 41, 45, 51, 70; 1909–27).

III. PRINTED SECONDARY WORKS

The Agrarian History of England and Wales, iv. *1500–1640*, J. Thirsk (ed.) (Cambridge, 1967).

Allison, K. J., 'The Sheep-Corn Husbandry of Norfolk in the Sixteenth and Seventeenth Centuries', *Ag. HR* 5 (1957), 12–30.

Anstruther, G., *Vaux of Harrowden: A Recusant Family* (Newport, Monmouthshire, 1953).

Appleby, A. B. 'Agrarian Capitalism or Seigneurial Reaction? The Northwest of England, 1500–1700', *AHR* 80/3 (1975), 574–94.

Appleby, A., 'Common Land and Peasant Unrest in Sixteenth-century England: A Comparative Note', *Peasant Studies Newsletter* (1975), 20-3.

—— *Famine in Tudor and Stuart England* (Stanford, Calif., 1978).

Ashton, R., *The City and the Court, 1603-1643* (Cambridge, 1979).

Baines, E., *The History of the County Palatine and Duchy of Lancaster*, ed. J. Croston (5 vols.; 1893).

Barnes, T. G., *Somerset, 1625-1640: A County's Government during the 'Personal Rule'* (Cambridge, Mass., 1961).

—— 'Star Chamber and the Sophistication of the Criminal Law', *Criminal Law Review* (1977), 316-26.

—— 'Star Chamber Litigants and their Counsel', *Legal Records and the Historian*, ed. J. H. Baker (R. Hist. Soc., Studies in History, 1978), 7-28.

Beer, B. L., *Rebellion and Riot: Popular Disorder in England during the Reign of Edward VI* (Kent, Ohio, 1982).

Beier, A. L., *Masterless Men: The Vagrancy Problem in England, 1560-1640* (1985).

—— 'Social Problems of Elizabethan London', *Journal of Interdisciplinary History* 9/2 (1978), 203-21.

—— 'The Social Problems of an Elizabethan Country Town: Warwick, 1589-90', in P. Clark (ed.), *Country Towns in Pre-industrial England* (New York, 1981).

—— 'Vagrants and the Social Order in Elizabethan England', *P. & P.* no. 64 (1974), 3-29.

Bellamy, J., *The Tudor Law of Treason: An Introduction* (1979).

Beresford, M., 'The Decree Rolls of Chancery as a Source for Economic History, 1547-c.1700', *Ec. HR*, 2nd ser. 32 (1979), 1-10.

—— 'The Deserted Villages of Warwickshire', *Trans. Birmingham Arch. Soc.* 66 (1945-6), 49-106.

—— 'Habitation Versus Improvement: The Debate on Enclosure by Agreement', in F. J. Fisher (ed.), *Essays in the Economic and Social History of Tudor and Stuart England in Honour of R. H. Tawney* (repr. Cambridge, 1974), 40-69.

Birch, T., *The Court and Times of Charles I* (2 vols.; 1848).

Blackwood, B. G., 'The Lancashire Cavaliers and their Tenants', *Trans. Hist. Soc. Lancs. Ches.* 117 (1965), 17-32.

Blanchard, I., 'Labour Productivity and Work Psychology in the English Mining Industry, 1400-1600', *Ec. HR*, 2nd ser. 31/1 (1972), 1-24.

—— 'Population Change, Enclosure, and the Early Tudor Economy', *Ec. HR*, 2nd ser. 23/3 (1970), 427-45.

Bloch, M., *French Rural History: An Essay on its Basic Characteristics*, trans. J. Sondheimer (Berkeley, Calif., 1966).

Boynton, L., 'The Tudor Provost-Marshal', *EHR* 77 (1962), 437-55.

Brewer, J. and Styles, J. (eds.), *An Ungovernable People: The English and their Law in the Seventeenth and Eighteenth Centuries* (New Brunswick, NJ, 1980).

Burke, P., 'Popular Culture in Seventeenth-century London', *London Journal* 3 (1977), 143–62.

Chalklin, C. W., *Seventeenth-century Kent: A Social and Economic History* (1965).

Chambers, E. K., *William Shakespeare: A Study of Facts and Problems* (2 vols.; repr. Oxford, 1963).

Charlesworth, A., *An Atlas of Rural Protest in Britain, 1548–1900* (Philadelphia, 1983).

Clark. P., *English Provincial Society from the Reformation to the Revolution: Religion, Politics and Society in Kent, 1500–1640* (Hassocks, Suss., 1977).

—— 'Popular Protest and Disturbance in Kent, 1558–1640', *Ec. HR*, 2nd ser. 29 (1976), 365–81.

Coleman, D. C., *Industry in Tudor and Stuart England* (Ec. Hist. Soc., 1975).

Court, W. H. B., *The Rise of the Midland Industries, 1600–1838* (repr. Oxford, 1953).

Cox, J. C., *The Royal Forests of England* (1905).

Davies, C. S. L., 'Slavery and Protector Somerset: The Vagrancy Act of 1547', *Ec. HR*, 2nd ser. 19 (1966), 533–49.

Davies, M. G., *The Enforcement of English Apprenticeship: A Study in Applied Mercantilism, 1563–1642* (Cambridge, Mass., 1956).

Dodds, M. H. and R., *The Pilgrimage of Grace, 1536–37 and the Exeter Conspiracy, 1538* (2 vols.; Cambridge, 1915).

Donald, M. B., *Elizabethan Monopolies: The History of the Company of Mineral and Battery Works from 1565 to 1604* (Edinburgh, 1961).

Dyer, A. D., *The City of Worcester in the Sixteenth Century* (Leicester, 1973).

Dyer, C., *Lords and Peasants in a Changing Society: The Estates of the Bishopric of Worcester, 680–1540* (Cambridge, 1980).

Eccles, M., *Shakespeare in Warwickshire* (Madison, Wisc., 1961).

Ellis [François], M. J., 'The Social and Economic Development of Halifax, 1558–1640', *Proc. Leeds Philos. and Lit. Soc.*, Literary and Historical Section, 11/8 (1966), 215–80.

—— 'A Study in the Manorial History of Halifax Parish in the Sixteenth and Early Seventeenth Centuries', *Yorks. Arch. Journal* 60 (1960–1), 250–64; 61 (1961), 420–42.

Emmison, F. G., *Elizabethan Life: Disorder, Mainly from Essex Sessions and Assize Records*, (Chelmsford, Essex Record Office Publications 56, 1970).

—— *Elizabethan Life: Home, Work, and Land: From Essex Wills and Sessions and Manorial Records* (Chelmsford, 1976).

Eversley, G. J. Shaw-Lefevre, Lord, *Commons, Forests and Footpaths* (1910).
Finch, M. E., *The Wealth of Five Northamptonshire Families, 1540-1640* (Northants. Rec. Soc. 19, 1956).
Finlay, R., *Population and Metropolis: The Demography of London, 1580-1650* (Cambridge, 1981).
Fisher, W. R., *The Forest of Essex: Its History, Laws and Ancient Customs* (1887).
Fletcher, A., *A County Community in Peace and War: Sussex, 1600-1660* (1975).
Flinn, M. W., 'Timber and the Advance of Technology: A Reconsideration', *Annals of Science* 15/2 (1959), 109-20.
Foster, F. F., *The Politics of Stability: A Portrait of the Rulers of Elizabethan London* (R. Hist. Soc., Studies in History, 1977).
Fox, L. and Russell, P., *Leicester Forest* (Leicester, 1948).
Frost, P., 'Yeomen and Metalsmiths: Livestock in the Dual Economy in South Staffordshire', *Ag. HR* 29 (1981), 29-41.
Gay, E. F., 'The Midland Revolt and the Inquisitions of Depopulation, 1607', *Trans. R. Hist. Soc.* 18 (1904), 195-244.
Goring, J., 'Social Change and Military Decline in Mid-Tudor England', *History* 60 (1975), 185-97.
Gough, J. W., *The Mines of Mendip* (Oxford, 1930).
Guy, J. A., *The Cardinal's Court: The Impact of Thomas Wolsey in Star Chamber* (Hassocks, Suss., 1977).
Halliwell, J. O., *The Marriage of Wit and Wisdom* (1846).
Hammersley, G., 'The Charcoal Iron Industry and its Fuel, 1540-1750', *Ec. HR*, new ser. 26 (1973), 593-613.
Hart, C. E., *The Free Miners of the Royal Forest of Dean and the Hundred of St. Briavels* (Gloucester, 1953).
—— *Royal Forest: A History of Dean's Woods as Producers of Timber* (Oxford, 1966).
Hay, D., 'Poaching and the Game Laws on Cannock Chase', in D. Hay *et al.* (eds.), *Albion's Fatal Tree: Crime and Society in Eighteenth-century England* (New York, 1975), 189-253.
Hey, D. G., *An English Rural Community: Myddle under the Tudors and Stuarts* (Leicester, 1974).
Hill, C., *The World Turned Upside Down: Radical Ideas during the English Revolution* (New York, 1972).
Hill, Sir Francis, *Medieval Lincoln* (Cambridge, 1965).
—— *Tudor and Stuart Lincoln* (Cambridge, 1956).
Hobsbawm, E. J., *Primitive Rebels: Studies in Archaic Forms of Social Movement in the 19th and 20th Centuries* (New York, 1965).
Hodgson, R. I., 'The Progress of Enclosure in County Durham, 1550-1870', in H. S. A. Fox and R. A. Butlin (eds.), *Change in the Countryside: Essays on Rural England, 1500-1900* (1979), 83-102.

Holdsworth, Sir William, *A History of English Law* (13 vols.; 1922–52).

Hoskins, W. G., *The Age of Plunder: King Henry's England, 1500–1547* (1976).

—— 'Harvest Fluctuations and English Economic History, 1480–1619', *Ag. HR* 12 (1964), 28–46.

—— *The Midland Peasant: The Economic and Social History of a Leicestershire Village* (1965).

—— *Provincial England: Essays in Social and Economic History* (repr. 1965).

—— 'The Reclamation of the Waste in Devon, 1550–1800', *Ec. HR* 13 (1943), 80–92.

—— and Stamp, L. D., *The Common Lands of England and Wales* (1963).

Hoyle, R. W., 'Lords, Tenants, and Tenant Right in the Sixteenth Century: Four Studies', *NH* 20 (1984), 38–63.

Jack, S. M., *Trade and Industry in Tudor and Stuart England* (1977).

James, M. E., *English Politics and the Concept of Honour, 1485–1642* (*P. & P.* Supplement 3, 1978).

—— *Family, Lineage and Civil Society: A Study of Society, Politics and Mentality in the Durham Region, 1500–1640* (Oxford, 1974).

—— 'The First Earl of Cumberland (1493–1542) and the Decline of Northern Feudalism', *NH* 1 (1966), 43–69.

—— *A Tudor Magnate and the Tudor State: Henry, Fifth Earl of Northumberland* (York, Borthwick Papers 30, 1966).

Jerrome, P., *Cloakbag and Common Purse: Enclosure and Copyhold in 16th Century Petworth* (Petworth, Suss., 1979).

Johnson, D. J., *Southwark and the City* (1969).

Jordan, W. K., *The Charities of Rural England, 1480–1660* (1961).

—— *Philanthropy in England, 1480–1660: A Study of the Changing Pattern of English Social Aspirations* (New York, 1959).

Kerridge, E., *Agrarian Problems in the Sixteenth Century and After* (1969).

—— *The Agricultural Revolution* (New York, 1967).

—— 'The Movement of Rent, 1540–1640', *Ec. HR*, 2nd ser. 6 (1953), 16–34.

Kirby, C. and E., 'The Stuart Game Prerogative', *EHR* 46 (1931), 239–54.

Landor, W. N., *Staffordshire Incumbents and Parochial Records, 1530–1680* (Wm. Salt Arch. Soc., 1915).

Laslett, P., *The World We Have Lost* (2nd edn.; New York, 1971).

Lehmberg, S. E., 'Star Chamber, 1485–1509', *The Huntington Library Quarterly* 24 (1961), 189–214.

Leonard, E. M., *The Early History of English Poor Relief* (repr. 1965).

—— 'The Inclosure of Common Fields in the Seventeenth Century', *Trans. R. Hist. Soc.*, 2nd ser. 18 (1905), 101–46.

Lindley, K. J., *Fenland Riots and the English Revolution* (1982).

Lindley, K., 'Riot Prevention and Control in Early Stuart London', *Trans. R. Hist. Soc.*, 5th ser. 33 (1983), 109–26.

Manning, B., *The English People and the English Revolution* (1976).

Manning, R. B., 'The Origins of the Doctrine of Sedition', *Albion* 12 (1980), 99–121.

—— 'The Prosecution of Sir Michael Blount, Lieutenant of the Tower, 1595', *BIHR* 57 (Nov. 1984), 216–24.

—— *Religion and Society in Elizabethan Sussex: A Study of the Enforcement of the Religious Settlement, 1558–1603* (Leicester, 1969).

—— 'Violence and Social Conflict in Mid-Tudor Rebellions', *JBS* 16 (spring 1977), 18–40.

Martin, J. E., 'Enclosure and the Inquisitions of Depopulation of 1607: An Examination of Dr. Kerridge's article "The Returns of the Inquisitions of Depopulation"', *Ag. HR* 30 (1982), 41–8.

—— *Feudalism to Capitalism: Peasant and Landlord in English Agrarian Development* (Atlantic Highlands, NJ, 1983).

Mitchell, R. J., and Leys, M. D. R., *A History of London Life* (1958).

Morrill, J. S., *The Revolt of the Provinces: Conservatives and Radicals in the English Civil War, 1630–1650* (1976).

Munsche, P. B., *Gentlemen and Poachers: The English Game Laws, 1671–1831* (Cambridge, 1981).

Nef, J. U., 'The Progress of Technology and the Growth of Large-Scale Industry in Great Britain, 1540–1640', in E. M. Carus-Wilson (ed.), *Essays in Economic History* (3 vols.; 1954), i. 88–107.

—— *The Rise of the British Coal Industry* (2 vols.; repr. 1966).

Nichols, J., *The History and Antiquities of the County of Leicester* (4 vols.; 1795–1815).

Norton, G., *Commentaries on the History, Constitution and Chartered Franchises of the City of London* (1829).

Palliser, D. M., *The Age of Elizabeth: England under the Later Tudors, 1547–1603* (1983).

—— *Tudor York* (Oxford, 1979).

Pam, D. O., *The Fight for Common Rights in Enfield and Edmonton, 1400–1600* (Edmonton Hundred Hist. Soc., occasional papers, new ser. 27; 1974).

Parker, L. A., 'The Agrarian Revolution at Cotesbach, 1501–1612', *Trans. Leics. Arch. Hist. Soc.* 24 (1948), 41–76.

—— 'The Depopulation Returns for Leicestershire in 1607', *Trans. Leics. Arch. Hist. Soc.* 23 (1947), 231–89.

Pearl, V., 'Change and Stability in Seventeenth-century London', *London Journal* 5 (May 1979), 3–34.

—— *London and the Outbreak of the Puritan Revolution: City Government and National Politics* (Oxford, 1964).

—— 'Social Policy in Early Modern London', in H. Lloyd-Jones (ed.) *History and Imagination: Essays in Honour of H. R. Trevor-Roper* (New York, 1981), 115–31.

Pettit, P. A. J., *The Royal Forests of Northamptonshire, 1558–1714* (Northants. Rec. Soc. 23, 1968).

Porter, J., 'Encroachment as an Element in the Rural Landscape', *Local Historian* 2 (Aug. 1974), 141–7.

Pound, J., *Poverty and Vagrancy in Tudor England* (1971).

Raistrick, A. and Jennings, B., *A History of Lead Mining in the Pennines* (1965).

Ramsay, G. D., *The City of London in International Politics at the Accession of Elizabeth Tudor* (Manchester, 1975).

Rappaport, S., 'Social Structure and Mobility in Sixteenth-century London, Part I', *London Journal* 9 (winter 1983), 107–35.

Schubert, H. R., *History of the British Iron and Steel Industry from c. 450 B.C. to A.D. 1775* (1957).

Sharp, B., *In Contempt of All Authority: Rural Artisans and Riot in the West of England, 1586–1660* (Berkeley, Calif., 1980).

Sharpe, R. R., *London and the Kingdom* (3 vols.; 1894).

Simpson, A. W. B., *An Introduction to the History of the Land Law* (Oxford, 1961).

Skipp, V. H. T., *Crisis and Development: An Ecological Case Study of the Forest of Arden, 1570–1674* (Cambridge, 1978).

—— 'Economic and Social Change in the Forest of Arden, 1530–1649', *Ag. HR* 18 (1970), 84–111.

Slack, P., 'Poverty and Politics in Salisbury, 1597–1666', in P. Clark and P. Slack (eds.), *Crisis and Order in English Towns, 1500–1700: Essays in Urban History* (Toronto, 1972), 164–203.

—— 'Vagrants and Vagrancy in England, 1598–1664', *Ec. HR*, new ser. 17 (1974), 360–79.

Slater, G., *The English Peasantry and the Enclosure of Common Fields* (repr. New York, 1968).

Smith, R. B., *Land and Politics in the England of Henry VIII; The West Riding of Yorkshire, 1539–1546* (Oxford, 1970).

Smith, S. R., 'The London Apprentices as Seventeenth-century Adolescents', *P. & P.* no. 61 (Nov. 1973), 149–61.

—— 'The Social and Geographical Origins of London Apprentices, 1630–1660', *The Guildhall Miscellany* 4/4 (Apr. 1973), 195–206.

Somerville, Sir Robert, *History of the Duchy of Lancaster* (2 vols.; 1953).

Spufford, M., *Contrasting Communities: English Villagers in the Sixteenth and Seventeenth Centuries* (Cambridge, 1974).

Stirling, B., *The Populace in Shakespeare* (repr. New York, 1965).

Stone, L., *The Crisis of the Aristocracy, 1558–1641* (New York, 1967).

Straker, E., *Wealden Iron* (repr. New York, 1969).

Supple, B. E., *Commercial Crisis and Change in England, 1600–1642* (Cambridge, 1964).

Tate, W. E., *The Enclosure Movement* (New York, 1967).

Tawney, R. H., *The Agrarian Problem in the Sixteenth Century* (repr. New York, 1967).

Thirsk, J., 'The Common Fields', in R. H. Hilton (ed.), *Peasants, Knights and Heretics: Studies in Medieval English Social History* (Cambridge, 1976), 10–32.

—— *English Peasant Farming: The Agrarian History of Lincolnshire from Tudor to Recent Times* (1957).

—— 'Horn and Thorn in Staffordshire: The Economy of a Pastoral County', *North Staffs. Journal of Field Studies* 9 (1969), 1–16.

—— 'Industries in the Countryside', in F. J. Fisher (ed.), *Essays in the Economic and Social History of Tudor and Stuart England in Honour of R. H. Tawney* (repr. Cambridge, 1974), 70–88.

—— 'The Local History of Enclosing and Engrossing', in J. Thirsk (ed.), *The Agrarian History of England and Wales*, iv. *1500–1640* (Cambridge, 1967).

—— 'Seventeenth-century Agriculture and Social Change', *Ag. HR* 18 (1970), 148–77.

Thomas, K., *Man and the Natural World: A History of the Modern Sensibility* (New York, 1983).

Thompson, E. P., 'The Moral Economy of the Crowd', *P. & P.* no. 50 (Feb. 1971), 76–136.

—— *Whigs and Hunters: The Origin of the Black Act* (New York, 1975).

Tomlins, Sir Thomas E., *The Law Dictionary* (2 vols.; 1820).

Trinder, B., *The Industrial Revolution in Shropshire* (1973).

Tupling, G. E., 'The Causes of the Civil War in Lancashire', *Trans. Lancs. Ches. Antiquarian Soc.* 65 (1956), 1–32.

—— *The Economic History of Rossendale* (Chetham Soc. 86; 1927).

Tyler, R. A. J., *Bloody Provost* (1980).

Unwin, G., *The Gilds and Companies of London* (repr. 1966).

Upton, A. F., *Sir Arthur Ingram, c.1565–1642: A Study of the Origins of an English Landed Family* (Oxford, 1961).

Walter, J., 'A "Rising of the People"? The Oxfordshire Rising of 1596', *P. & P.* no. 107 (May 1985), 90–143.

—— and Wrightson, K., 'Dearth and the Social Order in Early Modern England', *P. & P.* no. 71 (May 1976), 22–42.

Watts, S. J., 'Tenant-Right in Early Seventeenth-century Northumberland', *NH* 6 (1971), 65–75.

Wedgwood, J. C., *Staffordshire Parliamentary History* (Wm. Salt Arch. Soc., 1917), i. *1213–1603*.

Williams, P., *The Tudor Regime* (Oxford, 1979).

Wilson, C., *England's Apprenticeship, 1603–1763* (New York, 1965).
Wrightson, K., *English Society, 1580–1680* (1982).
—— and Levine, D., *Poverty and Piety in an English Village: Terling, 1525–1700* (1979).
Wrigley, E. A. and Schofield, R. S., *The Population History of England, 1541–1871* (Cambridge, Mass., 1981).
Youings, J., *Sixteenth-century England* (Harmondsworth, Middx., 1984).

IV. UNPUBLISHED THESES AND PAPERS

Barnes, T. G., 'Fines in the High Court of Star Chamber, 1596–1641' (typescript list in PRO Round Room).
Hammond, R. J., 'The Social and Economic Circumstances of Ket's Rebellion', Ph.D. thesis (London, 1934).

Index

Condover, Salop., m. of 61, 73, 265-6
Connington, Hunts., m. of 145, 250
Conquest, Sir Robert 250
convertible husbandry 10-11, 13-14, 23-4, 89, 220, 247-8, 251, 261
Cooke, Joseph 212
Coppinger, Sir Ambrose 63
Cotesbach, Leics. 90, 231, 234, 244-5
Cottenham, Cambs. 174-5
Cotton, Sir Robert 145-7, 250
Council in the Marches of Wales 67, 138, 175, 179-80, 266
Council in the North 165
Coventry 22, 103
Cox, Thomas 232
Cranbrook, Kent 274-5
Cranfield, Lionel, Earl of Middlesex 149
Craven, W. Yorks. 48-50, 301
crises, late-Elizabethan and early-Stuart 3, 65, 79-80, 82-4, 86-92, 102-7, 134, 157-8, 166, 168-9, 173, 178, 181-8, 193-4, 200-10, 220, 229, 245-6, 251, 258, 261, 311, 313-15, 318-19; mid-Tudor 27, 103, 199, 200; of subsistence 12-13, 314
Croft, Sir James 297-8
Cromwell, Sir Oliver 250
Cromwell, Oliver 104, 250
Cromwell, Thomas 49-50
crown estates 136-7, 139, 171, 240, 265; *see also* Lancaster, Duchy of
Cumberland, Henry Clifford, 1st Earl of 48-50
Cumberland, Francis Clifford, 3rd Earl of 301
Cuppeldike, Sir Thomas 40-1
Curwen, Sir Thomas 49

Dacre, Thomas Fiennes, 8th Lord 47

Dacre, Thomas Fiennes, 9th Lord 292-3
Dacre, Gregory Fiennes, 10th Lord 292-3
Danvers, family of 66
Darcy, Thomas, Lord 48, 50
Daventry, Northants. 103
Davies, Henry 304
Dawson, Dorothy, *alias* 'Captain Dorothy' 281
Dean, Forest of 127-8, 258-60, 262, 271-2, 274-6
dearth 15, 35, 79-80, 134, 157, 164, 200, 224-5, 229, 240-2, 245-6, 251-2, 313-14
Dekker, Thomas 212
demographic disaster 16, 174
demographic growth 4, 15, 23-4, 27, 29, 32-5, 59, 61, 79, 85, 106, 110, 127-9, 131, 135, 140-1, 147-51, 153, 158, 168, 170-8, 187-90, 196, 242, 255-67, 272, 277, 315-16
depopulation 23-4, 27, 29-30, 33, 85, 89-91, 106, 110, 157, 224, 229, 239-41, 244-5, 246-52, 288
Derby, Elizabeth, Countess of 281
Derby James Stanley, 7th Earl of 145, 280-2
diggers 6, 92, 174, 230, 232, 235
disafforestation 143, 174, 177, 186, 255-6, 258, 266
disparkment 128, 141
Dover, Robert 212
Drury Lane, Middx. 211, 213
Dudley, Sir Robert 90
Duffield Frith, Derbys. 262, 267
Dunchurch, Warws. 97, 245
Durham Cathedral, estates of the Dean and Chapter of 151
Dyer, Sir James 70

Edwards, John 76
Elizabeth I, Queen 136, 169-70, 180-1, 185, 187, 201, 203, 208-10, 284-5
Elkin, Thomas 297-98

Worcester, William Somerset, 3rd
  Earl of 271
Worcestershire Grand Jury 175-6,
  181
Worsley, Thomas 119
Wrightson, Keith 316
Wroth, Robert 69

Wroth, Sir Thomas 68-9
Wyatt, Sir Thomas 199-200
Wychwood Forest, Oxon. 271

Yarnton, Oxon. 225
York 52
York, Sir John 301